A Reasonable Affliction

1001 LOVE POEMS

To Read to Each Other

A Reasonable Affliction
1001 LOVE POEMS
To Read to Each Other

Edited by
Sally Ann Berk
and James Gordon Wakeman

BLACK DOG
& LEVENTHAL
PUBLISHERS
NEW YORK

Published by
BLACK DOG & LEVENTHAL PUBLISHERS, INC.
151 West 19th Street
New York, NY 10011

Distributed by
WORKMAN PUBLISHING COMPANY
708 Broadway
New York, NY 10003

Cover art "The Swing" by Jean Honore Fragonard
from Wallace Collection, London, Great Britain.
Used by permission of Art Resource, New York.

Design by Jonette Jakobson

Manufactured in the United States of America

ISBN: 1-884822-84-3

$\mathcal{C}$ONTENTS

Love the indescribable!
Love the ineffable!
For thousands of years,
great—and not so great—writers
have attempted to put into words
the magnificent and complicated
"Reasonable Affliction"
that rules us all.
From the florid verses of eighteenth century England
to the sparse haiku of Japan,
poets the world over continue to celebrate
that most complicated emotion—love.
As long as people live on the Earth,
the tradition of love poems will continue.
From "Roses are Red" to "How Do I Love Thee?"
scribes will always be here to offer us
their unique outlook on love.

Most of us struggle to find the right words to
express ourselves, and our love.
Here are one-thousand-and-one attempts
by some of the best, to help us.
Whether you are falling in or out of love,
these poems will help you
when you are at a loss for words.
Read them to your lover,
put them in your *billets-doux,*
sing them out in celebration,
use them to comfort you and renew you.
The power of love comes through
in each of these poems.

Use them with care.

Advice To The Lovelorn

The Bucking Bronco

Traditional, American

My love is a rider, wild horses he breaks,
But he promised to quit it all just for my sake;
He sold off his saddle, his spurs, and his rope,
And there'll be no more riding, and that's what I hope.
The first time I saw him was early last spring,
A-riding a bronco, a high-headed thing;
He laughed and he talked as they danced to and fro
He promised he'd not ride no other bronco.
My love has a gun that has gone to the bad,
Which makes all the ladies to feel very sad;
He give me some presents, among them a ring
But the return I gave him was a far better thing.
Now, all you young ladies that live on the Platte
Don't marry the cowboy who wears a white hat;
He'll pet you and court you and then be will go
And ride up the trail on another bronco.

Charm To Quell A Rival

Anonymous, Sanskrit

From out of the earth I dig this plant, an herb of most effectual power,
Wherewith one quells the rival wife and gains the husband for oneself.
Auspicious, with expanded leaves, sent by the gods, victorious plant,
Blow thou the rival wife away, and make my husband only mine.
Stronger am I, O Stronger one, yea, mightier than the mightier;
And she who is my rival wife is lower than the lowest dames.
Her very name I utter not: she takes no pleasure in this man.
Far into distance most remote drive we the rival wife away.
I am the conqueror, and thou, thou also art victorious:
As victory attends us both we will subdue my fellow-wife.
I have gained thee for vanquisher, have grasped thee with a
    stronger spell.
As a cow hastens to her calf, so let thy spirit speed to me, hasten like
    water on its way.

Written In A Lady's Prayer Book

John Wilmot, *Second Earl of Rochester*

Fling this useless book away,
And presume no more to pray.
Heaven is just, and can bestow
Mercy on none but those that mercy show.
With a proud heart maliciously inclined
Not to increase, but to subdue mankind,
In vain you vex the gods with your petition;
Without repentance and sincere contrition,
You're in a reprobate condition,
Phyllis, to calm the angry powers
And save my soul as well as yours,
Relieve poor mortals from despair,
And justify the gods that made you fair;
And in those bright and charming eyes
Let pity first appear, then love,
That we by easy steps may rise
Through all the joys on earth to those above.

A Curse

Daughter of K'ab Rabia

This is my curse on thee. God send thou love
One like thyself, unkind and obdurate,
That knowing Love's deep cautery, thou mayst writhe
In loneliness, and know my worth too late.

Round Robin

Bhartrihari

The maid my true heart loves would not my true love be;
She seeks another man; another maid loves he;
And me another maid her own true love would see;
O fie on her and him and Love and HER and me!

Give All To Love
Ralph Waldo Emerson

Give all to love;
Obey thy heart;
Friends, kindred, days,

Estate, good-fame,
Plans, credit and the Muse,
—Nothing refuse.

'Tis a brave master;
Let it have scope:
Follow it utterly,

Hope beyond hope:
High and more high
It dives into noon,

With wing unspent,
Untold intent;
But it is a god,

Knows its own path
And the outlets of the sky.
It was never for the mean;

It requireth courage stout.
Souls above doubt,
Valor unbending,

It will reward,—
They shall return
More than they were,

And ever ascending.
Leave all for love;
Yet, hear me, yet,

One word more thy heart behoved,
One pulse more of firm endeavor,
—Keep thee to-day,

To-morrow, forever,
Free as an Arab
Of thy beloved.

Cling with life to the maid;
But when the surprise,
First vague shadow of surmise

Flits across her bosom young,
Of a joy apart from thee,
Free be she, fancy-free;
Nor thou detain her vesture's hem,

Nor the palest rose she flung
From her summer diadem.
Though thou loved her as thyself,

As a self of purer clay,
Though her parting dims the day,
Stealing grace from all alive;

Heartily know,
When half-gods go,
The gods arrive.

Advice
Cynthia Heimel

Never judge someone by who he's in love with; judge him by his friends.
People fall in love with the most appalling people.
Take a cool, appraising glance at his pals.

To a Lady, Asking Him How Long He Would Love Her

Etheredge

It is not, Celia, in our power
To say how long our love will last;
It may be we within this hour
May lose those joys we now do taste:
The blessed, that immortal be,
From change in love are only free.
Then, since we mortal lovers are,
Ask not how long our love will last;
But while it does, let us take care
Each minute be with pleasure past.
Were it not madness to deny
To live, because we are sure to die?

To_____

John Keats

Had I a man's fair form, then might my sighs
  Be echoed swiftly through that ivory shell
  Thine ear, and find thy gentle heart; so well
  Would passion arm me for the enterprise:
But ah! I am no knight whose foeman dies;
  No cuirass glistens on my bosom's swell;
  I am no happy shepherd of the dell
  Whose lips have trembled with a maiden's eyes.
Yet must I dote upon thee,—call thee sweet,
  Sweeter by far than Hybla's honied roses
When steep'd in dew rich to intoxication.
  Ah! I will taste that dew, for me 'tis meet,
And when the moon her pallid face discloses,
  I'll gather some by spells, and incantation.

Arthur and Mollee

Traditional, English

As noble Sir Arthur one morning did ride,
With his hounds at his feet and his sword by his side,
He saw a fair maid sitting under a tree;
He asked her name, and she said 'twas Mollee.
"Oh, charming Mollee, you my butler shall be,
To draw the red wine for yourself and for me!
I'll make you a lady so high in degree,
If you will but love me, my charming Mollee!
"I'll give you fine ribbons, I'll give you fine rings,
I'll give you fine jewels and many fine things;
I'll give you a petticoat flounced to the knee,
If you will but love me, my charming Mollee!"
"I'll have none of your ribbons, and none of your rings,
None of your jewels and other fine things;
And I've got a petticoat suits my degree,
And I'll ne'er love a married man till his wife dee."
"Oh, charming Mollee, lend me then your penknife,
And I will go home and I'll kill my own wife;
I'll kill my own wife and my bairnies three,
If you will but love me, my charming Mollee!"
"Oh noble Sir Arthur, it must not be so,
Go home to your wife, and let nobody know;
For seven long years I will wait upon thee,
But I'll ne'er love a married man till his wife dee."
Now seven long years are gone and are past,
The old woman went to her long home at last;
The old woman died, and Sir Arthur was free,
And he soon came a-courting to charming Mollee.
Now charming Mollee in her carriage doth ride,
With her hounds at her feet and her lord by her side.
Now all ye fair maids take a warning by me,
And ne'er love a married man till his wife dee.

As I Went Out For A Ramble

Traditional, American

As I went out for a ramble,
I stopped in a little town,
I fell in love with a pretty little girl
And her eyes they were dark brown.
This girl I loved so dearly,
I loved her more than life,
But she was nothing but a young flirt
So she never could be my wife.
As I was walking one evening,
I walked around the park,
I found her in the arms of another boy,
God knows it broke my heart.
I went to her and asked her
As plain as words could be,
"Have you fell in love with another boy
And turned your back on me?"
She threw her arms around me
And in these words she said,
"I love you, dear, with all of my heart,
God knows, I'd rather be dead.

But your parents, they're against me;
They talk of me all the time,
And you are nothing but a hobo,
God knows you'll never be mine."
I turned away and left her,
I went on down the track;
And every step that I would take,
She seemed to say, "Come back."
Next morning I caught a freight train,
I went way down the line,
I said, "I'll go and ask her
If she'll try me one more time."
Now, boys, all take warning
From a friend that's tried and true.
Don't fall in love with such a young girl,
Her love will prove untrue.
God knows I've been a rambler,
I rambled all around;
But if she ever proves true to me
I'll marry and settle down.

Fancy

John Keats

Ever let the Fancy roam,
Pleasure never is at home:
At a touch sweet Pleasure melteth,
Like to bubbles when rain pelteth;
Then let winged Fancy wander
Through the thought still spread beyond her:
Open wide the mind's cage-door,
She'll dart forth, and cloudward soar.
O sweet Fancy! let her loose;
Summer's joys are spoilt by use,
And the enjoying of the Spring
Fades as does its blossoming;
Autumn's red-lipp'd fruitage too,
Blushing through the mist and dew,

Cloys with tasting: What do then?
Sit thee by the ingle, when
The sear faggot blazes bright,
Spirit of a winter's night;
When the soundless earth is muffled,
And the caked snow is shuffled
From the ploughboy's heavy shoon;
When the Night doth meet the Noon
In a dark conspiracy
To banish Even from her sky.
Sit thee there, and send abroad,
With a mind self-overaw'd,
Fancy, high-commission'd:—send her!
She has vassals to attend her:
She will bring, in spite of frost,
Beauties that the earth hath lost;
She will bring thee, all together,
All delights of summer weather;
All the buds and bells of May,
From dewy sward or thorny spray;
All the heaped Autumn's wealth,
With a still, mysterious stealth:
She will mix these pleasures up
Like three fit wines in a cup,
And thou shalt quaff it:—thou shalt hear
Distant harvest-carols clear;
Rustle of the reaped corn;
Sweet birds antheming the morn:
And, in the same moment—hark!
'Tis the early April lark,
Or the rooks, with busy caw,
Foraging for sticks and straw.
Thou shalt, at one glance, behold
The daisy and the marigold;
White-plum'd lilies, and the first
Hedge-grown primrose that hath burst;
Shaded hyacinth, always
Sapphire queen of the mid-May;
And every leaf, and every flower
Pearled with the self-same shower.

Thou shalt see the field-mouse peep
Meagre from its celled sleep;
And the snake all winter-thin
Cast on sunny bank its skin;
Freckled nest-eggs thou shalt see
Hatching in the hawthorn-tree,
When the hen-bird's wing doth rest
Quiet on her mossy nest;
Then the hurry and alarm
When the bee-hive casts its swarm;
Acorns ripe down-pattering,
While the autumn breezes sing.
Oh, sweet Fancy! let her loose;
Everything is spoilt by use:
Where's the cheek that doth not fade,
Too much gaz'd at? Where's the maid
Whose lip mature is ever new?
Where's the eye, however blue,
Doth not weary? Where's the face
One would meet in every place?
Where's the voice, however soft,
One would hear so very oft?
At a touch sweet Pleasure melteth
Like to bubbles when rain pelteth.
Let, then, winged Fancy find
Thee a mistress to thy mind:
Dulcet-eyed as Ceres' daughter,
Ere the God of Torment taught her
How to frown and how to chide;
With a waist and with a side
White as Hebe's, when her zone
Slipt its golden clasp, and down
Fell her girtle to her feet,
While she held the goblet sweet,
And Jove grew languid.—Break the mesh
Of the Fancy's silken leash;
Quickly break her prison-string
And such joys as these she'll bring.—
Let the winged Fancy roam,
Pleasure never is at home.

Would You Have A Young Virgin

Traditional, English

Would you have a young virgin of fifteen years,
You must tickle her fancy with sweets and dears,
Ever toying, and playing, and sweetly, sweetly,
Sing a love sonnet, and charm her ears.
Wittily, prettily talk her down,
Chase her, and praise her, if fair or brown,
   Sooth her, and smooth her,
   And teize her, and please her,
And touch but her smicket, and all's your own.
Do you fancy a widow well known in a man,
With a front of assurance come boldly on,
Let her rest not an hour, but briskly, briskly,
Put her in mind of how time steals on.
Rattle and prattle although she groan,
Rouse her and touse her from morn till noon,
   Show her some hour
   You're able to grapple
Then get but her writing's and all's your own.
Do you fancy a lass of a humour free?
That's kept by a fumbler of quality,
You must rail at her keeper and tell her, tell her,
Pleasure's best charm is variety.
Swear her more fairer than all the town
Try her and ply her when cully's gone
   Dog her and jog her
   And meet her and treat her
And kiss with two guineas and all's your own.

It Is Better

Stendhal

It is better to be silent that to say things at the wrong time that are too tender; what was appropriate ten seconds ago is so no longer, and hurts one's cause, rather than helps it.

One-and-Twenty

A.E. Houseman

When I was one-and-twenty
I heard a wise man say,
"Give crowns and poundsand guineas
But not your heart away;
Give pearls away and rubies
But keep your fancy free."
But I was one-and-twenty,
No use to talk to me.

When I was one-and-twenty
I heard him say again,
"The heart out of the bosom
Was never given in vain;
'Tis paid with sighs a-plenty
And sold for endless rue."
And I am two-and-twenty,
And oh, 'tis true, 'tis true!

Ladies Fair

Anna Hempstead Branch

Ladies fair, Oh, what are we
Fond or foolish or unwise?
That it is our lot to be
Made more lovely by men's eyes.

If our looks can shine more bright
It shall be at our own whim.
Let us dwell in native light
Without any thought of Him.

O my dears, we may not so!
Beauty comes not by desire!
But how soon we feel it grow
If they see us and admire.

When our souls in time of flower
Needs must blossom or repine,
They can wake us in an hour!
If they love us, how we shine!

Suddenly we hold our breath
While the trembling beauty grows.
We can feel it underneath,
And the sunshine lifts the rose!

Though we love you not, forbear!
Be not vexed that heard but nay!
Since your love has kept us fair
As the earth is with the day.

And our souls are robed with dew
In the old and vernal dress,
And we shine and are made new
With your love of loveliness.

Ladies Fair, oh, what are we?
Fond or foolish or unwise?
Still it is our lot to be
Made more lovely by men's eyes

Love At First Sight

Samuel Richardson

Love at first sight, supposes such as susceptibility of passion, as, however it may pass
in a man, very little becomes the delicacy of the female character.

DESIRE
Samuel Taylor Coleridge

Where true Love burns Desire is Love's pure flame ;
It is the reflex of our earthly frame,
That takes its meaning from the nobler part,
And but translates the language of the heart.

THE HEART
Pascal

The heart has its reasons which reason knows nothing of.

SONG
Louise Moulton

Fill the swift days full, my dear,
Since life is fleet;
Love, and hold fast, my dear,
He is so sweet—
Sweetest, dearest, fleetest comer,
Fledgling of the sudden summer.

Love, but not too well, my dear!
When skies are gray,
And the autumn winds are here,
Love will away—
Fleetest, vaguest, farthest rover,
When the summer's warmth is over.

LOVING IN TRUTH
Sir Philip Sydney

Loving in truth, and fain in verse my love to show,
That she, dear she, might take some pleasure of my pain:
Pleasure might cause her read, reading might make her know,
Knowledge might pity win, and pity grace obtain,
I sought fit words to paint the blackest face of woe,
Studying inventions fine, her wits to entertain:
Oft turning others' leaves to see if thence would flow

Some fresh and fruitful showers upon my sun-burn'd brain.
But words came halting forth, wanting Invention's stay,
Invention, Nature's child, fled step-dame Study's blows,
And others' feet still seem'd but strangers in my way.
Thus great with child to speak, and helpless in my throes,
Biting my trewand pen, beating myself for spite,
Fool, said my Muse to me, look in thy heart and write.

Envoy

Ernest Dowson

They are not long, the weeping and the laughter,
Love and desire and hate;
I think they have no portion in us after
    We pass the gate.

They are not long, the days of wine and roses:
Out of a misty dream
Our path emerges for a while, then closes
    Within a dream.

Sonnet XXXIV

Sappho

Venus! to thee, the Lesbian Muse shall sing,
The song, which Myttellenian youths admir'd,
When Echo, am'rous of the strain inspir'd,
Bade the wild rocks with madd'ning plaudits ring!
Attend my pray'r! O! Queen of rapture! bring
To these fond arms, he, whom my soul has fir'd;
From these fond arms remov'd; yet, still desir'd,
Though love, exulting, spreads his varying wing!
Oh! source of ev'ry joy! of ev'ry care
Blest Venus! Goddess of the zone divine!
To Phaon's bosom, Phaon's victim bear;
So shall her warmest, tend'rest vows be thine!
For Venus, Sappho shall a wreath prepare,
And Love be crown'd, immortal as the Nile!

To F—S S. O—D

Edgar Allan Poe

Thou wouldst be loved?—then let thy heart
From its present pathway part not!
Being everything which now thou art,
Be nothing which thou art not.
So with the world thy gentle ways,
Thy grace, thy more than beauty,
Shall be an endless theme of praise,
And love—a simple duty.

Sonnet 10

William Shakespeare

For shame, deny that thou bear'st love to any
Who for thyself art so unprovident.
Grant if thou wilt, thou art beloved of many,
But that thou none lov'st is most evident:
For thou art so possessed with murd'rous hate,
That 'gainst thy self thou stick'st not to conspire,
Seeking that beauteous roof to ruinate,
Which to repair should be thy chief desire.
O, change thy thought, that I may change my mind.
Shall hate be fairer lodged than gentle love?
Be as thy presence is, gracious and kind,
Or to thyself at least kind-hearted prove.
    Make thee another self for love of me,
    That beauty still may live in thine or thee.

Sonnet CXL

Petrarch

Love who within my thought does live and reign,
Who keeps his favored seat inside my heart,
Sometimes likes on my forehead to remain,
And there in arms displays his bow and dart.
She who taught us to love and suffer pain,
Who demands that desire and ardent hope
Be bound by reason, within worship's scope,
Feels for our daring an inner disdain.

Hence Love in fright again to the heart flies,
Abandoning all tasks, and tries to hide,
Trembles and weeps and comes no more outside.
What can I do, who fear my master's power,
But stay with him until the final hour?
Because he ends well who well loving dies.

$\mathcal{A}$ Nocturnall Upon St. Lucie's Day (Being The Shortest Day)

John Donne

Tis the yeares midnight, and it is the dayes,
Lucies, who scarce seaven houres herself unmaskes,
The Sunne is spend, and now his flasks
Send forth light squibs, no constant rayes;
The worlds whole sap is sunke:
The generall balme th' hydroptique earth hath drunk,
Whither, as to the beds-feet, life is shrunk,
Dead and enterr'd; yet all these seem to laugh,
Compar'd with mee, who am their Epitaph.

Study me then, you who shall lovers bee
At the next world, that is, at the next Spring:
For I am every dead thing,
In whom love wrought new Alchimie.
For his art did expresse
A quintessence even from nothingnesse,
From dull privations, and leane emptinesse:
He ruin'd mee, and I am re-begot
Of absence, darknesse, death; things which are not.

All others, from all things, draw all that's good,
Life, soule, forme, spirit, whence they being have;
I, by loves limbecke, am the grave
Of all, that's nothing.
Oft a flood
Have wee two wept, and so
Drownd the whole world, us two; oft did we grow
To be two Chaosses, when we did show
Care to ought else; and often absences
Withdrew our soules, and made us carcasses.

But I am by her death, (which word wrongs her)
Of the first nothing, the Elixer grown;
Were I a man, that I were one,
I needs must know; I should preferre,
If I were any beast,
Some ends, some means; Yea plants, yea stones detest,
And love; All, all some properties invest;
If I an ordinary nothing were,
As shadow, a light, and body must be here.

But I am None; nor will my Sunne renew.
You lovers, for whose sake, the lesser Sunne
At this time to the Goat is runne
To fetch new lust, and give it you,
Enjoy your summer all;
Since shee enjoyes her long nights festivall,
Let mee prepare towards her, and let mee call
This houre her Vigill, and her Eve, since this
Bothe the yeares, and the dayes deep midnight is.

*L*OVE AND BLACK MAGIC
Robert Graves

To the woods, to the woods is the
    wizard gone;
In his grotto the maiden sits alone.
She gazes up with a weary smile
At the rafter-hanging crocodile,
The slowly swinging crocodile.
Scorn has she of her master's gear,
Cauldron, alembic, crystal sphere,
Phial, philtre—"Fiddlededee
For all such trumpery trash!" quo' she.
"A soldier is the lad for me;
Hey and hither, my lad!
Oh, here have I ever lain forlorn:
My father died ere I was born,
Mother was by a wizard wed,
And oft I wish I had died instead—
Often I wish I were long time dead.

But, delving deep in my master's lore,
I have won of magic power such store
I can turn a skull—oh, fiddlededee
For all this curious craft!" quo' she.
"A soldier is the lad for me;
Hey and hither, my lad!
To bring my brave boy unto my arms,
What need have I of magic charms—
'Abracadabra!' and 'Prestopuff'?
I have but to wish, and that is enough.
The charms are vain, one wish is enough.
My master pledged my hand to a wizard;
Transformed would I be to toad or lizard
If e'er he guessed—but fiddlededee
For a black-browed sorcerer, now," quo' she.
"Let Cupid smile and the fiend must flee;
Hey and hither, my lad."

Quote
Sandra Bullock

"People ask me, 'What's the most dangerous thing you've ever done?' I say, 'Dating.'"

Quote
Curtis Judalet

" Love is as much of an object as an obsession, everybody wants it, everybody seeks it, but few ever achieve it, those who do will cherish it, be lost in it, and amoung all, never...never forget it. "

To My Heart, Bidding It Have No Fear
William Butler Yeats

Be you still, be you still, trembling heart;
Remember the wisdom out of the old days:
Him who trembles before the flame and the flood,
And the winds that blow through the starry ways,
Let the starry winds and the flame and the flood
Cover over and hide, for he has no part
With the proud, majestical multitude.

Quote
Thackeray

It is best to love wisely, no doubt; but to love foolishly is better than not to be able to love at all.

Sex
Woody Allen

Sex without love is an empty and meaningless experience, but as empty experiences go, it's one of the best.

Love
Unknown

That blissful intermission between meeting someone and realizing how much you hate them.

*L*OVE
Matt Groenig

Love is a snowmobile racing across the tundra and then suddenly
it flips over, pinning you underneath. At night, the ice weasels come."

*K*ISSES
Helen Rowland

A man snatches the first kiss, pleads for the second, demands the third,
takes the fourth, accepts the fifth—and endures all the rest.

*O*F HIS CYNTHIA
Lord Brooke Fulke Greville

Away with these self-loving lads,
Whom Cupid's arrow never glads.
Away, poor souls that lie and sleep;
    For Cupid is a meadow god
    And forceth none to kiss the rod.

God Cupid's shaft, like destiny.
Doth either good or ill decree;
Desert is born out of his bow,
Reward upon his feet does go.
    What fools are they that have not known
    That Love likes no laws but his own?

My songs thy be of Cynthia's praise,
I wear her ring on holy-days,
On every tree I write her name,
And every day I read the same.
    Where Honor Cupid's rival is,
    There miracles are seen of his.

If Cynthia crave her ring of me,
I blot her name out of the tree.
If doubt do darken things held dear,
Then well fare nothing once a year.
    For many run, but one must win
    Fools only hedge the cuckoo in,

The worth that worthiness should move
Is love, which is the due of love.
And love as well the shepherd can
As can the mighty nobleman.
    Sweet nymph, 'tis true you worthy be,
    Yet without love, nought worth to me.

*S*ONNET 13
William Shakespeare

O that you were your self, but love you are
No longer yours, than you your self here live,
Against this coming end you should prepare,
And your sweet semblance to some other give.
So should that beauty which you hold in lease
Find no determination, then you were
Your self again after your self's decease,
When your sweet issue your sweet form should bear.
Who lets so fair a house fall to decay,
Which husbandry in honour might uphold,
Against the stormy gusts of winter's day
And barren rage of death's eternal cold?
    O none but unthrifts, dear my love you know,
    You had a father, let your son say so.

*T*HE *T*HREE *S*ORTS *O*F *F*RIENDS
Samuel Taylor Coleridge

Though friendships differ endless in degree ,
The sorts , methinks, may be reduced to three.
Acquaintance many, and Conquaintance few;
    But for Inquaintance I know only two—
The friend I've mourned with, and the maid I woo!

*S*ONNET 79
William Shakespeare

Whilst I alone did call upon thy aid,
My verse alone had all thy gentle grace,
But now my gracious numbers are decayed,

And my sick muse doth give an other place.
I grant (sweet love) thy lovely argument
Deserves the travail of a worthier pen,
Yet what of thee thy poet doth invent,
He robs thee of, and pays it thee again,
He lends thee virtue, and he stole that word,
From thy behaviour, beauty doth he give
And found it in thy cheek: he can afford
No praise to thee, but what in thee doth live.
>   Then thank him not for that which he doth say,
>   Since what he owes thee, thou thy self dost pay.

A LECTURE UPON THE SHADOW
John Donne

Stand still, and I will read to thee
A lecture, love, in love's philosophy.
These three hours that we have spent,
Walking here, two shadows went
Along with us, which we ourselves produc'd.
But, now the sun is just above our head,
We do those shadows tread,
And to brave clearness all things are reduc'd.
So whilst our infant loves did grow,
Disguises did, and shadows, flow
From us, and our cares; but now 'tis not so.
That love has not attain'd the high'st degree,
Which is still diligent lest others see.

Except our loves at this noon stay,
We shall new shadows make the other way.
As the first were made to blind
Others, these which come behind
Will work upon ourselves, and blind our eyes.
If our loves faint, and westwardly decline,
To me thou, falsely, thine,
And I to thee mine actions shall disguise.
The morning shadows wear away,
But these grow longer all the day;
But oh, love's day is short, if love decay.
Love is a growing, or full constant light,
And his first minute, after noon, is night.

Thel's Motto (excerpts from "The Book of Thel")

William Blake

Does the Eagle know what is in the pit?
Or wilt thou go ask the Mole?
Can Wisdom be put in a silver rod?
Or Love in a golden bowl?

The daughters of the Seraphim led round their sunny flocks,
All but the youngest: she in paleness sought the secret air,
To fade away like morning beauty from her mortal day:
Down by the river of Adona her soft voice is heard,
And thus her gentle lamentation falls like morning dew:

"O life of this our spring! why fades the lotus of the water,
Why fade these children of the spring, born but to smile and fall?
Ah! Thel is like a wat'ry bow, and like a parting cloud;
Like a reflection in a glass; like shadows in the water;
Like dreams of infants, like a smile upon an infant's face;
Like the dove's voice; like transient day; like music in the air.
Ah! gentle may I lay me down, and gentle rest my head,
And gentle sleep the sleep of death, and gentle hear the voice
Of him that walketh in the garden in the evening time."

The Lily of the Valley, breathing in the humble grass,
Answer'd the lovely maid and said: "I am a wat'ry weed,
And I am very small and love to dwell in lowly vales;
So weak, the gilded butterfly scarce perches on my head.
Yet I am visited from heaven, and he that smiles on all
Walks in the valley and each morn over me spreads his hand,
Saying, 'Rejoice, thou humble grass, thou new-born lily-flower,
Thou gentle maid of silent valleys and of modest brooks;
For thou shalt be clothed in light, and fed with morning manna,
Till summer's heat melts thee beside the fountains and the springs
To flourish in eternal vales.' Then why should Thel complain?
Why should the mistress of the vales of Har utter a sigh?"

She ceas'd and smil'd in tears, then sat down in her silver shrine.

Thel answer'd: "O thou little virgin of the peaceful valley,
Giving to those that cannot crave, the voiceless, the o'er tired;

Thy breath doth nourish the innocent lamb, he smells thy milky garments,
He crops thy flowers while thou sittest smiling in his face,
Wiping his mild and meekin mouth from all contagious taints.
Thy wine doth purify the golden honey; thy perfume,
Which thou dost scatter on every little blade of grass that springs,
Revives the milked cow, and tames the fire-breathing steed.
But Thel is like a faint cloud kindled at the rising sun:
I vanish from my pearly throne, and who shall find my place?"

"Queen of the vales," the Lily answer'd, "ask the tender cloud,
And it shall tell thee why it glitters in the morning sky,
And why it scatters its bright beauty thro' the humid air.
Descend, O little Cloud, and hover before the eyes of Thel."

The Cloud descended, and the Lily bow'd her modest head
And went to mind her numerous charge among the verdant grass.

PLEASURE
Voltaire

Pleasure has its time; so, too, has wisdom. Make love in thy youth,
and in old age attend to thy salvation.

Agony and Ecstasy

REMEMBRANCE

Emily Brontë

Cold in the earth—and the deep snow piled above thee!
Far, far removed, cold in the dreary grave!
Have I forgot, my only Love, to love thee,
Severed at last by Time's all-severing wave?

Now, when alone, do my thoughts no longer hover
Over the mountains, on that northern shore,
Resting their wings where heath and fern leaves cover
Thy noble heart forever, ever more?

Cold in the earth—and fifteen wild Decembers,
From those brown hills, have melted into spring;
Faithful, indeed, is the spirit that remembers
After such years of change and suffering!

Sweet Love of youth, forgive, if I forget thee,
While the world's tide is bearing me along:
Other desires and other hopes beset me,
Hopes which obscure but cannot do thee wrong!

No later light has lightened up my heaven,
No second morn has ever shone for me;
All my life's bliss from thy dear life was given,
All my life's bliss is in the grave with thee.

But when the days of golden dreams had perished,
And even Despair was powerless to destroy,
Then did I learn how existence could be cherished,
Strengthened, and fed without the aid of joy.

Then did I check the tears of useless passion-
Weaned my young soul from yearning after thine;
Sternly denied its burning wish to hasten
Down to that tomb already more than mine!
And, even yet, I dare not let it languish,
Dare not indulge in memory's rapturous pain;
Once drinking deep of that divinest anguish,
How could I seek the empty world again?

DRIFTING DUCKWEED

Ts'ao Chih

Drifting duckweed floats on the clear water
Blown by the wind east and west.
Hair done up, I bade farewell to my parents,
To come to be my lord's mate.
Respectful and careful morning and night,
Without cause I got your accusations and blame.
In the past I was favoured with love and kindness,
In harmony and joy like harp and lute.
Why do you now reject me,
And separate us like east-star and west-star?
Dogwood itself has fragrance,
But not like the cassia and orchid;
Though you can love a new woman
It will be nothing like your old happiness.
Passing clouds return in time;
Shall, by chance, your love return?
Unsatisfied, unsatisfied, I look to the sky and sigh;
To what shall my anxious heart appeal?
The sun and moon stay not always in the same place;
Man's life is as insignificant as an overnight stay.
A sad wind comes and enters my breast;
Tears drop like falling dew.
I'll open this box and make some clothes,
Cut and sew the glossy silk and plain silk.

STAND FAST, O MY HEART

Anonymous, Egyptian

It fleeth away, my heart, quickly,
When I recall my love of thee,
Nor suffereth me to walk in human wise,
But is affrighted from its place
It suffereth me not to don a tunic,
Nor to attire myself with my fan.
I put not paint upon mine eyes,
Nor anoint myself at all.

Bide not, but get thee home,
Saith it to me as often as I recall him.
Act not the fool, O my heart;
Wherefore playest thou the madman?
Sit calm, until thy brother come to thee.
Let not the folk say concerning me,
A woman distraught with love.
Stand fast as often as thou recallest him,
O my heart, and do not flee.

Sweetest Love, I Do Not Go

John Donne

Sweetest love, I do not go,
    For weariness of thee,
    Nor in hope the world can show
      A fitter love for me;
        But since that I
    Must die at last, 'tis best
    To use myself in jest
      Thus by feign'd deaths to die.
    Yesternight the sun went hence,
    And yet is here today;
He hath no desire nor sense,
    Nor half so short a way:
      Then fear not me,
But believe that I shall make
Speedier journeys, since I take
    More wings and spurs than he.
O how feeble is man's power,
    That if good fortune fall,
Cannot add another hour,
    Nor a lost hour recall!

But come bad chance,
    And we join to'it our strength,
    And we teach it art and length,
      Itself o'er us to advance.
When thou sigh'st, thou sigh'st not wind,
    But sigh'st my soul away;
When thou weep'st, unkindly kind,
    My life's blood doth decay.
      It cannot be
That thou lov'st me, as thou say'st,
If in thine my life thou waste,
    That art the best of me.
Let not thy divining heart
    Forethink me any ill;
Destiny may take thy part,
    And may thy fears fulfil;
      But think that we
Are but turn'd aside to sleep;
They who one another keep
    Alive, ne'er parted be.

Mediocrity In Love Rejected

Thomas Carew

Give me more love or more disdain;
The torrid, or the frozen zone,
Bring equal ease unto my pain;
The temperate affords me none;
Either extreme, of love, or hate,
Is sweeter than a calm estate.

Give me a storm; if it be love,
Like Danae in that golden show'r
I swim in pleasure; if it prove
Disdain, that torrent will devour
My vulture-hopes; and he's possess'd
Of heaven, that's but from hell releas'd.

Then crown my joys, or cure my pain;
Give me more love, or more disdain.

NEVER SEEK TO TELL THY LOVE
William Blake

Never seek to tell thy love
Love that never told can be;
For the gentle wind does move
Silently, invisibly.

I told my love, I told my love,
I told her all my heart,
Trembling, cold, in ghastly fears—
Ah, she doth depart.

Soon as she was gone from me
A traveller came by
Silently, invisibly—
O, was no deny.

CUPID AND MY CAMPASPE
John Lyly

Cupid and my Campaspe played
At cards for kisses; Cupid paid.
He stakes his quiver, bow, and arrows,
His mother's doves and team of sparrows,
Loses them too; then down he throws
The coral of his lip, the rose
Growing on 's cheek (but none knows how),
With these the crystal of his brow,
And then the dimple of his chin:
All these did my Campaspe win.
At last he set her both his eyes;
She won, and Cupid blind did rise.
Oh Love! has she done this to thee?
What shall, alas, become of me?

SORROW SHATTERS MY HEART
Moses Ibn Ezra

Sorrow shatters my heart;
And men's distress it woth blame,
Because it follows love.

They censure it for its delight in the beautiful friend,
And because it loves him, even as its soul;
They rebuke it for the abundance of its tears
When it thinks and speaks of him,

They impute to him a blemish,
In that his face, bright as day,
Is framed a blackness of night.

Wherefore my heart swears by the life of Love,
That it will not listen to his detractors;
But the flame of its affection
It will hide in its innermost chambers, ever from the loved one,
That his heart may not be lifted up in pride.

Symptoms Of Love
Robert Graves

Love is a universal migraine,
A bright stain on the vision
Blotting out reason.

Symptoms of true love
Are leanness, jealousy,
Laggard dawns;

Are omens and nightmares -
Listening for a knock,
Waiting for a song:
For a touch of her fingers
In a darkened room,
For a searching look.

Take courage, lover!
Can you endure such grief
At any hand but hers?

She Walked Unaware
Patrick MacDonogh

Oh, she walked unaware of her own increasing beauty
That was holding men's thoughts from market or plough,
As she passed by intent on her womanly duties
And she passed without leisure to be wayward or proud;
Or if she had pride then it was not in her thinking
But thoughtless in her body like a flower of good breeding.
The first time I saw her spreading coloured linen

Beyond the green willow she gave me gentle greeting
With no more intention than the leaning willow tree.

Though she smiled without intention yet from that day forward
Her beauty filled like water the four corners of my being,
And she rested in my heart like a hare in the form
That is shaped to herself. And I that would be singing
Or whistling at all times went silently then,
till I drew her aside among straight stems of heeches
When the blackbird was sleeping and she promised that never
The fields would be ripe but I'd gather all sweetness,
A red moon of August would rise on our wedding.

October is spreading bright flame along stripped willows,
Low fires of the dogwood burn down to grey water,—
God pity me now and all desolate sinners
Demented with beauty! I have blackened my thought
In droughts of bad longing, and all brightness goes shrouded
Since he came with his rapture of wild words that mirrored
Her beauty and made her ungentle and proud.
Tonight she will spread her brown hair on his pillow,
But I shall be hearing the harsh cries of wild fowl.

Sonnet XII

Anna Seward

Chill'd by unkind Honora's alter'd eye,
"Why droops my heart with pining woe forlorn,"
Thankless for much of good?—what thousands, born
To ceaseless toll beneath this wintry sky,
Or to brave deathful oceans surging high,
Or fell Disease's fever'd rage to mourn,
How blest to them would seem my destiny!
How dear the comforts my rash sorrows scorn!—
Affection is repaid by causeless hate!
A plighted love is changed to cold disdain!
Yet suffer not thy wrongs to shroud thy fate,
But turn, my soul, to blessings which remain;
And let this truth the wise resolve create,
The Heart estranged no anguish can regain.

My Heart Is Lame
Charlotte Mew

My heart is lame with running after yours so fast
Such a long way,
Shall we walk slowly home, looking at all the things we passed
Perhaps to-day?
Home down the quiet evening roads under the quiet skies,
Not saying much,
You for a moment giving me your eyes
When you could bear my touch.
But not to-morrow. This has taken all my breath;
Then, though you look the same,
There may be something lovelier in Love's face in death
As your heart sees it, running back the way we came;
My heart is lame.

Greensleeves
Attributed to King Henry VIII of England

Alas, my love, you do me wrong,
To cast me off discourteously.
For I have loved you well and long,
Delighting in your company.
Greensleeves was all my joy
Greensleeves was my delight,
Greensleeves was my heart of gold,
And who but my Lady Greensleeves?
Your vows you've broken, like my heart,
Oh, why did you so enrapture me?
Now I remain in a world apart
But my heart remains in captivity.
I have been ready at your hand,
To grant whatever you would crave,
I have both wagered life and land,
Your love and good-will for to have.
If you intend thus to disdain,
It does the more enrapture me,
And even so, I still remain

A lover in captivity.
My men were clothed all in green,
And they did ever wait on thee;
All this was gallant to be seen,
And yet thou wouldst not love me.
Thou couldst desire no earthly thing,
but still thou hadst it readily.
Thy music still to play and sing;
And yet thou wouldst not love me.
Well, I will pray to God on high,
That thou my constancy mayst see,
And that yet once before I die,
Thou wilt vouchsafe to love me.
Ah, Greensleeves, now farewell, adieu,
To God I pray to prosper thee,
For I am still thy lover true,
Come once again and love me.

*T*o One Who Knows
Grace Grenwood

They told me, when I knew thee first,
Thou wert not made for loving,
That next St. Valentine's would see
Thy truant heart a-roving;

—That thou wouldst weary of my love,
Turn from me, and for ever!
That I would meekly bow and weep,
But chide the rover never.

Ah! those were mournful prophecies,
To cloud the sky of youth;
And thou and I, we little thought
So soon to test their truth!

We are that sad truth's witnesses,
Proofs manifest and living,—
Thou art for-getting this poor heart,
And I am still for-giving!

Hey Robin, Jolly Robin

Sir Thomas Wyatt

Robin, jolly Robin, tell me how thy Lady does.
Hey Robin, jolly Robin, tell me how thy Lady does.
Ay Robin, jolly Robin, tell me how thy leman doeth
Hey Robin, jolly Robin, and thou shalt know of mine.
My lady is unkind perde, alack why is she so?
She loveth another better than me, and yet she will say no.
I find no such doubleness, I find women true
My lady loveth me doubtless and will change for no new.
Thou art happy while that doth last but I say as I find,
That women's love is but a blast and turneth with the wind.

Out Upon It, I Have Loved

Sir John Suckling

Out upon it, I have loved
Three whole days together;
And am like to love three more,
If it hold fair weather.
Time shall moult away his wings
Ere he shall discover
In the whole wide world again
Such a constant lover.

But a pox upon't, no praise
There is due at all to me:
Love with me had made no stays,
Had it any been but she.

Had it any been but she
And that very face,
There had been at least ere this
A dozen in her place.

Restless Night

Tu Fu

As bamboo chill drifts into the bedroom,
Moonlight fills every corner of our
Garden. Heavy dew beads and trickles.
Stars suddenly there, sparse, next aren't.
Fireflies in dark flight flash. Waking
Waterbirds begin calling, one to another.
All things caught between shield and sword,
All grief empty, the clear night passes.

Sorrow, In Seven

Ts'ao Chih

A bright moon illumines the high building
With shimmering rays, just dancing back and forth.
Upstairs is an anxious minded woman,
Sadly sighing with endless sorrow.
I venture to ask who the sighing one is?
I am a wanderer's wife, she says.
My lord went off more than ten years ago,
While I have remained here always alone.
My lord is like dust on a clear road;
I am like mud in turbid water.
Floating, sinking, each in different circumstances;
When shall we reunite in harmony?
Would that I were the southwest wind,
To hurry off to the bosom of my lord.
If the bosom of my lord be not open to me,
Where can my poor self find refuge?

Modern Love: XVI

George Meredith

In our old shipwrecked days there was an hour,
When in the firelight steadily aglow,
Joined slackly, we beheld the red chasm grow
Among the clicking coals. Our library-bower

That eve was left to us: and hushed we sat
As lovers to whom Time is whispering.
From sudden-opened doors we heard them sing:
The nodding elders mixed good wine with chat.
Well knew we that Life's greatest treasure lay
With us, and of it was our talk. "Ah, yes!
Love dies!" I said: I never thought it less.
She yearned to me that sentence to unsay.
Then when the fire domed blackening, I found
Her cheek was salt against my kiss, and swift
Up the sharp scale of sobs her breast did lift:—
Now am I haunted by that taste! that sound!

Solitude
John Keats

O solitude! if I must with thee dwell,
    Let it not be among the jumbled heap
    Of murky buildings; climb with me the steep,—
Nature's observatory—whence the dell,
Its flowery slopes, its river's crystal swell,
    May seem a span; let me thy vigils keep
    'Mongst boughs pavillion'd, where the deer's swift leap
Startles the wild bee from the fox-glove bell.
But though I'll gladly trace these scenes with thee,
    Yet the sweet converse of an innocent mind,
Whose words are images of thoughts refin'd,
    Is my soul's pleasure; and it sure must be
Almost the highest bliss of human-kind,
    When to thy haunts two kindred spirits flee.

I Know You're Married
Anonymous, American

The day I met you my heart spoke to me
It said to love you through eternity
Not knowing that you were another's bride
I vowed I'd always be close by your side.

You know I love you and I always will
I know you're married but I love you still.
You broke a heart dear that would die for you
I'd give the world dear to belong to you
The game is over, now I know I've lost
My broken heart will have to pay the cost.

WHEN I HAVE FEARS
John Keats

When I have fears that I may cease to be
    Before my pen has gleaned my teeming brain,
    Before high-pile'd books in charact'ry
    Hold like rich garners the full ripened grain;
When I behold, upon the night's starred face
    Huge cloudy symbols of a high romance,
And think that I may never live to trace
    Their shadows with the magic hand of chance;
And when I feel, fair creature of an hour,
    That I shall never look upon thee more,
Never have relish in the faery power
    Of unreflecting love!—then on the shore
Of the wide world I stand alone, and think
Till love and Fame to nothingness do sink.

THE IMPERFECT LOVER
Siegfried Sassoon

I never asked you to be perfect—did I?—
Though often I've called you sweet, in the invasion
Of mastering love. I never prayed that you
Might stand, unsoiled, angelic and inhuman,
Pointing the way toward Sainthood like a sign-post.
Oh yes, I know the way to heaven was easy.
We found the little kingdom of our passion
That all can share who walk the road of lovers.
In wild and secret happiness we stumbled;
And gods and demons clamoured in our senses.
But I've grown thoughtful now. And you have lost

Your early-morning freshness of surprise
At being so utterly mine: you've learned to fear
The gloomy, stricken places in my soul,
And the occasional ghosts that haunt my gaze.
You made me glad; and I can still return
To you, the haven of my lonely pride:
But I am sworn to murder those illusions
That blossom from desire with desperate beauty:
And there shall be no falsehood in our failure;
Since, if we loved like beasts, the thing is done,
And I'll not hide it, though our heaven be hell.
You dream long liturgies of our devotion.
Yet, in my heart, I dread our love's destruction.
But, should you grow to hate me, I would ask
No mercy of your mood: I'd have you stand
And look me in the eyes, and laugh, and smite me.
Then I should know, at least, that truth endured,
Though love had died of wounds. And you could leave me
Unvanquished in my atmosphere of devils.

DOWN IN MY SALLY'S GARDEN

Traditional

Down in my Sally's garden,
Upon an ivy bush,
At morning and at twilight,
There sings a sweet song thrush.
His notes come clearly ringing,
And tidings to me tell,
And oh, I know already
My Sally loves me well.
I kissed her milk-white features
One silv'ry eve of May;
She whispered, "Won't you wander
Until the close of day?"

We wandered in her garden,
The flowers were wet with dew,
I saw the love-light beaming
In her fond eyes of blue.
Down in my Sally's garden,
Where snowy hawthorns blow,
My heart became love-weary
When I at last must go.
The bloom was on the hawthorn
That night I said farewell;
I left my Sally weeping
Down by an ivied dell.

Aye Wakin' Oh

Traditional, Scots

Summer is a pleasant time
Flowers of every color
The water is out the heugh
And I long for my true lover

Aye wakin' oh
Wakin' I am weary
Sleep I can get none
For thinking on my dearie
Aye wakin' oh

When first she came to town
The called her Grace MacFarland
But now she's gone away
They call her all folks darlin'

When I sleep I dream
And when I wake, I'm weary
Sleep I can get none
For thinking on my dearie

Her father loves her well
Her mother loves her better
And I love the lass myself
Woe is me, I can not get her

Lament

Princess Zeb-un-Nissa

Within my bosom stirs once more tonight
A voice of song. Love, ertswhile slumbering,
Intones his mystery, and the flowers of spring
Relive and bloom. Winter forbear to smite
My heart's late flowers. Listen! From left and right
Through the green boughs the bulbul's note is heard,
And, wing-clipt and imprisoned, my heart's bird
Flutters agaunst his barriers, wild for flight.

To _____

Elizabeth Barrett Browning

Mine is a wayward lay;
And, if its echoing rhymes I try to string,
   Proveth a truant thing,
Whenso some names I love, send it away!
   For then, eyes swimming o'er,
And clasped hands, and smiles in fondness meant,
   Are much more eloquent—
So it had fain begone, and speak no more!
   Yet shall it come again,
Ah, friend belov'd! if so thy wishes be,
   And, with wild melody,
I will, upon thine ear, cadence my strain—
   Cadence my simple line,
Unfashion'd by the cunning hand of Art,
   But coming from my heart,
To tell the message of its love to thine!
   As ocean shells, when taken
From Ocean's bed, will faithfully repeat
   Her ancient music sweet—
Ev'n so these words, true to my heart, shall waken!
   Oh! while our bark is seen,
Our little bark of kindly, social love,
   Down life's clear stream to move
Toward the summer shores, where all is green—
   So long thy name shall bring,
Echoes of joy unto the grateful gales,
   And thousand tender tales,
To freshen the fond hearts that round thee cling!
   Hast thou not look'd upon
The flowerets of the field in lowly dress?
   Blame not my simpleness —
Think only of my love!—my song is gone.

Sonnet V

Sappho

O! How can Love exulting Reason quell!
   How fades each nobler passion from his gaze!
   E'en Fame, that cherishes the Poet's lays,
That fame, ill-fated Sappho lov'd so well.
Lost is the wretch, who in his fatal spell
   Wastes the short Summer of delicious days,
   And from the tranquil path of wisdom strays,
In passion's thorny wild, forlorn to dwell.
   O ye! who in that sacred Temple smile
Where holy Innocence resides enshrin'd;
   Who fear not sorrow, and who know not guile,
Each thought compos'd, and ev'ry wish resign'd;
   Tempt not the path where pleasure's flow'ry wile
In sweet, but pois'nous fetters, holds the mind.

For That He Looked Not Upon Her

George Gascoigne

You must not wonder, though you think it strange,
To see me hold my louring head so low,
And that mine eyes take no delight to range
About the gleams which on your face do grow.
The mouse which once hath broken out of trap
Is seldom 'tice'd with the trustless bait,
But lies aloof for fear of more mishap,
And feedeth still in doubt of deep deceit.
The scorch'd fly, which once hath 'scaped the flame,
Will hardly come to play again with fire,
Whereby I learn that grievous is the game
Which follows fancy dazzled by desire:
So that I wink or else hold down my head,
Because your blazing eyes my bale have bred.

Ring Out Your Bells

Sir Philip Sydney

Ring out your bells, let mourning shows be spread,
For Love is dead.
All Love is dead, infected
With plague of deep disdain;
Worth as naught worth rejected,
And Faith fair scorn doth gain.
From so ungrateful fancy,
From such a female franzy,
From them that use men thus,
Good Lord, deliver us!

Weep, neighbors, weep; do you not hear it said
That Love is dead?
His deathbed peacock's folly,
His winding sheet is shame,
His will false-seeming holy,
His sole exec'tor blame.
From so ungrateful.

Let dirge be sung and trentals rightly read,
For Love is dead.
Sir Wrong his tomb ordaineth
My mistress, marble heart,
Which epitaph containeth,
"Her eyes were once his dart."
From so ungrateful…

Alas, I lie, rage hath this error bred;
Love is not dead.
Love is not dead, but sleepeth
In her unmatched mind,
Where she his counsel keepeth,
Till due desert she find.
Therefore from so vile fancy,
To call such wit a franzy,
Who Love can temper thus,
Good Lord, deliver us!

Love, That Doth Reign and Live Within My Thought

Henry Howard, Earl of Surrey

Love, that doth reign and live within my thought,
And built his seat within my captive breast,
Clad in the arms wherein with me he fought,
Oft in my face he doth his banner rest.
But she that taught me to love and suffer pain,
My doubtful hope and eke my hot desire
With shamefast look to shadow and refrain,
Her smiling grace converteth straight to ire.
And coward Love, then, to the heart apace
Taketh his flight, where he doth lurk and plain,
His purpose lost, and dare not show his face.
For my lord's guilt thus faultless bide I pain,
Yet from my lord shall not my foot remove:
Sweet is the death that taketh end by love.

Indifference

Edna St. Vincent Millay

I said,—for Love was laggard, O, Love was slow to come,—
"I'll hear his step and know his step when I am warm in bed;
But I'll never leave my pillow, though there be some
As would let him in—and take him in with tears!" I said.
I lay,—for Love was laggard, O, he came not until dawn,—
I lay and listened for his step and could not get to sleep;
And he found me at my window with my big cloak on,
All sorry with the tears some folks might weep!

Aucassin and Nicolette

Anonymous

When Aucassin heard Nicolette say that she would pass into a far country,
he was all in wrath.

"Fair sweet friend," quoth he, "thou shalt not go, for then thou wouldst be my death.
And the first man that saw thee and had the might withal, would take thee straightway
into his bed to be his leman. And once thou camest into a man's bed, and that bed not

mine, wit ye well that I would not tarry till I had found a knife to pierce my heart and slay myself. Nay, verily, wait so long I would not: but would hurl myself on it as soon as I could find a wall, or a black stone, thereon would I dash my head so mightily, that the eyes would start, and my brain hurts. Rather would I die even such a death, than know thou hadst lain in a man's bed, and that bed not mine."

Constancy
Michael Field

I love her with the seasons, with the winds,
As the stars worship, as anemones
Shudder in secret for the sun, as bees
Buzz round an open flower: in all kinds
My love is perfect, and in each she finds
Herself the goal: then why, intent to tease
And rob her delicate spirit of its ease,
Hastes she to range me with inconstant minds?
If she should die, if I were left at large
On earth without her—I, on earth, the same
Quick mortal with a thousand cries, her spell
She fears would break. And I confront the charge
As sorrowing, and as careless of my fame
As Christ intact before the infidel.

Song
William Blake

My silks and fine array,
My smiles and languish'd air,
By love are driv'n away;
And mournful lean Despair
Brings me yew to deck my grave;
Such end true lovers have.

His face is fair as heav'n
When springing buds unfold;
O why to him was't giv'n
Whose heart is wintry cold?

His breast is love's
    all-worshipp'd tomb,
Where all love's pilgrims come.

Bring me an axe and spade,
Bring me a winding sheet;
When I my grave have made
Let winds and tempests beat:
Then down I'll lie as cold as clay.
True love doth pass away!

Sorrow
Edna St. Vincent Millay

Sorrow like a ceaseless rain
Beats upon my heart.
People twist and scream in pain,—
Dawn will find them still again;
This has neither wax nor wane,
Neither stop nor start.

So_____
Fitz-Greene Halleck

The world is bright before thee,
Its summer flowers are thine,
Its calm blue sky is o'er thee,
Thy bosom Pleasure's shrine;
And thine the sunbeam given
To Nature's morning hour,
Pure, warm, as when from heaven
It burst on Eden's bower.
There is a song of sorrow,
The death-dirge of the gay,
That tells, ere dawn of morrow,
These charms may melt away,

That sun's bright beam be shaded,
That sky be blue no more,
The summer flowers be faded,
And youth's warm promise o'er.
Believe it not—though lonely
Thy evening home may be;
Though Beauty's bark can only
Float on a summer sea;
Though Time thy bloom is stealing,
There's still beyond his art
The wild-flower wreath of feeling,
The sunbeam of the heart.

That Spring Night
Lady Suwo

That spring night I spent
Pillowed on your arm
Never really happened
Except in a dream.
Unfortunately I am
Talked about anyway.

ꓝonnets From The Portuguese, XIII
Elizabeth Barrett Browning

And wilt thou have me fashion into speech
The love I bear thee, finding words enough,
And hold the torch out, while the winds are rough,
Between our faces, to cast light on each?—
I drop it at thy feet. I cannot teach
My hand to hold my spirit so far off
From myself—me—that I should bring thee proof
In words, of love hid in me out of reach.
Nay, let the silence of my womanhood
Commend my woman-love to thy belief,—
Seeing that I stand unwon, however wooed,
And rend the garment of my life, in brief,
By a most dauntless, voiceless fortitude,
Lest one touch of this heart convey its grief.

ℰlizabeth
Lizette Woodward Reese

Elizabeth, alack, Elizabeth!
Your lovely lilies blow,
Slim, love, still, love, beside the echoing stair.
The bees have found them out.
Row after row
Your pinks, those little blossoms with a breath
Blown from the east, and out the spice-trees there,
Nod up the paths; and roses white as death,
And roses red as love, grow everywhere;
For June is at the door.
Alack, alack, alack, Elizabeth!
Sweeter than June, why do you come no more?

ꓝonnet XVIII.
Sappho

Why art thou chang'd? O Phaon! tell me why?
    Love flies reproach, when passion feels decay;
    Or, I would paint the raptures of that day,

When, in sweet converse, mingling sigh with sigh,
I mark'd the graceful languor of thine eye
    As on a shady bank entranc'd we lay:
    O! Eyes! whose beamy radiance stole away
As stars fade trembling from the burning sky!
    Why art thou chang'd? dear source of all my woes!
Though dark my bosom's tint, through ev'ry vein
    A ruby tide of purest lustre flows,
Warm'd by thy love, or chill'd by thy disdain;
    And yet no bliss this sensate Being knows;
Ah! why is rapture so allied to pain?

A Song

Lizette Woodward Reese

Oh, Love, he went a-straying,
A long time ago!
I missed him in the Maying,
When blossoms were of snow;
So back I came by the old sweet way;
And for I loved him so, wept that he came not with me,
A long time ago!
Wide open stood my chamber door,
And one stepped forth to greet;
Gray Grief, strange Grief, who turned me sore
With words he spake so sweet.
I gave him meat; I gave him drink;
(And listened for Love's feet.)
How many years? I cannot think;
In truth, I do not know—
Ah, long time ago!
Oh, Love, he came not back again,
Although I kept me fair;
And each white May, in field and lane,
I waited for him there!
Yea, he forgot; but Grief stayed on,
And in Love's empty chair
Doth sit and tell of days long gone—
'Tis more than I can bear!

Sonnet XXXIII.
Sappho

I wake! delusive phantoms hence, away!
Tempt not the weakness of a lover's breast;
The softest breeze can shake the halcyon's nest,
And lightest clouds o'ercast the dawning ray!
'Twas but a vision! Now, the star of day
Peers, like a gem on Aetna's burning crest!
Welcome, ye Hills, with golden vintage drest;
Sicilian forests brown, and vallies gay!
A mournful stranger, from the Lesbian Isle,
Not strange, in loftiest eulogy of Song!
She, who could teach the Stoic's cheek to smile,
Thaw the cold heart, and chain the wond'ring throng,
Can find no balm, love's arrows to beguile;
Ah! Sorrows known too soon! and felt too long!

Sonnet 133
William Shakespeare

Beshrew that heart that makes my heart to groan
For that deep wound it gives my friend and me.
Is't not enough to torture me alone,
But slave to slavery my sweet'st friend must be?
Me from myself thy cruel eye hath taken,
And my next self thou harder hast engrossed.
Of him, myself, and thee, I am forsaken;
A torment thrice three fold thus to be crossed.
Prison my heart in thy steel bosom's ward,
But then my friend's heart let my poor heart bail;
Whoe'er keeps me, let my heart be his guard;
Thou canst not then use rigour in my gaol.
    And yet thou wilt, for I, being pent in thee,
    Perforce am thine and all that is in me.

Sonnet XXXVIII

Sappho

Oh Sigh! thou steal'st, the herald of the breast,
    The lover's fears, the lover's pangs to tell;
    Thou bid'st with timid grace the bosom swell,
Cheating the day of joy, the night of rest!
Oh! lucid Tears! with eloquence confest,
    Why on my fading cheek unheeded dwell,
    Meek, as the dew-drops on the floweret's bell
By ruthless tempests to the green-sod prest.
    Fond sigh be hush'd! congeal, O! slighted tear!
Thy feeble pow'rs the busy Fates control!
    Or if thy crystal streams again appear,
Let them, like Lethe's, oblivion roll:
    For Love the tyrant plays, when hope is near,
And she who flies the lover, chains the soul!

Ode: Who Can Support the Anguish of Love?

Ibn Al-Arabi

Who can support the anguish of love?
Who can drain the bitter draught of destiny?
    I said in my grief,
      In my burning passion:
"O would that he who caused my sickness
    Had tended me when I was sick!"
    He passsed by the house door
      Mocking, hiding himself;
      Veiling his head,
      And turning away.
His veiling did me no hurt;
I was only hurt by his having turned away from me.

Sad Love and Sad Song

Homei Iwanno

Holding a stone which has no voice,
I cry my world away with tears;
'Tis not for love as the other people say,

'Tis not for the pain which I suffer most,
'Tis more than my pain and love;
My flesh of burning thoughts will burn,
And my hot tears alone run down,
When the loneliness in my bosom comes to flow.
Nor God nor Death is in me;
If there is a thing, 'tis this loneliness:
Now I am prey of my own life,
And cry away this endless world with the stone;
It bears silence eternally growing,

$\mathcal{L}$OST
Narihira

I am so lost
In the black depths
Of the nights of love
That I can no longer tell
Dream from reality.

And I pour on it my own tears.

$\mathcal{S}$ONNET 111
William Shakespeare

O, for my sake do you with Fortune chide,
The guilty goddess of my harmful deeds,
That did not better for my life provide
Than public means which public manners breeds.
Thence comes it that my name receives a brand,
And almost thence my nature is subdued
To what it works in, like the dyer's hand.
Pity me then, and wish I were renewed,
Whilst, like a willing patient, I will drink
Potions of eisel 'gainst my strong infection;
No bitterness that I will bitter think,
Nor double penance to correct correction.
    Pity me then, dear friend, and I assure ye,
    Even that your pity is enough to cure me.

The Pearl

Hans Christian Andersen

There is a myth, a tale men tell:
Each mussel shell
That in the ocean's bitter deep doth lie,
When it has wrought its pearl, must straightway die.
O Love, though art the pearl my heart hath made.
And I am sore afraid.

Sonnet 28

William Shakespeare

How can I then return in happy plight
That am debarred the benefit of rest,
When day's oppression is not eased by night,
But day by night and night by day oppressed,
(And each, though enemies to either's reign,)
Do in consent shake hands to torture me,
The one by toil, the other to complain
How far I toil, still farther off from thee?
I tell the day, to please him, thou art bright
And dost him grace when clouds do blot the heaven:
So flatter I the swart-complexioned night,
When sparkling stars twire not thou gild'st the even.
But day doth daily draw my sorrows longer,
And night doth nightly make grief's length seem stronger

A Maiden To Her Mirror

Ella Wheeler Wilcox

He said he loved me! Then he called my hair
Silk threads wherewith sly Cupid strings his bow,
My cheek a rose leaf fallen on new snow;
And swore my round, full throat would bring despair
To Venus or to Psyche.
Time and care
Will fade these locks; the merry god, I trow,
Uses no grizzled cords upon his bow.
How will it be when I, no longer fair,

Plead for his kiss with cheeks whence long ago
The early snowflakes melted quite away,
The rose leaf died—and in whose sallow clay
Lie the deep sunken tracks of life's gaunt crow?
When this full throat shall wattle fold on fold,
Like some ripe peach left drying on a wall,
Or like a spent accordion, when all
Its music has exhaled—will love grow cold?

*S*onnet **CCXXIV**
Petrarch

If a loving belief, an artless heart,
A soft abandon, a courteous desire,
If honest wishes which a pure fire start,
An endless erring through a blind empire,
If on my forehead every thought revealed,
Or in some words broken as soon as heard,
And now by fear and now by shame repealed,
If in violet and love my face interred,
If holding someone else more than self dear,
Ever weeping and sighing without rest,
Feeding on grief, on anger and torment,
If burning when away and freezing near,
Are the causes why loving I am distressed,
Yours the sin, Lady, mine the punishment.

*T*he **Conquest of Love**
Jean Racine

I know that to the winds my reason is cast!
But since I have begun to speak at last,
I must go on and unto thee declare
A secret that I can no longer bear
In silence. Here before thee in distress
Thou seest a prince, of most rash haughtiness
A signal instance. I who in my pride
Was rebel against love, and who defied
His captive chains-I who would oft deplore

The shipwreck of weak mortals, from the shore
Thinking always to view the storm-ah, now,
Subjected to the universal law,
Do I behold myself swept far away
From every mooring. In one moment's fray
Was my presumptuous confidence o'erthrown.
This spirit doth finally a sovereign own.
For nearly six months, shamed and in despair,
Bearing the fatal arrow everywhere
That wounds me, I have struggled against thee
Vainly, and 'gainst myself. Present, I flee;
Absent, I seek thee. Even in the deeps
Of forests doth thine image haunt my steps,
Following; and to mine eyes alike the light
Of day recalleth and the shades of night
That loveliness I shun. All things combine
To make Hippolytus, despite him, thine.
My every effort fruitless proves; in vain
I seek to find my former self again.
My bow, my javelin, my chariot,
All weary me, and I remember not
The art which Neptune gave. The only noise
The woods hear is my sighings, and this voice
Mine idle coursers grow forgetful of.
It may be that so badly told a love
Will make thee, hearing me, to blush with shame
At having won it. Crude indeed and lame
The speech that tender thee my heart, and I
How strange a captive for how sweet a tie!
Yet thou shouldst find mine offering hence more dear.
Remember that I speak a tongue I ne'er
Have learned. Disdain of my ill-uttered plea,
Which would not have been made, except to thee.

*Y*ESTERDAY AND TO-MORROW

Paul Laurence Dunbar

Yesterday I held your hand,
Reverently I pressed it,
And its gentle yieldingness
From my soul I blessed it.

But to-day I sit alone,
Sad and sore repining;
Must our gold forever know
Flames for the refining?

Yesterday I walked with you,
Could a day be sweeter?
Life was all a lyric song
Set to tricksy meter.

Ah, to-day is like a dirge,
Place my arms around you,

Let me feel the same dear joy
As when first I found you.

Let me once retrace my steps,
From these roads unpleasant,
Let my heart and mind and soul
All ignore the present.

Yesterday the iron seared
And to-day means sorrow.
Pause, my soul, arise, arise,
Look where gleams the morrow.

$\mathcal{T}$HE LOVE SEAL
George Sylvester Viereck

A silver sea beneath the stars—
We paid to love his mystic rites,
And from thy lips I kissed the scars
Of fiercer joys and stranger nights.

What redder lips, what mouth of fate,
Till Buddha noddeth near the goal,
Shall, stronger still, obliterate
My one night's madness from thy soul?

I brand thee through eternity,
Upon thy blood I set my seal,
And boy and girl and change and sea
Cannot wipe out my mark or heal.

While the great life-snake sheds its coat,
I must rehearse my tragic part,
To kiss the love-wounds from thy throat,
And burn the iron in thy—heart.

$\mathcal{L}$IFE'S TRADES
Emily Dickinson

It 's such a little thing to weep,
So short a thing to sigh;
And yet by trades the size of these
We men and women die!

$\mathscr{F}$OR THE BOOK OF LOVE

Jules Laforgue

I may be dead to-morrow, uncaressed.
   My lips have never touched a woman's, none
   Has given me a look her soul, not one
Has ever held me swooning at her breast.

I have but suffered, for all nature, trees
   Whipped by the winds, wan flowers, the ashen sky,
   Suffered with all my nerves, minutely, I
Have suffered for my soul's impurities.

And I have spat on love, and, mad with pride,
   Slaughtered my flesh, and life's revenge I brave,
   And, while the whole world else was Instinct's slave,
With bitter laughter Instinct I defied.
In drawing rooms, the theater, the church,
   Before cold men, the greatest, most refined,
   And women with eyes jealous, Proud, or kind,
Whose tender souls no lust would seem to smirch,

I thought: this is the end for which they work.
   Beast coupling with the groaining beast they capture,
   And all this dirt for just three minutes' rapture!
Men, be correct! And women, Purr and smirk!

Ah! without the moon, what white nights,
What nightmares rich with ingenuity!
Don't I see your white swans there?
Doesn't someone come to turn the knob?

And it's your fault that I'm this way.
That my conscience sees double,
And my heart fishes in troubled water
For Eve, Gioconda and Dalila.

Oh, by the infinite circumflex
Of the archbeam of my cross-legged labors,
Come now-appease me just a little
With the why-and wherefore of your sex!

Unrequited
Madison Cawein

Passion? not hers, within whose virgin eyes
All Eden lay.—And I remember how
I drank the Heaven of her gaze with sighs
—She never sighed, nor gave me kiss or vow.

So have I seen a clear October pool,
Cold, liquid topaz, set within the sear
Gold of the woodland, tremorless and cool,
Reflecting all the heartbreak of the year.

Sweetheart? not she whose voice was music sweet;
Whose face was sweeter than melodious prayer.
Sweetheart I called her.—When did she repeat
Sweet to one hope or heart to one despair?

So have I seen a rose set round with thorn,
Sung to and sung to by a bird of spring,
And when, breast-pierced, the bird lay all forlorn,
The rose bloomed on, fair and unnoticing.

The Pains of Sleep
Samuel Taylor Coleridge

Ere on my bed my limbs I lay,
    It hath not been my use to pray
    With moving lips or bended knees—;
    But silently, by slow degrees,
My spirit I to Love compose,
    In humble trust mine eye-lids close,
    With reverential resignation,
    No wish conceived, no thought exprest,
    Only a sense of supplication—;
A sense o'er all my soul imprest
    That I am weak, yet not unblest,
    Since in me, round me, everywhere
    Eternal Strength and Wisdom are.
    But yester-night I prayed aloud
In anguish and in agony,

Up-starting from the fiendish crowd
Of shapes and thoughts that tortured me—:
A lurid light, a trampling throng,
Sense of intolerable wrong,
And whom I scorned, those only strong—!
Thirst of revenge, the powerless will
Still baffled, and yet burning still—!
Desire with loathing strangely mixed
On wild or hateful objects fixed.
Fantastic passions—! maddening brawl—!
And shame and terror over all!
Deeds to be hid which were not hid,
Which all confused I could not know
Whether I suffered, or I did—:
For all seemed guilt, remorse or woe,
My own or others still the same
Life-stifling fear, soul-stifling shame.
So two nights passed—: the night's dismay
Saddened and stunned the coming day.
Sleep, the wide blessing, seemed to me
Distemper's worst calamity.
The third night, when my own loud scream
Had waked me from the fiendish dream,
O'ercome with sufferings strange and wild,
I wept as if I had been a child—;
And having thus by tears subdued
My anguish to a milder mood,
Such punishments, I said, were due
To natures deepliest stained with sin,—
For aye entempesting anew
The unfathomable hell within,
The horror of their deeds to view,
To know and loathe, yet wish and do—!
Such griefs with such men well agree,
But wherefore, wherefore fall on me—?
To be beloved is all I need,
And whom I love, I love indeed.

PHYLLIS
Paul Laurence Dunbar

Phyllis ah, Phyllis, my life is a gray day,
Few are my years, but my griefs are not few,
Ever to youth should each day be a May-day,
Warm wind and rose-breath and diamonded dew—
Phyllis, ah, Phyllis, my life is a gray day.

Oh for the sunlight that shines on a May-day!
Only the cloud hangeth over my life.
Love that should bring me youth's happiest heyday
Brings me but seasons of sorrow and strife:
Phyllis, ah, Phyllis, my life is a gray day.

Sunshine or shadow, or gold day or gray day,
Life must be lived as our destinies rule;
Leisure or labor or work day or play day—
Feasts for the famous and fun for the fool;
Phyllis, ah, Phyllis, my life is a gray day.

TO M.—
Edgar Allan Poe

O! I care not that my earthly lot
  Hath little of Earth in it,
That years of love have been forgot
  In the fever of a minute:

I heed not that the desolate
  Are happier, sweet, than I,
But that you meddle with my fate
  Who am a passer-by.

It is not that my founts of bliss
  Are gushing—strange! with tears—
Or that the thrill of a single kiss
  Hath palsied many years-

Tis not that the flowers of twenty springs
  Which have wither'd as they rose
Lie dead on my heart-strings
  With the weight of an age of snows.

Not that the grass—O! may it thrive!
  On my grave is growing or grown—
But that, while I am dead yet alive
  I cannot be, lady, alone.

The Night

Emily Brontë

The night is darkening round me,
The wild winds coldly blow;
But a tyrant spell has bound me
And I cannot, cannot go.

The giant trees are bending
Their bare boughs weighed with snow,
And the storm is fast descending And yet
I cannot go.

Clouds beyond clouds above me,
Wastes beyond wastes below;
But nothing drear can move me;
I will not, cannot go.

Sonnet 27

William Shakespeare

Weary with toil, I haste me to my bed,
The dear respose for limbs with travel tired,
But then begins a journey in my head
To work my mind, when body's work's expired.
For then my thoughts (from far where I abide)
Intend a zealous pilgrimage to thee,
And keep my drooping eyelids open wide,
Looking on darkness which the blind do see.
Save that my soul's imaginary sight
Presents thy shadow to my sightless view,
Which like a jewel (hung in ghastly night)
Makes black night beauteous, and her old face new.
    Lo thus by day my limbs, by night my mind,
    For thee, and for my self, no quiet find.

I Would I Were A Careless Child

Lord Byron (George Gordon)

I would I were a careless child,
Still dwelling in my highland cave,
Or roaming through the dusky wild,
Or bounding o'er the dark blue wave;
The cumbrous pomp of Saxon pride,
Accords not with the freeborn soul,
Which loves the mountain's craggy side,
And seeks the rocks where billows roll.

Fortune! take back these cultured lands,
Take back this name of splendid sound!
I hate the touch of servile hands,
I hate the slaves that cringe around.
Place me among the rocks I love,
Which sound to Ocean's wildest roar;
I ask but this—again to rove
Through scenes my youth hath
      known before.

Few are my years, and yet I feel,
The world was ne'er designed for me:
Ah! why do dark'ning shades conceal,
The hour when man must cease to be?
Once I beheld a splendid dream,
A visionary scene of bliss:
Truth!—wherefore did thy hated beam,
Awake me to a world like this?
I loved—but those I loved are gone;
Had friends—my early friends are fled:
How cheerless feels the heart alone,
When all its former hopes are dead!
Though gay companions o'er the bowl,

Dispel awhile the sense of ill;
Though pleasure stirs the maddening soul,
The heart—the heart—is lonely still.

How dull! to hear the voice of those,
Whom rank or chance, whom wealth
      or power,
Have made, though neither friends
      nor foes,
Associates of the festive hour.
Give me again a faithful few,
In years and feelings still the same,
And I will fly the midnight crew,
Where boist'rous joy is but a name.

And woman, lovely woman! thou,
My hope, my comforter, my all!
How cold must be my bosom now,
When e'en thy smiles begin to pall!
Without a sigh I would resign,
This busy scene of splendid woe,
To make that calm contentment mine,
Which virtue knows, or seems to know.

Fain would I fly the haunts of men—
I seek to shun, not hate mankind;
My breast requires the sullen glen,
Whose gloom may suit a darken'd mind.
Oh! that to me the wings were given
Which bear the turtle to her nest!
Then would I cleave the vault of heaven,
To flee away and be at rest.

EXCHANGES
Ernest Dowson

All that I had I brought,
Little enough I know;
A poor rhyme roughly wrought,
A rose to match thy snow:
All that I had I brought.

Little enough I sought:
But a word compassionate,
A passing glance, or thought,
For me outside the gate:
Little enough I sought.

Little enough I found:
All that you had, perchance!
With the dead leaves on the ground,
I dance the devil's dance.
All that you had I found.

LOVE'S HUMILITY
Emily Dickinson

My worthiness is all my doubt,
His merit all my fear,
Contrasting which, my qualities
Do lowlier appear;
Let I should insufficient prove
For his beloved need,
The chiefest apprehension
Within my loving creed.
So I, the undivine abode
Of his elect content,
Conform my soul as 't were a church
Unto her sacrament.

HER DILEMMA (IN—CHURCH)
Thomas Hardy

The two were silent in a sunless church,
Whose mildewed walls, uneven paving-stones,
And wasted carvings passed antique research;
And nothing broke the clock's dull monotones.
Leaning against a wormy poppy-head,
So wan and worn that he could scarcely stand,
—For he was soon to die,—he softly said,
"Tell me you love me!"—holding hard her hand.
She would have given a world to breathe "yes" truly,
So much his life seemed hanging on her mind,
And hence she lied, her heart persuaded throughly,
'Twas worth her soul to be a moment kind.
But the sad need thereof, his nearing death,
So mocked humanity that she shamed to prize
A world conditioned thus, or care for breath
Where Nature such dilemmas could devise.

On Your Midnight Pallet Lying

A.E. Houseman

On your midnight pallet lying,
    Listen, and undo the door:
Lads that waste the light in sighing
    In the dark should sigh no more;
Night should ease a lover's sorrow;
Therefore, since I go to-morrow,
    Pity me before.
In the land to which I travel,
    The far dwelling, let me say—
Once, if here the couch is gravel,
    In a kinder bed I lay,
And the breast the darnel smothers
Rested once upon another's
    When it was not clay.

If Truth In Hearts That Perish.

A.E. Houseman

If truth in hearts that perish
    move the powers on high,
I think the love I bear you
    Should make you not to die.
Sure, sure, if stedfast meaning,
    If single thought could save,
The world might end to-morrow,
    You should not see the grave.
This long and sure-set liking,
    This boundless will to please,
—Oh, you should live for ever
    If there were help in these.
But now, since all is idle,
    To this lost heart be kind,
Ere to a town you journey
    Where friends are ill to find.

"Time Steals From Love"
Don Marquis

Time steals from Love all but Love's wings;
And how should aught but evil things,
Or any good but death, befall
Him that is thrall unto Time's thrall,
Slave to the lesser of these Kings?
O heart of youth that wakes and sings!
O golden vows and golden rings!
Life mocks you with the tale of all
Time steals from Love! O riven lute and writhen strings,
Dead bough whereto no blossom clings,
The glory was ephemeral!
Nor may our Autumn grief recall
The passion of the perished Springs
Time steals from Love!

On Monsieur's Departure
Elizabeth I

I grieve and dare not show my discontent,
I love and yet am forced to seem to hate,
I do, yet dare not say I ever meant,
I seem stark mute but inwardly do prate.
I am and not, I freeze and yet am burned,
Since from myself another self I turned.

My care is like my shadow in the sun,
Follows me flying, flies when I pursue it,
Stands and lies by me, doth what I have done.
His too familiar care doth make me rue it.
No means I find to rid him from my breast,
Till by the end of things it be supprest.

Some gentler passion slide into my mind,
For I am soft and made of melting snow;
Or be more cruel, love, and so be kind.
Let me or float or sink, be high or low.
Or let me live with some more sweet content,
Or die and so forget what love ere meant.

THE GALLERY

Andrew Marvell

Clora come view my Soul, and tell
Whether I have contriv'd it well.
Now all its several lodgings lye
Compos'd into one Gallery;
And the great Arras-hangings, made
Of various Faces, by are laid;
That, for all furniture, you'l find
Only your Picture in my Mind.
Here Thou art painted in the Dress
Of an Inhumane Murtheress;
Examining upon our Hearts
Thy fertile Shop of cruel Arts:
Engines more keen than ever yet
Adorned Tyrants Cabinet;
Of which the most tormenting are
Black Eyes, red Lips, and curled Hair.
But, on the other side, th' art drawn
Like to Aurora in the Dawn;
When in the East she slumb'ring lyes,
And stretches out her milky Thighs;
While all the morning Quire does sing,
And Manna falls, and Roses spring;
And, at thy Feet, the wooing Doves
Sit perfecting their harmless Loves.
Like an Enchantress here thou show'st,
Vexing thy restless Lover's Ghost;
And, by a Light obscure, dost rave
Over his Entrails, in the Cave;

Divining thence, with horrid Care,
How long thou shalt continue fair;
And (when inform'd) them throw'st away,
To be the greedy Vultur's prey.
But, against that, thou sit'st a float
Like Venus in her pearly Boat.
The Halcyons, calming all that's nigh,
Betwixt the Air and Water fly.
Or, if some rowling Wave appears,
A Mass of Ambergris it bears.
Nor blows more Wind than what may well
Convoy the Perfume to the Smell.
These Pictures and a thousand more,
Of Thee, my Gallery dost store;
In all the Forms thou can'st invent
Either to please me, or torment:
For thou alone to people me,
Art grown a num'rous Colony;
And a Collection choicer far
Then or White-hall's , or Mantua's were.
But, of these Pictures and the rest,
That at the Entrance likes me best:
Where the same Posture, and the Look
Remains, with which I first was took.
A tender Shepherdess, whose Hair
Hangs loosely playing in the Air,
Transplanting Flow'rs from the green Hill,
To crown her Head, and Bosome fill.

Philomela

Matthew Arnold

Hark! ah, the nightingale—
The tawny-throated!
Hark, from that moonlit cedar what a burst!
What triumph! hark!—what pain!

O wanderer from a Grecian shore,
Still, after many years, in distant lands,
Still nourishing in thy bewilder'd brain
That wild, unquench'd, deep-sunken, old-world pain—

Say, will it never heal?
And can this fragrant lawn
With its cool trees, and night,
And the sweet, tranquil Thames,
And moonshine, and the dew,
To thy rack'd heart and brain
Afford no balm?

Dost thou to-night behold,
Here, through the moonlight on this English grass,
The unfriendly palace in the Thracian wild?
Dost thou again peruse
With hot cheeks and sear'd eyes
The too clear web, and thy dumb sister's shame?
Dost thou once more assay
Thy flight, and feel come over thee,
Poor fugitive, the feathery change
Once more, and once more seem to make resound
With love and hate, triumph and agony,
Lone Daulis, and the high Cephissian vale?
Listen, Eugenia—
How thick the bursts come crowding through the leaves!
Again—thou hearest?
Eternal passion!
Eternal pain!

Self-Dependance

Matthew Arnold

Weary of myself, and sick of asking
What I am, and what I ought to be,
At this vessel's prow I stand, which bears me
Forwards, forwards, o'er the starlit sea.

And a look of passionate desire
O'er the sea and to the stars I send:
"Ye who from my childhood up have calm'd me,
Calm me, ah, compose me to the end!

"Ah, once more," I cried, "ye stars, ye waters,
On my heart your mighty charm renew;
Still, still let me, as I gaze upon you,
Feel my soul becoming vast like you!"

From the intense, clear, star-sown vault of heaven,
Over the lit sea's unquiet way,
In the rustling night-air came the answer:
"Wouldst thou be as these are? Live as they.

"Unaffrighted by the silence round them,
Undistracted by the sights they see,
These demand not that the things without them
Yield them love, amusement, sympathy.

"And with joy the stars perform their shining,
And the sea its long moon-silver'd roll;
For self-poised they live, nor pine with noting
All the fever of some differing soul.

Bounded by themselves, and unregardful
In what state God's other works may be,
In their own tasks all their powers pouring,
These attain the mighty life you see."

O air-born voice! long since, severely clear,
A cry like thine in mine own heart I hear:
"Resolve to be thyself; and know that he,
Who finds himself, loses his misery!"

Song: How Sweet I Roam'd From Field To Field

William Blake

How sweet I roam'd from field to field,
    And tasted all the summer's pride,
'Till I the prince of love beheld,
    Who in the sunny beams did glide!

He shew'd me lilies for my hair,
    And blushing roses for my brow;
He led me through his gardens fair,
    Where all his golden pleasures grow.

With sweet May dews my wings were wet,
    And Phoebus fir'd my vocal rage;
He caught me in his silken net,
    And shut me in his golden cage.

He loves to sit and hear me sing,
    Then, laughing, sports and plays with me;
Then stretches out my golden wing,
    And mocks my loss of liberty.

Song: Memory, Hither Come

William Blake

Memory, hither come,
    And tune your merry notes;
And, while upon the wind
    Your music floats,

I'll pore upon the stream
    Where sighing lovers dream,
And fish for fancies as they pass
    Within the watery glass.

I'll drink of the clear stream,
    And hear the linnet's song;
And there I'll lie and dream
    The day along:

And, when night comes, I'll go
    To places fit for woe,
Walking along the darken'd valley
    With silent Melancholy.

Sonnet 16

William Shakespeare

But wherefore do not you a mightier way
Make war upon this bloody tyrant Time?
And fortify your self in your decay
With means more blessed than my barren rhyme?
Now stand you on the top of happy hours,
And many maiden gardens yet unset,
With virtuous wish would bear you living flowers,
Much liker than your painted counterfeit:
So should the lines of life that life repair
Which this (Time's pencil) or my pupil pen
Neither in inward worth nor outward fair
Can make you live your self in eyes of men.
    To give away your self, keeps your self still,
    And you must live drawn by your own sweet skill.

Sonnet 60

William Shakespeare

Like as the waves make towards the pebbled shore,
So do our minutes hasten to their end,
Each changing place with that which goes before,
In sequent toil all forwards do contend.
Nativity once in the main of light,
Crawls to maturity, wherewith being crowned,
Crooked eclipses 'gainst his glory fight,
And Time that gave, doth now his gift confound.
Time doth transfix the flourish set on youth,
And delves the parallels in beauty's brow,
Feeds on the rarities of nature's truth,
And nothing stands but for his scythe to mow.
    And yet to times in hope, my verse shall stand
    Praising thy worth, despite his cruel hand.

Sonnet 64

William Shakespeare

When I have seen by Time's fell hand defaced
The rich-proud cost of outworn buried age,
When sometime lofty towers I see down-rased,
And brass eternal slave to mortal rage.
When I have seen the hungry ocean gain
Advantage on the kingdom of the shore,
And the firm soil win of the watery main,
Increasing store with loss, and loss with store.
When I have seen such interchange of State,
Or state it self confounded, to decay,
Ruin hath taught me thus to ruminate
That Time will come and take my love away.
　　This thought is as a death which cannot choose
　　But weep to have, that which it fears to lose.

Sonnet 125

William Shakespeare

Were't aught to me I bore the canopy,
With my extern the outward honouring,
Or laid great bases for eternity,
Which proves more short than waste or ruining?
Have I not seen dwellers on form and favour
Lose all, and more by paying too much rent
For compound sweet; forgoing simple savour,
Pitiful thrivers in their gazing spent?
No, let me be obsequious in thy heart,
And take thou my oblation, poor but free,
Which is not mixed with seconds, knows no art,
But mutual render, only me for thee.
　　Hence, thou suborned informer, a true soul
　　When most impeached, stands least in thy control.

THE END
Sharon Mesmer

Ample purple shadows between me and you,
this heart a calm palmetto grandly glamorous and tragic.
You, my favorite song, forever young and in one place,
my personal summer burbling up a broken flight of stairs.
The screen door slams at midnight.
Invisible schoolgirl emerges from plaid like old flaubert in egypt,
like every melodrama dreamed by a bunch of bad maryanns.
The bright sidewalks where spontaneous romance once occured
now just reminders of my poverty.
I'm really living the oriental life now,
in a perpetual dread of saying something gauche,
wasting long days on a mossy stained mattress,
dreaming the affair between the old andalusian sheik
and the little girl from mecca.
Pitiful shitheads, I won't get anywhere in this world if I don't learn
to lie about everything.
Oh, will you please screw me in cuban moonlight so's I can write
a few good poems?

DELIA: XLV
Samuel Daniel

Care-charmer Sleep, son of the sable Night,
Brother to Death, in silent darkness born:
Relieve my languish, and restore the light,
With dark forgetting of my cares, return;
And let the day be time enough to mourn
  The shipwreck of my ill-adventur'd youth:
  Let waking eyes suffice to wail their scorn,
  Without the torment of the night's untruth.
Cease dreams, th' imagery of our day-desires,
To model forth the passions of the morrow;
Never let rising sun approve you liars,
To add more grief to aggravate my sorrow.
Still let me sleep, embracing clouds in vain;
And never wake to feel the day's disdain.

$\mathcal{S}$ONNET 129

William Shakespeare

Th' expense of spirit in a waste of shame
Is lust in action, and till action, lust
Is perjured, murd'rous, bloody full of blame,
Savage, extreme, rude, cruel, not to trust,
Enjoyed no sooner but despised straight,
Past reason hunted, and no sooner had
Past reason hated as a swallowed bait,
On purpose laid to make the taker mad.
Mad in pursuit and in possession so,
Had, having, and in quest, to have extreme,
A bliss in proof and proved, a very woe,
Before a joy proposed behind a dream.
    All this the world well knows yet none knows well,
    To shun the heaven that leads men to this hell.

$\mathcal{W}$HAT DOES IT AVAIL ME?

Louise Labé

Then what does it avail me, that you once
Sang so divinely of my golden hair?
And that you once, in passion could declare
That my two eyes were like two separate suns
Whose fires the god had gathered from above
To strike you down? And what of all those hot,
Distracted tears and deathless vows? And what
Was this your stratagem? That you appear
  Enslaved while you enslave me? O, my dear,
  Forgive me this suspicion! Dazed, drawn under
  By all this grief, I know not what to do
  Except once more console myself that you
  Also will grieve, wherever you may wander.

Ye Flowery Banks

Robert Burns

Ye flowery banks o' bonnie Doon,
How can ye blume sae fair?
How can ye chant, ye little birds,
And I sae fu' o' care?

Thou'll break my heart, thou bonnie bird,
That sings upon the bough;
Thou minds me o' the happy days,
When my fause love was true.

Thou'll break my heart, thou bonnie bird,
That sings beside thy mate;
For sae I sat, and sae I sang,
And wist na o' my fate.

Aft hae I rov'd by bonnie Doon
To see the wood-bine twine,
And ilka bird sang o' its luve,
And sae did I o' mine.

Wi' lightsome heart I pu'd a rose
Frae aff its thorny tree;
And my fause luver staw my rose
But left the thorn wi' me.

THE PAIN OF LOVE

Sonnet 137
William Shakespeare

Thou blind fool, Love, what dost thou to mine eyes
That they behold and see not what they see?
They know what beauty is, see where it lies,
Yet what the best is take the worst to be.
If eyes corrupt by over partial looks,
Be anchored in the bay where all men ride,
Why of eyes' falsehood hast thou forged hooks,
Whereto the judgment of my heart is tied?
Why should my heart think that a several plot,
Which my heart knows the wide world's common place?
Or mine eyes seeing this, say this is not,
To put fair truth upon so foul a face?
    In things right true my heart and eyes have erred,
    And to this false plague are they now transferred.

A Song
Paul Laurence Dunbar

Thou art the soul of a summer's day,
Thou art the breath of the rose.
But the summer is fled
And the rose is dead
Where are they gone, who knows, who knows?

Thou art the blood of my heart o' hearts,
Thou art my soul's repose,
But my heart grows numb
And my soul is dumb
Where art thou, love, who knows, who knows?

Thou art the hope of my after years
Sun for my winter snows
But the years go by
'Neath a clouded sky.
Where shall we meet, who knows, who knows?

Jealousy
Iris Litt

I try not to think
of what they are doing now
and, wherever it is, of why
he is doing it with her
instead of me
and I try not to remember
    what it was like
when he did do it with me

but the mind insists
on remembering
what was delicious
and, after the memory,
begging for another taste.
I tell my mind every time
that it is all grown up now
and when it asks for him
the answer is No
and when it asks Why
I say, Because I say so.

Parted
Paul Laurence Dunbar

She wrapped her soul in a lace of lies,
With a prime deceit to pin it;
And I thought I was gaining a fearsome prize,
So I staked my soul to win it.

We wed and parted on her complaint,
And both were a bit of barter,
Tho' I'll confess that I'm no saint,
I'll swear that she's no martyr.

The Blacksmith
Traditional, English

A blacksmith courted me, nine months and better.
He fairly won my heart, wrote me a letter.
With his hammer in his hand, he looked so clever,
And if I was with my love, I'd live forever.

And where is my love gone, with his cheek like roses,
And his good black billycock on, decked with primroses?
I'm afraid the scorching sun will shine and burn his beauty,
And if I was with my love, I'd do my duty.

Strange news is come to town, strange news is carried,
Strange news flies up and down that my love is married.

I wish them both much joy, though they don't hear me
And may God reward him well for the slighting of me.

'What did you promise when you sat beside me?
You said you would marry me, and not deny me.'
'If I said I'd marry you, it was only for to try you,
So bring your witness, love, and I'll never deny you.'

'Oh, witness have I none save God Almighty.
And He'll reward you well for slighting of me.'
Her lips grew pale and white, it made her poor heart tremble
To think she loved one, and he proved deceitful.

ℬLUE EYES

Traditional, American

'Twould been better for us both had we never
In this wide and wicked world had never met,
But the pleasure we both seemed to gather
I'm sure, love, I'll never forget.

    Oh, I'm thinking tonight of my blue eyes
    Who is sailing far over the sea.
    I'm thinking tonight of my blue eyes
    And I wonder if he ever thinks of me.

Oh, you told me once, dear, that you loved me;
You vowed that we never would part.
But a link in the chain has been broken
Leavin' me with a sad and aching heart.
When the cold, cold grave shall enclose me
Will you come near and shed just one tear?
Will you say to the strangers around you
A poor heart you have broken lies here?

When We Fight
Lesléa Newman

milk curdle in coffee
toast burn
hot water run out
shampoo empty
tire flat
bus late
rain come
umbrella break
shoelace snap
stocking run
button fall off coat
glove disappear
pocketbook vanish
earring break
nail polish chip
typewriter key stick
white out spill
xerox machine jam
envelope don't seal
stamps stuck together
check bounce

pizza burn mouth
tomato sauce on white blouse
heel break off left shoe
key fall down sewer
mail box empty
answering machine silent
cat miss litter box
dog vomit
toilet overflow
lettuce rot in crisper
finger cut instead of onion
meat spoil
bread green
soda flat
newspaper don't come
TV fuzzy
plant on window sill die
pages fall out of book
pen run dry
light bulb burn out
heart stop

Bill Bailey
Hughie Cannon

On one summer's day,
Sun was shinin' fine,
The lady love of old Bill Bailey
Was hangin' clothes on the line
In her back yard, and weepin' hard.
She married a B&O brakeman
That took and threw her down,
Bellerin' like a prune-fed calf
With a big gang hanging round
And to that crowd, she hollered loud:

Won't you come home, Bill Bailey

Won't you come home?
She moans the whole day long.
I'll do the cookin', darling
I'll pay the rent,
I know I've done you wrong;
'Member that rainy eve that
I threw you out,
With nothing but a fine-tooth comb?
I know I'm to blame,
Well, ain't that a shame
Bill Bailey won't you please come home.

Bill drove by that door
In an automobile,
A great big diamond, coach and footman
Hear that lady squeal.
He's all alone
I heard her groan.
She hollered through the door
Bill Bailey, is you sore?
Stop a minute, listen to me
Won't I see you no more?
Bill winks his eye
As he heard her cry:

COME KISS ME LOVE

Anonymous

Come kiss me love, before you leave me
   Come kiss the one you have betrayed
   And when I'm dead, love, come and see me
   And throw sweet flowers upon my grave

Once I loved you with all my heart and soul
   I thought your love was all for me
   Until a stranger came and caught your eye
   I found you cared no more for me
Many's the night with you I've rambled
   Many's the night with you I've lain
   Thinking your love was mine forever
   And now I find it was all in vain

FOR THAT HE LOOKED NOT UPON HER

George Gascoigne

You must not wonder, though you think it strange,
To see me hold my louring head so low,
And that mine eyes take no delight to range
About the gleams which on your face do grow.
The mouse which once hath broken out of trap
Is seldom 'tice'd with the trustless bait,
But lies aloof for fear of more mishap,
And feedeth still in doubt of deep deceit.
The scorche'd fly, which once hath 'scaped the flame,
Will hardly come to play again with fire,
Whereby I learn that grievous is the game
Which follows fancy dazzled by desire:
        So that I wink or else hold down my head,
        Because your blazing eyes my bale have bred.

BANCHORY'S LANDS

Traditional, Scots

Banchory's lands are bonny when spring comes in the year
Wi' lasses sweet an' mony, but neen sae sweet's my dear.
There's neen sae sweet's my only dear, to lee wad be a sin
For she in fact micht weel be styled the flooer o' Banchory's lands.

She is a charming creature, both humourous frank and free
And mony's the nicht she'd gi'en consent to open the door to me.
And mony's the nicht she's gi'en consent to rise and lat me in
My wish be wi' you bonny lass, she stays at Hattonsburn.

For love of her I'm sore oppressed and greaved in my mind
My restless heart within my breast nae comfort there can find.
My restless heart within my breast nae comfort finds ava,
It's all for Bett o' Banchory's lands she's flooer outoor them a.

But curse upon cruel fortune while days and years do sway
For in a moment sinks our views or lifts them to the skies.
Or in a moment lifts our views or sinks them in the deep,
It disappoints the constant swain or leaves the maid to weep.

'Twas on a mid-summer's evening as I went to the fair,
And gazing all around me I spied my true love there
And gazing round and round about she was always in my view,
But words of her I couldna get for all that I could do.

It was on a mid-Lanterns as Phoebus left the sky
While I did sing with all my might my true love passed by
While I did sing with all my might my true love passed home,
And mony an anxious look she gave to see fin I would come.

Fareweel false lover unto you I bid you now adieu
For I have been most constant unto you, unto you,
My kind Providence protect you with his unerring hand
And perhaps you may prove constant unto some other man.

FRANKIE AND JOHNNY

Traditional, American

Frankie and Johnnie were lovers,
Oh, Lordie how they could love!
They swore to be true to each other,
Just as true as the stars above,
He was her man, but he done her wrong.
Frankie and Johnnie went walking
John in his brand new suit.
Then, "oh good Lawd," says Frankie
"Don't my Johnnie look real cute!"
He was her man, but he done her wrong.
Frankie she was a good woman,
And Johnnie was a good man,
And every dollar that she made
Went right into Johnnie's hand,
He was her man, but he done her wrong.
Frankie went down to the corner,
Just for a bucket of beer.
She said to the fat bartender,
"Has my lovinest man been here?"
He was her man, but he done her wrong.
"I don't want to cause you no trouble,

I don't want to tell you no lie;
But I saw your man an hour ago
With a gal named Nellie Bly,
And if he's your man, he's a-doing you wrong."
Frankie looked over the transom,
And found, to her great surprise,
That there on the bed sat Johnnie,
A-lovin' up Nellie Bly.
He was her man, but he done her wrong.
Frankie drew back her kimono;
She took out her little forty-four;
Root-a-toot-toot, three times she shot
Right through that hardwood floor,
She shot her man, 'cause he done her wrong.
Roll me over easy,
Roll me over slow,
Roll me on de right side,
'Cause de bullet hurt me so.
I was her man, but I done her wrong.
The judge said to the jury
"It's as plain as plain can be
This woman shot her lover
It's murder in the second degree.
He was her man, though he done her wrong.
This story has no moral
This story has no end
This story only goes to show
That there ain't no good in men
They'll do you wrong, just as sure as you're born.

The Kiss
Sara Teasdale

I hoped that he would love me more,
And he has kissed my mouth
But I am like a stricken bird
That cannot reach the south.

For though I know he loves me,
Tonight my heart is sad;
His kiss was not so wonderful
As all the dreams I had.

In Former Days We'd Both Agree

Bhartrihari

In former days we'd both agree
That you were me, and I was you.
What has now happened to us two,
That you are you, and I am me?

OMother, I Cannot Mind My Wheel

Landor, Walter Savage

Mother, I cannot mind my wheel;
My fingers ache, my lips are dry:
Oh! if you felt the pain I feel!
But Oh, who ever felt as I!

No longer could I doubt him true;
All other men may use deceit:
He always said my eyes were blue,
And often swore my lips were sweet.

Deserted

Harriet Monroe

O love, my love, it's over then—
Your heart flies free;
And it's now no more us two again,
The door on you and me.
And it's now no more the supper spread,
The stove singing low.
Oh, worlds away your feet are led,
Where bold winds blow.
Oh, seas between and worlds away
Our paths run now.
Go, for more dead than coffined clay
Is love's dead vow.
Go, may your bread be sweet, your rest
As soft and deep be
As when you slept upon my breast
And gave the world for me.

Go, for my heart cries out with pain,
With joy cries out.
Go! you've unwound the golden chain—
Love's hope, love's doubt.
Go! you were mine—now mine shall be
The whole brave world.
My spirit flutters and is free,
With wings unfurled.
Out of my little house of bliss,
O lost love sweet,
Out of my grief and loneliness
Now will I rise to greet
The beggar in the street below,
The saint who prays above;
And each will be—oh, well I know!—
You—you, lost love.

THE RESOLVE

Sir Walter Scott

My wayward fate I needs must 'plain,
Though bootless be the theme;
I loved, and was beloved again,
Yet all was but a dream:
For, as her love was quickly got,
So it was quickly gone;
No more I'll bask in flame so hot,
But coldly dwell alone.
Not maid more bright than maid was e'er
My fancy shall beguile,
By flattering word, or feigned tear,
By gesture, look, or smile:
No more I'll call the shaft fair shot,
Till it has fairly flown,
Nor scorch me at a flame so hot;
I'll rather freeze alone.
Each ambush'd Cupid I'll defy,
In cheek, or chin, or brow,
And deem the glance of woman's eye
As weak as woman's vow:
I'll lightly hold the lady's heart,
That is but lightly won;
I'll steel my breast to beauty's art,
And learn to live alone.

The flaunting torch soon blazes out,
The diamond's ray abides;
The flame its glory hurls about,
The gem its lustre hides;
Such gem I fondly deem'd was mine,
And glow'd a diamond stone,
But, since each eye may see it shine,
I'll darkling dwell alone.
No waking dream shall tinge my thought
With dyes so bright and vain,
No silken net, so slightly wrought,
Shall tangle me again:
No more I'll pay so dear for wit,
I'll live upon mine own,
Nor shall wild passion trouble it,
I'll rather dwell alone.
And thus I'll hush my heart to rest—
Thy loving labor's lost;
Thou shalt no more be wildly blest,
To be so strangely crost;
The widow'd turtles mateless die,
The phoenix is but one;
They seek no loves, no more will I—
I'll rather dwell alone.

THE MAID OF NEIDPATH

Sir Walter Scott

O lovers' eyes are sharp to see,
And lovers' ears in hearing;
And love, in life's extremity,
Can lend an hour of cheering.
Disease had been in Mary's bower,
And slow decay from mourning,

Though now she sits on Neidpath's tower,
To watch her love's returning.
All sunk and dim her eyes so bright,
Her form decay'd by pining,
Till through her wasted hand, at night,
You saw the taper shining;
By fits, a sultry hectic hue
Across her cheek was flying;
By fits, so ashy pale she grew,
Her maidens thought her dying.
Yet keenest powers to see and hear
Seem'd in her frame residing;
Before the watch-dog pricked his ear
She heard her lover's riding;
Ere scarce a distant form was ken'd,
She knew, and waved to greet him;
And o'er the battlement did bend,
As on the wing to meet him.
He came—he pass'd—an heedless gaze,
As o'er some stranger glancing;
Her welcome, spoke in faltering phrase,
Lost in his courser's prancing.
The castle arch, whose hollow tone
Returns each whisper spoken,
Could scarcely catch the feeble moan
Which told her heart was broken.

*S*ONNET 10

Edmund Spenser

Unrighteous Lord of love, what law is this
That me thou makest thus tormented be:
The whiles she lordeth in licentious blisse
Of her free will, scorning both thee and me.
See how the Tyrannesse doth joy to see
The huge massacres which her eyes do make:
And humbled harts brings captives unto thee,
That thou of them mayst mightie vengeance take.
But her proud heart doe thou a little shake

And that high look, with which she doth comptroll
All this worlds pride, bow to a baser make,
And all her faults in thy black booke enroll.
That I may laugh at her in equall sort,
As she doth laugh at me and makes my pain her sport.

Sympathy Canteen
Robert Homem

She follows me like disease
    we sit at a table
There are crowds
      The men tell stories
        & the girls blush & laugh

There are burning butterflies
    in her eyes—raging & screaming—
Her eyes are unhappy green bottles
    of broken glass
I don't know her anymore
    She says she knows me—well—

Her hands are cupped like shells
    Her hair is brown seaweed
      She speaks of suicide

This time I'm not listening
    It's 4:47pm late afternoon
    & I hate the traffic at this time—

Woman
Oliver Goldsmith

When lovely woman stops to folly,
And finds too late that men betray,
What charm can soothe her melancholy?
What art can wash her tears away?

The only art her guilt to cover,
To hide her shame from ev'ry eye,
To give repentance to her lover,
And wring his bosom is—to die.

Sonnet VI, Bluebeard
Edna St. Vincent Millay

This door you might not open, and you did;
So enter now, and see for what slight thing
You are betrayed...Here is no treasure hid,
No cauldron, no clear crystal mirroring
The sought-for truth, no heads of women slain
For greed like yours, no writhings of distress,
But only what you see...Look yet again—
An empty room, cobwebbed and comfortless.
Yet this alone out of my life I kept
Unto myself, lest any know me quite;
And you did so profane me when you crept
Unto the threshold of this room to-night
That I must never more behold your face.
This now is yours. I seek another place.

Betrayed
Lizette Woodward Reese

She is false, O Death, she is fair!
Let me hide my head on thy knee;
Blind mine eyes, dull mine ears, O Death!
She hath broke my heart for me!
Give me a perfect dream;
Find me a rare, dim place;
But let not her voice come nigh,
And keep out her face—her face!

Tell Me Some Way
Lizette Woodward Reese

Oh, you who love me not, tell me some way
Whereby I may forget you for a space;
Nay, clean forget you and your lovely face—
Yet well I know how vain this prayer I pray.
All weathers hold you. Can I make the May
Forbid her boughs blow white in every place?

Or rob June of her rose that comes apace?
Cheat of their charm the elder months and gray?
Aye, were you dead, you could not be forgot:
So sparse the bloom along the lanes would be;
Such sweetness out the briery hedges fled;
My tears would fall that you had loved me not,
And bitterer tears that you had gone from me;
Living, you break my heart, so would you dead!

Sonnet XXVII

Sappho

Oh! ye bright Stars! that on the Ebon fields
　　Of Heav'n's empire, trembling seems to stand;
　　'Till rosy morn unlocks her portal bland,
Where the proud Sun his fiery banner wields!
To flames, less fierce than mine, your lustre yields,
　　And pow'rs more strong my countless tears command;
　　Love strikes the feeling heart with ruthless hand,
And only spares the breast which dullness shields!
　　Since, then, capricious nature but bestows
The fine affections of the soul, to prove
　　A keener sense of desolating woes,
Far, far from me the empty boast remove;
　　If bliss from coldness, pain from passion flows,
Ah! who would wish to feel, or learn to love?

Song

William Blake

My silks and fine array,
My smiles and languish'd air,
By love are driv'n away;
And mournful lean Despair
Brings me yew to deck my grave;
Such end true lovers have.

His face is fair as heav'n
When springing buds unfold;

O why to him was't giv'n
Whose heart is wintry cold?
His breast is love's all-worshipp'd tomb,
Where all love's pilgrims come.

Bring me an axe and spade,
Bring me a winding sheet;
When I my grave have made
Let winds and tempests beat:
Then down I'll lie as cold as clay.
True love doth pass away!

Sonnet 134
William Shakespeare

So, now I have confessed that he is thine
And I myself am mortgaged to thy will,
Myself I'll forfeit, so that other mine
Thou wilt restore to be my comfort still.
But thou wilt not, nor he will not be free,
For thou art covetous, and he is kind;
He learned but surety-like to write for me
Under that bond that him as fist doth bind.
The statute of thy beauty thou wilt take,
Thou usurer that put'st forth all to use,
And sue a friend came debtor for my sake;
So him I lose through my unkind abuse.
    Him have I lost, thou hast both him and me;
    He pays the whole, and yet am I not free.

Sonnet 40
William Shakespeare

Take all my loves, my love, yea take them all;
What hast thou then more than thou hadst before?
No love, my love, that thou mayst true love call;
All mine was thine, before thou hadst this more.
Then if for my love, thou my love receivest,
I cannot blame thee for my love thou usest;
But yet be blamed, if thou this self deceivest

By wilful taste of what thy self refusest.
I do forgive thy robbery, gentle thief,
Although thou steal thee all my poverty;
And yet love knows it is a greater grief
To bear love's wrong, than hate's known injury.
 Lascivious grace, in whom all ill well shows,
 Kill me with spites; yet we must not be foes.

ℛUMOR LAETALIS
Peter Abelard (attributed to)

I am constantly wounded
By the deadly gossip that adds
Insult to injury, that
Punished me mercilessly
With the news of your latest
Scandal in my ears. Wherever
I go the smirking fame of each
Fresh despicable infamy
Has run on ahead of me.
Can't you learn to be cautious
About your lecheries?
Hide your practices in darkness;
Keep away from raised eyebrows.
If you must murder love, do it
Covertly, with your candied
Prurience and murmured lewdness.

You were never the heroine
Of dirty stories in the days
When love bound us together.
Now those links are broken, desire
Is frozen, and you are free
To indulge every morbid lust,
And filthy jokes about your

Latest amour are the delight
Of every cocktail party.
Your boudoir is a brothel;
Your salon is a saloon;
Even your sensibilities
And your depraved innocence
Are only special premiums,
Rewards of a shameful commerce.

O the heartbreaking memory
Of days like flowers, and your
Eyes that shone like Venus the star
In our brief nights, and the soft bird
Flight of your love about me;
And now your eyes are as bitter
As a rattlesnake's dead eyes
And your disdain as malignant.
Those who give off the smell of coin
You warm in bed; I who have
Love to bring am not even
Allowed to speak to you now.
You receive charlatans and fools;
I have only swindling
Memory of poisoned honey.

$\mathcal{U}$NTITLED
Matt Groenig

Love is a perky elf dancing a merry little jig and then suddenly he turns on you
with a miniature machine gun.

$\mathcal{A}$ BROKEN APPOINTMENT
Thomas Hardy

You did not come,
And marching Time drew on, and wore me numb.
Yet less for loss of your dear presence there
Than that I thus found lacking in your make
That high compassion which can overbear
Reluctance for pure loving kindness' sake
Grieved I, when, as the hope-hour stroked its sum,
You did not come.
You love not me,
And love alone can lend you loyalty;
I know and knew it.
But, unto the store
Of human deeds divine in all but name,
Was it not worth a little hour or more
To add yet this:
Once you, a woman, came
To soothe a time-torn man; even though it be
You love me not?

$\mathcal{Y}$OU LOVED ME
Marina Tsvetaeva

You loved me. And your lies had their own probity.
There was a truth behind every falsehood.
Your love went far beyond any possible
     boundary as no one else's could.

Your love seemed to last even longer
     than time itself. Now you wave your hand—
and suddenly your love for me is over!
That is the truth in five words.

The Lover and the Moon

Paul Laurence Dunbar

A lover whom duty called over the wave,
With himself communed: "Will my love be true
If left to herself? Had I better not sue
Some friend to watch over her, good and grave?

But my friend might fail in my need," he said,
"And I return to find love dead.
Since friendships fade like the flow'rs of June,
I will leave her in charge of the stable moon."

Then he said to the moon: "O dear old moon,
Who for years and years from thy throne above
Hast nurtured and guarded young lovers and love,
My heart has but come to its waiting June,

And the promise time of the budding vine;
Oh, guard thee well this love of mine."
And he barked him then while all was still,
And the pale moon answered and said, "I will."

And he sailed in his ship o'er many seas,
And he wandered wide o'er strange far strands:
in isles of the south and in Orient lands,
Where pestilence lurks in the breath of the breeze.

But his star was high, so he braved the main,
And sailed him blithely home again;
And with joy he bended his footsteps soon
To learn of his love from the matron moon.

She sat as of yore, in her olden place,
Serene as death, in her silver chair.
A white rose gleamed in her whiter hair,
And the tint of a blush was on her face.

At sight of the youth she sadly bowed
And hid her face 'neath a gracious cloud.
She faltered faint on the night's dim marge,
"But how," spoke the youth, "have you kept your charge?"

The moon was sad at a trust ill-kept;
The blush went out in her blanching cheek,
And her voice was timid and low and weak,
As she made her plea and sighed and wept.

"Oh, another prayed and another pled,
 And I couldn't resist," she answering said;
"But love still grows in the hearts of men:
Go forth, dear youth, and love again."

But he turned him away from her proffered grace.
"Thou art false, O moon, as the hearts of men,
I will not, will not love again."
And he turned sheer 'round with a soul-sick face

To the sea, and cried: "Sea, curse the moon,
Who makes her vows and forgets so soon."
And the awful sea with anger stirred,
And his breast heaved hard as he lay and heard.

And ever the moon wept down in rain,
And ever her sighs rose high in wind;
But the earth and sea were deaf and blind,
And she wept and sighed her griefs in vain.

And ever at night, when the storm is fierce,
The cries of a wraith through the thunders pierce;
And the waves strain their awful hands on high
To tear the false moon from the sky.

THE INEVITABLE
Emily Dickinson

While I was fearing it, it came,
But came with less of fear,
Because that fearing it so long
Had almost made it dear.
There is a fitting dismay,
A fitting despair.

'Tis harder knowing it is due,
Than knowing it is here.
The trying on the utmost,
The morning it is new,
Is terribler than wearing it
A whole existence through.

The Blight of Love

Mary Tucker

Many long years ago, I loved a youth,
Who seemed the soul of honor and of truth—
He charmed my heart with some unholy spell,
He was a serpent, whom I loved so well.

The blush of girlhood had just ting'd my cheek;
He knew me young—perchance he thought me weak.
'Tis said, he often boasted of his power,
To gather for his own each new-blown flower.

My simple language can not well describe
How first he stood before me in his pride;
His form was cast in beauty's manly mould;
His eyes shot fire, and his hair was gold.

Fain, fain would I describe to you his glance;
One look enough, to throw me in a trance;
His flute-like voice—ah! from my sleep I woke,
When on mine ear the cadence gently broke.

A month passed by: he lingered by my side,
Longed for the time, when I should be his bride;
Ah! bitter ending, of that month of years,
A life of sorrow, and a life of tears.

The scathing truth, like any lightning stroke,
Fell'd me to earth, and my poor heart was broke;
He, frightened, turned and left me, with my woe,
For, in my wrath, I sternly bade him go.

I've never loved again; for there, and then,
All my faith vanished in the truth of men.
Of that short month, 'tis seldom that I speak,
And to forget my youth, in vain I seek.

DESERTED
Harriet Monroe

O love, my love, it's over then—
Your heart flies free;
And it's now no more us two again,
The door on you and me.
And it's now no more the supper spread,
The stove singing low.
Oh, worlds away your feet are led,
Where bold winds blow.
Oh, seas between and worlds away
Our paths run now.
Go, for more dead than coffined clay
Is love's dead vow.
Go, may your bread be sweet, your rest
As soft and deep be
As when you slept upon my breast
And gave the world for me.

Go, for my heart cries out with pain,
With joy cries out.
Go! you've unwound the golden chain—
Love's hope, love's doubt.
Go! you were mine—now mine shall be
The whole brave world.
My spirit flutters and is free,
With wings unfurled.
Out of my little house of bliss,
O lost love sweet,
Out of my grief and loneliness
Now will I rise to greet
The beggar in the street below,
The saint who prays above;
And each will be—oh, well I know!—
You—you, lost love.

A DIVINE IMAGE
William Blake

Cruelty has a Human heart
And Jealousy a Human Face,
Terror, the Human Form Divine,
And Secrecy, the Human Dress.

The Human Dress is forged Iron,
The Human Form, a fiery Forge,
The Human Face, a Furnace seal'd,
The Human Heart, its hungry Gorge.

Revulsion

Thomas Hardy

Though I waste watches framing words to fetter
Some spirit to mine own in clasp and kiss,
Out of the night there looms a sense 'twere better
To fail obtaining whom one fails to miss.
For winning love we win the risk of losing,
And losing love is as one's life were riven;
It cuts like contumely and keen ill-using
To cede what was superfluously given.
Let me then feel no more the fateful thrilling
That devastates the love-worn wooer's frame,
The hot ado of fevered hopes, the chilling
That agonizes disappointed aim!
So may I live no junctive law fulfilling,
And my heart's table bear no woman's name.

The Tryst

Mary Tucker

I waited full two hours, or more,
Beneath the old pine tree,
Where oft I've lingered twilight hours,
Watching, my Love, for thee.

I waited till the shadows grew
Like giants, grim and grey;
I waited till night's coming chased
The shadows far away.

I waited for, I knew not what;
But, oh, I waited there,
Hoping, perchance, some ray to find,
To lighten my despair.

A year ago last May, I sat
Beneath the old pine-tree;
My tryst was not a broken one,
For, Love, you came to me.

I waited, and my spirit called
Thy spirit, Love, to me;
No tryst was ever broken there
Beneath the old pine-tree.

Love's Draft

Paul Laurence Dunbar

The draft of love was cool and sweet
You gave me in the cup,
But, ah, love's fire is keen and fleet,
And I am burning up.

Unless the tears I shed for you
Shall quench this burning flame,
It will consume me through and through,
And leave but ash—a name.

A Poison Tree

William Blake

I was angry with my friend:
I told my wrath , my wrath did end.
I was angry with my foe:
I told it not, my wrath did grow.

And I watered it in fears,
Night and morning with my tears;
And I sunned it with smiles,
And with soft deceitful wiles.

And it grew both day and night,
Till it bore an apple bright.
And my foe beheld it shine,
And he knew it was mine,

And into my garden stole,
When the night had veild the pole;
In the morning glad I see
My foe outstretchd beneath the tree.

IX

Emily Dickinson

Poor little heart!
Did they forget thee?
Then dinna care! Then dinna care!
Proud little heart!
Did they forsake thee?
Be debonair! Be debonair!
Frail little heart!
I would not break thee:
Could'st credit me? Could'st credit me?
Gay little heart!
Like morning glory
Thou 'll wilted be; thou 'll wilted be!

Amabel

Thomas Hardy

I marked her ruined hues,
Her custom-straitened views,
And asked, "Can there indwell
    My Amabel?"
I looked upon her gown,
Once rose, now earthen brown;
The change was like the knell
    Of Amabel.

Her step's mechanic ways
Had lost the life of May's;
Her laugh, once sweet in swell,
    Spoilt Amabel.
I mused: "Who sings the strain
I sang ere warmth did wane?
Who thinks its numbers spell
    His Amabel?"—

Knowing that, though Love cease,
Love's race shows undecrease;
All find in dorp or dell
    An Amabel.
—I felt that I could creep
To some housetop, and weep,
That Time the tyrant fell
    Ruled Amabel!

I said (the while I sighed
That love like ours had died),
"Fond things I'll no more tell
    To Amabel,
But leave her to her fate,
And fling across the gate,
'Till the Last Trump, farewell,
    O Amabel!'"

No Second Troy

William Butler Yeats

Why should I blame her that she filled my days
With misery, or that she would of late
Have taught to ignorant men most violent ways,
Or hurled the little streets upon the great,
Had they but courage equal to desire?
What could have made her peaceful with a mind
That nobleness made simple as a fire,
With beauty like a tightened bow, a kind
That is not natural in an age like this,
Being high and solitary and most stern?
Why, what could she have done being what she is?
Was there another Troy for her to burn?

Aedh Thinks of Those Who Have Spoken
Evil Of His Beloved

William Butler Yeats

Half close your eyelids, loosen your hair,
And dream about the great and their pride;
They have spoken against you everywhere,
But weigh this song with the great and their pride;
I made it out of a mouthful of air,
Their children's children shall say they have lied.

Sonnet 4

William Shakespeare

Unthrifty loveliness why dost thou spend,
Upon thy self thy beauty's legacy?
Nature's bequest gives nothing but doth lend,
And being frank she lends to those are free:
Then beauteous niggard why dost thou abuse,
The bounteous largess given thee to give?
Profitless usurer why dost thou use
So great a sum of sums yet canst not live?
For having traffic with thy self alone,
Thou of thy self thy sweet self dost deceive,
Then how when nature calls thee to be gone,
What acceptable audit canst thou leave?
   Thy unused beauty must be tombed with thee,
   Which used lives th' executor to be.

Sonnet 62

William Shakespeare

Sin of self-love possesseth all mine eye,
And all my soul, and all my every part;
And for this sin there is no remedy,
It is so grounded inward in my heart.
Methinks no face so gracious is as mine,
No shape so true, no truth of such account,
And for my self mine own worth do define,

As I all other in all worths surmount.
But when my glass shows me my self indeed
beated and chopt with tanned antiquity,
Mine own self-love quite contrary I read:
Self, so self-loving were iniquity.
      'Tis thee (my self) that for my self I praise,
      Painting my age with beauty of thy days.

Sonnet 92
William Shakespeare

But do thy worst to steal thy self away,
For term of life thou art assured mine,
And life no longer than thy love will stay,
For it depends upon that love of thine.
Then need I not to fear the worst of wrongs,
When in the least of them my life hath end,
I see, a better state to me belongs
Than that, which on thy humour doth depend.
Thou canst not vex me with inconstant mind,
Since that my life on thy revolt doth lie,
O what a happy title do I find,
Happy to have thy love, happy to die!
      But what's so blessed-fair that fears no blot?
      Thou mayst be false, and yet I know it not.

Sonnet 8
William Shakespeare

Music to hear, why hear'st thou music sadly?
Sweets with sweets war not, joy delights in joy:
Why lov'st thou that which thou receiv'st not gladly,
Or else receiv'st with pleasure thine annoy?
If the true concord of well-tuned sounds,
By unions married do offend thine ear,
They do but sweetly chide thee, who confounds
In singleness the parts that thou shouldst bear:
Mark how one string sweet husband to another,
Strikes each in each by mutual ordering;

Resembling sire, and child, and happy mother,
Who all in one, one pleasing note do sing:
Whose speechless song being many, seeming one,
Sings this to thee, 'Thou single wilt prove none'.

Sonnet 35

William Shakespeare

No more be grieved at that which thou hast done,
Roses have thorns, and silver fountains mud,
Clouds and eclipses stain both moon and sun,
And loathsome canker lives in sweetest bud.
All men make faults, and even I in this,
Authorizing thy trespass with compare,
My self corrupting salving thy amiss,
Excusing thy sins more than thy sins are:
For to thy sensual fault I bring in sense,
Thy adverse party is thy advocate,
And 'gainst my self a lawful plea commence:
Such civil war is in my love and hate,
    That I an accessary needs must be,
    To that sweet thief which sourly robs from me.

Sonnet 70

William Shakespeare

That thou art blamed shall not be thy defect,
For slander's mark was ever yet the fair,
The ornament of beauty is suspect,
A crow that flies in heaven's sweetest air.
So thou be good, slander doth but approve,
Thy worth the greater being wooed of time,
For canker vice the sweetest buds doth love,
And thou present'st a pure unstained prime.
Thou hast passed by the ambush of young days,
Either not assailed, or victor being charged,
Yet this thy praise cannot be so thy praise,
To tie up envy, evermore enlarged,
    If some suspect of ill masked not thy show,
    Then thou alone kingdoms of hearts shouldst owe.

Sonnet 72
William Shakespeare

O lest the world should task you to recite,
What merit lived in me that you should love
After my death (dear love) forget me quite,
For you in me can nothing worthy prove.
Unless you would devise some virtuous lie,
To do more for me than mine own desert,
And hang more praise upon deceased I,
Than niggard truth would willingly impart:
O lest your true love may seem false in this,
That you for love speak well of me untrue,
My name be buried where my body is,
And live no more to shame nor me, nor you.
    For I am shamed by that which I bring forth,
    And so should you, to love things nothing worth.

Sonnet 74
William Shakespeare

But be contented when that fell arrest,
Without all bail shall carry me away,
My life hath in this line some interest,
Which for memorial still with thee shall stay.
When thou reviewest this, thou dost review,
The very part was consecrate to thee,
The earth can have but earth, which is his due,
My spirit is thine the better part of me,
So then thou hast but lost the dregs of life,
The prey of worms, my body being dead,
The coward conquest of a wretch's knife,
Too base of thee to be remembered,
    The worth of that, is that which it contains,
    And that is this, and this with thee remains.

Sonnet 86
William Shakespeare

Was it the proud full sail of his great verse,
Bound for the prize of (all too precious) you,
That did my ripe thoughts in my brain inhearse,
Making their tomb the womb wherein they grew?
Was it his spirit, by spirits taught to write,
Above a mortal pitch, that struck me dead?
No, neither he, nor his compeers by night
Giving him aid, my verse astonished.
He nor that affable familiar ghost
Which nightly gulls him with intelligence,
As victors of my silence cannot boast,
I was not sick of any fear from thence.
　　　But when your countenance filled up his line,
　　　Then lacked I matter, that enfeebled mine.

Sonnet 93
William Shakespeare

So shall I live, supposing thou art true,
Like a deceived husband, so love's face,
May still seem love to me, though altered new:
Thy looks with me, thy heart in other place.
For there can live no hatred in thine eye,
Therefore in that I cannot know thy change,
In many's looks, the false heart's history
Is writ in moods and frowns and wrinkles strange.
But heaven in thy creation did decree,
That in thy face sweet love should ever dwell,
Whate'er thy thoughts, or thy heart's workings be,
Thy looks should nothing thence, but sweetness tell.
　　　How like Eve's apple doth thy beauty grow,
　　　If thy sweet virtue answer not thy show.

Sonnet 94

William Shakespeare

They that have power to hurt, and will do none,
That do not do the thing, they most do show,
Who moving others, are themselves as stone,
Unmoved, cold, and to temptation slow:
They rightly do inherit heaven's graces,
And husband nature's riches from expense,
Tibey are the lords and owners of their faces,
Others, but stewards of their excellence:
The summer's flower is to the summer sweet,
Though to it self, it only live and die,
But if that flower with base infection meet,
The basest weed outbraves his dignity:
    For sweetest things turn sourest by their deeds,
    Lilies that fester, smell far worse than weeds.

Sonnet 1: Dost See How Unregarded Now

Sir John Suckling

Dost see how unregarded now
That piece of beauty passes?
There was a time when I did vow
To that alone;
But mark the fate of faces;
The red and white works now no more on me
Than if it could not charm, or I not see.
And yet the face continues good,
And I have still desires, Am still the selfsame flesh and blood,
As apt to melt
And suffer from those fires;
Oh some kind pow'r unriddle where it lies,
Whether my heart be faulty, or her eyes?
She ev'ry day her man does kill,
And I as often die;
Neither her power then, nor my will
Can question'd be.
What is the mystery?
Sure beauty's empires, like to greater states,
Have certain periods set, and hidden fates.

Sonnet 99

William Shakespeare

The forward violet thus did I chide,
Sweet thief, whence didst thou steal thy sweet that smells,
If not from my love's breath? The purple pride
Which on thy soft check for complexion dwells,
In my love's veins thou hast too grossly dyed.
The lily I condemned for thy hand,
And buds of marjoram had stol'n thy hair,
The roses fearfully on thorns did stand,
One blushing shame, another white despair:
A third nor red, nor white, had stol'n of both,
And to his robbery had annexed thy breath,
But for his theft in pride of all his growth
A vengeful canker eat him up to death.
  More flowers I noted, yet I none could see,
  But sweet, or colour it had stol'n from thee.

Sonnet 100

William Shakespeare

Where art thou Muse that thou forget'st so long,
To speak of that which gives thee all thy might?
Spend'st thou thy fury on some worthless song,
Darkening thy power to lend base subjects light?
Return forgetful Muse, and straight redeem,
In gentle numbers time so idly spent,
Sing to the ear that doth thy lays esteem,
And gives thy pen both skill and argument.
Rise resty Muse, my love's sweet face survey,
If time have any wrinkle graven there,
If any, be a satire to decay,
And make time's spoils despised everywhere.
  Give my love fame faster than Time wastes life,
  So thou prevent'st his scythe, and crooked knife.

Sonnet 103

William Shakespeare

Alack what poverty my muse brings forth,
That having such a scope to show her pride,
The argument all bare is of more worth
Than when it hath my added praise beside.
O blame me not if I no more can write!
Look in your glass and there appears a face,
 That over-goes my blunt invention quite,
Dulling my lines, and doing me disgrace.
Were it not sinful then striving to mend,
To mar the subject that before was well?
For to no other pass my verses tend,
Than of your graces and your gifts to tell.
 And more, much more than in my verse can sit,
 Your own glass shows you, when you look in it.

Sonnet 112

William Shakespeare

Your love and pity doth th' impression fill,
Which vulgar scandal stamped upon my brow,
For what care I who calls me well or ill,
So you o'er-green my bad, my good allow?
You are my all the world, and I must strive,
To know my shames and praises from your tongue,
None else to me, nor I to none alive,
That my steeled sense or changes right or wrong.
In so profound abysm I throw all care
Of others' voices, that my adder's sense,
To critic and to flatterer stopped are:
Mark how with my neglect I do dispense.
 You are so strongly in my purpose bred,
 That all the world besides methinks are dead.

LITTLE QUEENIE
Sharon Mesmer

Dirt-dark she was, a beast of burden,
looming large and nurse-like in my garden.
The autumn leaves fell like a gentle rain;
I told her I loved her, she said,
"Tell me again."

Little Queenie she was: cleap clothes and roses.
She smelled like a church, she had valentine poses.
My pious bones were broken like a waiting slave's
when she said, "You ain't no angel
but you sure are brave."

She ruined my roof, now I'm drowning in light;
she broke my boat, but I drifted upstream;
I'm so drunk in this world there's no tale to tell;
she said, "Once you leave me
you'll be an angel."

Transition's skin is so transparent:
kerosene colors in a tall glass furnace.
Like Penelope I'm waiting on her pure war love,
on a bare white bed
under a bare light bulb.

SONNET 114
William Shakespeare

Or whether doth my mind being crowned with you
Drink up the monarch's plague this flattery?
Or whether shall I say mine eye saith true,
And that your love taught it this alchemy?
To make of monsters, and things indigest,
Such cherubins as your sweet self resemble,
Creating every bad a perfect best
As fast as objects to his beams assemble:
O 'tis the first, 'tis flattery in my seeing,
And my great mind most kingly drinks it up,
Mine eye well knows what with his gust is 'greeing,

And to his palate doth prepare the cup.
　　If it be poisoned, 'tis the lesser sin,
　　That mine eye loves it and doth first begin.

Sonnet 118
William Shakespeare

Like as to make our appetite more keen
With eager compounds we our palate urge,
As to prevent our maladies unseen,
We sicken to shun sickness when we purge.
Even so being full of your ne'er-cloying sweetness,
To bitter sauces did I frame my feeding;
And sick of welfare found a kind of meetness,
To be diseased ere that there was true needing.
Thus policy in love t' anticipate
The ills that were not, grew to faults assured,
And brought to medicine a healthful state
Which rank of goodness would by ill be cured.
　　But thence I learn and find the lesson true,
　　Drugs poison him that so feil sick of you.

Sonnet 119
William Shakespeare

What potions have I drunk of Siren tears
Distilled from limbecks foul as hell within,
Applying fears to hopes, and hopes to fears,
Still losing when I saw my self to win!
What wretched errors hath my heart committed,
Whilst it hath thought it self so blessed never!
How have mine eyes out of their spheres been fitted
In the distraction of this madding fever!
O benefit of ill, now I find true
That better is, by evil still made better.
And ruined love when it is built anew
Grows fairer than at first, more strong, far greater.
　　So I return rebuked to my content,
　　And gain by ills thrice more than I have spent.

SONNET 121

William Shakespeare

'Tis better to be vile than vile esteemed,
When not to be, receives reproach of being,
And the just pleasure lost, which is so deemed,
Not by our feeling, but by others' seeing.
For why should others' false adulterate eyes
Give salutation to my sportive blood?
Or on my frailties why are frailer spies,
Which in their wills count bad what I think good?
No, I am that I am, and they that level
At my abuses, reckon up their own,
I may be straight though they themselves be bevel;
By their rank thoughts, my deeds must not be shown
    Unless this general evil they maintain,
    All men are bad and in their badness reign.

MEDIOCRITY IN LOVE REJECTED

Thomas Carew

Give me more love, or more disdain;
The torrid or the frozen zone
Bring equal ease unto my pain;
The temperate affords me none:
Either extreme, of love or hate,
Is sweeter than a calm estate.

Give me a storm, if it be love,
Like Danaë in that golden shower,
I swim in pleasure; if it prove
Disdain, that torrent will devour
My vulture hopes; and he's possessed
Of heaven that's from hell released.
Then crown my joys, or cure my pain;
Give me love or more disdain.

Sonnet 124

William Shakespeare

If my dear love were but the child of state,
It might for Fortune's bastard be unfathered,
As subject to time's love or to time's hate,
Weeds among weeds, or flowers with flowers gathered.
No it was builded far from accident,
It suffers not in smiling pomp, nor falls
Under the blow of thralled discontent,
Whereto th' inviting time our fashion calls:
It fears not policy that heretic,
Which works on leases of short-numbered hours,
But all alone stands hugely politic,
That it nor grows with heat, nor drowns with showers.
  To this I witness call the fools of time,
  Which die for goodness, who have lived for crime.

Sonnet 148

William Shakespeare

O me! what eyes hath love put in my head,
Which have no correspondence with true sight,
Or if they have, where is my judgment fled,
That censures falsely what they see aright?
If that be fair whereon my false eyes dote,
What means the world to say it is not so?
If it be not, then love doth well denote,
Love's eye is not so true as all men's: no,
How can it? O how can love's eye be true,
That is so vexed with watching and with tears?
No marvel then though I mistake my view,
The sun it self sees not, till heaven clears.
  O cunning love, with tears thou keep'st me blind,
  Lest eyes well-seeing thy foul faults should find.

Sonnet 149

William Shakespeare

Canst thou O cruel, say I love thee not,
When I against my self with thee partake?
Do I not think on thee when I forgot
Am of my self, all-tyrant, for thy sake?
Who hateth thee that I do call my friend,
On whom frown'st thou that I do fawn upon,
Nay if thou lour'st on me do I not spend
Revenge upon my self with present moan?
What merit do I in my self respect,
That is so proud thy service to despise,
When all my best doth worship thy defect,
Commanded by the motion of thine eyes?
    But love hate on for now I know thy mind,
    Those that can see thou lov'st, and I am blind.

Song

Sir John Suckling

Why so pale and wan, fond lover?
Prithee, why so pale?
Will, when looking well can't move her,
Looking ill prevail?
Prithee, why so pale?

Why so dull and mute, young sinner?
Prithee why so mute?
Will, when speaking well can't win her,
Saying nothing do't?
Prithee why so mute?

Quit, quit, for shame; this will not move,
This cannot take her.
If of herself she will not love,
Nothing will make her:
The devil take her!

Sonnet 150

William Shakespeare

O from what power hast thou this powerful might,
With insufficiency my heart to sway,
To make me give the lie to my true sight,
And swear that brightness doth not grace the day?
Whence hast thou this becoming of things ill,
That in the very refuse of thy deeds,
There is such strength and warrantise of skill,
That in my mind thy worst all best exceeds?
Who taught thee how to make me love thee more,
The more I hear and see just cause of hate?
O though I love what others do abhor,
With others thou shouldst not abhor my state.
　　If thy unworthiness raised love in me,
　　More worthy I to be beloved of thee.

Song:

If You Refuse Me Once, And Think Again

Sir John Suckling

If you refuse me once, and think again,
I will complain.
You are deceiv'd, love is no work of art,
It must be got and born,
Not made and worn,
By every one that hath a heart.
Or do you think they more than once can die,
Whom you deny?
Who tell you of a thousand deaths a day,
Like the old poets feign
And tell the pain
They met, but in the common way?
　　Or do you think 't too soon to yield,
And quit the field?
Nor is that right, they yield that first entreat;
Once one may crave for love,
But more would prove   This heart too little, that too great.

Oh that I were all soul, that I might prove
For you as fit a love
As you are for an angel; for I know,
None but pure spirits are fit loves for you.
You are all ethereal; there's in you no dross,
Nor any part that's gross.
Your coarsest part is like a curious lawn,
The vestal relics for a covering drawn.
Your other parts, part of the purest fire
That e'er Heav'n did inspire,
Makes every thought that is refin'd by it
A quintessence of goodness and of wit.
Thus have your raptures reach'd to that degree
In love's philosophy,
That you can figure to yourself a fire
Void of all heat, a love without desire.
Nor in divinity do you go less;
You think, and you profess,
That souls may have a plenitude of joy,
Although their bodies meet not to employ.
But I must needs confess, I do not find
The motions of my mind
So purified as yet, but at the best
My body claims in them an interest.
I hold that perfect joy makes all our parts
As joyful as our hearts.
Our senses tell us, if we please not them,
Our love is but a dotage or a dream.
How shall we then agree? you may descend,
But will not, to my end.
I fain would tune my fancy to your key,
But cannot reach to that obstructed way.
There rests but this, that whilst we sorrow here,
Our bodies may draw near;
And, when no more their joys they can extend,
Then let our souls begin where they did end.

&d Goes the Way of All Flesh

Sharon Mesmer

Jealousy, lend me your ear,
  your ear
of crime and crucifixes.
And lend me your jealousy,
Ed,
Ed, lend me your arena boots
and broken bones,
your suicides set in Italy,
your evasive action
which follows passion.
Ed,
your greasy luck.

I first saw you in the parade of
pick-up men, whispering,
"Let's make this Uptown."
I next saw you in the gallery
with your torso
and family.
Then I saw you selling girlskins
by the side of the road—her severed head:
omen of quarrels and remorse.
And now your brain is on me like a bad song,
and your smell is in me like a tomb,
and true love is upon you,
Ed,
like an ill-fitting suit.
You are making swains
of my old dead lovers, lurking
in the luck of death, feasting
on its flank,
without your soul, without your shirt.

I dreamt I pissed on your playing cards,
I dreamt you were the company whore,
I dreamt you were the long tall Sally,
the mustang sally, the fire
of unknown origin,

milling in my milieu
swilling in my swarm,
        my malaise enflamed,
born blue
with a parlour mark,
Ed.

Sonnet 145
William Shakespeare

Those lips that Love's own hand did make,
Breathed forth the sound that said 'I hate',
To me that languished for her sake:
But when she saw my woeful state,
Straight in her heart did mercy come,
Chiding that tongue that ever sweet,
Was used in giving gentle doom:
And taught it thus anew to greet:
'I hate' she altered with an end,
That followed it as gentle day,
Doth follow night who like a fiend
From heaven to hell is flown away.
        'I hate', from hate away she threw,
        And saved my life saying 'not you'.

Sally Silver
Sharon Mesmer

Pale slope of nape and neckbone
Icy jut of jaw and cheekbone
Odor of two nights ago:
Sally Silver
smooth as sable

Hand mirror and trousseau
Travelling pretty picture show
A hand from nowhere, a cloud of dust
A salty dog she can count on:
Sally Silver
sad as silk

Let's play the radio till the curtains rot
Let's rock in the sand till the horses run
Let's rise like fog

Sally Silver
Voice of blue-green forest morning
One more holster in the middle of winter
Starfish give birth inside her belly:
Sally Silver
cool as milk

DISDAIN RETURNED
Thomas Carew

He that loves a rosy cheek,
Or a coral lip admires,
Or from star-like eyes doth seek
Fuel to maintain his fires;
As old Time makes these decay,
So his flames must waste away.

But a smooth and steadfast mind,
Gentle thoughts and calm desires,
Hearts with equal love combin'd,
Kindle never-dying fires.
Where these are not, I despise
Lovely cheeks, or lips, or eyes.

No tears, Celia, now shall win
My resolv'd heart to return;
I have search'd thy soul within,
And find nought, but pride, and scorn;
I have learn'd thy arts, and now
Can disdain as much as thou.
Some power, in my revenge, convey
That love to her I cast away.

To Mary

William Cowper

The twentieth year is well nigh past,
Since first our sky was overcast;
Ah, would that this might be the last!
My Mary!

Thy spirits have a fainter flow,
I see thee daily weaker grow—
'Twas my distress that brought thee low,
My Mary!

Thy needles, once a shining store,
For my sake restless heretofore,
Now rust disus'd, and shine no more,
My Mary!

For though thou gladly wouldst fulfil
The same kind office for me still,
Thy sight now seconds not thy will,
My Mary!

But well thou play'dst the housewife's part,
And all thy threads with magic art
Have wound themselves about this heart,
My Mary!

Thy indistinct expressions seem
Like language utter'd in a dream;
Yet me they charm, whate'er the theme,
My Mary!

Thy silver locks, once auburn bright,
Are still more lovely in my sight
Than golden beams of orient light,
My Mary!

For, could I view nor them nor thee,
What sight worth seeing could I see?
The sun would rise in vain for me,
My Mary!

Partakers of thy sad decline,
Thy hands their little force resign;
Yet gently press'd, press gently mine,
My Mary!

Such feebleness of limbs thou prov'st,
That now at ev'ry step thou mov'st
Upheld by two; yet still thou lov'st,
My Mary!

And still to love, though press'd with ill,
In wintry age to feel no chill,
With me is to be lovely still,
My Mary!

But ah! by constant heed I know,
How oft the sadness that I show
Transforms thy smiles to looks of woe,
My Mary!

And should my future lot be cast
With much resemblance of the past,
Thy worn-out heart will break at last,
My Mary!

The Quarry

Juan Boscan

As trails a sadly wounded deer the hound
Who scents the hoofprints on the bloody way,
And loudly baying follows through the day
Until he finds him stretched upon the gound,
Thus, Lady, have you followed me and found
my death and my dishonor, on your prey
Have hurled your fury and your power to slay
until despair encloses me around.
At seeing that my heart was wounded sore
Unceasingly you stalked it to and fro
Striking again the place from which it bled;
Your only aim, in hot pursit once more
Relentlessly to seek and overthrow,
And then to kill, when strength and hope had fled.

Elegy V: His Picture
John Donne

Here take my picture; though I bid farewell
Thine, in my heart, where my soul dwells, shall dwell.
Tis like me now, but I dead, 'twill be more
When we are shadows both, than 'twas before.
When weather-beaten I come back, my hand
Perhaps with rude oars torn, or sun beams tann'd,
My face and breast of haircloth, and my head
With care's rash sudden storms being o'erspread,
My body'a sack of bones, broken within,
And powder's blue stains scatter'd on my skin;
If rival fools tax thee to'have lov'd a man
So foul and coarse as, oh, I may seem then,
This shall say what I was, and thou shalt say,
Do his hurts reach me? doth my worth decay?
Or do they reach his judging mind, that he
Should now love less, what he did love to see?
That which in him was fair and delicate,
Was but the milk which in love's childish state
Did nurse it; who now is grown strong enough
To feed on that, which to disus'd tastes seems tough."

Protestation
Bertans de Born

O let me, Lady, silence calumny
And end these lies envy has laid on me.
In God's name, I pray you! Let them not confuse
Your heart that is all faith and courtesy,
Complaisance, truth and tender loyalty,
However they assail me with abuse.

At first cast may I lose my hawk in air,
See falcons strike it at my wrist and tear
It from me, to pluck it to the bloodied bone,
If ever the love I have of you could bear
I look upon another with desire to share
That bed whereon I get no rest alone.

And now that I may utterly disencumber
My course from shame the protest shall be sombre:
If ever I have failed toward you in thought
When we shall be alone in the high chamber
May my powers fail and my heart not remember
To send blood into my veins for the bout.

If I sit down to tables may my luck
Change so I cannot win by hook or crook;
When I start gaming may the dice conspire
Always to fall upon the lowest stroke;
If ever I sought another and forsook
You whom alone I love, alone desire.

May I share Altafort with other lords
And in the tower may we be four swards
And no love lost among the lot.
But rather
May I go always covered round with guards
Crossbowmen, leeches, sergeants and gatewards,
If ever I had heart to love another.

O Lady, leave me for another knight
Nor let me know where to avenge the slight;
May the winds fail me when beyond the sea,
And the King's porters drub me from his sight;
In press of battle may I take first flight;
If they lie not who tell of me.

Lady, I have a goshawk, finely mewed,
Swift to the wild duck, trained and unsubdued
By any bird that flies, heron or swan
Or even the black eagle, and I would
Gladly for your sake see her droop immewed,
Sullen and slow to fly, fat as a capon.

Envious liars, feinting with calumny,
Since through my lady you have troubled me,
You were advised to leave me well alone.

TAM GLEN

Robert Burns

My heart is a-breaking, dear Tittie,
Some counsel unto me come len';
To anger them a' is a pity,
But what will I do wi' Tam Glen?
I'm thinking, wi' sic a braw fellow,
In poortith I might mak a fen':
What care I in riches to wallow,
If I mauna marry Tam Glen?
There's Lowrie, the laird o' Dumeller,
Guid-day to you,"—brute! he comes ben:
He brags and he blaws o' his siller,
But when will he dance like Tam Glen?
My minnie does constantly deave me,
And bids me beware o' young men;
They flatter, she says, to deceive me;
But wha can think sae o' Tam Glen?
My daddie says, gin I'll forsake him,
He'll gie me guid hunder marks ten:
But, if it's ordain'd I maun take him,
O wha will I get but Tam Glen?
Yestreen at the valentines' dealing,
My heart to my mou gied a sten:
For thrice I drew ane without failing,
And thrice it was written, "Tam Glen!"
The last Halloween I was waukin
My droukit sark-sleeve, as ye ken:
His likeness cam up the house staukin,
And the very gray breeks o' Tam Glen!
Come counsel, dear Tittie, don't tarry;
I'll gie ye my bonie black hen,
Gif ye will advise me to marry
Thee dearly, Tam Glen.

LOVE AND BEAUTY

Sonnet 18

William Shakespeare

Shall I compare thee to a summer's day?
Thou art more lovely and more temperate.
Rough winds do shake the darling buds of May,
And summer's lease hath all too short a date.
Sometime too hot the eye of heaven shines,
And often is his gold complexion dimmed;
And every fair from fair sometime declines,
By chance, or nature's changing course untrimmed;
But thy eternal summer shall not fade,
Nor lose possession of that fair thou ow'st,
Nor shall Death brag thou wand'rest in his shade,
When in eternal lines to time thou grow'st.
    So long as men can breathe or eyes can see,
    So long lives this, and this gives life to thee.

She Walks In Beauty

Lord Byron (George Gordon)

She walks in beauty, like the night
    Of cloudless climes and starry skies;
And all that's best of dark and bright
    Meet in her aspect and her eyes:
Thus mellow'd to that tender light
    Which heaven to gaudy day denies.

One shade the more, one ray the less,
    Had half impair'd the nameless grace
Which waves in every raven tress,
    Or softly lightens o'er her face;
Where thoughts serenely sweet express
    How pure, how dear their dwelling-place.

And on that cheek, and o'er that brow,
    So soft, so calm, yet eloquent,
The smiles that win, the tints that glow,
    But tell of days in goodness spent,
A mind at peace with all below,
    A heart whose love is innocent!

Sonnet 130

William Shakespeare

My mistress' eyes are nothing like the sun;
Coral is far more red, than her lips' red;
If snow be white, why then her breasts are dun;
If hairs be wires, black wires grow on her head.
I have seen roses damasked, red and white,
But no such roses see I in her cheeks,
And in some perfumes is there more delight
Than in the breath that from my mistress reeks.
I love to hear her speak, yet well I know
That music hath a far more pleasing sound.
I grant I never saw a goddess go.
My mistress when she walks treads on the ground.
    And yet by heaven I think my love as rare
    As any she belied with false compare.

Alice

Paul Laurence Dunbar

Know you, winds that blow your course
Down the verdant valleys,
That somewhere you must, perforce,
Kiss the brow of Alice?

When her gentle face you find,
Kiss it softly, naughty wind.
Roses waving fair and sweet
Thro' the garden alleys,
Grow into a glory meet
For the eye of Alice;

Let the wind your offering bear
Of sweet perfume, faint and rare.
Lily holding crystal dew
In your pure white chalice,
Nature kind hath fashioned you
Like the soul of Alice;
It of purest white is wrought,
Filled with gems of crystal thought.

To _____

John Keats

Hadst thou liv'd in days of old,
  O what wonders had been told
Of thy lively countenance,
And thy humid eyes that dance
In the midst of their own brightness;
In the very fane of lightness.
Over which thine eyebrows, leaning,
Picture out each lovely meaning:
In a dainty bend they lie,
Like to streaks across the sky,
Or the feathers from a crow,
Fallen on a bed of snow.
Of thy dark hair that extends
Into many graceful bends:
As the leaves of Hellebore
Turn to whence they sprung before.
And behind each ample curl
Peeps the richness of a pearl.
Downward too flows many a tress
With a glossy waviness;
Full, and round like globes that rise
From the censer to the skies
Through sunny air. Add too, the sweetness
Of thy honied voice; the neatness
Of thine ankle lightly turn'd:
With those beauties, scarce discern'd,
Kept with such sweet privacy,
That they seldom meet the eye
Of the little loves that fly
Round about with eager pry.
Saving when, with freshening lave,
Thou dipp'st them in the taintless wave;
Like twin water lillies, born
In the coolness of the morn.

O, if thou hadst breathed then,
Now the Muses had been ten.
Couldst thou wish for lineage higher
Than twin sister of Thalia?
At least forever, evermore,
Will I call the Graces four.
Hadst thou liv'd when chivalry
Lifted up her lance on high,
Tell me what thou wouldst have been?
Ah! I see the silver sheen
Of thy broidered, floating vest
Cov'ring half thine ivory breast;
Which, O heavens! I should see,
But that cruel destiny
Has placed a golden cuirass there;
Keeping secret what is fair.
Like sunbeams in a cloudlet nested
Thy locks in knightly casque are rested:
O'er which bend four milky plumes
Like the gentle lilly's blooms
Springing from a costly vase.
See with what a stately pace
Comes thine alabaster steed;
Servant of heroic deed!
O'er his loins, his trappings glow
Like the northern lights on snow.
Mount his back! thy sword unsheath!
Sign of the enchanter's death;
Bane of every wicked spell;
Silencer of dragon's yell.
Alas! thou this wilt never do:
Thou art an enchantress too,
And wilt surely never spill
Blood of those whose eyes can kill.

Annie Laurie
William Douglas

Maxwellton's braes are bonnie,
Where early fa's the dew,
And it's there that Annie Laurie
Gave me her promise true
Gave me her promise true,
Which ne'er forgot will be,
And for bonnie Annie Laurie
I'd lay me doon and dee.
Her brow is like the snowdrift,
Her throat is like the swan,
Her face is the fairest
That e'er the sun shone on.

That e'er the sun shone on,
And dark blue is her e'e,
And for bonnie Annie Laurie,
I'd lay me doon and dee.
Like dew on the gowan lying
Is the fa' o' her fairy feet.
And like winds in the summer sighing,
Her voice is low and sweet.
Her voice is low and sweet,
And she's a' the world to me,
And for bonnie Annie Laurie,
I'd lay me doon and dee.

Sonnet 24
William Shakespeare

Mine eye hath played the painter and hath steeled
Thy beauty's form in table of my heart;
My body is the frame wherein 'tis held,
And perspective it is best painter's art.
For through the painter must you see his skill,
To find where your true image pictured lies,
Which in my bosom's shop is hanging still,
That hath his windows glazed with thine eyes.
Now see what good turns eyes for eyes have done:
Mine eyes have drawn thy shape, and thine for me
Are windows to my breast, wherethrough the sun
Delights to peep, to gaze therein on thee.
    Yet eyes this cunning want to grace their art,
    They draw but what they see, know not the heart.

A Love Song

Anonymous, Egyptian

One alone, a sister without her peer,
Comelier than all mankind.
Behold, she is like the Star-goddess arising
At the beginning of the happy year;
Of sheen surpassing, of radiant skin,
Lovely of eyes wherewith to gaze,
Sweet are her lips wherewith to speak,
She hath not a word too much;
Long of neck and radiant of nipple,
Of true sapphire is her hair;
Her arm surpasseth gold,
Her fingers ar like lotus-lilies,
Drooping of buttocks, firm-girt in her midst;
Her legs show forth her beauty.
Fair of gait she treadeth upon the earth,
She hath captured my heart in her embrace,
She maketh the necks of all men
To be turned away dazzled at the sight of her.
Joyous is whoso embraceth her,
He is like the chiefest of lusty youths.
One regardeth her going forth abroad
Even as hers yonder, the Only One.

Love in the Moonlight

Bhartrihari

My love within a forest walked alone,
All in a moonlit dale;
And here awhile she rested, weary grown,
And from her shoulders threw the wimpled veil
To court the little gale.

I peering through the thicket saw it all,
The yellow moonbeams fall,
I saw them mirrored from her bosom fly
Back to the moon on high.

Sonnet 127
William Shakespeare

In the old age black was not counted fair,
Or, if it were, it bore not beauty's name.
But now is black beauty's successive heir,
And beauty slandered with a bastard shame;
For since each hand hath put on nature's power,
Fairing the foul with art's false borrowed face,
Sweet beauty hath no name, no holy bower,
But is profaned, if not lives in disgrace.
Therefore my mistress' eyes are raven black,
Her eyes so suited, and they mourners seem,
At such who, not born fair, no beauty lack,
Slandering creation with a false esteem:
    Yet so they mourn, becoming of their woe,
    That every tongue says beauty should look so.

Beauty's Queen
Kisai of Merv

Beauty's queen by lovers guarded,
You whose cheeks the moon doth glass,
Where you glance, narcissus blooming;
    The moon rising, where you pass!

Oh, your face and hair—the fairest
Book of white and black is this!
Cheek and tress are sin and penance,
    Lips and eye are bale and bliss.

Of Beauty
Sir Richard Fanshawe

Let us use it while we may
Snatch those joys that haste away!
Earth her winter coat may cast,
And renew her beauty past:
But, our winter come, in vain
We solicit spring again;
And when our furrows snow shall cover,
Love may return but never lover.

Elizabeth of Bohemia
Sir Henry Wotton

You meaner beauties of the night,
    That poorly satisfy our eyes
More by your number than your light,
    You common people of the skies;
    What are you when the moon shall rise?

You curious chanters of the wood,
    That warble forth Dame Nature's lays,
Thinking your passions understood
    By your weak accents; what's your praise
    When Philomel her voice shall raise?

You violets that first appear,
    By your pure purple mantles known
Like the proud virgins of the year,
    As if the spring were all your own;
    What are you when the rose is blown?

So, when my mistress shall be seen
    In form and beauty of her mind,
By virtue first, then choice, a Queen.
    Tell me, if she were not designed
    Th' eclipse and glory of her kind!

To Cloris
Sir Charles Sedley

Cloris, I cannot say your eyes
Did my unwary heart surprise;
Nor will I swear it was your face,
Your shape, or any nameless grace:
For you are so entirely fair,
To love a part, injustice were;
No drowning man can know which drop
Of water his last breath did stop;
So when the stars in heaven appear,
And join to make the night look clear;
The light we no one's bounty call,
but the obliging gift of all.
He that does lips or hands adore,
Deserves them only, and no more;
But I love all, and every part,
And nothing less can ease my heart.
Cupid, that lover, weakly strikes,
Who can express what 'tis he likes.

Go, Lovely Rose—
Edmund Waller

Go, lovely Rose—
    Tell her that wastes her time and me,
    That now she knows,
When I resemble her to thee,
How sweet and fair she seems to be.

    Tell her that's young,
And shuns to have her graces spied,
    That hadst thou sprung
In deserts where no men abide,
Thou must have uncommended died.

    Small is the worth
Of beauty from the light retired:
    Bid her come forth,
Suffer herself to be desired,
And not blush so to be admired.

    Then die—that she
The common fate of all things rare
    May read in thee;
How small a part of time they share
That are so wondrous sweet and fair!

Elegy, Written At The Sea-Side, And Addressed To Miss Honora Sneyd
Anna Seward

I write, Honora, on the sparkling sand!—
The envious waves forbid the trace to stay:
Honora's name again adorns the strand!
Again the waters bear their prize away!
So Nature wrote her charms upon thy face,
The cheek's light bloom, the lip's envermeil'd dye,
And every gay, and every witching grace,
That Youth's warm hours, and Beauty's stores supply.
But Time's stern tide, with cold Oblivion's wave,
Shall soon dissolve each fair, each fading charm;

E'en Nature's self, so powerful, cannot save
Her own rich gifts from this o'erwhelming harm.
Love and the Muse can boast superior power,
Indelible the letters they shall frame;
They yield to no inevitable hour,
But will on lasting tablets write thy name.

To Eva
Ralph Waldo Emerson

O fair and stately maid, whose eyes
Were kindled in the upper skies
At the same torch that lighted mine;
For so I must interpret still
Thy sweet dominion o'er my will,
A sympathy divine.
Ah! let me blameless gaze upon
Features that seem at heart my own;
Nor fear those watchful sentinels,
Who charm the more their glance forbids,
Chaste-glowing, underneath their lids,
With fire that draws while it repels.

O Love, Thy Hair!
Kamal ud-Din

O love, thy hair! thy locks of night and musk!
The very wind therein doth lose his way,
While in the perfumed darkness he would stray;
And my heart, too, is lost in scented dusk.

Thy crescent brows irradiate the night;
Love, of thy lips and tresses give thou me —
Thy breast is like a restless, heaving sea;
Thine eyes are stars of sorrow and delight.

Yet grieve not that I grieve, Soul of the Sea —
What is my heart that thou shouldst comfort it
With wine or song, with smile or dance or wit?
Dust of thy threshold is enough for me.

Fast bound am I, as are thy tresses long,
And bent am I, as bend thy brows so fair.
Low to the earth, I fall, as falls thy hair,
And clasp thy feet, as thy small sandals' thong.

Who once hath loved thy pale and fervent face,
To him the rose is dead and cold the flame,
Deaf to all music save the voice and name,
Blind to all beauty save thy subtle grace.

Love, The Light Giver
Michelangelo Buonarotti

With your fair eyes and charming light I see,
    For which my own blind eyes would peer in vain;
    Stayed by your feet the burden I sustain
    Which my lame feet find all too strong for me;
Wingless upon your pinions I fly;
    Heavenward your spirit stirreth me to strain;
    E'en as you will, I blush and blanch again,
    Freeze in the sun, burn 'neath a frosty sky.
Your will includes and is the lord of mine;
    Life to my thoughts within your heart is given;
    My words begin to breathe upon your breath:
    Like to the moon am I, that cannot shine
Alone; for lo! our eyes see nought in heaven
Save what the living sun illumineth.

Upon Julia's Clothes
Robert Herrick

Whenas in silks my Julia goes,
Then, then, methinks, how sweetly flows
    That liquefaction of her clothes.

Next, when I cast mine eyes, and see
That brave vibration each way free,
    O how that glittering taketh me!

To Helen
Edgar Allen Poe

Helen, thy beauty is to me
    Like those Nicean barks of yore,
That gently, o'er a perfumed sea,
    The weary, way-worn wanderer bore
To his own native shore.

On desperate seas long wont to roam,
    Thy hyacinth hair, thy classic face,
Thy Naiad airs have brought me home
    To the glory that was Greece
And the grandeur that was Rome.

Lo! in yon brilliant window-niche
    How statue-like I see thee stand,
The agate lamp within thy hand!
    Ah, Psyche, from the regions which
Are Holy Land!

To Some Ladies
John Keats

What though while the wonders of nature exploring,
    I cannot your light, mazy footsteps attend;
Nor listen to accents, that almost adoring,
    Bless Cynthia's face, the enthusiast's friend:
Yet over the steep, whence the mountain stream rushes,
    With you, kindest friends, in idea I rove;
Mark the clear tumbling crystal, its passionate gushes,
    Its spray that the wild flower kindly bedews.
Why linger you so, the wild labyrinth strolling?
    Why breathless, unable your bliss to declare?
Ah! you list to the nightingale's tender condoling,
    Responsive to sylphs, in the moon beamy air.
'Tis morn, and the flowers with dew are yet drooping,
    I see you are treading the verge of the sea:
And now! ah, I see it—you just now are stooping
    To pick up the keep-sake intended for me.

If a cherub, on pinions of silver descending,
 Had brought me a gem from the fret-work of heaven;
And smiles, with his star-cheering voice sweetly blending,
 The blessings of Tighe had melodiously given;
It had not created a warmer emotion
 Than the present, fair nymphs, I was blest with from you
Than the shell, from the bright golden sands of the ocean
 Which the emerald waves at your feet gladly threw.
For, indeed, 'tis a sweet and peculiar pleasure,
 (And blissful is he who such happiness finds,)
To possess but a span of the hour of leisure,
 In elegant, pure, and aerial minds.

MADRIGAL

Anon

My Love in her attire doth show her wit,
 It doth so well become her;
For every season she hath dressing fit,
 For Winter, Spring, and Summer.
   No beauty she doth miss
    When all her robes are on:
   But Beauty's self she is
    When all her robes are gone.

1816, TRANSLATED FROM RONSARD

John Keats

Nature withheld Cassandra in the skies
   For more adornment a full thousand years;
She took their cream of Beauty's fairest dyes,
   And shap'd and tinted her above all Peers:
Meanwhile Love kept her dearly with his wings,
   And underneath their shadow fill'd her eyes
With such a richness that the cloudy Kings
   Of high Olympus utter'd slavish sighs.
When from the Heavens I saw her first descend
   My heart took fire, and only burning pains
They were my pleasures- they my Life's sad end;
   Love pour'd her beauty into my warm veins...

To_____

John Keats

Had I a man's fair form, then might my sighs
  Be echoed swiftly through that ivory shell
  Thine ear, and find thy gentle heart; so well
Would passion arm me for the enterprize:
But ah! I am no knight whose foeman dies;
  No cuirass glistens on my bosom's swell;
  I am no happy shepherd of the dell
Whose lips have trembled with a maiden's eyes.
Yet must I dote upon thee,—call thee sweet,
  Sweeter by far than Hybla's honied roses
    When steep'd in dew rich to intoxication.
Ah! I will taste that dew, for me 'tis meet,
  And when the moon her pallid face discloses,
    I'll gather some by spells, and incantation.

To G. A. W.

John Keats

Nymph of the downward smile, and sidelong glance,
  In what diviner moments of the day
  Art thou most lovely? When gone far astray
Into the labyrinths of sweet utterance?
Or when serenely wand'ring in a trance
  Of sober thought? Or when starting away,
  With careless robe, to meet the morning ray,
Thou spar'st the flowers in thy mazy dance?
Haply 'tis when thy ruby lips part sweetly,
  And so remain, because thou listenest:
But thou to please wert nurtured so completely
  That I can never tell what mood is best.
I shall as soon pronounce which grace more neatly
  Trips it before Apollo than the rest.

Sonnet To_____

John Brainard

She was a lovely one—her shape was light
And delicately flexible; her eye
Might have been black, or blue,— but it was bright,
Though beaming not on every passer-by;
T'was very modest, and a little shy.
The eyelash seemed to shade the very cheek;
That had the color of a sunset sky,
Not rosy—but a soft and heavenly streak
For which the arm might strike—the heart might break—
And a soft gentle voice, that kindly sweet
Accosted one she chanced to overtake,
While walking slowly on iambic feet,
in tones that fell as soft as heaven's own dew—
Who was it! dear young Lady, was it you?

If Love...

Luis de Gongora.

If Love, within the feathers of his nest,
Imprisoned my heart, what will he do now,
When in thy eyes, O Lady of sweet brow,
He flies in armour clad, though yet undressed?
I was stung, amid the violets pressed,
By the asp that lives midst the lilies bough;
As fragrant Dawn equal power hadst thou
As now, when Sun, thou dost shimmer full crest.
I'll greet the light in grave voice rent with pain,
As the kind nightingale in prison bound
Gives voice to grievances with sweet refrain.
I'll tell how with rays I saw thy brow gain
A crown, and that thy loveliness renowned
Doth cause birds to sing and men tears attain.

To Beauty

Anna Hempstead Branch

I would not have thee far away
By whom I must be led.
I needs must have thee every day
To be my meat and bread.

For if there be unlovely things
Wherein no radiance glows,
I'll kiss them till their folded wings
Shall blossom like the rose!

Oh, be thou beautiful, I'll say,—
And save me with delight!
Then each dark thing will smile like day
Between me and the night.

I'll listen till I make them speak,
By need will make them wise!
As love calls blushes to the cheek
Or laughter to the eyes.

For where love lays its trusting kiss
There Beauty needs must be
And so I'll turn the world to bliss
Until it shines like thee.

My Love's A Match

Alfred P. Graves

My love's a match in beauty
For every flower that blows,
Her little ear's a lily,
Her velvet cheeks a rose;
Her locks lke gilly gowans
Hang golden to her knee.
If I were King of Ireland,
My Queen she'd surely be.

Her eyes are fond forget-me-nots,
And no such snow is seen
Upon the heaving hawthorn bush
As crests her bodice green.
The thrushes when she's talking
Sit listening on the tree.
If I were King of Ireland,
My Queen she'd surely be.

Helen Of Troy
Christopher Marlowe

Was this the face that launched a thousand ships?
And burnt the topless towers of Ilium?
Sweet Helen, make me immortal with a kiss:
Her lips suck forth my soul, see where it flies;
Come Helen, come give my soul again.
Here I will dwell, for heaven be in these lips,
And all is dross that is not Helen.

Sonnet I
Edna St. Vincent Millay

Thou art not lovelier than lilacs,—no,
Nor honeysuckle; thou art not more fair
Than small white single poppies,
—I can bear Thy beauty; though
I bend before thee, though
From left to right, not knowing where to go,
I turn my troubled eyes, nor here nor there
Find any refuge from thee, yet I swear
So has it been with mist,—with moonlight so.
Like him who day by day unto his draught
Of delicate poison adds him one drop more
Till he may drink unharmed the death of ten,
Even so, inured to beauty, who have quaffed
Each hour more deeply than the hour before,
I drink—and live—what has destroyed some men.

A Girl
Michael Field

Her soul a deep-wave pearl
Dim, lucent of all lovely mysteries;
A face flowered for heart's ease,
A brow's grace soft as seas
Seen through faint forest-trees:
A mouth, the lips apart,
Like aspen-leaflets trembling in the breeze
From her tempestuous heart.
Such: and our souls so knit,
I leave a page half-writ—
The work begun
Will be to heaven's conception done,
If she come to it.

To—, With A Rose

Sidney Lanier

I asked my heart to say
Some word whose worth my love's devoir might pay
Upon my Lady's natal day.

Then said my heart to me:
Learn from the rhyme that now shall come to thee
What fits thy Love most lovingly.

This gift that learning shows;
For, as a rhyme unto its rhyme-twin goes,
I send a rose unto a Rose.

32 Song

Gil Vicente

Grace and beauty has the maid;
Could anything more lovely be?

Sailor, you who live on ships,
Did you ever see
Any ship or sail or star
As beautiful as she?

Knight of war, in armour clad,
Did you ever see
Horse or arms or battle-field
As beautiful as she?

Shepherd, you who guard your flock,
Did you ever see
Cattle, valem or mountain range
As beautiful as she?

*W*HEN MY BONNIE DANCES

Fenton Johnson

When my Bonnie dances earth is mine,
And a thousand kingdoms I can see;
I am thrilled with joy and love and hope,
And my sweetheart's goodness comes to me.

In her eye the vision Hellas knew,
In her step the dream o' wanton Rome;
And in garb o' white she mocks a queen,
As she finds within my heart a home.

When my Bonnie dances fields are green,
Blood stained roses bloom, and asphodel;
And Beloved walks awhile with me,
Where I wooed her in a lonely dell.

Rivers feel the warmth o' sunlit gaze,
Sweet canary sings within the grove,
And I nod as music sways my nymph
Where the sprites of Nature lightly rove.

When my Bonnie dances, music's stream,
Silv'ry white as glows the old moon's breast,
Flows into the liquid veins of Youth,
Warmer than a maiden's fond caress;

And the spheres of Heaven, all attuned,
To the rhythmic measure sets the world,
While the flowers that sleep on eve of snow
From their beds their petals gay unfurl.

Oh, my Bonnie, thou hast won a crown,
Love and worship from tile world of youth,
And through dancing graceful thou hast carved
On our hearts the magic legend TRUTH;

Long may Bonnie live and drink the sweets
Men call living, God above call life,
Long may Bonnie live and never know
Woe and sorrow, bitterness and strife.

Sonnet 37
Edmund Spenser

What guyle is this, that those her golden tresses,
She doth attyre under a net of gold:
And with sly skill so cunningly them dresses,
That which is gold or heare, may scarse be told?
Is it that mens frayle eyes, which gaze too bold,
She may entangle in that golden snare:
And being caught may craftily enfold,
Theyr weaker harts, which are not wel aware?
Take heed therefore, myne eyes, how ye doe stare
Henceforth too rashly on that guilefull net,
In which if ever ye entrapped are,
Out of her bands ye by no meanes shall get.
Fondnesse it were for any being free,
To covet fetters, though they golden bee.

Sonnet XIII.
Sappho

Bring, bring to deck my brow, ye Sylvan girls,
A roseate wreath; nor for my waving hair
The costly band of studded gems prepare,
Of sparkling crysolite or orient pearls:
Love, o'er my head his canopy unfurls,
His purple pinions fan the whisp'ring air;
Mocking the golden sandal, rich and rare,
Beneath my feet the fragrant woodbine curls.
Bring the thin robe, to fold about my breast,
White as the downy swan; while round my waist
Let leaves of glossy myrtle bind the vest,
Not idly gay, but elegantly chaste!
Love scorns the nymph in wanton trappings drest;
And charms the most concealed, are doubly grac'd.

La Bella Donna Della Mia Mente
Oscar Wilde

My limbs are wasted with a flame,
    My feet are sore with travelling,
For calling on my Lady's name
    My lips have now forgot to sing.
O Linnet in the wild-rose brake
    Strain for my Love thy melody,
O Lark sing louder for love's sake,
    My gentle Lady passeth by.
She is too fair for any man
    To see or hold his heart's delight,
Fairer than Queen or courtezan
    Or moon-lit water in the night.
Her hair is bound with myrtle leaves,
    (Green leaves upon her golden hair!)
Green grasses through the yellow sheaves
    Of autumn corn are not more fair.
Her little lips, more made to kiss
    Than to cry bitterly for pain,
Are tremulous as brook-water is,
    Or roses after evening rain.
Her neck is like white melilote
    Flushing for pleasure of the sun,
The throbbing of the linnet's throat
    Is not so sweet to look upon.
As a pomegranate, cut in twain,
    White-seeded, is her crimson mouth,
Her cheeks are as the fading stain
    Where the peach reddens to the south.
O twining hands! O delicate
    White body made for love and pain!
O House of love! O desolate
    Pale flower beaten by the rain!

Sonnet CCXIII

Petrarch

Graces that heaven's bounty gives to tew:
A rare virtue not found in humankind,
Under blond hair a wise and ripened mind,
And in a humble woman beauty true;
A loveliness unique in excellence,
And the singing that one hears in the heart,
The heavenly gait, the dear and ardent sense
That breaks the hardest, curbs the highest art;
The eyes that every heart can petrify,
Puissant to lighten darkness, the abyss,
And to steal souls from bodies where they stormed;
And the speech full of reasons pure and high,
With the sighs sweetly broken for my bliss:
By these magicians I have been transformed.

A Dream Shape

Madison Cawein

With moon-white hearts that held a gleam
I gathered wild-flowers in a dream,
And shaped a woman, whose sweet blood
Was odour of the wildwood bud.

From dew, the starlight arrowed through,
I wrought a woman's eyes of blue;
The lids that on her eyeballs lay,
Were rose-pale petals of the May.

Out of a rosebud's veins I drew
The flagrant crimson beating through
The languid lips of her, whose kiss
Was as a poppy's drowsiness.

Out of the moonlight and the air
I wrought the glory of her hair,
That o'er her eyes blue heaven lay
Like some gold cloud o'er dawn of day.

I took the music of the breeze
And water, whispering in the trees,
And shaped the soul that breathed below
A woman's blossom breasts of snow.

A shadow's shadow in the glass
Of sleep, my spirit saw her pass:
And thinking of it now, meseems
We only live within our dreams.

For in that time she was to me
More real than our reality;
More real than Earth, more real than I—
The unreal things that pass and die.

Love In The Valley

George Meredith

Under yonder beech-tree single on the green-sward,
Couched with her arms behind her golden head,
Knees and tresses folded to slip and ripple idly,
Lies my young love sleeping in the shade.
Had I the heart to slide an arm beneath her,
Press her parting lips as her waist I gather slow,
Waking in amazement she could not but embrace me:
Then would she hold me and never let me go?
Shy as the squirrel and wayward as the swallow
Swift as the swallow along the river's light
Circleting the surface to meet his mirrored winglets,
Fleeter she seems in her stay than in her flight.
Shy as the squirrel that leaps among the pine-tops,
Wayward as the swallow overhead at set of sun,
She whom I love is hard to catch and conquer,
Hard, but O the glory of the winning were she won!
When her mother tends her before the laughing mirror,
Tying up her laces, looping up her hair,
Often she thinks, were this wild thing wedded,
More love should I have, and much less care.
When her mother tends her before the lighted mirror,
Loosening her laces, combing down her curls,
Often she thinks, were this wild thing wedded,
I should miss but one for many boys and girls.
Heartless she is as the shadow in the meadows
Flying to the hills on a blue and breezy noon.
No, she is athirst and drinking up her wonder:
Earth to her is young as the slip of the new moon.
Deals she an unkindness, 'tis but her rapid measure,
Even as in a dance; and her smile can heal no less:
Like the swinging May-cloud that pelts the flowers with hailstones
Off a sunny border, she was made to bruise and bless.
Lovely are the curves of the white owl sweeping
Wavy in the dusk lit by one large star.
Lone on the fir-branch, his rattle-note unvaried,
Brooding o'er the gloom, spins the brown eve-jar.

Darker grows the valley, more and more forgetting:
So were it with me if forgetting could be willed.
Tell the grassy hollow that holds the bubbling well-spring,
Tell it to forget the source that keeps it filled.
Stepping down the hill with her fair companions,
Arm in arm, all against the raying West
Boldly she sings, to the merry tune she marches,
Brave in her shape, and sweeter unpossessed.
Sweeter, for she is what my heart first awaking
Whispered the world was; morning light is she.
Love that so desires would fain keep her changeless;
Fain would fling the net, and fain have her free.
 Happy happy time, when the white star hovers
Low over dim fields fresh with bloomy dew,
Near the face of dawn, that draws athwart the darkness,
Threading it with colour, as yewberries the yew.
Thicker crowd the shades while the grave East deepens
Glowing, and with crimson a long cloud swells.
Maiden still the morn is; and strange she is, and secret;
Strange her eyes; her cheeks are cold as cold sea-shells.
Sunrays, leaning on our southern hills and lighting
Wild cloud-mountains that drag the hills along,
Oft ends the day of your shifting brilliant laughter
Chill as a dull face frowning on a song.
Ay, but shows the South-West a ripple-feathered bosom
Blown to silver while the clouds are shaken and ascend
Scaling the mid-heavens as they stream, there comes a sunset
Rich, deep like love in beauty without end.
When at dawn she sighs, and like an infant to the window
Turns grave eyes craving light, released from dreams,
Beautiful she looks, like a white water-lily
Bursting out of bud in havens of the streams.
When from bed she rises clothed from neck to ankle
In her long nightgown sweet as boughs of May,
Beautiful she looks, like a tall garden lily
Pure from the night, and splendid for the day.
Mother of the dews, dark eye-lashed twilight,
Low-lidded twilight, o'er the valley's brim,
Rounding on thy breast sings the dew-delighted skylark,

Clear as though the dewdrops had their voice in him.
Hidden where the rose-flush drinks the rayless planet,
Fountain-full he pours the spraying fountain-showers.
Let me hear her laughter, I would have her ever
Cool as dew in twilight, the lark above the flowers.
All the girls are out with their baskets for the primrose;
Up lanes, woods through, they troop in joyful bands.
My sweet leads: she knows not why, but now she totters,
Eyes the bent anemones, and hangs her hands.
Such a look will tell that the violets are peeping,
Coming the rose: and unaware a cry
Springs in her bosom for odours and for colour,
Covert and the nightingale; she knows not why.
Kerchiefed head and chin she darts between her tulips,
Streaming like a willow grey in arrowy rain: ·
Some bend beaten cheek to gravel, and their angel
She will be; she lifts them, and on she speeds again.
Black the driving raincloud breasts the iron gateway:
She is forth to cheer a neighbour lacking mirth.
So when sky and grass met rolling dumb for thunder
Saw I once a white dove, sole light of earth.
Prim little scholars are the flowers of her garden,
Trained to stand in rows, and asking if they please.
I might love them well but for loving more the wild ones:
O my wild ones! they tell me more than these.
You, my wild one, you tell of honied field-rose,
Violet, blushing eglantine in life; and even as they,
They by the wayside are earnest of your goodness,
You are of life's, on the banks that line the way.
Peering at her chamber the white crowns the red rose,
Jasmine winds the porch with stars two and three.
Parted is the window; she sleeps; the starry jasmine
Breathes a falling breath that carries thoughts of me.
Sweeter unpossessed, have I said of her my sweetest?
Not while she sleeps: while she sleeps the jasmine breathes,
Luring her to love; she sleeps; the starry jasmine
Bears me to her pillow under white rose-wreaths.
Yellow with birdfoot-trefoil are the grass-glades;
Yellow with cinquefoil of the dew-grey leaf;

Yellow with stonecrop; the moss-mounds are yellow;
Blue-necked the wheat sways, yellowing to the sheaf:
Green-yellow bursts from the copse the laughing yaffle;
Sharp as a sickle is the edge of shade and shine:
Earth in her heart laughs looking at the heavens,
Thinking of the harvest: I look and think of mine.
This I may know: her dressing and undressing
Such a change of light shows as when the skies in sport
Shift from cloud to moonlight; or edging over thunder
Slips a ray of sun; or sweeping into port
White sails furl; or on the ocean borders
White sails lean along the waves leaping green.
Visions of her shower before me, but from eyesight
Guarded she would be like the sun were she seen.
Front door and back of the mossed old farmhouse
Open with the morn, and in a breezy link
Freshly sparkles garden to stripe-shadowed orchard,
Green across a rill where on sand the minnows wink.
Busy in the grass the early sun of summer
Swarms, and the blackbird's mellow fluting notes
Call my darling up with round and roguish challenge:
Quaintest, richest carol of all the singing throats!
Cool was the woodside; cool as her white dairy
Keeping sweet the cream-pan; and there the boys from school,
Cricketing below, rushed brown and red with sunshine;
O the dark translucence of the deep-eyed cool!
Spying from the farm, herself she fetched a pitcher
Full of milk, and tilted for each in turn the beak.
Then a little fellow, mouth up and on tiptoe,
Said, "I will kiss you": she laughed and leaned her cheek.
Doves of the fir-wood walling high our red roof
Through the long noon coo, crooning through the coo.
Loose droop the leaves, and down the sleepy roadway
Sometimes pipes a chaffinch; loose droops the blue.
Cows flap a slow tail knee-deep in the river,
Breathless, given up to sun and gnat and fly.
Nowhere is she seen; and if I see her nowhere,
Lightning may come, straight rains and tiger sky.
O the golden sheaf, the rustling treasure-armful!

O the nutbrown tresses nodding interlaced!
O the treasure-tresses one another over
Nodding! O the girdle slack about the waist!
Slain are the poppies that shot their random scarlet
Quick amid the wheatears: wound about the waist,
Gathered, see these brides of Earth one blush of ripeness!
O the nutbrown tresses nodding interlaced!
Large and smoky red the sun's cold disk drops,
Clipped by naked hills, on violet shaded snow:
Eastward large and still lights up a bower of moonrise,
Whence at her leisure steps the moon aglow.
Nightlong on black print-branches our beech-tree
Gazes in this whiteness: nightlong could I.
Here may life on death or death on life be painted.
Let me clasp her soul to know she cannot die!
Gossips count her faults; they scour a narrow chamber
Where there is no window, read not heaven or her.
 "When she was tiny," one aged woman quavers,
Plucks at my heart and leads me by the ear.
Faults she had once as she learnt to run and tumbled:
Faults of feature some see, beauty not complete.
Yet, good gossips, beauty that makes holy
Earth and air, may have faults from head to feet.
Hither she comes; she comes to me; she lingers,
Deepens her brown eyebrows, while in new surprise
High rise the lashes in wonder of a stranger;
Yet am I the light and living of her eyes.
Something friends have told her fills her heart to brimming,
Nets her in her blushes, and wounds her, and tames.—
Sure of her haven, O like a dove alighting,
Arms up, she dropped: our souls were in our names.
Soon will she lie like a white-frost sunrise.
Yellow oats and brown wheat, barley pale as rye,
Long since your sheaves have yielded to the thresher,
Felt the girdle loosened, seen the tresses fly.
Soon will she lie like a blood-red sunset.
Swift with the to-morrow, green-winged Spring!
Sing from the South-West, bring her back the truants,
Nightingale and swallow, song and dipping wing.

Soft new beech-leaves, up to beamy April
Spreading bough on bough a primrose mountain, you,
Lucid in the moon, raise lilies to the skyfields,
Youngest green transfused in silver shining through:
Fairer than the lily, than the wild white cherry:
Fair as in image my seraph love appears
Borne to me by dreams when dawn is at my eyelids:
Fair as in the flesh she swims to me on tears.
Could I find a place to be alone with heaven,
I would speak my heart out: heaven is my need.
Every woodland tree is flushing like the dog-wood,
Flashing like the whitebeam, swaying like the reed.
Flushing like the dog-wood crimson in October;
Streaming like the flag-reed South-West blown;
Flashing as in gusts the sudden-lighted white beam:
All seem to know what is for heaven alone.

SONG

Anonymous, Spanish

Three Moorish girls I loved
In Jaén
Axa and Fátima and Marién.

Three Moorish girls so gay
Went olive-picking there,
And found them plucked away
In Jaén,
Axa and and Fátima and Marién.

And found them plucked away,
And turned back in dismay,
And pale and sad were they
in Jaén
Axa and Fátima and Marién.

Three Moorish girls so fair,
Three Moorish girls so fair,
Went apple-plucking there
In Jaén
Axa and Fátima and Marién.

In The Gold Room
Oscar Wilde

A Harmony.

Her ivory hands on the ivory keys
  Strayed in a fitful fantasy,
Like the silver gleam when the poplar trees
  Rustle their pale leaves listlessly,
Or the drifting foam of a restless sea
When the waves show their teeth in the flying breeze.
Her gold hair fell on the wall of gold
  Like the delicate gossamer tangles spun
On the burnished disk of the marigold,
  Or the sun-flower turning to meet the sun
  When the gloom of the jealous night is done,
And the spear of the lily is aureoled.
And her sweet red lips on these lips of mine
  Burned like the ruby fire set
In the swinging lamp of a crimson shrine,
  Or the bleeding wounds of the pomegranate,
  Or the heart of the lotus drenched and wet
With the spilt-out blood of the rose-red wine.

Rose-Cheeked Laura
Thomas Campion

Rose-cheeked Laura, come
Sing thou smoothly with they beauty's
Silent music,either one
Sweetly gracing
Lovely forms do flow
From concert divinely framed;
Heav'n is music, and thy beauty's
Birth is heavenly.
These dull notes we sing
Discords need for helps to grace them;
Only beauty purely loving
Knows no discord,
But still moves delight,
Like clear springs renewed by flowing,
Ever perfect, ever in them-Selves eternal

THE TOLLMAN'S DAUGHTER
Madison Cawein

She stood waist-deep among the briars:
Above in twisted lengths were rolled
The sunset's tangled whorls of gold,
Blown from the west's cloud-pillared fires.

And in the hush no sound did mar,
You almost heard o'er hill and dell,
Deep, bubbling over, star on star,
The night's blue cisterns slowly well.

A crane, like some dark crescent, crossed
The sunset, winging towards the west;
While up the east her silver breast
Of light the moon brought, white as frost.

So have I painted her, you see,
The tollman's daughter.—What an arm
And throat was hers! and what a form!
—Art dreams of such divinity.

What braids of night to hold and kiss!
There is no pigment anywhere
A man might use to picture this
—The splendour of her raven hair.

A face as beautiful and bright,
As rosy fair as twilight skies,
Lit with the stars of hazel eyes
And eyebrowed black with pencilled night.

For her, I know, where'er she trod
Each dewdrop raised a looking-glass
To flash her beauty from the grass;
That wild-flowers bloomed along the sod,

And whispered perfume when she smiled;
The wood-bird hushed to hear her song,
Or, all enamoured, tame, not wild,
Before her feet flew fluttering long.

The brook went mad with melody,
Eddied in laughter when she kissed
With naked feet its amethyst—
And I—I fell in love; ah me!

AEDH TELLS OF THE PERFECT BEAUTY
William Butler Yeats

O cloud-pale eyelids, dream-dimmed eyes
The poets labouring all their days
To build a perfect beauty in rhyme
Are overthrown by a woman's gaze
And by the unlabouring brood of the skies:
And therefore my heart will bow, when dew
Is dropping sleep, until God burn time,
Before the unlabouring stars and you.

Beauty

Madison Cawein

High as a star, yet lowly as a flower,
Unknown she takes her unassuming place
At Earth's proud masquerade—the appointed hour
Strikes, and, behold! the marvel of her face.

Rose In Gray

Philip Henry Savage

Lightly moves the silver moon
Through these glimmering nights of June,
Lightly falls, and in the shine
Of her moon-rays hyaline,
Lifts the nightfall and the hush
From the red rose on the bush,
And the rose's heart discovers
To her nightly wandering lovers
I could tell you, Phyllis dear,
How the rose looked faint and clear
In the moonlight; how she burned
Like the sacred fire inurned;
Distant, with the far-withdrawn
Sweet shamefacedness of dawn;
Quaintly cool, with yet the glow
Of a lamp through falling snow.
So; but when I whisper,
"Sweet, take my hand, come let us see 't,"
'T is the very smothered rose
In your milk-white cheek that glows.

Sonnet 1

William Shakespeare

From fairest creatures we desire increase,
That thereby beauty's rose might never die,
But as the riper should by time decease,
His tender heir might bear his memory:
But thou contracted to thine own bright eyes,
Feed'st thy light's flame with self-substantial fuel,
Making a famine where abundance lies,
Thy self thy foe, to thy sweet self too cruel:
Thou that art now the world's fresh ornament,
And only herald to the gaudy spring,
Within thine own bud buriest thy content,
And tender churl mak'st waste in niggarding:
    Pity the world, or else this glutton be,
    To eat the world's due, by the grave and thee.

An Epitaph
Walter De La Mare

Here lies a most beautiful lady,
Light of step and heart was she;
I think she was the most beautiful lady
That ever was in the West Country.

But beauty vanishes, beauty passes;
However rare—rare it be;
And when I crumble,who will remember
This lady of the West Country.

The Secret Rose
William Butler Yeats

Far off, most secret, and inviolate Rose,
Enfold me in my hour of hours; where those
Who sought thee in the Holy Sepulchre,
Or in the wine vat, dwell beyond the stir
And tumult of defeated dreams; and deep
Among pale eyelids, heavy with the sleep
Men have named beauty. Thy great leaves enfold
The ancient beards, the helms of ruby and gold
Of the crowned Magi; and the king whose eyes
Saw the Pierced Hands and Rood of elder rise
In druid vapour and make the torches dim;
Till vain frenzy awoke and he died; and him
Who met Fand walking among flaming dew
By a gray shore where the wind never blew,
And lost the world and Emer for a kiss;
And him who drove the gods out of their liss,
And till a hundred morns had flowered red,
Feasted and wept the barrows of his dead;
And the proud dreaming king who flung the crown
And sorrow away, and calling bard and clown
Dwelt among wine-stained wanderers in deep woods;
And him who sold tillage, and house, and goods,
And sought through lands and islands numberless years,
Until he found with laughter and with tears,
A woman, of so shining loveliness,
That men threshed corn at midnight by a tress,
A little stolen tress. I, too, await
The hour of thy great wind of love and hate.

When shall the stars be blown about the sky,
Like the sparks blown out of a smithy, and die?
Surely thine hour has come, thy great wind blows,
Far off, most secret, and inviolate Rose?

Sonnet 3

William Shakespeare

Look in thy glass and tell the face thou viewest,
Now is the time that face should form another,
Whose fresh repair if now thou not renewest,
Thou dost beguile the world, unbless some mother.
For where is she so fair whose uneared womb
Disdains the tillage of thy husbandry?
Or who is he so fond will be the tomb,
Of his self-love to stop posterity?
Thou art thy mother's glass and she in thee
Calls back the lovely April of her prime,
So thou through windows of thine age shalt see,
Despite of wrinkles this thy golden time.
    But if thou live remembered not to be,
    Die single and thine image dies with thee.

Sonnet 5

William Shakespeare

Those hours that with gentle work did frame
The lovely gaze where every eye doth dwell
Will play the tyrants to the very same,
And that unfair which fairly doth excel:
For never-resting time leads summer on
To hideous winter and confounds him there,
Sap checked with frost and lusty leaves quite gone,
Beauty o'er-snowed and bareness every where:
Then were not summer's distillation left
A liquid prisoner pent in walls of glass,
Beauty's effect with beauty were bereft,
Nor it nor no remembrance what it was.
    But flowers distilled though they with winter meet,
    Leese but their show, their substance still lives sweet.

Sonnet 14

William Shakespeare

Not from the stars do I my judgement pluck,
And yet methinks I have astronomy,
But not to tell of good, or evil luck,
Of plagues, of dearths, or seasons' quality,
Nor can I fortune to brief minutes tell;
Pointing to each his thunder, rain and wind,
Or say with princes if it shall go well
By oft predict that I in heaven find.
But from thine eyes my knowledge I derive,
And constant stars in them I read such art
As truth and beauty shall together thrive
If from thy self, to store thou wouldst convert:
    Or else of thee this I prognosticate,
    Thy end is truth's and beauty's doom and date.

Sonnet 20

William Shakespeare

A woman's face with nature's own hand painted,
Hast thou the master mistress of my passion,
A woman's gentle heart but not acquainted
With shifting change as is false women's fashion,
An eye more bright than theirs, less false in rolling:
Gilding the object whereupon it gazeth,
A man in hue all hues in his controlling,
Which steals men's eyes and women's souls amazeth.
And for a woman wert thou first created,
Till nature as she wrought thee fell a-doting,
And by addition me of thee defeated,
By adding one thing to my purpose nothing.
    But since she pricked thee out for women's pleasure,
    Mine be thy love and thy love's use their treasure.

Sonnet 95

William Shakespeare

How sweet and lovely dost thou make the shame,
Which like a canker in the fragrant rose,
Doth spot the beauty of thy budding name!
O in what sweets dost thou thy sins enclose!
That tongue that tells the story of thy days,
(Making lascivious comments on thy sport)
Cannot dispraise, but in a kind of praise,
Naming thy name, blesses an ill report.
O what a mansion have those vices got,
Which for their habitation chose out thee,
Where beauty's veil doth cover every blot,
And all things turns to fair, that eyes can see!
    Take heed (dear heart) of this large privilege,
    The hardest knife ill-used doth lose his edge.

Sonnet 132

William Shakespeare

Thine eyes I love, and they as pitying me,
Knowing thy heart torment me with disdain,
Have put on black, and loving mourners be,
Looking with pretty ruth upon my pain.
And truly not the morning sun of heaven
Better becomes the grey cheeks of the east,
Nor that full star that ushers in the even
Doth half that glory to the sober west
As those two mourning eyes become thy face:
O let it then as well beseem thy heart
To mourn for me since mourning doth thee grace,
And suit thy pity like in every part.
    Then will I swear beauty herself is black,
    And all they foul that thy complexion lack.

David To Bathsheba
Don Marquis

Very red are the roses of Sharon,
But redder thy mouth,
There is nard, there is myrrh, in En Gedi,
From the uplands of Lebanon, heavy
With balsam, the winds
Drift freighted and scented and cedar—
But thy mouth is more precious than spices!
Thy breasts are twin lilies of Kedron;
White lilies, that sleep
In the shallows where loitering Kedron
Broadens out and is lost in the Jordan;
Globed lilies, so white
That David, thy King, thy beloved
Declareth them meet for his gardens.
Under the stars very strangely
The still waters gleam;
Deep down in the waters of Hebron
The soul of the starlight is sunken,
But deep in thine eyes
Stirs a more wonderful secret
Than pools ever learn of the starlight.

Sonnet 7
William Shakespeare

Lo in the orient when the gracious light
Lifts up his burning head, each under eye
Doth homage to his new-appearing sight,
Serving with looks his sacred majesty,
And having climbed the steep-up heavenly hill,
Resembling strong youth in his middle age,
Yet mortal looks adore his beauty still,
Attending on his golden pilgrimage:
But when from highmost pitch with weary car,
Like feeble age he reeleth from the day,
The eyes (fore duteous) now converted are

From his low tract and look another way:
So thou, thy self out-going in thy noon:
Unlooked on diest unless thou get a son.

Sonnet 12

William Shakespeare

When I do count the clock that tells the time,
And see the brave day sunk in hideous night,
When I behold the violet past prime,
And sable curls all silvered o'er with white:
When lofty trees I see barren of leaves,
Which erst from heat did canopy the herd
And summer's green all girded up in sheaves
Borne on the bier with white and bristly beard:
Then of thy beauty do I question make
That thou among the wastes of time must go,
Since sweets and beauties do themselves forsake,
And die as fast as they see others grow,
   And nothing 'gainst Time's scythe can make defence
   Save breed to brave him, when he takes thee hence

Sonnet 21

William Shakespeare

So is it not with me as with that muse,
Stirred by a painted beauty to his verse,
Who heaven it self for ornament doth use,
And every fair with his fair doth rehearse,
Making a couplement of proud compare
With sun and moon, with earth and sea's rich gems:
With April's first-born flowers and all things rare,
That heaven's air in this huge rondure hems.
O let me true in love but truly write,
And then believe me, my love is as fair,
As any mother's child, though not so bright
As those gold candles fixed in heaven's air:
   Let them say more that like of hearsay well,
   I will not praise that purpose not to sell.

Sonnet 54
William Shakespeare

O how much more doth beauty beauteous seem,
By that sweet ornament which truth doth give!
The rose looks fair, but fairer we it deem
For that sweet odour, which doth in it live:
The canker blooms have full as deep a dye,
As the perfumed tincture of the roses,
Hang on such thorns, and play as wantonly,
When summer's breath their masked buds discloses:
But for their virtue only is their show,
They live unwooed, and unrespected fade,
Die to themselves. Sweet roses do not so,
Of their sweet deaths, are sweetest odours made:
    And so of you, beauteous and lovely youth,
    When that shall vade, by verse distills your truth.

Andrea Del Sarto
(Called "The Faultless Painter")
Robert Browning

But do not let us quarrel any more,
No, my Lucrezia; bear with me for once:

Sit down and all shall happen as you wish.
You turn your face, but does it bring your heart?
I'll work then for your friend's friend, never fear,
Treat his own subject after his own way,
Fix his own time, accept too his own price,
And shut the money into this small hand
When next it takes mine. Will it? tenderly?
Oh, I'll content him,—but to-morrow, Love!
I often am much wearier than you think,
This evening more than usual, and it seems
As if—forgive now—should you let me sit
Here by the window with your hand in mine
And look a half-hour forth on Fiesole,
Both of one mind, as married people use,
Quietly, quietly the evening through,

I might get up to-morrow to my work
Cheerful and fresh as ever. Let us try.
To-morrow, how you shall be glad for this!
Your soft hand is a woman of itself,
And mine the man's bared breast she curls inside.
Don't count the time lost, neither; you must serve
For each of the five pictures we require:
It saves a model. So! keep looking so—
My serpentining beauty, rounds on rounds!
How could you ever prick those perfect ears,
Even to put the pearl there! oh, so sweet—
My face, my moon, my everybody's moon,
Which everybody looks on and calls his,
And, I suppose, is looked on by in turn,
While she looks—no one's: very dear, no less.
You smile? why, there's my picture ready made,
There's what we painters call our harmony!
A common greyness silvers everything,—
All in a twilight, you and I alike
You, at the point of your first pride in me
(That's gone you know),—but I, at every point;
My youth, my hope, my art, being all toned down
To yonder sober pleasant Fiesole.
There's the bell clinking from the chapel-top;
That length of convent-wall across the way
Holds the trees safer, huddled more inside;
The last monk leaves the garden; days decrease,
And autumn grows, autumn in everything.
Eh? the whole seems to fall into a shape
As if I saw alike my work and self
And all that I was born to be and do,
A twilight-piece. Love, we are in God's hand.
How strange now, looks the life he makes us lead;
So free we seem, so fettered fast we are!
I feel he laid the fetter: let it lie!
This chamber for example—turn your head—
All that's behind us! You don't understand
Nor care to understand about my art,
But you can hear at least when people speak:

And that cartoon, the second from the door
It is the thing, Love! so such things should be—
Behold Madonna!—I am bold to say.
I can do with my pencil what I know,
What I see, what at bottom of my heart
I wish for, if I ever wish so deep—
Do easily, too—when I say, perfectly,
I do not boast, perhaps: yourself are judge,
Who listened to the Legate's talk last week,
And just as much they used to say in France.
At any rate 'tis easy, all of it!
No sketches first, no studies, that's long past:
I do what many dream of, all their lives,
Dream? strive to do, and agonize to do,
And fail in doing. I could count twenty such
On twice your fingers, and not leave this town,
Who strive—you don't know how the others strive
To paint a little thing like that you smeared
Carelessly passing with your robes afloat,—
Yet do much less, so much less, Someone says,
(I know his name, no matter)—so much less!
Well, less is more, Lucrezia: I am judged.
There burns a truer light of God in them,
In their vexed beating stuffed and stopped-up brain,
Heart, or whate'er else, than goes on to prompt
This low-pulsed forthright craftsman's hand of mine.
Their works drop groundward, but themselves, I know,
Reach many a time a heaven that's shut to me,
Enter and take their place there sure enough,
Though they come back and cannot tell the world.
My works are nearer heaven, but I sit here.
The sudden blood of these men! at a word—
Praise them, it boils, or blame them, it boils too.
I, painting from myself and to myself,
Know what I do, am unmoved by men's blame
Or their praise either. Somebody remarks
Morello's outline there is wrongly traced,
His hue mistaken; what of that? or else,
Rightly traced and well ordered; what of that?

Speak as they please, what does the mountain care?
Ah, but a man's reach should exceed his grasp,
Or what's a heaven for? All is silver-grey,
Placid and perfect with my art: the worse!
I know both what I want and what might gain,
And yet how profitless to know, to sigh
Had I been two, another and myself,
Our head would have o'erlooked the world!" No doubt.
Yonder's a work now, of that famous youth
The Urbinate who died five years ago.
(Tis copied, George Vasari sent it me.)
Well, I can fancy how he did it all,
Pouring his soul, with kings and popes to see,
Reaching, that heaven might so replenish him,
Above and through his art—for it gives way;
That arm is wrongly put—and there again—
A fault to pardon in the drawing's lines,
Its body, so to speak: its soul is right,
He means right—that, a child may understand.
Still, what an arm! and I could alter it:
But all the play, the insight and the stretch—
Out of me, out of me! And wherefore out?
Had you enjoined them on me, given me soul,
We might have risen to Rafael, I and you!
Nay, Love, you did give all I asked, I think—
More than I merit, yes, by many times.
But had you—oh, with the same perfect brow,
And perfect eyes, and more than perfect mouth,
And the low voice my soul hears, as a bird
The fowler's pipe, and follows to the snare —
Had you, with these the same, but brought a mind!
Some women do so. Had the mouth there urged
God and the glory! never care for gain.
The present by the future, what is that?
Live for fame, side by side with Agnolo!
Rafael is waiting: up to God, all three!"
I might have done it for you. So it seems:
Perhaps not. All is as God over-rules.
Beside, incentives come from the soul's self;

The rest avail not. Why do I need you?
What wife had Rafael, or has Agnolo?
In this world, who can do a thing, will not;
And who would do it, cannot, I perceive:
Yet the will's somewhat—somewhat, too, the power—
And thus we half-men struggle. At the end,
God, I conclude, compensates, punishes.
Tis safer for me, if the award be strict,
That I am something underrated here,
Poor this long while, despised, to speak the truth.
I dared not, do you know, leave home all day,
For fear of chancing on the Paris lords.
The best is when they pass and look aside;
But they speak sometimes; I must bear it all.
Well may they speak! That Francis, that first time,
And that long festal year at Fontainebleau!
I surely then could sometimes leave the ground,
Put on the glory, Rafael's daily wear,
In that humane great monarch's golden look,—
One finger in his beard or twisted curl
Over his mouth's good mark that made the smile,
One arm about my shoulder, round my neck,
The jingle of his gold chain in my ear,
I painting proudly with his breath on me,
All his court round him, seeing with his eyes,
Such frank French eyes, and such a fire of souls
Profuse, my hand kept plying by those hearts,—
And, best of all, this, this, this face beyond,
This in the background, waiting on my work,
To crown the issue with a last reward!
A good time, was it not, my kingly days?
And had you not grown restless... but I know—
Tis done and past: 'twas right, my instinct said:
Too live the life grew, golden and not grey,
And I'm the weak-eyed bat no sun should tempt
Out of the grange whose four walls make his world.
How could it end in any other way?
You called me, and I came home to your heart.
The triumph was—to reach and stay there; since

I reached it ere the triumph, what is lost?
Let my hands frame your face in your hair's gold,
You beautiful Lucrezia that are mine!
Rafael did this, Andrea painted that;
The Roman's is the better when you pray,
But still the other's Virgin was his wife—"
Men will excuse me. I am glad to judge
Both pictures in your presence; clearer grows
My better fortune, I resolve to think.
For, do you know, Lucrezia, as God lives,
Said one day Agnolo, his very self,
To Rafael . . . I have known it all these years . . .
When the young man was flaming out his thoughts
Upon a palace-wall for Rome to see,
(Too lifted up in heart because of it)
Friend, there's a certain sorry little scrub
Goes up and down our Florence, none cares how,
Who, were he set to plan and execute
As you are, pricked on by your popes and kings,
Would bring the sweat into that brow of yours!"
To Rafael's!—And indeed the arm is wrong.
I hardly dare…yet, only you to see,
Give the chalk here—quick, thus, the line should go!
Ay, but the soul! he's Rafael! rub it out!
Still, all I care for, if he spoke the truth,
What he? why, who but Michel Agnolo?
(Do you forget already words like those?)
If really there was such a chance, so lost,—
Is, whether you're—not grateful—but more pleased.
Well, let me think so. And you smile indeed!
This hour has been an hour! Another smile?
If you would sit thus by me every night
I should work better, do you comprehend?
I mean that I should earn more, give you more.
See, it is settled dusk now; there's a star;
Morello's gone, the watch-lights show the wall,
The cue-owls speak the name we call them by.
Come from the window, love,—come in, at last,
Inside the melancholy little house

We built to be so gay with. God is just.
King Francis may forgive me: oft at nights
When I look up from painting, eyes tired out,
The walls become illumined, brick from brick
Distinct, instead of mortar, fierce bright gold,
That gold of his I did cement them with!
Let us but love each other. Must you go?
That Cousin here again? he waits outside?
Must see you—you, and not with me? Those loans?
More gaming debts to pay? you smiled for that?
Well, let smiles buy me! have you more to spend?
While hand and eye and something of a heart
Are left me, work's my ware, and what's it worth?
I'll pay my fancy. Only let me sit
The grey remainder of the evening out,
Idle, you call it, and muse perfectly
How I could paint, were I but back in France,
One picture, just one more—the Virgin's face,
Not yours this time! I want you at my side
To hear them—that is, Michel Agnolo—
Judge all I do and tell you of its worth.
Will you? To-morrow, satisfy your friend.
I take the subjects for his corridor,
Finish the portrait out of hand—there, there,
And throw him in another thing or two
If he demurs; the whole should prove enough
To pay for this same Cousin's freak. Beside,
What's better and what's all I care about,
Get you the thirteen scudi for the ruff!
Love, does that please you? Ah, but what does he,
The Cousin! what does he to please you more?
I am grown peaceful as old age to-night.
I regret little, I would change still less.
Since there my past life lies, why alter it?
The very wrong to Francis!—it is true
I took his coin, was tempted and complied,
And built this house and sinned, and all is said.
My father and my mother died of want.
Well, had I riches of my own? you see

How one gets rich! Let each one bear his lot.
They were born poor, lived poor, and poor they died:
And I have laboured somewhat in my time
And not been paid profusely. Some good son
Paint my two hundred pictures—let him try!
No doubt, there's something strikes a balance. Yes,
You loved me quite enough. it seems to-night.
This must suffice me here. What would one have?
In heaven, perhaps, new chances, one more chance—
Four great walls in the New Jerusalem,
Meted on each side by the angel's reed,
For Leonard, Rafael, Agnolo and me
To cover—the three first without a wife,
While I have mine! So—still they overcome
Because there's still Lucrezia,—as I choose.

Again the Cousin's whistle! Go, my Love.

*M*Y LAST DUCHESS
Robert Browning

FERRARA

That's my last Duchess painted on the wall,
Looking as if she were alive. I call
That piece a wonder, now: Fr'a Pandolf's hands
Worked busily a day, and there she stands.
Will 't please you sit and look at her? I said
"Fr'a Pandolf" by design, for never read
Strangers like you that pictured countenance,
The depth and passion of its earnest glance,
But to myself they turned (since none puts by
The curtain I have drawn for you, but I)
And seemed as they would ask me, if they durst,
How such a glance came there; so, not the first
Are you to turn and ask thus. Sir, 'twas not
Her husband's presence only, called that spot
Of joy into the Duchess' cheek: perhaps
"Over my Lady's wrist too much," or "Paint
Must never hope to reproduce the faint
Half-flush that dies along her throat"; such stuff

Was courtesy, she thought, and cause enough
For calling up that spot of joy. She had
A heart…how shall I say?…too soon made glad,
Too easily impressed; she liked whate'er
She looked on, and her looks went everywhere.
Sir, 'twas all one! My favour at her breast,
The dropping of the daylight in the West,
The bough of cherries some officious fool
Broke in the orchard for her, the white mule
She rode with round the terrace—all and each
Would draw from her alike the approving speech,
Or blush, at least. She thanked men,—good; but thanked
Somehow… know not how… as if she ranked
My gift of a nine-hundred-years-old name
With anybody's gift. Who'd stoop to blame
This sort of trifling? Even had you skill
In speech—(which I have not)—to make your will
Quite clear to such an one, and say, "Just this
Or that in you disgusts me; here you miss,
Or there exceed the mark"—and if she let
Herself be lessoned so, nor plainly set
Her wits to yours, forsooth, and made excuse,
—E'en then would be some stooping; and I chuse
Never to stoop. Oh, sir, she smiled, no doubt,
Whene'er I passed her; but who passed without
Much the same smile? This grew; I gave commands;
Then all smiles stopped together. There she stands
As if alive. Will 't please you rise? We'll meet
The company below, then. I repeat,
The Count your Master's known munificence
Is ample warrant that no just pretence
Of mine for dowry will be disallowed;
Though his fair daughter's self, as I avowed
At starting, is my object. Nay, we'll go
Together down, Sir! Notice Neptune, though,
Taming a sea-horse, thought a rarity,
Which Claus of Innsbruck cast in bronze for me.

Sonnet 101
William Shakespeare

O truant Muse what shall be thy amends,
For thy neglect of truth in beauty dyed?
Both truth and beauty on my love depends:
So dost thou too, and therein dignified:
Make answer Muse, wilt thou not haply say,
'Truth needs no colour with his colour fixed,
Beauty no pencil, beauty's truth to lay:
But best is best, if never intermixed'?
Because he needs no praise, wilt thou be dumb?
Excuse not silence so, for't lies in thee,
To make him much outlive a gilded tomb:
And to be praised of ages yet to be.
    Then do thy office Muse, I teach thee how,
    To make him seem long hence, as he shows now.

Sonnet 81
From "Amoretti"
Edmund Spenser

Fayre is my love, when her fayre golden heares,
With the loose wynd ye waving chance to marke:
Fayre when the rose in her red cheekes appeares,
Or in her eyes the fyre of love does sparke.
Fayre when her brest lyke a rich laden barke,
With pretious merchandize she forth does lay:
Fayre when that cloud of pryde, which oft does dark
Her goodly light with with smiles she drives away.
But fayrest she, when she so doth display,
The gate with pearles and rubyes richly dight:
Throgh which her words so wise do make their way
To beare the message of her gentle spright.
The rest be works of natures wonderment,
But this the worke of harts astonishment.

DELIA: VI

Samuel Daniel

Fair is my love, and cruel as she's fair:
Her brow shades frowns although her eyes are sunny,
Her smiles are lightning though her pride despair,
And her disdains are gall, her favours honey;
A modest maid, deck'd with a blush of honour,
Whose feet do tread green paths of youth and love,
The wonder of all eyes that look upon her:
Sacred on earth, design'd a saint above.
Chastity and beauty, which were deadly foes,
Live reconciled friends within her brow;
And had she pity to conjoin with those,
Then who had heard the plaints I utter now?
For had she not been fair and thus unkind,
My muse had slept, and none had known my mind.

DELIA: XXXI

Samuel Daniel

Look, Delia, how we 'steem the half-blown rose,
The image of thy blush and summer's honour,
Whilst in her tender green she doth enclose
That pure sweet beauty time bestows upon her.
No sooner spreads her glory in the air
But straight her full-blown pride is in declining;
She then is scorn'd that late adorn'd the fair:
So clouds thy beauty after fairest shining.
No April can revive thy wither'd flowers,
Whose blooming grace adorns thy beauty now;
Swift speedy time, feather'd with flying hours,
Dissolves the beauty of the fairest brow.
O let not then such riches waste in vain,
But love whilst that thou mayst be lov'd again.

DELIA: XLVI

Samuel Daniel

Let others sing of knights and paladines
In aged accents and untimely words;
Paint shadows in imaginary lines
Which well the reach of their high wits records:
But I must sing of thee, and those fair eyes
Authentic shall my verse in time to come,
When yet th' unborn shall say, "Lo where she lies
Whose beauty made him speak that else was dumb."
These are the arks, the trophies I erect,
That fortify thy name against old age;
And these thy sacred virtues must protect
Against the dark, and time's consuming rage.
Though th' error of my youth they shall discover,
Suffice they show I liv'd and was thy lover.

SONG

Gil Vicente

Grace and Beauty has the maid;
Could anything more lovely be?

Sailor, you who live on ships,
Did you ever see
Any ship or sail or star
As beautiful as she?

Knight of war, in armour clad,
Did you ever see
Horse or arms or battle-field
As beautiful as she?

Shepherd, you who guard your flock,
Did you ever see
Cattle, vale, or mountain range
As beautiful as she?

CELEBRATING LOVE

Love, Love

Pedro Calderon de la Barca

What is the glory far above
All else in human life?
Love! Love!
There is no form in which the fire
Of love its traces has impressed not.
Man lives far more in love's desire
Than by life's breath, soon possessed not.
If all that lives must love or lie,
All shapes on earth, or sea, or sky,
With one consent, to Heaven cry
That the glory far above
All else in life is—

Love! O, Love!
Thou melancholy thought, which art
So fluttering and so sweet, to thee
When did I give the liberty
Thus to afflict my heart?
What is the cause of this new power
Which doth my fevered being move,
Momently raging more and more?
What subtle pain is kindled now,
Which from my heart doth overflow
Into my senses?

Love! O, Love!

Sonnet 25

William Shakespeare

Let those who are in favour with their stars
Of public honour and proud titles boast,
Whilst I whom fortune of such triumph bars,
Unlooked for joy in that I honour most.
Great princes' favourites their fair leaves spread
But as the marigold at the sun's eye,
And in themselves their pride lies buried,
For at a frown they in their glory die.
The painful warrior famoused for might,
After a thousand victories once foiled,
Is from the book of honour razed quite,
And all the rest forgot for which he toiled.
    Then happy I that love and am beloved
    Where I may not remove, nor be removed.

Love In A Life
Robert Browning

I

Room after room,
I hunt the house through
We inhabit together.
Heart, fear nothing, for, heart, thou shalt find her—
Next time, herself!—not the trouble behind her
Left in the curtain, the couch's perfume!
As she brushed it, the cornice-wreath blossomed anew:
Yon looking-glass gleamed at the wave of her feather.

II

Yet the day wears,
And door succeeds door;
I try the fresh fortune—
Range the wide house from the wing to the centre.
Still the same chance! she goes out as I enter.
Spend my whole day in the quest,—who cares?
But 'tis twilight, you see,—with such suites to explore,
Such closets to search, such alcoves to importune

The Presence Of Love
Samuel Taylor Coleridge

And in Life's noisiest hour,
There whispers still the ceaseless Love of Thee,
The heart's Self-solace and soliloquy.
You mould my Hopes, you fashion me within ;
And to the leading Love-throb in the Heart
Thro' all my Being, thro' my pulses beat ;
You lie in all my many Thoughts, like Light,
Like the fair light of Dawn, or summer Eve
On rippling Stream, or cloud-reflecting Lake.
And looking to the Heaven, that bends above you,
How oft ! I bless the Lot, that made me love you.

Love Among The Ruins

Robert Browning

Where the quiet-coloured end of evening smiles,
Miles and miles
On the solitary pastures where our sheep
Half-asleep
Tinkle homeward thro' the twilight, stray or stop
As they crop—
Was the site once of a city great and gay,
(So they say)
Of our country's very capital, its prince
Ages since
Held his court in, gathered councils, wielding far
Peace or war.
Now the country does not even boast a tree,
As you see,
To distinguish slopes of verdure, certain rills
From the hills
Intersect and give a name to, (else they run
Into one)
Where the domed and daring palace shot its spires
Up like fires
O'er the hundred-gated circuit of a wall
Bounding all
Made of marble, men might march on nor be prest
Twelve abreast.
And such plenty and perfection, see, of grass
Never was!
Such a carpet as, this summer-time, o'er-spreads
And embeds
Every vestige of the city, guessed alone,
Stock or stone—
Where a multitude of men breathed joy and woe
Long ago;
Lust of glory pricked their hearts up, dread of shame
Struck them tame;
And that glory and that shame alike, the gold
Bought and sold.

Now—the single little turret that remains
On the plains,
By the caper overrooted, by the gourd
Overscored,
While the patching houseleek's head of blossom winks
Through the chinks—
Marks the basement whence a tower in ancient time
Sprang sublime,
And a burning ring, all round, the chariots traced
As they raced,
And the monarch and his minions and his dames
Viewed the games.
And I know, while thus the quiet-coloured eve
Smiles to leave
To their folding, all our many-tinkling fleece
In such peace,
And the slopes and rills in undistinguished grey
Melt away—
That a girl with eager eyes and yellow hair
Waits me there
In the turret whence the charioteers caught soul
For the goal,
When the king looked, where she looks now, breathless, dumb
Till I come.
But he looked upon the city, every side,
Far and wide,
All the mountains topped with temples, all the glades'
Colonnades,
All the causeys, bridges, aqueducts,—and then
All the men!
When I do come, she will speak not, she will stand,
Either hand
On my shoulder, give her eyes the first embrace
Of my face,
Ere we rush, ere we extinguish sight and speech
Each on each.
In one year they sent a million fighters forth
South and North,

And they built their gods a brazen pillar high
As the sky
Yet reserved a thousand chariots in full force—
Gold, of course.
O heart! oh blood that freezes, blood that burns!
Earth's returns
For whole centuries of folly, noise and sin!
Shut them in,
With their triumphs and their glories and the rest!
Love is best.

Sonnet 29
William Shakespeare

When, in disgrace with Fortune and men's eyes,
I all alone beweep my outcast state,
And trouble deaf heaven with my bootless cries,
And look upon myself and curse my fate,
Wishing me like to one more rich in hope,
Featured like him, like him with friends possessed,
Desiring this man's art, and that man's scope,
With what I most enjoy contented least;
Yet in these thoughts my self almost despising,
Haply I think on thee, and then my state,
Like to the lark at break of day arising
From sullen earth, sings hymns at heaven's gate;
    For thy sweet love remembered such wealth brings,
    That then I scorn to change my state with kings.

Fine Knacks For Ladies
Anonymous

Fine knacks for ladies, cheap, choice, brave and new!
Good pennyworths-but money cannot move:
I keep a fair but for the fair to view;
A beggar may be liberal of love.
    Though all my wares be trash, the heart is true,
    The heart is true.

Great gifts are guiles and look for gifts again;
My trifles come as treasures from my mind.
It is a precious jewel to be plain;
Sometimes in shell the orient's pearls we find.
Of others take a sheaf, of me a grain!
    Of me a grain!

Within this pack pins, points, laces, and gloves,
And divers toys fitting a country fair;
But in my heart, where duty serves and loves,
Turtles and twins, court's brood, a heavenly pair.
Happy the heart that thinks of no removes!
    Of no removes!

Love, That Doth Reign and Live Within My Thought

Henry Howard, *Earl of Surrey*

Love, that doth reign and live within my thought,
And built his seat within my captive breast,
Clad in the arms wherein with me he fought,
Oft in my face he doth his banner rest.
But she that taught me love and suffer pain,
My doubtful hope and eke my hot desire
With shamefast look to shadow and refrain,
Her smiling grace converteth straight to ire.
And coward Love, then, to the heart apace
Taketh his flight, where he doth lurk and plain,
His purpose lost, and dare not show his face.
For my lord's guilt thus faultless bide I pain,
Yet from my lord shall not my foot remove:
Sweet is the death that taketh end by love.

Song

Paul Laurence Dunbar

A bee that was searching for sweets one day
Through the gate of a rose garden happened to stray.
In the heart of a rose he hid away,
And forgot in his bliss the light of day,
As sipping his honey he buzzed in song;

Though day was waning, he lingered long,
For the rose was sweet, so sweet.
A robin sits pluming his ruddy breast,
And a madrigal sings to his love in her nest:
"Oh, the skies they are blue, the fields are green,
And the birds in your nest will soon be seen!"
She hangs on his words with a thrill of love,
And chirps to him as he sits above,
For the song is sweet, so sweet.

A maiden was out on a summer's day
With the winds and the waves and the flowers at play;
And she met with a youth of gentle air,
With the light of the sunshine on his hair.
Together they wandered the flowers among;
They loved, and loving they lingered long,
For to love is sweet, so sweet.

My Sweetest Lesbia

Thomas Campion

My sweetest Lesbia, let us live and love
And though the sager sort our deeds reprove,
Let us not weigh them. Heaven's great lamps do dive
Into their west, and straight again revive,
But soon as once set is our little light,
Then must we sleep one ever-during night.

If all would lead their lives in love like me,
Then bloody swords and armor should not be;
No drum nor trumpet peaceful sleeps should move,
Unless alarm came from the camp of love.
But fools do live, and waste their little light,
And seek with pain their ever-during night.

When timely death my life and fortune ends,
Let not my hearse be vexed with mourning friends,
But let all lovers, rich in triumph, come
And with sweet pastimes grace my happy tomb;
And Lesbia, close up thou my little light,
And crown with love my ever-during night.

FLICKER

Traditional, American

The flicker of the campfire, the wind in the pines
The stars in the heavens, the moon that shines
A place where people gather to meet friends of all kinds
A place where old man trouble is always left behind
So give me the light of a campfire, warm and bright
And give me some friends to sing with, I'll be here all night
Love is where you find it; I've found mine right here
Just you and me and the campfire and songs we love to hear
So give me the light of a campfire, warm and bright
And give me some friends to sing with, I'll be here all night
Love is where you find it; I've found mine right here
Just you and me and the campfire and songs we love to hear

LOVE POEM

Kathleen Raine

Because I love
 There is an invisible way across the sky,
 Birds travel by that way, the sun and moon
 And all the stars travel that path by night.
Because I love
 There is a river flowing all night long.
Because I love
 All night the river flows into my sleep,
 Ten thousand living things are sleeping in my arms,
 And sleeping wake, and flowing are at rest.

LOVE'S APPARITION AND EVANISHMENT:
AN ALLEGORIC ROMANCE

Samuel Taylor Coleridge

Like a lone Arab, old and blind,
Some caravan had left behind,
Who sits beside a ruin'd well,
Where the shy sand-asps bask and swell;
And now he hangs his ag'ed head aslant,
And listens for a human sound—in vain!
And now the aid, which Heaven alone can grant,

Upturns his eyeless face from Heaven to gain—
Even thus, in vacant mood, one sultry hour,
Resting my eye upon a drooping plant,
With brow low-bent, within my garden-bower,
I sate upon the couch of camomile;
And—whether 'twas a transient sleep, perchance,
Flitted across the idle brain, the while
I watch'd the sickly calm with aimless scope,
In my own heart; or that, indeed a trance,
Turn'd my eye inward—thee, O genial Hope,
Love's elder sister! thee did I behold
Drest as a bridesmaid, but all pale and cold,
With roseless cheek, all pale and cold and dim,
Lie lifeless at my feet!
And then came Love, a sylph in bridal trim,
And stood beside my seat;
She bent, and kiss'd her sister's lips,
As she was wont to do;—
Alas! 'twas but a chilling breath
Woke just enough of life in death
To make Hope die anew.

*T*HE KISS

Coventry Patmore

"I saw you take his kiss!" "Tis true."
   "O, modesty!" "Twas strictly kept:
He thought me asleep; at least I knew
   He thought I thought he thought I slept."

*E*ROS

Ralph Waldo Emerson

The sense of the world is short,
—Long and various the report,
—To love and be beloved;
Men and gods have not outlearned it;
And, how oft soe'er they're turned it,
Not to be improved.

$\mathcal{P}$HYLLIS CORYDON CLUTCHED TO HIM
Catullus

Phyllis Corydon clutched to him
Her head at rest beneath his chin.
He said, "If I don't love you more
than ever maid was loved before
I shall (if this the years not prove)
in Afric or the Indian grove
some green-eyed lion serve for food."
amor, to show that he was pleased,
approvingly (in silence) sneezed.
Then Phyllis slightly raised her head
(her lips were full & wet & red)
to kiss the sweet eyes full of her:
"Corydon mine, with me prefer
always to serve unique Amor:
my softer flesh the fire licks
more greedily and deeper sticks."
Amor, to show that he was pleased,
approvingly (in silence) sneezed.
So loving & loved so, they rove
between twin auspices of Love.
Corydon sets in his eye-lust
Phyllis before all other dust;
Phyllis on Corydon expends
Her nubile toys, Lover's dividends.
Could Venus yield more love-delight"
than here she grants in Love's requite?

$\mathcal{I}$F LOVE...
Luis de Gongora

If Love, within the feathers of his nest,
Imprisoned my heart, what will he do now,
When in thy eyes, O Lady of sweet brow,
He flies in armour clad, though yet undressed?
I was stung, amid the violets pressed,
By the asp that lives midst the lilies bough;
As fragrant Dawn equal power hadst thou
As now, when Sun, thou dost shimmer full crest.
I'll greet the light in grave voice rent with pain,

As the kind nightingale in prison bound
Gives voice to grievances with sweet refrain.
I'll tell how with rays I saw thy brow gain
A crown, and that thy loveliness renowned
Doth cause birds to sing and men tears attain.

*L*OVE'S EMBLEMS

Grace Greenwood

There was a rose, that blushing grew
Within my life's young bower;
The angels sprinkled holy dew
Upon the blessed flower.

I glory to resign it, love,
Though it was dear to me;
Amid thy laurels twine it, love,
It only blooms for thee.

There was a rich and radiant gem
I long kept hid from sight;
Lost from some seraph's diadem,
It shone with heaven's own light!

The world could never tear it, love,
That gem of gems, from me;
Yet on thy fond breast wear it, love,
It only shines for thee.

There was a bird came to my breast,
When I was very young;
I only knew that sweet bird's nest,
To me she only sung.

But, ah! one summer day, love,
I saw that bird depart!
The truant flew thy way, love,
And nestled in thy heart!

An Offering To Anna

Grace Greenwood

I send this ring of braided hair,
A simple gift, to thee,
One more fond pledge of perfect trust,
And perfect peace, from me.

Thou 'lt wear it for our dear love's sake,
So fresh and pure and strong,
Far sweeter than the dreams of fame,
Of romance, or of song.

And when snows fall, or spring-flowers wave,
My cold, still breast ahoy,
Dear, faithful heart, thou'lt wear it then
In memory of our love.

Bird of my bosom! blessed shape
Of joy and song thou art;
Sweet soul of tenderness and truth,
Soft nestled in my heart.

Thou say'st that heart is Poesy's harp,
A lute which Pleasure plays,
And Love's own dimpled fingers wake
To gay or mournful lays.

Then grieve not, should strains sad or harsh
Rise sometimes from its strings,
When thou dost jar the silver chords
With the fluttering of thy wings.

The Sign

Bhartrihari

O fair Acoka-tree, with my love's own red
Thy bows are all aflame;
Whither, I pray thee, has my wanton fled?
This way I know she came.

In vain thy nodding in the wind, thy sigh
Of ignorance assumed;
I know because my flower-love wandered by

For joy thy branches bloomed.

I know thee: ever with thy buds unblown,
Till touched by maiden's foot;
And thou so fair- one fairest maid alone
Hath trod upon thy root.

To My Dearest Lucasia
Katherine Fowler Philips

Come, my Lucasia, since we see
    That miracles Men's Faith do move,
By wonder and by prodigy
    To the dull angry World let's prove
    There's a Religion in our Love.
For Though we were design'd t'agree,
    That Fate no liberty destroys,
But our Election is as free
    As Angels, who with greedy choice
    Are yet determin'd to their joys.
Our hearts are doubled by the loss,
    Here Mixture is Addition grown;
We both diffuse, and both ingross:
    And we whose minds are so much one,
    Never, yet ever are alone.
We court our own Captivity
    Than Thrones more great and innocent:
`Twere banishment to be set free,
    Since we wear fetters whose intent
    Not Bondage is but Ornament
Divided joys are tedious found,
    And griefs united easier grow:
We are our selves but by rebound,
    And all our Titles shuffled so,
    Both Princes, and both Subjects too.
Our Hearts are mutual Victims laid,
    While they (such power in Friendship lies)
Are Altars, Priests, and Off'rings made:
    And each Heart which thus kindly dies,
    Grows deathless by the Sacrifice.

*L*OVE

George Herbert

Love bade me welcome, yet my soul drew back,
Guilty of dust and sin.
But quick-eye'ed Love, observing me grow slack
From my first entrance in,
Drew nearer to me, sweetly questioning
If I lack'd anything.

"A guest," I answer'd, "worthy to be here";
Love said, "You shall be he."
"I, the unkind, the ungrateful? ah my dear,
I cannot look on thee."
Love took my hand and smiling did reply,
"Who made the eyes but I?"

"Truth, Lord, but I have marr'd them; let my shame
Go where it doth deserve."
"And know you not," says Love, "who bore the blame?"
"My dear, then I will serve."
"You must sit down," says Love, "and taste my meat."
So I did sit and eat.

*S*ONNET **XLIII**

Elizabeth Barrett Browning

How do I love thee? Let me count the ways.
I love thee to the depth and breadth and height
My soul can reach, when feeling out of sight
For the ends of Being and ideal Grace.
I love thee to the level of everyday's
Most quiet need, by sun and candle-light.
I love thee freely, as men strive for Right;
I love thee purely, as they turn from Praise.
I love thee with the passion put to use
In my old griefs, and with my childhood's faith.
I love thee with a love I seemed to lose
With my lost saints,—I love thee with the breath,
Smiles, tears, of all my life! —and, if God choose,
I shall but love thee better after death.

In Love Made Visible

May Swenson

In love are we made visible

As in a magic bath
are unpeeled
to the sharp pit
so long concealed

With love's alertness
we recognize
the soundless whimper
of the soul
behind the eyes
A shaft opens
and the timid thing
at last leaps to surface
with full-spread wing

The fingertips of love discover
more than the body's smoothness
They uncover a hidden conduit
for the transfusion
of empathies that circumvent
the mind's intrusion

In love are we set free
Objective bone
and flesh no longer insulate us
to ourselves alone
We are released
and flow into each other's cup
Our two frail vials pierced
drink each other up

The Sun Rising

John Donne

Busy old fool, unruly Sun,
    Why dost thou thus,
Through windows and through curtains call on us?
Must to thy motions lovers' seasons run?
    Saucy pedantic wretch, go chide
    Late School-boys, and sour 'prentices,
    Go tell court-huntsmen that the King will ride,
    Call country ants to harvest offices;
Love, all alike, no season knows, not clime,
Nor hours, days, months, which are the rugs of time.

Thy beams, so reverend and strong
    Why shouldst thou think?
I could eclipse and cloud them with a wink,
But that I would not lose her sight so long:
    If her eyes have not blinded thine,
    Look, and tomorrow late tell me,
    Whether both the Indias of spice and mine
    Be where thou left'st them, or lie here with me.
Ask for those kings whom thou saw'st yesterday,
And thou shalt hear, "All here in one bed lay."

She's all States, and all Princes I;
    Nothing else is.
Princes do but play us; compared to this,
All honour's mimic; all wealth alchemy
    Thou, Sun, art half as happy as we,
    In that the world's contracted thus;
    Thine age asks case, and since thy duties be
    To warm the world, that's done in warming us,
Shine here to us, and thou art everywhere;
This bed thy centre is, these walls thy sphere.

Song To Celia, From "Volpone"

Ben Jonson

Come my Celia, let us prove,
While we may, the sports of love.
Time will not be ours for ever:
He at length our good will sever.
Spend not then his gifts in vain;
Suns that set may rise again,
But if once we lose this light
'Tis, with us, perpetual night.
Why should we defer our joys?
Fame and rumour are but toys.
Cannot we delude the eyes
Of a few poor household spies?
Or his easier ears beguile,
So removed by our wile?
'Tis no sin love's fruit to steal,
But the sweet theft to reveal;
To be taken, to be seen,
These have crimes accounted been.

The Orchard

Gretel Ehrlich

We go into it at night,
In Wyoming an orchard is the
only city around—so many blossoms going up
into trees like lights
and windfall apples like lives
coming down.

In the pickup, heads on the tailgate,
we lie on last year's hay and wait
for the orchard to bloom
A great horned owl sweeps between
trees as if to cropdust the rising
sap with white for the flowers.

"The first blossom to come," you say,
"I'll give the apple that grows there to you."

Another owl lands
on a bare branch and drops
a plug of micebones to the roots.
Under him, the tree does not think of
the sap's struggle.
I listen to your heart. Divided by
beats and rests, it says yes, then no, then yes.

Above us the Milky Way seams the sky and is
stirred by a hand too big to see.
We watch the stars.

Tonight so many of them fall.

ODE TO PSYCHE

John Keats

O Goddess! hear these tuneless numbers, wrung
    By sweet enforcement and remembrance dear,
And pardon that thy secrets should be sung
    Even into thine own soft-conched ear:
Surely I dreamt to-day, or did I see
    The winged Psyche with awaken'd eyes?
I wander'd in a forest thoughtlessly,
    And, on the sudden, fainting with surprise,
Saw two fair creatures, couched side by side
    In deepest grass, beneath the whisp'ring roof
    Of leaves and trembled blossoms, where there ran
      A brooklet, scarce espied:
'Mid hush'd, cool-rooted flowers, fragrant-eyed,
    Blue, silver-white, and budded Tyrian,
They lay calm-breathing on the bedded grass;
    Their arms embraced, and their pinions too;
    Their lips touch'd not, but had not bade adieu,
As if disjoined by soft-handed slumber,
And ready still past kisses to outnumber
    At tender eye-dawn of aurorean love:
      The winged boy I knew;

But who wast thou, O happy, happy dove?
    His Psyche true!
O latest born and loveliest vision far
  Of all Olympus' faded hierarchy!
Fairer than Phoebe's sapphire-region'd star,
  Or Vesper, amorous glow-worm of the sky;
Fairer than these, though temple thou hast none,
    Nor altar heap'd with flowers;
Nor virgin-choir to make delicious moan
    Upon the midnight hours;
No voice, no lute, no pipe, no incense sweet
  From chain-swung censer teeming;
No shrine, no grove, no oracle, no heat
  Of pale-mouth'd prophet dreaming.
O brightest! though too late for antique vows,
  Too, too late for the fond believing lyre,
When holy were the haunted forest boughs,
  Holy the air, the water, and the fire;
Yet even in these days so far retir'd
  From happy pieties, thy lucent fans,
  Fluttering among the faint Olympians,
I see, and sing, by my own eyes inspired.
So let me be thy choir, and make a moan
    Upon the midnight hours;
Thy voice, thy lute, thy pipe, thy incense sweet
  From swinged censer teeming;
Thy shrine, thy grove, thy oracle, thy heat
  Of pale-mouth'd prophet dreaming.
Yes, I will be thy priest, and build a fane
  In some untrodden region of my mind,
Where branched thoughts, new grown with pleasant pain,
  Instead of pines shall murmur in the wind:
Far, far around shall those dark-cluster'd trees
  Fledge the wild-ridged mountains steep by steep;
And there by zephyrs, streams, and birds, and bees,
  The moss-lain Dryads shall be lull'd to sleep;
And in the midst of this wide quietness
A rosy sanctuary will I dress

With the wreath'd trellis of a working brain,
  With buds, and bells, and stars without a name,
With all the gardener Fancy e'er could feign,
  Who breeding flowers, will never breed the same:
And there shall be for thee all soft delight
  That shadowy thought can win,
A bright torch, and a casement ope at night,
  To let the warm Love in!

Kissing My Kate
Robert Burns

O, merry hae I been teethin a heckle
An merry hae I been shapin a spoon!
O, merry hae I been cloutin a kettle,
An kissin my Katie when a' was done!
O, a' the lang day I ca' at my hammer,
An a' the lang day I whistle and sing!
O, a' the lang night I cuddle my kimmer,
An a' the lang night as happy's a king!
Bitter in dool, I lickit my winnins
O marrying Bess, to gie her a slave:
Blest be the hour she cool'd in her linens
And blythe be the bird that sings on her grave
Come to my arms, my Katie, my Katie,
An come to my arms, and kiss me again!
Drunken or sober, here's to thee, Katie,
An blest be the day I did it again!

At Midsummer, For Jeanine
Norman Dubie

We had been in the tall grass for hours—
Sleep coming on some barrier of bells
Waking you—you stretched, the moon lost
In clouds, the gravestones below us
To the north had moved
West to a hill, the white rounded stones,
All at cruel angles to the ground,

Had been black and white heifers resting
Between the stream with its ledges of quartz marl.

Earlier you had thought the stream
Moved like clear muscle and sinew
With their hooks
In the narrow runners of limestone.
You stretched, your breasts uncovered—
You had hurt your back lifting seed basins
Out in the shed; eased,
Touching me you think of Kabir saying:

Worlds are being told like beads.
The day began with the famous airs of a catbird,
A white unstruck music, you were downstairs
Sweeping mouse dirt out of the cupboards.
Now, down in the grass I am awake. I look over
To the north. And say: It's gone? The gravestones?
You smile and cross over me like a welcome storm.

*T*o Charlotte Cushman
Sidney Lanier

Look where a three-point star shall weave his beam
Into the slumb'rous tissue of some stream,
Till his bright self o'er his bright copy seem
Fulfillment dropping on a come-true dream;

So in this night of art thy soul doth show
Her excellent double in the steadfast flow
Of wishing love that through men's hearts doth go:
At once thou shin'st above and shin'st below.

E 'en when thou strivest there within Art's sky
(Each star must o'er a strenuous orbit fly),
Full calm thine image in our love doth lie,
A Motion glassed in a Tranquillity.

So triple-rayed, thou mov'st, yet stay'st, serene—
Art's artist,
Love's dear woman,
Fame's good queen!

It Was A Lover And His Lass

Traditional, Scots

It was a lover and his lass
  With a hey and a ho and a hey nonni no
  With a hey nonni nonni no
That o'er the green cornfields did pass
  In springtime, in springtime
  In springtime, the only pretty ring time
  When the birds do sing
  Hey ding a ding a ding
  Hey ding a ding a ding
  Hey ding a ding a ding
  Sweet lovers love the spring
Between the acres of rye...
These pretty country folks would lie...
And therefore take the present time...
For love is crowned with the prime...

Red, Red Rose

Robert Burns

O my Luve's like a red, red rose
That's newly sprung in June:
O my Luve's like the melodie
That's sweetly play'd in tune!

As fair thou art, my bonnie lass,
So deep in love am I:
And I will love thee still, my dear,
Till a' the seas gang dry:

Till a' the seas gang dry, my dear,
And the rocks melt with the sun;
I will luve thee still my dear,
When the sands of life shall run.

And fare thee weel, my only Luve,
And fare thee weel a while!
And I will come again, my Luve,
Tho' it were ten thousand mile.

Night Visiting Song

Traditional, Scots

The time has come, I can no longer tarry
This morning's tempest I must shortly brave
To cross the moors and high towering mountains
Until I'm in the arms of the one I love
And when he came to his true love's dwelling
He knelt down gently upon a stane
And whispered softly into the window
"Does my own true love lie there alane?"
She lifted her head from off her down-white pillow
She's lifted the blankets from off her breast
And raised herself up onto an elbow
"Who's that disturbing me from my night's rest?"
"It's I, it's I, it's I, your own true lover
Oh open the door, love and let me in
For I am wet love, and also wearied
For I am wet love, into the skin"
She raised herself up with the greatest of pleasure
She's raised her up and she's let him in
And all night long they rolled in each other's arms
Until the long night was past and gone
And when the long night was past and over
And when the small cocks began to crow
He shook her hand, aye, they've kissed and parted
He's saddled and mounted and away did go

The Riddle Song

Traditional

I gave my love a cherry that has no stone,
I gave my love a chicken that has no bone,
I gave my love a ring that has no end,
I gave my love a baby with no cryen.
How can there be a cherry that has no stone?
How can there be a chicken that has no bone?
How can there be a ring that has no end?
How can there be a baby with no cryen?

A cherry, when it's blooming, it has no stone,
A chicken when it's pipping, it has no bone,
A ring when it's rolling, it has no end,
A baby when it's sleeping, has no cryen.

Scotch And Soda

Anonymous, American

Scotch and soda, mud in your eye
Baby, do I feel high
O me o my, do I feel high
Dry martini, jigger of gin
O what a spell you got me in
O my, do I feel high
People won't believe me
They'll think that I'm just braggin'
That I could feel the way I do
And still be on the wagon
All I need is one of your smiles
Sunshine of your eye
Do I feel higher than a kite can fly
Give me loving, Baby, I feel high

An Hour With Thee

Sir Walter Scott

An hour with thee! When earliest day
Dapples with gold the eastern gray,
Oh, what can frame my mind to bear
The toil and turmoil, cark and care,
New griefs, which coming hours unfold,
And sad remembrance of the old?
One hour with thee.
One hour with thee! When burning June
Waves his red flag at pitch of noon;
What shall repay the faithful swain,
His labor on the sultry plain;
And, more than cave or sheltering bough,
Cool feverish blood and throbbing brow?
One hour with thee.

One hour with thee! When sun is set,
Oh, what can teach me to forget
The thankless labors of the day;
The hopes, the wishes, flung away;
The increasing wants, and lessening gains,
The master's pride, who scorns my pains?
One hour with thee.

LOVERS
Siegfried Sassoon

You were glad tonight: and now you've gone away.
Flushed in the dark, you put your dreams to bed;
But as you fall asleep I hear you say
Those tired sweet drowsy words we left unsaid.
Sleep well: for I can follow you, to bless
And lull your distant beauty where you roam;
And with wild songs of hoarded loveliness
Recall you to these arms that were your home.

CURRENTS
Tina Koyama

Each night a dark river flows over the edge of your heart,
its hard current pulling you toward the pain at the end of your dream.
If I could, I would give you fins, a streamlined body, scales or a pair of gills,
whatever would help you swim back up that long rush of water, home again.
I would walk along the river, watch your shadow slide between rocks
     that rake the water,
your gills filtering fragments of air. Bright as coins, your scales would flash
     in the chilled light.
Upstream is where I would wait.
But tonight, you ask only for quiet in the curve of my arms, a space
     too small for anything but breathing.
It is all I can give you.
Love's swift current roars past me in the dark as you sleep.

*L*OVE POEM

Kathleen Raine

Because I love
    There is an invisible way across the sky,
    Birds travel by that way, the sun and moon
    And all the stars travel that path by night.
Because I love
    There is a river flowing all night long.
Because I love
    All night the river flows into my sleep,
    Ten thousand living things are sleeping in my arms,
    And sleeping wake, and flowing are at rest.

*M*Y HIGHLAND LASSIE, O

Robert Burns

Nae gentle dames, tho' e'er sae fair,
Shall ever be my muse's care;
Their titles a' are empty show;
Gie me my Highland Lassie, O.
Within the glen sae bushy, O,
Aboon the plain sae rushy, O,
I sit me down wi' right good will,
To sing my Highland Lassie, O.
Oh, were yon hills and valleys mine,
Yon palace and yon gardens fine!
The world then the love should know
I bear my Highland Lassie, O.
Within the glen...
But fickle fortune frowns on me,
And I maun cross the raging sea;
But while my crimson currents flow
I'll love my highland Lassie, O.
Within the glen...
Altho' thro' foreign climes I range,
I know her heart will never change,
For her bosom burns with honor's glow,
My faithful highland Lassie, O.

Within the glen...
For her I'll dare the billows' roar,
For her I'll trace a distant shore,
That Indian wealth may lustre throw
Around my Highland Lassie, O.
Within the glen...
She has my heart, she has my hand,
By sacred troth and honor's band!
Till the mortal stroke shall lay me low,
I'm thine, my highland Lassie, O.
Farewell the glen sae bushy, O!
Farewell the plain sae rushy, O!
To other lands I now must go,
To sing my Highland Lassie, O!

THE PRESENCE OF LOVE
Samuel Taylor Coleridge

And in Life's noisiest hour,
There whispers still the ceaseless Love of Thee,
The heart's Self-solace and soliloquy.
You mould my Hopes, you fashion me within;
And to the leading Love-throb in the Heart
Thro' all my Being, thro' my pulses beat;
You lie in all my many Thoughts, like Light,
Like the fair light of Dawn, or summer Eve
On rippling Stream, or cloud-reflecting Lake.
And looking to the Heaven, that bends above you,
How oft! I bless the Lot, that made me love you.

LOVE
Henry David Thoreau

Love is the burden of all nature's odes; the song of the birds is an epithalamium,
a hymeneal. The marriage of the flowers spots the meadows and fringes the hedges with
pearls and diamonds. In the deep waters, in the high air, in woods and pastures, and the
bowels of the earth, this is the employment and condition of all things.

ALISON

Anonymous

Bytuene Mersh and Averil,
    When spray biginneth to springe,
The lutel foul hath hire wyl
    On hyre lud to synge.
    Ich libbe in love-longinge
    For semlokest of alle thinge —
    He may me blisse bringe;
Icham in hire baundoun
    An hendy hap ichabbe yhent-
    Ichot from hevene it is me sent:
    From alle wymmen mi love is lent
And lyht on Alysoun.

On heu hire her is fayr ynoh,
    Hire browe broune, hire eye blake—
With lossum chere he on me loh-
    With middel smal and wel ymake.
    Bote he me wolle to hire take,
    Forte buen hire owen make,
    Longe to lyven ichulle forsake
And feye fallen adoun
    An hendy hap ...

Nightes when I wende and wake-
    Forthi myn wonges waxeth won-
Levedi, al for thine sake
    Longinge is ylent me on.
    In world nis non so wyter mon
    That al hire bounte telle con.
    Hire swyre is whittore then the swon,
And feyrest may in toune.
    An hendy hap...

Icham for wowyng al forwake,
    Wery so water in wore,
Lest eny reve me my make
    Ichabbe y-yerned yore.
    Betere is tholien whyle sore
    Then mournen evermore.
    Geynest under gore,
Herkne to my roun.
    An hendy hap ...

DESTINY

Edwin Arnold

Somewhere there waiteth in this wold of ours
    For one line soul another lonely soul,
Each choosing each through all the weary hours
    And meeting strangely at one sudden goal.
Then blend they, like green leeaves with golden flowers,
    Into one beautiful and perfect whole;
And life's long night is ended, and the way
    Lies open onward to eternal day.

Nightfall

Michael Field

She sits beside: through four low panes of glass
The sun, a misty meadow, and the stream;
Falling through rounded elms the last sunbeam
Through night's thick fibre sudden barges pass
With great forelights of gold, with trailing mass
Of timber: rearward of their transient glearn
The shadows settle, and profounder dream
Enters, fulfils the shadows. Vale and grass
Are now no more; a last leaf strays about,
Then every wandering ceases; we remain.
Clear dusk, the face of wind is on the sky:
The eyes I love lift to the upper pane —
Their voice gives note of welcome quietly
"I love the air in which the stars come out."

The Pleasure of Love

Duc de la Rouchefoucauld

The pleasure of love is in loving, and one is happier in the passion one feles
than in the passion one arouses in another

Sweet, Can I Sing

Arthur Symons

Sweet, can I sing you the song of your kisses?
How soft is this one, how subtle this is,
How fluttering swift as a bird's kiss that is,
As a bird that taps at a leafy lattice;
How this one clings and how that uncloses
From bud to flower in the way of roses;
And this through laughter and that through weeping
Swims to the brim where Love lies sleeping;
And this in a pout I snatch, and capture
That in ecstasy of rapture,
When the odorous red-rose petals part
That my lips may find their way to the heart
Of the rose of the world, your lips, my rose.
But no song knows
The way of my heart to the heart of my rose.

_A_ Stolen Kiss

George Wither

Now gentle sleep hath closed up those eyes
Which, waking, kept my boldest thoughts in awe;
And free access unto thy sweet lip lies,
From whence I long the rosy breath to draw.

Methinks not wrong it were, if I should steal
From those two melting rubies one poor kiss;
None sees the theft that would the theft reveal,
Nor rob I her of aught that she can miss;

Nay should I twenty kisses take away,
There would be little sign I would do so;
Why then ashould I this robbery delay?
O, she may wake, and therewith angry grow!
Well, if she do, I'lll back restore that one,
And twenty hundred thousand more for loan.

_U_nbosoming

Michael Field

The love that breeds
In my heart for thee!
As the iris is full, brimful of seeds,
And all that it flowered for among the reeds
Is packed in a thousand vermilion-beads
That push, and riot, and squeeze, and clip,
Till they burst the sides of the silver scrip,
And at last we see
What the bloom, with its tremulous, bowery fold
Of zephyr-petal at heart did hold:
So my breast is rent
With the burden and strain of its great content;
For the summer of fragrance and sighs is dead,
The harvest-secret is burning red,
And I would give thee, after my kind,
The final issues of heart and mind.

MAIDS, NOT TO YOU MY MIND DOTH CHANGE
Michael Field

Maids, not to you my mind doth change;
Men I defy, allure, estrange,
Prostrate, make bond or free:
Soft as the stream beneath the plane
To you I sing my love's refrain;
Between us is no thought of pain,
Peril, satiety.
Soon doth a lover's patience tire,
But ye to manifold desire
Can yield response, ye know
When for long, museful days I pine,
The presage at my heart divine;
To you I never breathe a sign
Of inward want or woe.
When injuries my spirit bruise,
Allaying virtue ye infuse
With unobtrusive skill:
And if care frets ye come to me
As fresh as nymph from stream or tree,
And with your soft vitality
My weary bosom fill.

WHEN A BELOVED HAND
Matthew Arnold

When a beloved hand is laid in ours,
When, jaded with the rush and glare
Of the interminable hours,
Our eyes can in another's eyes read clear,
When our world-deafened ear
Is by the tones of a loved voice caressed, —
A bolt is shot back somewhere in our breast,
And a lost pulse of feeling stirs again.
The eye sinks inward, and the heart lies plain,
And what we mean, we say, and what we would, we know!
A man becomes aware of his life's flow,

And hears its winding murmur, and he sees
The meadows where it glides, the sun, the breeze.

And there arrives a lull in the hot race,
Wherein he doth for ever chase
That flying and elusive shadow, rest.
An air of coolness plays upon his face,
And an unwonted calm pervades his breast.
And then he thinks he knows
The hills where his life rose,
And the sea where it goes.

In a Gondola
Robert Browning

The moth's kiss, first!
Kiss me as if you made me believe
You were not sure, this ve,
How my face, your flower, had pursed
Its petals up; so, here and there
You brush it, till I grow aware
Who wants me, and wide ope I burst.

The bee's kiss now!
Kiss me as if you enter'd gay
My heart at some noonday,
A bud that dare not disallow
The claim. So all is render'd up,
And passively its shattered cup
Over your head to sleep I bow.

From "The Rubaiyat"
Omar Khayyam

A Book of Verses underneath the Bough,
A Jug of Wine, a Loaf of Bread—
and ThouBeside me singing in the Wilderness—
Oh, Wilderness were Paradise e'now!

From "The Rubaiyat"
Omar Khayyam

And if the Wine you drink, the Lip you pressEnd in what
All begins and ends in—Yes;
Think then you are To-day what YesterdayYou were—
To-morrow You shall not be less.

The Definition of Love
Andrew Marvell

My love is of a birth as rare
As 'tis for object strange and high;
It was begotten by Despair
Upon Impossibility.

Magnanimous Despair alone
Could show me so divine a thing
Where feeble Hope could ne'er have flown,
But vainly flapp'd its tinsel wing.

And yet I quickly might arrive
Where my extended soul is fixt,
But Fate does iron wedges drive,
And always crowds itself betwixt.

For Fate with jealous eye does see
Two perfect loves, nor lets them close;
Their union would her ruin be,
And her tyrannic pow'r depose.

And therefore her decrees of steel
Us as the distant poles have plac'd,
(Though love's whole world on us doth wheel)
Not by themselves to be embrac'd;

Unless the giddy heaven fall,
And earth some new convulsion tear;
And, us to join, the world should all
Be cramp'd into a planisphere.

As lines, so loves oblique may well
Themselves in every angle greet;
But ours so truly parallel,
Though infinite, can never meet.

Therefore the love which us doth bind,
But Fate so enviously debars,
Is the conjunction of the mind,
And opposition of the stars.

The Aeolian Harp

Samuel Taylorge Coleridge

My pensive Sara! thy soft cheek reclined
Thus on mine arm, most soothing sweet it is
To sit beside our Cot, our Cot o'ergrown
With white-flower'd Jasmin, and the broad-leav'd Myrtle,
 (Meet emblems they of Innocence and Love!)
And watch the clouds, that late were rich with light,
Slow saddenning round, and mark the star of eve
Serenely brilliant (such should Wisdom be)
Shine opposite! How exquisite the scents
Snatch'd from yon bean-field ! and the world so hush'd!
The stilly murmur of the distant Sea
Tells us of silence.

And that simplest Lute,
Plac'd length-ways in the clasping casement, hark!
How by the desultory breeze caress'd,
Like some coy maid half-yielding to her lover,
It pours such sweet upbraiding, as must needs
Tempt to repeat the wrong! And now, its strings
Boldlier swept, the long sequacious notes
Over delicious surges sink and rise,
Such a soft floating witchery of sound
As twilight Elfins make, when they at eve
Voyage on gentle gales from Faery-Land,
Where Melodies round honey-dropping flowers,
Footless and wild, like birds of Paradise,
Nor pause, nor perch, hovering on untam'd wing!
O! the one Life within us and abroad,
Which meets all motion and becomes its soul,
A light in sound, a sound-like power in light,
Rhythm in all thought, and joyance every where
Methinks, it should have been impossible
Not to love all things in a world so fill'd;
Where the breeze warbles, and the mute still air
Is Music slumbering on her instrument.
And thus, my Love! as on the midway slope

Of yonder hill I stretch my limbs at noon,
Whilst thro' my half-clos'd eye-lids I behold
The sunbeams dance, like diamonds, on the main,
And tranquil muse upon tranquility;
Full many a thought uncall'd and undetain'd,
And many idle flitting phantasies,
Traverse my indolent and passive brain,
As wild and various, as the random gales
That swell and flutter on this subject Lute!
And what if all of animated nature
Be but organic Harps diversly fram'd,
That tremble into thought, as o'er them sweeps
Plastic and vast, one intellectual breeze,
At once the Soul of each, and God of all?
But thy more serious eye a mild reproof
Darts, O beloved Woman! nor such thoughts
Dim and unhallow'd dost thou not reject,
And biddest me walk humbly with my God.
Meek Daughter in the Family of Christ!
Well hast thou said and holily disprais'd
These shapings of the unregenerate mind;
Bubbles that glitter as they rise and break
On vain Philosophy's aye-babbling spring.
For never guiltless may I speak of him,
The Incomprehensible! save when with awe
I praise him, and with Faith that inly feels;
Who with his saving mercies healed me,
A sinful and most miserable man,
Wilder'd and dark, and gave me to possess
Peace, and this Cot, and thee, heart-honour'd Maid !

$\mathcal{D}$ESIRE

Samuel Taylor Coleridge

Where true Love burns Desire is Love's pure flame;
It is the reflex of our earthly frame,
That takes its meaning from the nobler part,
And but translates the language of the heart.

A Birthday

Christina Rossetti

My heart is like a singing bird
Whose nest is in a watered shoot;
My heart is like an apple-tree
Whose boughs are bent with thickset fruit;
My heart is like a rainbow shell
That paddles in a halcyon sea;
My heart is gladder than all these
Because my love is come to me.
Raise me a dais of silk and down;
Hang it with vair and purple dyes;
Carve it in doves and pomegranates,
And peacocks with a hundred eyes;
Work it in gold and silver grapes,
In leaves and silver fleurs-de-lys;
Because the birthday of my life
come, my love is come to me.

*T*he Dream

Edna St. Vincent Millay

Love, if I weep it will not matter,
    And if you laugh I shall not care;
Foolish am I to think about it,
    But it is good to feel you there.

Love, in my sleep I dreamed of waking,—
    White and awful the moonlight reached
Over the floor, and somewhere, somewhere,
    There was a shutter loose, —it screeched!

Swung in the wind,—and no wind blowing!—
    I was afraid, and turned to you,
Put out my hand to you for comfort, —
    And you were gone! Cold, cold as dew,

Under my hand the moonlight lay!
    Love, if you laugh I shall not care,
But if I weep it will not matter,—
    Ah, it is good to feel you there!

THE REVELATION
Coventry Patmore

An idle poet, here and there,
    Looks around him; but, for all the rest,
The world, unfathomably fair,
    Is duller than a witling's jest.
Love wakes men, once a lifetime each;
    They lift their heavy lids, and look;
And, lo, what one sweet page can teach,
    They read with joy, then shut the book.
And some give thanks, and some blaspheme
    And most forget; but, either way,
That and the Child's unheeded dream
Is all the light of all their day.

FIREFLIES
Rabindranath Tagore

I touch God in my song
    as the hill touches the far-away sea
    with its waterfall.
The butterfly counts not months but moments,
    and has time enough.
Let my love, like sunlight, surround you
    and yet give you illumined freedom.
Love remains a secret even when spoken,
    for only a lover truly knows that he is loved.
Emancipation from the bondage of the soil
    is no freedom for the tree.
In love I pay my endless debt to thee
    for what thou art.

SONNET 141
William Shakespeare

In faith I do not love thee with mine eyes,
For they in thee a thousand errors note,
But 'tis my heart that loves what they despise,

Who in despite of view is pleased to dote.
Nor are mine ears with thy tongue's tune delighted,
Nor tender feeling to base touches prone,
Nor taste, nor smell, desire to be invited
To any sensual feast with thee alone:
But my five wits, nor my five senses can
Dissuade one foolish heart from serving thee,
Who leaves unswayed the likeness of a man,
Thy proud heart's slave and vassal wretch to be:
    Only my plague thus far I count my gain,
    That she that makes me sin, awards me pain.

Sonnets From The Portuguese, XIV
Elizabeth Barrett Browning

If thou must love me, let it be for nought
Except for love's sake only. Do not say
'I love her for her smile—her look—her way
Of speaking gently,—for a trick of thought
That falls in well with mine, and certes brought
A sense of pleasant ease on such a day'—
For these things in themselves, Beloved, may
Be changed, or change for thee,—and love, so wrought,
May be unwrought so. Neither love me for
Thine own dear pity's wiping my cheeks dry,—
A creature might forget to weep, who bore
Thy comfort long, and lose thy love thereby!
But love me for love's sake, that evermore
Thou mayst love on, through love's eternity.

My Love
Ono no Yoshiki

My love
Is like the grasses
Hidden in the deep mountain:
Though its abundance increases,
There is none that knows.

A Thought Of May
Lizette Woodward Reese

All that long, mad March day, in the dull town,
I had a thought of May —alas, alas!
The dogwood boughs made whiteness up and down;
The daffodils were burning in the grass;
And there were bees astir in lane and street,
And scent of lilacs blowing tall and lush;
While hey, the wind, that pitched its voice so sweet,
It seemed an angel talked behind each bush!
The west grew very golden, roofs turned black.
I saw one star above the gables bare.
The door flew open.
Love, you had come back.
I held my arms; you found the old way there.
In its old place you laid your yellow head,
And at your kiss the mad March weather fled!

How Do I Know?
Bevington

How do I know you good?—my dear, my dear,
How do I know?
Because, at thought of you the bonds fall off
That plagued me so;
Because for love of you my very life
Has changed its flow.

How do I know you good? Because, dear love,
In needing you,
My inmost soul most urgently desires
Great goodness too;
Pure skies alone can win a turbid sea
To perfect blue.

One little lovely victory for your sake
O'er my mad blood,
One little hour when higher than myself
I knew I stood,
One stillness, dear, has taught the blessed truth,
My love is good.
'Tis so I know you good—my dear, my dear;

My heart is new;
For your sweet sake 'tis less than virtue now
To be quite true;
Ay! easy to be patient, pure, and brave,
Quite good—for you.

Sonnet XV

Sappho

Now, round my favor'd grot let roses rise,
To strew the bank where Phaon wakes from rest;
O! happy buds! to kiss his burning breast,
And die, beneath the lustre of his eyes!
Now, let the timbrels echo to the skies,
Now damsels sprinkel cassia on his vest,
With od'rous wreaths of constant myrtle drest,
And flow'rs, deep tinted with the rainbow's dyes!
From cups of porphyry let nectar flow,
Rich as the perfume of Phoenicia's vine!
Now let his dimpling cheek with rapture glow,
While round his heart love's mystic fetters twine;
And let the Grecian Lyre its aid bestow,
In songs of triumph, to proclaim him mine!

Sonnet 115

William Shakespeare

Those lines that I before have writ to lie,
Even those that said I could not love you dearer.
Yet then my judgment knew no reason why,
My most full flame should afterwards burn clearer.
But reckoning Time, whose millioned accidents
Creep in 'twixt vows, and change decrees of kings,
Tan sacred beauty, blunt the sharp'st intents,
Divert strong minds to the course of alt'ring things.
Alas, why fearing of time's tyranny,
Might I not then say, "Now I love you best,"
When I was certain o'er incertainty,
Crowning the present, doubting of the rest?
    Love is a babe; then might I not say so,
    To give full growth to that which still doth grow.

Sonnet 80
William Shakespeare

O, how I faint when I of you do write,
Knowing a better spirit doth use your name,
And in the praise thereof spends all his might,
To make me tongue-tied speaking of your fame.
But since your worth, wide as the ocean is,
The humble as the proudest sail doth bear,
My saucy bark, inferior far to his,
On your broad main doth wilfully appear.
Your shallowest help will hold me up afloat
Whilst he upon your soundless deep doth ride;
Or, being wrecked, I am a worthless boat,
He of tall building, and of goodly pride.
　　Then if he thrive, and I be cast away,
　　The worst was this: my love was my decay.

I Have Got Her
Fujiwara no Kamatari

I have got her,
Have got Yamasuko;
She who for any man
Was thought hard to get,
Yamasuko I have got!

Love
Madhu

Everything in this world is colorful
when you are in love you heard the voice of
clouds songs of skylark sound of waves
but when you are in sorrow
everything lost his own color
so ever think about the color
heart is full of joy not the nature
and ever be in a love

$\mathcal{U}$NTITLED

Anonymous, Egyptian

He is the love-wolf
gobbling in my cave,
within...the pebbles beneath
moring a tree
of the bread
offered to the gods.

$\mathcal{L}$OVE SONG

Anonymous

Herself hath given back my life to me,
Herself hath yielded far
More than had ever hoped my misery.
And when she recklessly
Gave herself wholly unto Love and me,
Beauty in heaven afar
Laughed from her joyous star.

Too great desire hath overwhelmed me,
My heart's not great enough
For this huge joy that overmastered me,
What time my love
Made in her arms another man of me,
And all the gathered honey of her lips
Drained in one yielded kiss.

Again, again, I dream the freedom given
Of her soft breast,
And am so come, another god, to heaven
Among the rest.
Yea, and serene would govern gods and men,
If I might find again
My hand upon her breast.

The Crossing

Anonymous, Egyptian

I dwell upon your love
through the night and all
the day, through the hours
I lie asleep and when
I wake again at dawn.

Your beauty nourishes hearts.
Your voice creates desire.
It makes my body strong.
"He is weary."
So may I say whenever
There is no other girl
in harmony with his heart.
I am the only one.

Surprised by Joy

William Wordsworth

I turned to share the transport —Oh! with whom
But Thee, deep buried in the silent tomb,
That spot which no vicissitude can find?
Love, faithful love, recalled thee to my mind—
But how could I forget thee Through what power,
Even for the least division of an hour,
Have I been so beguiled as to be blind
To my most grievous loss!—That thought's return
Was the worst pang that sorrow ever bore,
Save one, one only, when I stood forlorn,
Knowing my heart's best treasure was no more;
That neither present time, nor years inborn
Could to my sight that heavenly face restore.

Inscription For A Statue of Love

F.M. Arouet de Voltaire

Whoer'er you are, your master see,
He is, he was, or is to be.

Song

Gil Vicente

If thou art sleeping, maiden,
Awake and open thy door.
'Tis the break of day, and we must away
O'er meadow, and mount, and moor,

Wait not to find thy slippers,
But come with thy naked feet;
We shall have to pass through the dewy grass
And waters wide and fleet.

The Flower Song

Anonymous, Egyptian

My heart has a portion of yours.
I do its will for you
when I am in your arms.
My prayer is the paint of my eyes.
The sight of you makes bright
my eyes. I come close
to see your love for me.
Beloved lord of my heart!
How lovely my hour with you!
It flows forever for me
since I first lay with you.
Whether in sorrow or joy,
you have exalted my heart.
Never leave me, I beg.

XI

Emily Dickinson

I 've got an arrow here;
Loving the hand that sent it,
I the dart revere.
Fell, they will say, in 'skirmish'!
Vanquished, my soul will know,
By but a simple arrow
Sped by an archer's bow.

MASS OF LOVE

Anonymous, Spanish

Dawn of a bright June morning,
The birthday of Saint John,
When ladies and their lovers
To hear High Mass are gone.

Yonder goes my lady,
Among them all, the best;
In colored silk mantilla
And many skirts she's dressed.

Embroidered is her bodice
With gems of pearl and gold.
Her lips of beauty rare
Beguiling sweetness hold.

Faint the touch of rouge
On cheeks of fairest white,
Sparkling blue her eyes
With subtle art made bright.

Proudly church she entered
Radiant as sun above,
Ladies died of envy
And courtiers, of love.

A singer in the choir
His place lost in the creed;
The priest who read the lesson
The pages did not heed,

And acolytes beside him
No order could restore;
Instead of Amen, Amen,
They sang Amor, Amor.

TO HER

Paul Laurence Dunbar

Your presence like a benison to me
Wakes my sick soul to dreamful ecstasy,
I fancy that some old Arabian night
Saw you my houri and my heart's delight.
And wandering forth beneath the passionate moon
Your love-strung zither and my soul in tune,
We knew the joy, the haunting of the pain
That like a flame thrills through me now again.
To-night we sit where sweet the spice winds blow,
A wind the northland lacks and ne'er shall know,
With clasped hands and spirits all aglow
As in Arabia in the long ago.

The Roses of Sa'adi
Marceline Desbordes-Valmore

I wanted this morning to bring you a gift of roses;
But I took so many in my wide belt,
The tightened knots could not contain them all,

And burst asunder. The roses taking wing
On the wind, were all blown out to sea,
Following the water, never to return;

The waves were red with them as if aflame.
This evening my dress bears their perfume still:
You may take from it now their frangrant souvenir.

All That Love Asks
Ella Wheeler Wilcox

"All that I ask," says Love, "is just to stand
And gaze, unchided, deep in thy dear eyes;
For in their depths lies largest Paradise.
Yet, if perchance one pressure of thy hand
Be granted me, then joy I thought complete
Were still more sweet."

"All that I ask," says Love, "all that I ask,
Is just thy hand clasp. Could I brush thy cheek
As zephyrs brush a rose leaf, words are weak
To tell the bliss in which my soul would bask.
There is no language but would desecrate
A joy so great."

"All that I ask, is just one tender touch
Of that soft cheek. Thy pulsing palm in mine,
Thy dark eyes lifted in a trust divine
And those curled lips that tempt me overmuch
Turned where I may not seize the supreme bliss
Of one mad kiss.

"All that I ask," says Love, "of life, of death.
Or of high heaven itself, is just to stand,
Glance melting into glance, hand twined in hand,
The while I drink the nectar of thy breath,

In one sweet kiss, but one, of all thy store,
I ask no more."

"All that I ask "—nay, self-deceiving Love,
Reverse thy phrase, so thus the words may fall,
In place of "all I ask," say, "I ask all,"
All that pertains to earth or soars above,
All that thou weft, art, will be, body, soul,
Love asks the whole.

Love In A Zeppelin
George Sylvester Viereck

Below us rolled the earth. We were
Like clouds above the dust and din.
We heard Saint Peter's violin,
For Heaven's gate drew near us there:
We rode upon the Zeppelin,
The strong-ribbed dolphin of the air.

A magic carpet was the plain,
Men crawled like ants that seemed to doze.
A thousand poplars stood in rows
Like soldiers marching in a lane.
Your mouth, the envy of the rose,
Drank in the sunshine llke champagne.

And then the glass grew bright for us
With wine.
Like happy boy and maid
We drank to all hearts unafraid
Who bravely walk the perilous
Ways of the air to shame the shade
Of Phaethon and Icarus.

Leander for his Love's sake hurled
Himself into the deep, but I
More blessed than Hero's lover, fly
Above green meadows dew-bepearled,
While at my side I clasp on high
The fairest lady in the world.

God's lifted finger, looms a spire,
And now the city's windows gleam.
Our shadow races with the stream
And still the ship climbs high and higher,
But not so high as soars my dream,
But not so swift as my desire.

My lady laughs.Oh Cruel One:
All ships pay toll unto the sea,
But I can build a craft for thee,
That earth itself shall not outrun,
And lift on wings of melody
My heart's desire to the sun.

All ships pay toll unto the sea,
Death sounds the last bell of delight;
Like the earth earthy, and the night,
Love's pleasant face at last shall be:
But she who shares a poet's flight
May share his immortality.

CHANSON
Oscar Wilde

A RING of gold and a milk-white dove
    Are goodly gifts for thee,
And a hempen rope for your own love
    To hang upon a tree.
For you a House of Ivory
    (Roses are white in the rose-bower)!
A narrow bed for me to lie
    (White, O white, is the hemlock flower)!
Myrtle and jessamine for you
    (O the red rose is fair to see)!
For me the cypress and the rue
    (Fairest of all is rose-mary)!
For you three lovers of your hand
    (Green grass where a man lies dead)!
For me three paces on the sand
    (Plant lilies at my head)!

LYRICS OF LOVE, LYRIC TWO
Fenton Johnson

This is the hour, my love, the hour of tryst;
The earth is sleeping in the cool of dusk,
The lily-of-the valley nods and sways,
The air is drooping with the perfumed musk.

Ah! open wide, my love, thy garden' gate;
Eftsoons the ancient moon will ply her barge,
For thee I bring sweet Cupid's rosary,
To thee a book of kisses do I charge.

When Eden's glory thrived, fair Eve was won
At such an hour as this, our trysting hour,
And burning Romeo, when Night was Queen,
Enthralled young Juliet within her bower.

Then blest be every hour that Love holds sway,
And sweet the roses of the eventide.
Then blest the crucial moment of this life,
When down the stream of passion sweethearts glide

WAITING

Emily Dickinson

I sing to use the waiting,
My bonnet but to tie,
And shut the door unto my house;
No more to do have I,
Till, his best step approaching,
We journey to the day,
And tell each other how we sang
To keep the dark away.

DISCOVERY

Madison Cawein

What is it now that I shall seek
Where woods dip downward, in the hills;
A mossy nook, a ferny creek,
And May among the daffodils.

Or in the valley's vistaed glow,
Past rocks of terraced trumpet-vines,
Shall I behold her coming slow,
Sweet May, among the columbines?

With red-bud cheeks and bluet eyes,
Big eyes, the homes of happiness,
To meet me with the old surprise,
Her hoiden hair all bonnetless.

Who waits for me, where, note for note,
The birds make glad the forest trees?
A dogwood blossom at her throat,
My May among th' anemones.

As sweetheart breezes kiss the blooms,
And dewdrops drink the moonlight's gleam,
My soul shall kiss her lips' perfumes,
And drink the magic of her dreams.

A VALENTINE

Matilda Betham-Edwards

What shall I send my sweet today,
When all the woods attune in love?
And I would show the lark and dove,
That I can love as well as they.
I'll send a locket full of hair, -
But no, for it might chance to lie
Too near her heart, and I should die
Of love's sweet envy to be there.
A violet is sweet to give, -
Ah, stay! she'd touch it with her lips,
And, after such complete eclipse,
How could my soul consent to live?
I'll send a kiss, for that would be
The quickest sent, the lightest borne,
And well I know tomorrow morn
She'll send it back again to me.
Go, happy winds; ah, do not stay,
Enamoured of my lady's cheek,
But hasten home, and I'll bespeak
Your services another day!

*S*ERENADE

Edgar Allan Poe

So sweet the hour, so calm the time,
I feel it more than half a crime,
When Nature sleeps and stars are mute,
To mar the silence ev'n with lute.
At rest on ocean's brilliant dyes
An image of Elysium lies:
Seven Pleiades entranced in Heaven,
Form in the deep another seven:
Endymion nodding from above
Sees in the sea a second love.
Within the valleys dim and brown,
And on the spectral mountain's crown,

The wearied light is dying down,
And earth, and stars, and sea, and sky
Are redolent of sleep, as I
Am redolent of thee and thine
Enthralling love, my Adeline.
But list, O list,—so soft and low
Thy lover's voice tonight shall flow,
That, scarce awake, thy soul shall deem
My words the music of a dream.
Thus, while no single sound too rude
Upon thy slumber shall intrude,
Our thoughts, our souls—O God above!
In every deed shall mingle, love.

Song

Nedim

Come, let's grant the joy to this heart of ours that founders in distress:
Let's go to the pleasure gardens, come, my sauntering cypress…
Look, at the quay, a six-oared boat is waiting in readiness-
Let's go to the pleasure gardens, come, my sauntering cypress…
Let's laugh and play, let's enjoy the world to the hilt while we may,
Drink nectar at the fountain which was unveiled the other day,
And watch the gargoyle sputter the elixir of life away-
Let's go to the pleasure gardens, come, my sauntering cypress.
First, for a while, let's take a stroll around the pond at leisure,
And gaze in marvel at that palace of heavenly pleasure;
Now and then, let's sing songs or recite poems for good measure-
Let's go to the pleasure gardens, come, my sauntering cypress .
Get your mother's leave, say it's for holy prayers this Friday:
Out of time's tormenting clutches let us both steal a day
And slinking through the secret roads and alleys down to the quay,
Let's go to the pleasure gardens, come, my sauntering cypress .
Just you and I, and a singer with exquisiste airs-and yet
Another: with your kind permission, Nedim, the mad poet;
Let's forget our boon companions today, my joyful coquette-
Let's go to the pleasure gardens, come, my sauntering cypress.

SATISFIED
Emily Dickinson

One blessing had I, than the rest
So larger to my eyes
That I stopped gauging, satisfied,
For this enchanted size.
It was the limit of my dream,
The focus of my prayer,—
A perfect, paralyzing bliss
Contented as despair.
I knew no more of want or cold,
Phantasms both become,
For this new value in the soul,
Supremest earthly sum.
The heaven below the heaven above
Obscured with ruddier hue.
Life's latitude leant over-full;
The judgment perished, too.
Why joys so scantily disburse,
Why Paradise defer,
Why floods are served to us in bowls,—
I speculate no more.

THE OCEAN OF YOUR EYES
Poorvi Vora and Susan Chacko

This edge of sunlight, as evening descends,
the meeting point of dark and light,
'fore tomorrow begins and this day ends:
a pause between the day and the night.
Eternal for a moment,
Transient in a moment,
on this edge of sunlight, for a fraction of time.
the impatience of lips; arms in contact;
our union needs not to attest, misbelieve
or blame, what need is there to deceive?
The evening sun sets in the depths of your eyes
as in peaceful sleep the homedweller lies
and the traveller takes to the road with a sigh.

To F—

Edgar Allan Poe

Beloved! amid the earnest woes
    That crowd around my earthly path-
(Drear path, alas! where grows
    Not even one lonely rose)-
My soul at least a solace hath
In dreams of thee, and therein knows
    An Eden of bland repose.

And thus thy memory is to me
    Like some enchanted far-off isle
In some tumultuous sea-
    Some ocean throbbing far and free
With storms- but where meanwhile
    Serenest skies continually
Just o'er that one bright island smile.

Afton Water

Robert Burns

Flow gently, sweet Afton, among thy Green braes,
Flow gently, I'll sing thee a song in thy praise;
My Mary's asleep by thy murmuring stream,
Flow gently, sweet Afton, disturb not her dream.

Thou stock-dove whose echo resounds through the glen,
Ye wild whistling blackbirds in yon thorny den,
Thou green-crested lapwing, thy screaming forbear,
I charge you disturb not my slumbering fair.

How lofty, sweet Afton, thy neighboring hills,
Far marked with the courses of clear winding rills;
There daily I wander as noon rises high,
My flocks and my Mary's sweet cot in my eye.

How pleasant thy banks and green valleys below,
Where wild in the woodlands the primroses blow;
There oft as mild evening weeps over the lea,
The sweet-scented birk shades my Mary and me.

Thy crystal stream, Afton, how lovely it glides,
And winds by the cot where my Mary resides;
How wanton the waters her snowy feet lave,
As gathering sweet flowerets she stems thy clear wave.

Flow gently, sweet Afton, among thy Green braes,
Flow gently, sweet river, the theme of my lays;
My Mary's asleep by thy murmuring stream,
Flow gently, sweet Afton, disturb not her dream.

Love's Alchemy

John Donne

Some that have deeper digg'd love's mine than I,
Say, where his centric happiness doth lie;
    I have lov'd, and got, and told,
But should I love, get, tell, till I were old,
I should not find that hidden mystery
    Oh, 'tis imposture all!
And as no chemic yet th' elixir got,
    But glorifies his pregnant pot
    If by the way to him befall
Some odoriferous thing, or medicinal,
    So, lovers dream a rich and long delight,
    But get a winter-seeming summer's night.

Our ease, our thrift, our honour, and our day,
Shall we for this vain bubble's shadow pay?
    Ends love in this, that my man
Can be as happy'as I can, if he can
Endure the short scorn of a bridegroom's play?
    That loving wretch that swears
'Tis not the bodies marry, but the minds,
    Which he in her angelic finds,
    Would swear as justly that he hears,
In that day's rude hoarse minstrelsy, the spheres.
    Hope not for mind in women; at their best
    Sweetness and wit, they'are but mummy, possess'd.

Love Is A Sickness

Samuel Daniel

Love is a sickness full of woes,
All remedies refusing;
A plant that with most cutting grows,
Most barren with best using.
Why so?
More we enjoy it, more it dies;
If not enjoyed, sighing cries
Heigh Ho!

Love is a torment of the mind,
A tempest everlasting;
And Jove hath made it of a kind
Not well, nor full, nor fasting.
Why so?
More we enjoy it, more it dies;
If not enjoyed, sighing cries
Heigh Ho!

A Late Walk

Robert Frost

When I go up through the mowing field,
The heedless aftermath,
Smooth-laid like thatch with the heavy dew,
Half closes the garden path.
And when I come to the garden ground,
The whir of sober birds
Up from the tangle of withered weeds
Is sadder than any words.
A tree beside the wall stands bare,
But a leaf that lingered brown,
Disturbed, I doubt not, by my thought,
Comes softly rattling down.
I end not far from my going forth
By picking the faded blue
Of the last remaining aster flower
To carry again to you.

IV

e e cummings

when god lets my body be
From each brave eye shall sprout a tree fruit that dangles there
    from
the purpled world will dance upon
Between my lips which did sing
    a rose shall beget the spring that maidens whom passion wastes
    will lay between their little breasts

My strong fingers beneath the snow
Into strenuous birds shall go my love walking in the grass
    their wings will touch with her face and all the while shall my heart be
    With the bulge and nuzzle of the sea

XVIII

Emily Dickinson

He touched me, so I live to know
That such a day, permitted so,
I groped upon his breast.
It was a boundless place to me,
And silenced, as the awful sea
Puts minor streams to rest.
And now, I 'm different from before,
As if I breathed superior air,
Or brushed a royal gown;
My feet, too, that had wandered so,
My gypsy face transfigured now
To tenderer renown.

A DEEP-SWORN VOW

William Butler Yeats

Others because you did not keep
That deep-sworn vow have been friends of mine;
Yet always when I look death in the face,
When I clamber to the heights of sleep,
Or when I grow excited with wine,
Suddenly I meet your face.

THE HEART OF THE WOMAN
William Butler Yeats

O what to me the little room
That was brimmed up with prayer and rest;
He bade me out into the gloom,
And my breast lies upon his breast.
O what to me my mother's care,
The house where I was safe and warm;
The shadowy blossom of my hair
Will hide us from the bitter storm.
O hiding hair and dewy eyes,
I am no more with life and death,
My heart upon his warm heart lies,
My breath is mixed into his breath.

A POET TO HIS BELOVED
William Yeats

I bring you with reverent hands
The books of my numberless dreams;
White woman that passion has worn
As the tide wears the dove-gray sands,
And with heart more old than the horn
That is brimmed from the pale fire of time:
White woman with numberless dreams
I bring you my passionate rhyme.

YOU SMILE UPON YOUR FRIEND TO-DAY
A.E. Houseman

You smile upon your friend to-day,
   To-day his ills are over;
You hearken to the lover's say,
   And happy is the lover.
'Tis late to hearken, late to smile,
   But better late than never:
I shall have lived a little while
   Before I die for ever.

THE STARS LOOK AT LOVE

Heinrich Heine

When young hearts break with passion
The starts break into laughter,
They laugh and, in their fashion,
Gossip a long time after:

"Poor souls, those mortals languish
With Love; 'tis all they cherish.
It pays them back with anguish
And pain until they perish.

"We never can discover
This Love, so brief abd breathless,
So fatal to each lover—
And hence we stars are deathless."

LOVE

Johann Ludwig Tieck

Love must think in music sweetly,
for all thought is too remote.
Only music can denote
all that love desires completely.
Love we know and know her only
when the voice of music sounds;
while her magic still abounds,
love can never leave us lonely.
Love would die a sterile death,
did not music lend her breath.

SONNET 15

William Shakespeare

When I consider every thing that grows
Holds in perfection but a little moment.
That this huge stage presenteth nought but shows
Whereon the stars in secret influence comment.
When I perceive that men as plants increase,
Cheered and checked even by the self-same sky:

Vaunt in their youthful sap, at height decrease,
And wear their brave state out of memory.
Then the conceit of this inconstant stay,
Sets you most rich in youth before my sight,
Where wasteful time debateth with decay
To change your day of youth to sullied night,
    And all in war with Time for love of you,
    As he takes from you, I engraft you new.

Sonnet 23
William Shakespeare

As an unperfect actor on the stage,
Who with his fear is put beside his part,
Or some fierce thing replete with too much rage,
Whose strength's abundance weakens his own heart;
So I for fear of trust, forget to say,
The perfect ceremony of love's rite,
And in mine own love's strength seem to decay,
O'ercharged with burthen of mine own love's might:
O let my looks be then the eloquence,
And dumb presagers of my speaking breast,
Who plead for love, and look for recompense,
More than that tongue that more hath more expressed.
    O learn to read what silent love hath writ,
    To hear with eyes belongs to love's fine wit.

Sonnet 91
William Shakespeare

Some glory in their birth, some in their skill,
Some in their wealth, some in their body's force,
Some in their garments though new-fangled ill:
Some in their hawks and hounds, some in their horse.
And every humour hath his adjunct pleasure,
Wherein it finds a joy above the rest,
But these particulars are not my measure,
All these I better in one general best.
Thy love is better than high birth to me,
Richer than wealth, prouder than garments' costs,

Of more delight than hawks and horses be:
And having thee, of all men's pride I boast.
    Wretched in this alone, that thou mayst take,
    All this away, and me most wretchcd make.

THE NAME
Don Marquis

It shifts and shifts from form to form,
It drifts and darkles, gleams and glows;
It is the passion of the storm,
The poignance of the rose;
Through changing shapes, through devious ways,
By noon or night, through cloud or flame,
My heart has followed all my days
Something I cannot name.
In sunlight on some woman's hair,
Or starlight in some woman's eyne,
Or in low laughter smothered where
Her red lips wedded mine,
My heart hath known, and thrilled to know,
This unnamed presence that it sought;
And when my heart hath found it so,
"Love is the name," I thought.
Sometimes when sudden afterglows
In futile glory storm the skies
Within their transient gold and rose
The secret stirs and dies;
Or when the trampling morn walks o'er
The troubled seas, with feet of flame,
My awed heart whispers,
"Ask no more, For Beauty is the name!"
Or dreaming in old chapels where
The dim aisles pulse with murmurings
That part are music, part are prayer
—(Or rush of hidden wings)
Sometimes I lift a startled head
To some saint's carven countenance,
Half fancying that the lips have said,
All names mean God, perchance!"

ACROSS THE NIGHT

Don Marquis

Much listening through the silences,
Much staring through the night,
And lo! the dumb blind distances
Are bridged with speech and sight!

Magician Thought, informed of Love,
Hath fixed her on the air—
Oh, Love and I laughed down the fates
And clasped her, here as there!

Across the eerie silences
She came in headlong flight,
She stormed the serried distances,
She trampled space and night!

Oh, foolish scientists might give
This miracle a name —
But Love and I care but to know
That when we called she came.

And since I find the distances
Subservient to my thought,
And of the sentient silences
More vital speech have wrought,

Then she and I will mock Death's self,
For all his vaunted might —
There are no gulfs we dare not leap,
As she leapt through the night!

SEA CHANGES

Don Marquis

(Morning) We stood among the boats and nets;
We saw the swift clouds fall,
We watched the schooners scamper in
Before the sudden squall;

—The jolly squall strove lustily
To whelm the sheltered street—

The merry squall that piled the seas
About the patient headland's knees

And chased the fishing fleet.
She laughed; as if with wings her mirth
Arose and left the wingless earth
And all tame things behind;

Rose like a bird, wild with delight
Whose briny pinions flash in flight
Through storm and sun and wind.
Her laughter sought those skies because

Their mood and hers were one,
For she and I were drunk with love
And life and storm and sun!
And while she laughed, the Sun himself

Leapt laughing through the rain
And struck his harper hand along
The ringing coast; and that wind-song
Whose joy is mixed with pain

Forgot the undertone of grief
And joined the jocund strain,
And over every hidden reef
Whereon the waves broke merrily
Rose jets and sprays of melody
And leapt and laughed again.

New From Babylon

Don Marquis

"Archaeologists have discovered a love-letter among the ruins of Babylon."
— Newspaper report.

The world hath just one tale to tell, and it is very old,
A little tale—a simple tale—a tale that's easy told:

"There was a youth in Babylon who greatly loved a maid!"
The world hath just one song to sing, but sings it unafraid,

A little song—a foolish song—the only song it hath:
"There was a youth in Ascalon who loved a girl in Gath!"

Homer clanged it, Omar twanged it, Greece and Persia knew!
—Nimrod's reivers, Hiram's weavers, Hindu, Kurd, and Jew —

Crowning Tyre, Troy afire, they have dreamed the dream;
Tiber-side and Nilus-tide brightened with the gleam —

Oh, the suing, sighing, wooing, sad and merry hours,
Blisses tasted, kisses wasted, building Babel's towers!

Hearts were aching, hearts were breaking, lashes wet with dew,
When the ships touched the lips of islands Sappho knew;

Yearning breasts and burning breasts, cold at last, are hid
Amid the glooms of carven tombs in Khufu's pyramid—

Though the sages, down the ages, smile their cynic doubt,
Man and maid, unafraid, put the schools to rout;

Seek to chain love and retain love in the bonds of breath,
Vow to hold love, bind and fold love even unto death!

The dust of forty centuries has buried Babylon,
And out of all her lovers dead rises only one;

Rises with a song to sing and laughter in his eyes,
The old song—the only song—for all the rest are lies!

For, oh, the world has just one dream, and it is very old—
'Tis youth's dream —a silly dream—but it is flushed with gold!

THE DEFINITION OF LOVE

Andrew Marvell

My Love is of a birth as rare
As 'tis for object strange and high:
It was begotten by despair
Upon Impossibility.
Magnanimous Despair alone.
Could show me so divine a thing,
Where feeble Hope could ne'r have flown
But vainly flapt its Tinsel Wing.
And yet I quickly might arrive
Where my extended Soul is fixt,
But Fate does Iron wedges drive,

And alwaies crouds it self betwixt.
For Fate with jealous Eye does see.
Two perfect Loves; nor lets them close:
Their union would her ruine be,
And her Tyrannick pow'r depose.
And therefore her Decrees of Steel
Us as the distant Poles have plac'd,
(Though Loves whole World on us doth wheel)
Not by themselves to be embrac'd.
Unless the giddy Heaven fall,
And Earth some new Convulsion tear;
And, us to joyn, the World should all
Be cramp'd into a Planisphere .
As Lines so Loves Oblique may well
Themselves in every Angle greet:
But ours so truly Paralel,
Though infinite can never meet.
Therefore the Love which us doth bind,
But Fate so enviously debarrs,
Is the Conjunction of the Mind,
And Opposition of the Stars.

Inscription
Ann Hamilton

It is not hard to tell of a rose
That in another's garden grows,
Or the green shadow of a tree
That has cooled others, but not me,
Or the star-radience of a sky
That heaven possesses, but not I;
The rose is a scent, the tree a shade,
The sky a temple God has made,
But you are mine—a flame that endures
To warm my soul as it warms yours—
How can I praise it when its light
Is the fierce pen with which I write?
Back to the rose. I cannot see
When sunlight is so close to me.

Gather Me The Rose
William Ernest Henley

O gather me the rose, the rose,
    While yet in flower we find it,
    For summer smiles, but summer goes,
    And winter waits behind it.
    For with the dream foregone, foregone,
    The deed foreborn forever,
    The worm Regret will canker on,
    And time will turn him never.

So were it well to love, my love,
    And cheat of any laughter
    The fate beneath us, and above,
    The dark before and after.
    The myrtle and the rose, the rose,
    The sunshine and the swallow,
    The dream that comes, the wish that goes
    The memories that follow!

Be My Mistress Short Or Tall
Robert Herrick

Be my mistress short or tall
And distorted therewithall
Be she likewise one of those
That an acre hath of nose
Be her teeth ill hung or set

And her grinders black as jet
Be her cheeks so shallow too
As to show her tongue wag through
Hath she thin hair, hath she none
She's to me a paragon.

Jenny Kissed Me
Leigh Hunt

Jenny kiss'd me when we met,
Jumping from the chair she sat in;
Time, you thief, who love to get
Sweets into your list, put that in!

Say I'm weary, say I'm sad,
Sat that health and wealth have miss'd me,
Say I'm growing old, but add,
Jenny kiss'd me.

Barter
Sara Teasdale

Life has loveliness to sell,
All beautiful and splendid things,
Blue waves whitened on a cliff,
Soaring fire that sways and sings,
And children's faces looking up,
Holding wonder like a cup.
Life has loveliness to sell
Music like a curve of gold,
Scent of pine trees in the rain,

Eyes that love you, arms that hold,
And for your spirit's still delight,
Holy thoughts that star the night.
Spend all you have for loveliness,
Buy it and never count the cost;
For one white singing hour of peace
Count many a year of strife well lost,
And for a breath of ecstacy
Give all you have been, or could be.

She Comes Not

Herbert Trench

She comes not when Noon is on the roses—
    Too bright is Day.
She comes not to the Soul till it reposes
    From work and play.
But when Night is on the hills, and the great Voices
    Roll in from Sea,
By starlight and candle-light and dreamlight
    She comes to me.

I Travelled Among Unknown Men

William Wordsworth

I travelled among unknown men,
    In lands beyond the sea;
Nor, England! did I know till then
    What love I bore to thee.

'Tis past, that melancholy dream!
    Nor will I quit thy shore
A second time; for still I seem
    To love thee more and more.

Among thy mountains did I feel
    The joy of my desire;
And she I cherished turned her wheel
    Beside an English fire.

Thy mornings showed, thy nights concealed,
    The bowers where Lucy played;
And thine too is the last green field
    That Lucy's eyes surveyed.

The Apache Wedding Prayer
Anonymous

Now you will feel no rain,
For each of you will be shelter to the other.
Now you will feel no cold,
For each of you will be warmth to the other
Now there is no more loneliness,
For each of you will be companion to the other.
Now you are two bodies,
But there is only one life before you.
Go now to your dwelling place
To enter into the days of your togetherness
And may your days be good and long upon the earth.

The Presence Of Love
Samuel Taylor Coleridge

And in Life's noisiest hour,
There whispers still the ceaseless Love of Thee,
The heart's Self-solace and soliloquy.

You mould my Hopes, you fashion me within ;
And to the leading Love-throb in the Heart
Thro' all my Being, thro' my pulses beat ;
You lie in all my many Thoughts, like Light,
Like the fair light of Dawn, or summer Eve
On rippling Stream, or cloud-reflecting Lake.
And looking to the Heaven, that bends above you,
How oft ! I bless the Lot, that made me love you.

Sigh No More
William Shakespeare

Sigh no more, ladies, sigh no more
 Men were deceivers ever;
One foot in sea, and one on shore,
 To one thing constant never.
  Then sigh not so,
  But let them go,
 And be you blith and bonny,

Converting all your sounds of woe
Into Hey nonny, nonny.
Sing no more ditties, sing no more
Of dumps so dull and heavy;
The fraud of men was ever so,
Since summer first was leavy.
Then sigh not so,
But let them go,
And be you blith and bonny,
Converting all your sounds of woe
Into Hey nonny, nonny.

To Love

C.S. Lewis

Love anything and your heart will be wrung and possibly broken.
If you want to make sure of keeping it intact you must give it to no one,
not even an animal. Wrap it carefully round with hobbies and little luxuries;
avoid all entanglements. Lock it up save in the casket or coffin of your selfishness.
But in that casket—safe, dark, motionless, airless—it will change.
It will not be broken; it will become unbreakable, impenetrable, irredeemable.
    To love is to be vulnerable.

Carpe Diem

William Shakespeare

O mistress mine, where are you roaming?
O stay and hear! your true-love's coming
    That can sing both high and low;
Trip no further, pretty sweeting
Journey's end in lovers' meeting—
    Every wise man's son doth know
What is love? 'tis not hereafter;
Present mirth hath present laughter;
    What's to come is still unsure:
In delay there lies no plenty,—
Then come kiss me, Sweet and twenty,
    Youth's a stuff will not endure.

Untitled
Judy Garland

For twas not into my ear you whispered but into my heart.
Twas not my lips you kissed, but my soul.

A Kiss
Christian Nestell Bovee

It is the passion that is in a kiss that gives to it its sweetness; it is
the affection in a kiss that sanctifies it.

To Madame A.P. Kern
Alexander Pushkin

I can remember our first meeting,
When like a miracle you came
Before my eyes, a swiftly fleeting
Vision of beauty's purest flame.

Amid the miseries that oppressed me,
Amid the world's vain, foolish cries,
For long your gentle voice caressed me,
Your features gleamed before my eyes.

The years went by, wild storms swept past me,
Scattering many a youthful dream;
I lost the voice that once caressed me,
I lost that face's heavenly gleam.

Shut in my prison's dark damnatiion,
Before me stretched dumb days, dead years,
Deprived of God, of inspiration,
Deprived of love, of life, of tears.

Then from its trance arose in greeting
My soul, as once again you came
Before my eyes, a swiftly fleeting
Vision of Beauty's purest flame.

My heart is beating with elation:
As from the grave again they rise—
Glory of God and inspiration,
Life, love and tears to fill my eyes.

SONNET 11

William Shakespeare

As fast as thou shalt wane so fast thou grow'st,
In one of thine, from that which thou departest,
And that fresh blood which youngly thou bestow'st,
Thou mayst call thine, when thou from youth convertest,
Herein lives wisdom, beauty, and increase,
Without this folly, age, and cold decay,
If all were minded so, the times should cease,
And threescore year would make the world away:
Let those whom nature hath not made for store,
Harsh, featureless, and rude, barrenly perish:
Look whom she best endowed, she gave thee more;
Which bounteous gift thou shouldst in bounty cherish:
    She carved thee for her seal, and meant thereby,
    Thou shouldst print more, not let that copy die.

SONNET 33

William Shakespeare

Full many a glorious morning have I seen,
Flatter the mountain tops with sovereign eye,
Kissing with golden face the meadows green;
Gilding pale streams with heavenly alchemy:
Anon permit the basest clouds to ride,
With ugly rack on his celestial face,
And from the forlorn world his visage hide
Stealing unseen to west with this disgrace:
Even so my sun one early morn did shine,
With all triumphant splendour on my brow,
But out alack, he was but one hour mine,
The region cloud hath masked him from me now.
    Yet him for this, my love no whit disdaineth,
    Suns of the world may stain, when heaven's sun staineth.

LOVE

H.L. Mencken

"Love is the triumph of imagination over intelligence."

From "Wind, Sand and Stars"
Antoine de Saint-Exupery

Love is not just looking at each other, it's looking in the same direction.

Sonnet 37
William Shakespeare

As a decrepit father takes delight,
To see his active child do deeds of youth,
So I, made lame by Fortune's dearest spite
Take all my comfort of thy worth and truth.
For whether beauty, birth, or wealth, or wit,
 Or any of these all, or all, or more
Entitled in thy parts, do crowned sit,
I make my love engrafted to this store:
So then I am not lame, poor, nor despised,
Whilst that this shadow doth such substance give,
That I in thy abundance am sufficed,
And by a part of all thy glory live:
    Look what is best, that best I wish in thee,
    This wish I have, then ten times happy me.

Sonnet 46
William Shakespeare

Mine eye and heart are at a mortal war,
How to divide the conquest of thy sight,
Mine eye, my heart thy picture's sight would bar,
My heart, mine eye the freedom of that right,
My heart doth plead that thou in him dost lie,
(A closet never pierced with crystal eyes)
But the defendant doth that plea deny,
And says in him thy fair appearance lies.
To side this title is impanelled
A quest of thoughts, all tenants to the heart,
And by their verdict is determined
The clear eye's moiety, and the dear heart's part.
    As thus, mine eye's due is thy outward part,
    And my heart's right, thy inward love of heart.

Sonnet 56

William Shakespeare

Sweet love renew thy force, be it not said
Thy edge should blunter be than appetite,
Which but to-day by feeding is allayed,
To-morrow sharpened in his former might.
So love be thou, although to-day thou fill
Thy hungry eyes, even till they wink with fulness,
To-morrow see again, and do not kill
The spirit of love, with a perpetual dulness:
Let this sad interim like the ocean be
Which parts the shore, where two contracted new,
Come daily to the banks, that when they see:
Return of love, more blest may be the view.
 Or call it winter, which being full of care,
 Makes summer's welcome, thrice more wished, more rare.

Sonnet 57

William Shakespeare

Being your slave what should I do but tend,
 Upon the hours, and times of your desire?
I have no precious time at all to spend;
Nor services to do till you require.
Nor dare I chide the world-without-end hour,
Whilst I (my sovereign) watch the clock for you,
Nor think the bitterness of absence sour,
When you have bid your servant once adieu.
Nor dare I question with my jealous thought,
Where you may be, or your affairs suppose,
But like a sad slave stay and think of nought
Save where you are, how happy you make those.
 So true a fool is love, that in your will,
 (Though you do any thing) he thinks no ill.

Sonnet 69

William Shakespeare

Those parts of thee that the world's eye doth view,
Want nothing that the thought of hearts can mend:
All tongues (the voice of souls) give thee that due,
Uttering bare truth, even so as foes commend.
Thy outward thus with outward praise is crowned,
But those same tongues that give thee so thine own,
In other accents do this praise confound
By seeing farther than the eye hath shown.
They look into the beauty of thy mind,
And that in guess they measure by thy deeds,
Then churls their thoughts (although their eyes were kind)
To thy fair flower add the rank smell of weeds:
    But why thy odour matcheth not thy show,
    The soil is this, that thou dost common grow.

Sonnet 78

William Shakespeare

So oft have I invoked thee for my muse,
And found such fair assistance in my verse,
As every alien pen hath got my use,
And under thee their poesy disperse.
Thine eyes, that taught the dumb on high to sing,
And heavy ignorance aloft to fly,
Have added feathers to the learned's wing,
And given grace a double majesty.
Yet be most proud of that which I compile,
Whose influence is thine, and born of thee,
In others' works thou dost but mend the style,
And arts with thy sweet graces graced be.
    But thou art all my art, and dost advance
    As high as learning, my rude ignorance.

Sonnet 82
William Shakespeare

I grant thou wert not married to my muse,
And therefore mayst without attaint o'erlook
The dedicated words which writers use
Of their fair subject, blessing every book.
Thou art as fair in knowledge as in hue,
Finding thy worth a limit past my praise,
And therefore art enforced to seek anew,
Some fresher stamp of the time-bettering days.
And do so love, yet when they have devised,
What strained touches rhetoric can lend,
Thou truly fair, wert truly sympathized,
In true plain words, by thy true-telling friend.
    And their gross painting might be better used,
    Where cheeks need blood, in thee it is abused.

Sonnet 96
William Shakespeare

Some say thy fault is youth, some wantonness,
Some say thy grace is youth and gentle sport,
Both grace and faults are loved of more and less:
Thou mak'st faults graces, that to thee resort:
As on the finger of a throned queen,
The basest jewel will be well esteemed:
So are those errors that in thee are seen,
To truths translated, and for true things deemed.
How many lambs might the stern wolf betray,
If like a lamb he could his looks translate!
How many gazers mightst thou lead away,
if thou wouldst use the strength of all thy state!
    But do not so, I love thee in such sort,
    As thou being mine, mine is thy good report.

Sonnet 126

William Shakespeare

O thou my lovely boy who in thy power,
Dost hold Time's fickle glass his fickle hour:
Who hast by waning grown, and therein show'st,
Thy lovers withering, as thy sweet self grow'st.
If Nature (sovereign mistress over wrack)
As thou goest onwards still will pluck thee back,
She keeps thee to this purpose, that her skill
May time disgrace, and wretched minutes kill.
Yet fear her O thou minion of her pleasure,
She may detain, but not still keep her treasure!
Her audit (though delayed) answered must be,
And her quietus is to render thee.

Sonnet 143

William Shakespeare

Lo as a careful huswife runs to catch,
One of her feathered creatures broke away,
Sets down her babe and makes all swift dispatch
In pursuit of the thing she would have stay:
Whilst her neglected child holds her in chase,
Cries to catch her whose busy care is bent,
To follow that which flies before her face:
Not prizing her poor infant's discontent;
So run'st thou after that which flies from thee,
Whilst I thy babe chase thee afar behind,
But if thou catch thy hope turn back to me:
And play the mother's part, kiss me, be kind.
    So will I pray that thou mayst have thy Will,
    If thou turn back and my loud crying still.

Sonnet 144

William Shakespeare

Two loves I have of comfort and despair,
Which like two spirits do suggest me still,
The better angel is a man right fair:
The worser spirit a woman coloured ill.
To win me soon to hell my female evil,

Tempteth my better angel from my side,
And would corrupt my saint to be a devil:
Wooing his purity with her foul pride.
And whether that my angel be turned fiend,
Suspect I may, yet not directly tell,
But being both from me both to each friend,
I guess one angel in another's hell.
	Yet this shall I ne'er know but live in doubt,
	Till my bad angel fire my good one out.

$\mathscr{P}$ROLONG THE NIGHT

Rene Vivien

Prolong the night, Goddess who sets us aflame!
Hold back from us the golden-sandalled dawn!
Already on the sea the first faint gleam
Of day is coming on.
Sleeping under your veils, protect us yet,
Having forgotten the cruelty day may give!
The wine of darkness, wine of the stars let
Overwhelm us with love!
Since no one knows what dawn will come,
Bearing the dismal future with its sorrows
In its hands, we tremble at full day, our dream
Fears all tomorrows.
Oh! keeping our hands on our still-closed eyes,
Let us vainly recall the joys that take flight!
Goddess who delights in the ruin of the rose,
Prolong the night!

$\mathscr{F}$IRE LOGS

Carl Sandburg

Nancy Hanks dreams by the fire;
Dreams, and the logs sputter,
And the yellow tongues climb.
Red lines lick their way in flickers.
Oh, sputter, logs.
Oh, dream, Nancy.
Time now for a beautiful child.
Time now for a tall man to come.

SONG: LOVE STILL HAS SOMETHING OF THE SEA

Sir Charles Sedley

Love still has something of the sea,
From whence his Mother rose;
No time his slaves from doubt can free,
Nor give their thoughts repose.
They are becalm'd in clearest days,
And in rough weather tost;
They wither under cold delays,
Or are in tempests lost.
One while they seem to touch the port,
Then straight into the main
Some angry wind in cruel sport
Their vessel drives again.
At first disdain and pride they fear,
Which, if they chance to 'scape,
Rivals and falsehood soon appear
In a more dreadful shape.
By such degrees to joy they come,
And are so long withstood,
So slowly they receive the sum,
It hardly does them good.
'Tis cruel to prolong a pain;
And to defer a joy,
Believe me, gentle Celemene,
Offends the winged boy.
An hundred thousand oaths your fears
Perhaps would not remove,
And if I gaz'd a thousand years,
I could no deeper love.

SONG: RARELY, RARELY, COMEST THOU

Percy Bysshe Shelley

Rarely, rarely, comest thou,
Spirit of Delight!
Wherefore hast thou left me now
Many a day and night?
Many a weary night and day

'Tis since thou are fled away.
How shall ever one like me
Win thee back again?
With the joyous and the free
Thou wilt scoff at pain.
Spirit false! thou hast forgot
All but those who need thee not.
As a lizard with the shade
Of a trembling leaf,
Thou with sorrow art dismay'd;
Even the sighs of grief
Reproach thee, that thou art not near,
And reproach thou wilt not hear.
Let me set my mournful ditty
To a merry measure;
Thou wilt never come for pity,
Thou wilt come for pleasure;
Pity then will cut away
Those cruel wings, and thou wilt stay.
I love all that thou lovest,
Spirit of Delight!
The fresh Earth in new leaves dress'd,
And the starry night;
Autumn evening, and the morn
When the golden mists are born.
I love snow, and all the forms
Of the radiant frost;
I love waves, and winds, and storms,
Everything almost
Which is Nature's, and may be
Untainted by man's misery.
I love tranquil solitude,
And such society
As is quiet, wise, and good;
Between thee and me What difference?
but thou dost possess
The things I seek, not love them less.
I love Love—though he has wings,
And like light can flee,

But above all other things,
Spirit, I love thee—
Thou art love and life! Oh come,
Make once more my heart thy home.

A Song—When First I Saw Thee

Park Benjamin

When first I saw thee, to my breast
Love came-a not unwelcome guest:
From thy sweet eyes I saw him dart-
Those eyes! the portals of thy heart.

Indeed it seemeth strange that he
Should leave his home to dwell with me:
Yet I the little rover keep
Within my bosom, soft and deep.

Must I for him the cage unbar
To plume his wings and haste afar?
Oh say not "yes," delicious maid;
But rather grant thy gentle aid

To keep the pretty prisoner where
He cannot sport in Freedom's air;
Or only be allowed to flee
From thee and back again to me.

Epithalamion

Edmund Spenser

Ye learned sisters, which have oftentimes
Beene to me ayding, others to adorne,
Whom ye thought worthy for your gracefull rymes,
That even the greatest did not greatly scorne
To heare theyr names sung in your simple layes,
But joyed in theyr praise;
And when ye list your owne mishaps to mourne,
Which death, or love, or fortunes wreck did rayse,
Your string could soone to sadder tenor turne,
And teach the woods and waters to lament

Your doleful dreriment:
Now lay those sorrowfull complaints aside,
And having all your heads with girland crownd,
Helpe me mine owne loves prayses to resound;
Ne let the same of any be envide:
So Orpheus did for his owne bride:
So I unto my selfe alone will sing;
The woods shall to me answer, and my eccho ring.
Early, before the worlds light giving lampe
His golden beame upon the hils doth spred,
Having disperst the nights unchearefull dampe,
Doe ye awake, and, with fresh lustyhed,
Go to the bowre of my beloved love,
My truest turtle dove:
Bid her awake; for Hymen is awake,
And long since ready forth his maske to move,
With his bright tead that flames with many a flake,
And many a bachelor to waite on him,
In theyr fresh garments trim.
Bid her awake therefore, and soone her dight,
For lo! the wished day is come at last,
That shall, for al the paynes and sorrowes past,
Pay to her usury of long delight:
And whylest she doth her dight,
Doe ye to her of joy and solace sing,
That all the woods may answer, and your eccho ring.
Bring with you all the nymphes that you can heare,
Both of the rivers and the forrests greene,
And of the sea that neighbours to her neare,
Al with gay girlands goodly wel beseene.
And let them also with them bring in hand
Another gay girland,
For my fayre love, of lillyes and of roses,
Bound truelove wize with a blew silke riband.
And let them make great store of bridale poses,
And let them eeke bring store of other flowers,
To deck the bridale bowers.
And let the ground whereas her foot shall tread,
For feare the stones her tender foot should wrong,

Be strewed with fragrant flowers all along,
And diapred lyke the discolored mead.
Which done, doe at her chamber dore awayt,
For she will waken strayt;
The whiles doe ye this song unto her sing
The woods shall to you answer, and your eccho ring.
Ye nymphes of Mulla, which with carefull heed
The silver scaly trouts doe tend full well,
And greedy pikes which use therein to feed,
(Those trouts and pikes all others doo excell)
And ye likewise which keepe the rushy lake,
Where none doo fishes take,
Bynd up the locks the which hang scatterd light,
And in his waters, which your mirror make,
Behold your faces as the christall bright,
That when you come whereas my love doth lie,
No blemish she may spie.
And eke ye lightfoot mayds which keepe the dere
That on the hoary mountayne use to towre,
And the wylde wolves, which seeke them to devoure,
With your steele darts doo chace from comming neer,
Be also present heere,
To helpe to decke her, and to help to sing,
That all the woods may answer, and your eccho ring.
Wake now, my love, awake! for it is time:
The rosy Morne long since left Tithones bed,
All ready to her silver coche to clyme,
And Phoebus gins to shew his glorious hed.
Hark how the cheerefull birds do chaunt theyr laies,
And carroll of loves praise!
The merry larke hir mattins sings aloft,
The thrush replyes, the mavis descant playes,
The ouzell shrills, the ruddock warbles soft,
So goodly all agree, with sweet consent,
To this dayes merriment.
Ah! my deere love, why doe ye sleepe thus long,
When meeter were that ye should now awake,
T'awayt the comming of your joyous make,

And hearken to the birds love-learned song,
The deawy leaves among?
For they of joy and pleasance to you sing,
That all the woods them answer, and theyr eccho ring.
My love is now awake out of her dreame,
And her fayre eyes, like stars that dimmed were
With darksome cloud, now shew theyr goodly beames
More bright then Hesperus his head doth rere.
Come now, ye damzels, daughters of delight,
Helpe quickly her to dight.
But first come ye, fayre Houres, which were begot,
In Joves sweet paradice, of Day and Night,
Which doe the seasons of the year allot,
And al that ever in this world is fayre
Do make and still repayre.
And ye three handmayds of the Cyprian Queene,
The which doe still adorne her beauties pride,
Helpe to addorne my beautifullest bride:
And as ye her array, still throw betweene
Some graces to be seene:
And as ye use to Venus, to her sing,
The whiles the woods shal answer, and your eccho ring.
Now is my love all ready forth to come:
Let all the virgins therefore well awayt,
And ye fresh boyes, that tend upon her groome,
Prepare your selves, for he is comming strayt.
Set all your things in seemely good aray,
Fit for so joyfull day,
That joyfulst day that ever sunne did see.
Faire Sun, shew forth thy favourable ray,
And let thy lifull heat not fervent be,
For feare of burning her sunshyny face,
Her beauty to disgrace.
O fayrest Phoebus, father of the Muse,
If ever I did honour thee aright,
Or sing the thing that mote thy mind delight,
Doe not thy servants simple boone refuse,
But let this day, let this one day be myne,

Let all the rest be thine.
Then I thy soverayne prayses loud wil sing,
That all the woods shal answer, and theyr eccho ring.
Harke how the minstrels gin to shrill aloud
Their merry musick that resounds from far,
The pipe, the tabor, and the trembling croud,
That well agree withouten breach or jar,
But most of all the damzels doe delite,
When they their tymbrels smyte,
And thereunto doe daunce and carrol sweet,
That all the sences they doe ravish quite,
The whyles the boyes run up and downe the street,
Crying aloud with strong confused noyce,
As if it were one voyce.
'Hymen, Io Hymen, Hymen,' they do shout,
That even to the heavens theyr shouting shrill
Doth reach, and all the firmament doth fill;
To which the people, standing all about,
As in approvance doe thereto applaud,
And loud advaunce her laud,
And evermore they 'Hymen, Hymen' sing,
That al the woods them answer, and theyr eccho ring.
Loe! where she comes along with portly pace,
Lyke Phoebe, from her chamber of the east,
Arysing forth to run her mighty race,
Clad all in white, that seemes a virgin best.
So well it her beseemes, that ye would weene
Some angell she had beene,
Her long loose yellow locks lyke golden wyre,
Sprinckled with perle, and perling flowres atweene,
Doe lyke a golden mantle her attyre,
And being crowned with a girland greene,
Seeme lyke some mayden queene.
Her modest eyes, abashed to behold
So many gazers as on her do stare,
Upon the lowly ground affixed are;
Ne dare lift up her countenance too bold,
But blush to heare her prayses sung so loud,
So farre from being proud.

Nathlesse doe ye still loud her prayses sing,
That all the woods may answer, and your eccho ring.
Tell me, ye merchants daughters, did ye see
So fayre a creature in your towne before,
So sweet, so lovely, and so mild as she,
Adornd with beautyes grace and vertues store?
Her goodly eyes lyke saphyres shining bright,
Her forehead yvory white,
Her cheekes lyke apples with the sun hath rudded,
Her lips lyke cherryes charming men to byte,
Her brest like to a bowle of creame uncrudded,
Her paps lyke lyllies budded,
Her snowie necke lyke to a marble towre,
And all her body like a pallace fayre,
Ascending uppe, with many a stately stayre,
To honors seat and chastities sweet bowre.
Why stand ye still, ye virgins, in amaze,
Upon her so to gaze,
Whiles ye forget your former lay to sing,
To which the woods did answer, and your eccho ring.
But if ye saw that which no eyes can see,
The inward beauty of her lively spright,
Garnisht with heavenly guifts of high degree,
Much more then would ye wonder at that sight,
And stand astonisht lyke to those which red
Medusaes mazeful hed.
There dwels sweet Love and constant Chastity,
Unspotted Fayth, and comely Womanhood,
Regard of Honour, and mild Modesty;
There Vertue raynes as queene in royal throne,
And giveth lawes alone,
The which the base affections doe obay,
And yeeld theyr services unto her will;
Ne thought of thing uncomely ever may
Thereto approch to tempt her mind to ill.
Had ye once seene these her celestial threasures,
And unrevealed pleasures,
Then would ye wonder, and her prayses sing,
That al the woods should answer, and your eccho ring.

Open the temple gates unto my love,
Open them wide that she may enter in,
And all the postes adorne as doth behove,
And all the pillours deck with girlands trim,
For to receyve this saynt with honour dew,
That commeth in to you.
With trembling steps and humble reverence,
She commeth in before th' Almighties vew:
Of her, ye virgins, learne obedience,
When so ye come into those holy places,
To humble your proud faces.
Bring her up to th' high altar, that she may
The sacred ceremonies there partake,
That which do endlesse matrimony make;
And let the roring organs loudly play
The praises of the Lord in lively notes,
The whiles with hollow throates
The choristers the joyous antheme sing,
That al the woods may answere, and their eccho ring.
Behold, whiles she before the altar stands,
Hearing the holy priest that to her speakes,
And blesseth her with his two happy hands,
How the red roses flush up in her cheekes,
And the pure snow with goodly vermill stayne,
Like crimsin dyde in grayne:
That even th' angels, which continually
About the sacred altare doe remaine,
Forget their service and about her fly,
Ofte peeping in her face, that seemes more fayre,
The more they on it stare.
But her sad eyes, still fastened on the ground,
Are governed with goodly modesty,
That suffers not one looke to glaunce awry,
Which may let in a little though unsownd.
Why blush ye, love, to give to me your hand,
The pledge of all our band?
Sing, ye sweet angels, Alleluya sing,
That all the woods may answere, and your eccho ring.
Now al is done; bring home the bride againe,

Bring home the triumph of our victory,
Bring home with you the glory of her gaine,
With joyance bring her and with jollity.
Never had man more joyfull day then this,
Whom heaven would heape with blis.
Make feast therefore now all this live long day;
This day for ever to me holy is;
Poure out the wine without restraint or stay,
Poure not by cups, but by the belly full,
Poure out to all that wull,
And sprinkle all the postes and wals with wine,
That they may sweat, and drunken be withall.
Crowne ye God Bacchus with a coronall.
And Hymen also crowne with wreathes of vine;
And let the Graces daunce unto the rest,
For they can doo it best:
The whiles the maydens doe theyr carroll sing,
The which the woods shal answer, and theyr eccho ring.
Ring ye the bels, ye yong men of the towne,
And leave your wonted labors for this day:
This day is holy; doe ye write it downe,
That ye for ever it remember may.
This day the sunne is in his chiefest hight,
With Barnaby the bright,
From whence declining daily by degrees,
He somewhat loseth of his heat and light,
When once the Crab behind his back he sees.
But for this time it ill ordained was,
To chose the longest day in all the yeare,
And shortest night, when longest fitter weare:
Yet never day so long, but late would passe.
Ring ye the bels, to make it weare away,
And bonefires make all day,
And daunce about them, and about them sing:
That all the woods may answer, and your eccho ring.
Ah! when will this long weary day have end,
And lende me leave to come unto my love?
How slowly do the houres theyr numbers spend!

How slowly does sad Time his feathers move!
Hast thee, O fayrest planet, to thy home
Within the westerne fome:
Thy tyred steedes long since have need of rest,
Long though it be, at last I see it gloome,
And the bright evening star with golden creast
Appeare out of the east.
Fayre childe of beauty, glorious lampe of love,
That all the host of heaven in rankes doost lead,
And guydest lovers through the nightes dread,
How chearefully thou lookest from above,
And seemst to laugh atweene thy twinkling light,
As joying in the sight
Of these glad many, which for joy doe sing,
That all the woods them answer, and their eccho ring!
Now ceasse, ye damsels, your delights forepast;
Enough is it that all the day was youres:
Now day is doen, and night is nighing fast:
Now bring the bryde into the brydall boures.
The night is come, now soone her disaray,
And in her bed her lay;
Lay her in lillies and in violets,
And silken courteins over her display,
And odourd sheetes, and Arras coverlets.
Behold how goodly my faire love does ly,
In proud humility!
Like unto Maia, when as Jove her tooke
In Tempe, lying on the flowry gras,
Twixt sleepe and wake, after she weary was
With bathing in the Acidalian brooke.
Now it is night, ye damsels may be gon,
And leave my love alone.
And leave likewise your former lay to sing:
The woods no more shal answere, nor your eccho ring.
Now welcome, night! thou night so long expected,
That long daies labour doest at last defray,
And all my cares, which cruell Love collected,
Hast sumd in one, and cancelled for aye:

Spread thy broad wing over my love and me,
That no man may us see,
And in thy sable mantle us enwrap,
From feare of perrill and foule horror free.
Let no false treason seeke us to entrap,
Nor any dread disquiet once annoy
The safety of our joy:
But let the night be calme and quietsome,
Without tempestuous storms or sad afray:
Lyke as when Jove with fayre Alcmena lay,
When he begot the great Tirynthian groome:
Or lyke as when he with thy selfe did lie,
And begot Majesty.
And let the mayds and yongmen cease to sing:
Ne let the woods them answer, nor theyr eccho ring.
Let no lamenting cryes, nor dolefull teares,
Be heard all night within, nor yet without:
Ne let false whispers, breeding hidden feares,
Breake gentle sleepe with misconceived dout.
Let no deluding dreames, nor dreadul sights,
Make sudden sad affrights;
Ne let house-fyres, nor lightnings helplesse harmes,
Ne let the Pouke, nor other evill sprights,
Ne let mischivous witches with theyr charmes,
Ne let hob goblins, names whose sense we see not,
Fray us with things that be not.
Let not the shriech oule, nor the storke be heard,
Nor the night raven that still deadly yels,
Nor damned ghosts cald up with mighty spels,
Nor griesly vultures make us once affeard:
Ne let th' unpleasant quyre of frogs still croking
Make us to wish theyr choking.
Let none of these theyr drery accents sing;
Ne let the woods them answer, nor theyr eccho ring.
But let stil Silence trew night watches keepe,
That sacred Peace may in assurance rayne,
And tymely Sleep, when it is tyme to sleepe,
May poure his limbs forth on your pleasant playne,

The whiles an hundred little winged loves,
Like divers fethered doves,
Shall fly and flutter round about our bed,
And in the secret darke, that none reproves,
Their prety stealthes shall worke, and snares shal spread
To filch away sweet snatches of delight,
Conceald through covert night.
Ye sonnes of Venus, play your sports at will:
For greedy Pleasure, careless of your toyes,
Thinks more upon her paradise of joyes,
Then what ye do, albe it good or ill.
All night therefore attend your merry play,
For it will soone be day:
Now none doth hinder you, that say or sing,
Ne will the woods now answer, nor your eccho ring.
Who is the same which at my window peepes?
Or whose is that faire face that shines so bright?
Is it no Cinthia, she that never sleepes,
But walkes about high heaven al the night?
O fayrest goddesse, do thou not envy
My love with me to spy:
For thou likewise didst love, though now unthought,
And for a fleece of woll, which privily
The Latmian shephard once unto thee brought,
His pleasures with thee wrought.
Therefore to us be favorable now;
And sith of wemens labours thou hast charge,
And generation goodly dost enlarge,
Encline thy will t' effect our wishfull vow,
And the chast wombe informe with timely seed,
That may our comfort breed:
Till which we cease our hopefull hap to sing,
Ne let the woods us answere, nor our eccho ring.
And thou, great Juno, which with awful might
The lawes of wedlock still dost patronize
And the religion of the faith first plight
With sacred rites hast taught to solemnize,
And eeke for comfort often called art
Of women in their smart,

Eternally bind thou this lovely bank,
And all thy blessings unto us impart.
And thou, glad Genius, in whose gentle hand
The bridale bowre and geniall bed remaine,
Without blemish or staine,
And the sweet pleasures of theyr loves delight
With secret ayde doest succour and supply,
Till they bring forth the fruitfull progeny,
Send us the timely fruit of this same night.
And thou, fayre Hebe, and thou, Hymen free,
Grant that it may so be.
Til which we cease your further prayse to sing,
Ne any words shal answer, nor your eccho ring.
And ye high heavens, the temple of the gods,
In which a thousand torches flaming bright
Doe burne, that to us wretched earthly clods
In dreadful darknesse lend desired light,
And all ye powers which in the same remayne,
More then we men can fayne,
Poure out your blessing on us plentiously,
And happy influence upon us raine,
That we may raise a large posterity,
Which from the earth, which they may long possesse
With lasting happinesse,
Up to your haughty pallaces may mount,
And for the guerdon of theyr glorious merit,
May heavenly tabernacles there inherit,
Of blessed saints for to increase the count.
So let us rest, sweet love, in hope of this,
And cease till then our tymely joyes to sing:
The woods no more us answer, nor our eccho ring.
 Song, made in lieu of many ornaments
With which my love should duly have bene dect,
Which cutting off through hasty accidents,
Ye would not stay your dew time to expect,
But promist both to recompens,
Be unto her a goodly ornament,
And for a short time an endless moniment.

When Thou Must Home To Shades Of Underground

Thomas Campion

When thou must home to shades of underground,
And there arriv'd, a new admired guest,
The beauteous spirits do engirt thee round,
White Iope, blithe Helen, and the rest,
To hear the stories of thy finish'd love
From that smooth tongue whose music hell can move;

Then wilt thou speak of banqueting delights,
Of masques and revels which sweet youth did make,
Of tourneys and great challenges of knights,
And all these triumphs for thy beauty's sake:
When thou hast told these honours done to thee,
Then tell, O tell, how thou didst murder me.

Ingrateful Beauty Threatened

Thomas Carew

Know Celia, since thou art so proud,
Twas I that gave thee thy renown;
Thou hadst, in the forgotten crowd
Of common beauties, liv'd unknown,
Had not my verse exhal'd thy name,
And with it imp'd the wings of fame.

That killing power is none of thine,
I gave it to thy voice, and eyes;
Thy sweets, thy graces, all are mine;
Thou art my star, shin'st in my skies;
Then dart not from thy borrow'd sphere
Lightning on him that fix'd thee there.

Tempt me with such affrights no more,
Lest what I made, I uncreate;
Let fools thy mystic forms adore,
I'll know thee in thy mortal state;
Wise poets that wrapp'd Truth in tales,
Knew her themselves, through all her veils.

Epitaph On The Lady Mary Villiers

Thomas Carew

This little vault, this narrow room,
Of Love, and Beauty, is the tomb;
The dawning beam that began to clear
Our clouded sky, lies darken'd here,
Forever set to us, by death
Sent to inflame the world beneath.
'Twas but a bud, yet did contain
More sweetness than shall spring again;
A budding star that might have grown
Into a sun, when it had blown.
This hopeful beauty did create
New life in Love's declining state;
But now his empire ends, and we
From fire and wounding darts are free;
His brand, his bow, let no man fear,
The flames, the arrows, all lie here.

The Spring

Thomas Carew

Now that the winter's gone, the earth hath lost
Her snow-white robes, and now no more the frost
Candies the grass, or casts an icy cream
Upon the silver lake or crystal stream;
But the warm sun thaws the benumbed earth,
And makes it tender; gives a sacred birth
To the dead swallow; wakes in hollow tree
The drowsy cuckoo, and the humble-bee.
Now do a choir of chirping minstrels bring
In triumph to the world the youthful Spring.
The valleys, hills, and woods in rich array
Welcome the coming of the long'd-for May.
Now all things smile, only my love doth lour;
Nor hath the scalding noonday sun the power
To melt that marble ice, which still doth hold
Her heart congeal'd, and makes her pity cold.

The ox, which lately did for shelter fly
Into the stall, doth now securely lie
In open fields; and love no more is made
By the fireside, but in the cooler shade
Amyntas now doth with his Chloris sleep
Under a sycamore, and all things keep
Time with the season; only she doth carry
June in her eyes, in her heart January.

Summer
John Clare

Come we to the summer, to the summer we will come,
For the woods are full of bluebells and the hedges full of bloom,
And the crow is on the oak a-building of her nest,
And love is burning diamonds in my true lover's breast;
She sits beneath the whitethorn a-plaiting of her hair,
And I will to my true lover with a fond request repair;
I will look upon her face, I will in her beauty rest,
And lay my aching weariness upon her lovely breast.

The clock-a-clay is creeping on the open bloom of May,
The merry bee is trampling the pinky threads all day,
And the chaffinch it is brooding on its grey mossy nest
In the whitethorn bush where I will lean upon my lover's breast;
I'll lean upon her breast and I'll whisper in her ear
That I cannot get a wink o'sleep for thinking of my dear;
I hunger at my meat and I daily fade away
Like the hedge rose that is broken in the heat of the day

Dejection: An Ode
Samuel Taylor Coleridge

Late, late yestreen I saw the new Moon,
With the old Moon in her arms;
And I fear, I fear, my Master dear!
We shall have a deadly storm.
                    —"Ballad of Sir Patrick Spence"

1.

Well! If the Bard was weather-wise, who made
The grand old ballad of Sir Patrick Spence,
This night, so tranquil now, will not go hence
Unroused by winds, that ply a busier trade
Than those which mould yon cloud in lazy flakes,
Or the dull sobbing draft, that moans and rakes
Upon the strings of this Aeolian lute,
Which better far were mute.
For lo! the New-moon winter-bright!
And overspread with phantom light,
(With swimming phantom light o'erspread
But rimmed and circled by a silver thread)
I see the old Moon in her lap, foretelling
The coming-on of rain and squally blast.
And oh! that even now the gust were swelling,
And the slant night-shower driving loud and fast!
Those sounds which oft have raised me, whilst they awed,
And sent my soul abroad,
Might now perhaps their wonted impulse give,
Might startle this dull pain, and make it move and live!

2.

A grief without a pang, void, dark, and drear,
A stifled, drowsy, unimpassioned grief,
Which finds no natural outlet, no relief,
In word, or sigh, or tear—
O Lady! in this wan and heartless mood,
To other thoughts by yonder throstle woo'd,
All this long eve, so balmy and serene,
Have I been gazing on the western sky,
And its peculiar tint of yellow green:
And still I gaze—and with how blank an eye!
And those thin clouds above, in flakes and bars,
That give away their motion to the stars;
Those stars, that glide behind them or between,
Now sparkling, now bedimmed, but always seen:
Yon crescent Moon, as fixed as if it grew
In its own cloudless, starless lake of blue;

I see them all so excellently fair,
I see, not feel, how beautiful they are!

3.

My genial spirits fail;
And what can these avail
To lift the smothering weight from off my breast?
It were a vain endeavour,
Though I should gaze for ever
On that green light that lingers in the west:
I may not hope from outward forms to win
The passion and the life, whose fountains are within.

4.

O Lady! we receive but what we give,
And in our life alone does Nature live:
Ours is her wedding garment, ours her shroud!
And would we aught behold, of higher worth,
Than that inanimate cold world allowed
To the poor loveless ever-anxious crowd,
Ah! from the soul itself must issue forth
A light, a glory, a fair luminous cloud
Enveloping the Earth—
And from the soul itself must there be sent
A sweet and potent voice, of its own birth,
Of all sweet sounds the life and element!

5.

O pure of heart! thou need'st not ask of me
What this strong music in the soul may be!
What, and wherein it doth exist,
This light, this glory, this fair luminous mist,
This beautiful and beauty-making power.
Joy, virtuous Lady! Joy that ne'er was given,
Save to the pure, and in their purest hour,
Life, and Life's effluence, cloud at once and shower,
Joy, Lady! is the spirit and the power,
Which wedding Nature to us gives in dower
A new Earth and new Heaven,

Undreamt of by the sensual and the proud—
Joy is the sweet voice, Joy the luminous cloud—
We in ourselves rejoice!
And thence flows all that charms or ear or sight,
All melodies the echoes of that voice,
All colours a suffusion from that light.

6.

There was a time when, though my path was rough,
This joy within me dallied with distress,
And all misfortunes were but as the stuff
Whence Fancy made me dreams of happiness:
For hope grew round me, like the twining vine,
And fruits, and foliage, not my own, seemed mine.
But now afflictions bow me down to earth:
Nor care I that they rob me of my mirth;
But oh! each visitation
Suspends what nature gave me at my birth,

My shaping spirit of Imagination.
For not to think of what I needs must feel,
But to be still and patient, all I can;
And haply by abstruse research to steal
From my own nature all the natural man—
This was my sole resource, my only plan:
Till that which suits a part infects the whole,
And now is almost grown the habit of my soul.

7.

Hence, viper thoughts, that coil around my mind,
Reality's dark dream!
I turn from you, and listen to the wind,
Which long has raved unnoticed. What a scream
Of agony by torture lengthened out
That lute sent forth! Thou Wind, that rav'st without,
Bare crag, or mountain-tairn, or blasted tree,
Or pine-grove whither woodman never clomb,
Or lonely house, long held the witches' home,
Methinks were fitter instruments for thee,

Mad lutanist! who in this month of showers,
Of dark-brown gardens, and of peeping flowers,
Mak'st devils' yule, with worse than wintry song,
The blossoms, buds, and timorous leaves among.
Thou actor, perfect in all tragic sounds!
Thou mighty poet, e'en to frenzy bold!
What tell'st thou now about?
'Tis of the rushing of an host in rout,
With groans, of trampled men, with smarting wounds—
At once they groan with pain, and shudder with the cold!
But hush! there is a pause of deepest silence!
And all that noise, as of a rushing crowd,
With groans, and tremulous shudderings—all is over—
It tells another tale, with sounds less deep and loud!
A tale of less affright,
And tempered with delight,
As Otway's self had framed the tender lay,—
Tis of a little child
Upon a lonesome wild,
Nor far from home, but she hath lost her way:
And now moans low in bitter grief and fear,
And now screams loud, and hopes to make her mother hear.

8.

'Tis midnight, but small thoughts have I of sleep:
Full seldom may my friend such vigils keep!
Visit her, gentle Sleep! with wings of healing,
And may this storm be but a mountain-birth,
May all the stars hang bright above her dwelling,
Silent as though they watched the sleeping Earth!
With light heart may she rise,
Gay fancy, cheerful eyes,
Joy lift her spirit, joy attune her voice;
To her may all things live, from pole to pole,
Their life the eddying of her living soul!
O simple spirit, guided from above,
Dear Lady! friend devoutest of my choice,
Thus mayest thou ever, evermore rejoice.

Love's Apparition And Evanishment: An Allegoric Romance

Samuel Taylor Coleridge

Like a lone Arab, old and blind,
Some caravan had left behind,
Who sits beside a ruin'd well,
Where the shy sand-asps bask and swell;
And now he hangs his ag'ed head aslant,
And listens for a human sound—in vain!
And now the aid, which Heaven alone can grant,
Upturns his eyeless face from Heaven to gain;—
Even thus, in vacant mood, one sultry hour,
Resting my eye upon a drooping plant,
With brow low-bent, within my garden-bower,
I sate upon the couch of camomile;
And—whether 'twas a transient sleep, perchance,
Flitted across the idle brain, the while
I watch'd the sickly calm with aimless scope,
In my own heart; or that, indeed a trance,
Turn'd my eye inward—thee, O genial Hope,
Love's elder sister! thee did I behold
Drest as a bridesmaid, but all pale and cold,
With roseless cheek, all pale and cold and dim,
Lie lifeless at my feet!
And then came Love, a sylph in bridal trim,
And stood beside my seat;
She bent, and kiss'd her sister's lips,
As she was wont to do;—
Alas! 'twas but a chilling breath
Woke just enough of life in death
To make Hope die anew.

Inscription For A Statue Of Love

F.M. Arouet de Voltaire

Whoe'er you are, your master see,
    He is, he was. or is to be.

No Marvel Is It

Bernard de Ventadour

No marvel is it if I sing
Better than other minstrels all:
For more than they I am Love's thrall,
And all myself therein I fling,-
Knowledge and sense, body and soul,
And whatso power I have beside;
The rein that doth my being guide
Impels me to this only goal.

His heart is dead whence did not spring
Love's odor, sweet and magical;
His life doth ever on him pall
Who knoweth not that blessed thin;
Yea! God, who doth my life control,
Were cruel did he bid me bide
A month, or even a day, denied
The love whose rapture I extol.
How keen, how exquisite the sting
Of that sweet odor! At its call
An hundred times a day I fall
And faint, an hundred rise and sing.
So fair the semblance of my dole.
'Tis lovelier than another's pride:
If such the ill doth me betide,
Good hap were more than I could thole.

Yet haste, kind heaven! the sundering
True swains from false, great hearts from small!
The traitor in the dust bin crawl!
The faithless to confession bring!
Ah! If I were the master sole
Of all earth's treasures multiplied,
To see my Lady satisfied
Of my pure faith, I'd give the whole.

Softly Sighs The April Air
Arnaut Daniel

Softly sighs the April air,
    Ere the coming of the May,
Of the tranquil night aware,
    Murmur nightingale and jay;
Then, when dewy dawn doth rise,
    Every bird in his own tongue
Wakes his mate with happy cries;
    All their joy abroad is flung.

Gladness, lo! is everywhere
    When the first leaf sees the day;
And shall I alone despair,
    Turing from sweet love away?
Something to my heart replies,
    Thou too wast for rapture strung;
Wherefore else the dreams that rise
    Round thee when the year is young?

One, than Helen yet more fair,
    Loveliest blossom of the May,
Rose-tints hath and sunny hair,
    And a gracious mien and gay;
Heart that scorneth all disguise,
    Lips where pearls of truth are hung,
God, who gives all sovereignties,
    Knows her like was never sung.

Though she lead through long despair,
    I would never say her nay,
If one kiss-reward how rare!
    Each new trial might repay.
Swift returns I'd then devise,
    Many labors, but not long.
Following so fir a prize
    I could nevermore go wrong.

ℰLEGY IX: THE AUTUMNAL

John Donne

No spring nor summer beauty hath such grace
As I have seen in one autumnal face.
Young beauties force our love, and that's a rape,
This doth but counsel, yet you cannot scape.
If 'twere a shame to love, here 'twere no shame;
Affection here takes reverence's name.
Were her first years the golden age? That's true,
But now she's gold oft tried and ever new.
That was her torrid and inflaming time,
This is her tolerable tropic clime.
Fair eyes, who asks more heat than comes from hence,
He in a fever wishes pestilence.
Call not these wrinkles, graves; if graves they were,
They were Love's graves, for else he is no where.
Yet lies not Love dead here, but here doth sit
Vow'd to this trench, like an anachorit;
And here till hers, which must be his death, come,
He doth not dig a grave, but build a tomb.
Here dwells he; though he sojourn ev'rywhere
In progress, yet his standing house is here:
Here where still evening is, not noon nor night,
Where no voluptuousness, yet all delight.
In all her words, unto all hearers fit,
You may at revels, you at council, sit.
This is Love's timber, youth his underwood;
There he, as wine in June, enrages blood,
Which then comes seasonabliest when our taste
And appetite to other things is past.
Xerxes' strange Lydian love, the platan tree,
Was lov'd for age, none being so large as she,
Or else because, being young, nature did bless
Her youth with age's glory, barrenness.
If we love things long sought, age is a thing
Which we are fifty years in compassing;
If transitory things, which soon decay,
Age must be loveliest at the latest day.
But name not winter faces, whose skin's slack,

Lank as an unthrift's purse, but a soul's sack;
Whose eyes seek light within, for all here's shade;
Whose mouths are holes, rather worn out than made;
Whose every tooth to a several place is gone,
To vex their souls at resurrection:
Name not these living death's-heads unto me,
For these, not ancient, but antique be.
I hate extremes, yet I had rather stay
With tombs than cradles, to wear out a day.
Since such love's natural lation is, may still
My love descend, and journey down the hill,
Not panting after growing beauties. So,
I shall ebb on with them who homeward go.

To The First

Lord Byron (George Gordon)

In him inexplicably mix'd appear'd
Much to be lov'd and hated, sought and fear'd.
Opinion varying o'er his hidden lot,
In praise or railing ne'er his name forgot;
His silence form'd a theme for others' prate;
They guess'd—they gaz'd—they fain would know his fate.
What had he been? what was he, thus unknown,
Who walk'd their world, his lineage only known?
A hater of his kind? yet some would say,
With them he could seem gay amidst the gay;
But own'd that smile, if oft observ'd and near,
Wan'd in its mirth and wither'd to a sneer;
That smile might reach his lip but pass'd not by,
None e'er could trace its laughter to his eye.
Yet there was softness too in his regard,
At times, a heart as not by nature hard,
But once perceiv'd, his spirit seem'd to chide
Such weakness as unworthy of its pride,
And steel'd itself, as scorning to redeem
One doubt from others' half withheld esteem;
In self-inflicted penance of a breast
Which tenderness might once have wrung from rest;

In vigilance of grief that would compel
The soul to hate for having lov'd too well.

There was in him a vital sign of all:
As if the worst had fall'n which could befall,
He stood a stranger in this breathing world,
An erring spirit from another hurl'd;
A thing of dark imaginings, that shap'd
By choice the perils he by chance escap'd;
But 'scap'd in vain, for in their memory yet
His mind would half exult and half regret.
With more capacity for love than earth
Bestows on most of mortal mould and birth,
His early dreams of good outstripp'd the truth,
And troubled manhood follow'd baffled youth;
With thought of years in phantom chase misspent,
And wasted powers for better purpose lent;
And fiery passions that had pour'd their wrath
In hurried desolation o'er his path,
And left the better feelings all at strife
In wild reflection o'er his stormy life;
But haughty still and loth himself to blame,
He call'd on Nature's self to share the shame,
And charg'd all faults upon the fleshly form
She gave to clog the soul and feast the worm;
Till he at last confounded good and ill,
And half mistook for fate the acts of will.
Too high for common selfishness, he could
At times resign his own for others' good,
But not in pity, not because he ought,
But in some strange perversity of thought,
That sway'd him onward with a secret pride
To do what few or none would do beside;
And this same impulse would, in tempting time,
Mislead his spirit equally in crime;
So much he soar'd beyond, or sunk beneath,
The men with whom he felt condemn'd to breathe,
And long'd by good or ill to separate
Himself from all who shared his mortal state.
His mind abhorring this had fix'd her throne

Far from the world, in regions of her own:
Thus coldly passing all that pass'd below,
His blood in temperate seeming now would flow:
Ah! happier if it ne'er with guilt had glow'd,
But ever in that icy smoothness flow'd!
T'is true, with other men their path he walk'd,
And like the rest in seeming did and talk'd,
Nor outrag'd Reason's rules by flaw nor start,
His madness was not of the head, but heart;
And rarely wander'd in his speech, or drew
His thoughts so forth as to offend the view.

With all that chilling mystery of mien,
And seeming gladness to remain unseen,
He had (if 't were not nature's boon) an art
Of fixing memory on another's heart.
It was not love perchance, nor hate, nor aught
That words can image to express the thought;
But they who saw him did not see in vain,
And once beheld, would ask of him again

*E*PISTLE TO AUGUSTA
Lord Byron (George Gordon)

My sister! my sweet sister! if a name
Dearer and purer were, it should be thine.
Mountains and seas divide us, but I claim
No tears, but tenderness to answer mine:
Go where I will, to me thou art the same
A lov'd regret which I would not resign.
There yet are two things in my destiny—
A world to roam through, and a home with thee.

The first were nothing—had I still the last,
It were the haven of my happiness;
But other claims and other ties thou hast,
And mine is not the wish to make them less.
A strange doom is thy father's son's, and past
Recalling, as it lies beyond redress;
Revers'd for him our grandsire's fate of yore—
He had no rest at sea, nor I on shore.

If my inheritance of storms hath been
In other elements, and on the rocks
Of perils, overlook'd or unforeseen,
I have sustain'd my share of worldly shocks,
The fault was mine; nor do I seek to screen
My errors with defensive paradox;
I have been cunning in mine overthrow,
The careful pilot of my proper woe.

Mine were my faults, and mine be their reward.
My whole life was a contest, since the day
That gave me being, gave me that which marr'd
The gift—a fate, or will, that walk'd astray;
And I at times have found the struggle hard,
And thought of shaking off my bonds of clay:
But now I fain would for a time survive,
If but to see what next can well arrive.

Kingdoms and empires in my little day
I have outliv'd, and yet I am not old;
And when I look on this, the petty spray
Of my own years of trouble, which have roll'd
Like a wild bay of breakers, melts away:
Something—I know not what—does still uphold
A spirit of slight patience; not in vain,
Even for its own sake, do we purchase pain.

Perhaps the workings of defiance stir
Within me—or perhaps a cold despair,
Brought on when ills habitually recur,
Perhaps a kinder clime, or purer air
For even to this may change of soul refer,
(And with light armour we may learn to bear),
Have taught me a strange quiet, which was not
The chief companion of a calmer lot.

I feel almost at times as I have felt
In happy childhood; trees, and flowers, and brooks,
Which do remember me of where I dwelt
Ere my young mind was sacrific'd to books,
Come as of yore upon me, and can melt

My heart with recognition of their looks;
And even at moments I could think I see
Some living thing to love—but none like thee.

Here are the Alpine landscapes which create
A fund for contemplation; to admire
Is a brief feeling of a trivial date;
But something worthier do such scenes inspire:
Here to be lonely is not desolate,
For much I view which I could most desire,
And, above all, a lake I can behold
Lovelier, not dearer, than our own of old.

Oh that thou wert but with me!—but I grow
The fool of my own wishes, and forget
The solitude which I have vaunted so
Has lost its praise in this but one regret;
There may be others which I less may show;
I am not of the plaintive mood, and yet
I feel an ebb in my philosophy,
And the tide rising in my alter'd eye.

I did remind thee of our own dear Lake,
By the old Hall which may be mine no more.
Leman's is fair; but think not I forsake
The sweet remembrance of a dearer shore:
Sad havoc Time must with my memory make
Ere that or thou can fade these eyes before;
Though, like all things which I have lov'd, they are
Resign'd for ever, or divided far.

The world is all before me; I but ask
Of Nature that with which she will comply—
It is but in her summer's sun to bask,
To mingle with the quiet of her sky,
To see her gentle face without a mask,
And never gaze on it with apathy.
She was my early friend, and now shall be
My sister—till I look again on thee.

I can reduce all feelings but this one;
And that I would not; for at length I see

Such scenes as those wherein my life begun,
The earliest—even the only paths for me—
Had I but sooner learnt the crowd to shun,
I had been better than I now can be;
The passions which have torn me would have slept;
I had not suffer'd, and thou hadst not wept.

With false Ambition what had I to do?
Little with Love, and least of all with Fame;
And yet they came unsought, and with me grew,
And made me all which they can make—a name,
Yet this was not the end I did pursue;
Surely I once beheld a nobler aim.
But all is over—I am one the more
To baffled millions which have gone before.

And for the future, this world's future may
From me demand but little of my care;
I have outliv'd myself by many a day,
Having surviv'd so many things that were;
My years have been no slumber, but the prey
Of ceaseless vigils; for I had the share
Of life which might have fill'd a century,
Before its fourth in time had pass'd me by.

And for the remnant which may be to come
I am content; and for the past I feel
Not thankless, for within the crowded sum
Of struggles, happiness at times would steal,
And for the present, I would not benumb
My feelings further. Nor shall I conceal
That with all this I still can look around,
And worship Nature with a thought profound.

For thee, my own sweet sister, in thy heart
I know myself secure, as thou in mine;
We were and are—I am, even as thou art—
Beings who ne'er each other can resign;
It is the same, together or apart,
From life's commencement to its slow decline
We are entwin'd—let death come slow or fast,
The tie which bound the first endures the last!

Manfred: Incantation
Lord Byron (George Gordon)

When the moon is on the wave,
And the glow-worm in the grass,
And the meteor on the grave,
And the wisp on the morass;
When the falling stars are shooting,
And the answer'd owls are hooting,
And the silent leaves are still
In the shadow of the hill,
Shall my soul be upon thine,
With a power and with a sign.

Though thy slumber may be deep,
Yet thy spirit shall not sleep;
There are shades which will not vanish,
There are thoughts thou canst not banish;
By a power to thee unknown,
Thou canst never be alone;
Thou art wrapt as with a shroud,
Thou art gather'd in a cloud;
And for ever shalt thou dwell
In the spirit of this spell.

Though thou seest me not pass by,
Thou shalt feel me with thine eye
As a thing that, though unseen,
Must be near thee, and hath been;
And when in that secret dread
Thou hast turn'd around thy head,
Thou shalt marvel I am not
As thy shadow on the spot,
And the power which thou dost feel
Shall be what thou must conceal.

And a magic voice and verse
Hath baptiz'd thee with a curse;
And a spirit of the air
Hath begirt thee with a snare;
In the wind there is a voice

Shall forbid thee to rejoice;
And to thee shall night deny
All the quiet of her sky;
And the day shall have a sun,
Which shall make thee wish it done.

From thy false tears I did distil
An essence which hath strength to kill;
From thy own heart I then did wring
The black blood in its blackest spring;
From thy own smile I snatch'd the snake,
For there it coil'd as in a brake;
From thy own lip I drew the charm
Which gave all these their chiefest harm;
In proving every poison known,
I found the strongest was thine own.

By thy cold breast and serpent smile,
By thy unfathom'd gulfs of guile,
By that most seeming virtuous eye,
By thy shut soul's hypocrisy;
By the perfection of thine art
Which pass'd for human thine own heart;
By thy delight in others' pain,
And by thy brotherhood of Cain,
I call upon thee! and compel
Thyself to be thy proper Hell!

And on thy head I pour the vial
Which doth devote thee to this trial;
Nor to slumber, nor to die,
Shall be in thy destiny;
Though thy death shall still seem near
To thy wish, but as a fear;
Lo! the spell now works around thee,
And the clankless chain hath bound thee;
O'er thy heart and brain together
Hath the word been pass'd—now wither!

The Clod And The Pebble
William Blake

"Love seeketh not itself to please,
Nor for itself hath any care,
But for another gives its ease,
And builds a Heaven in Hell's despair."

So sung a little Clod of Clay
Trodden with the cattle's feet,
But a Pebble of the brook
Warbled out these metres meet:

"Love seeketh only self to please,
To bind another to its delight,
Joys in another's loss of ease,
And builds a Hell in Heaven's despite."

The Buried Life
Arnold Matthew

Light flows our war of mocking words, and yet,
Behold, with tears mine eyes are wet!
I feel a nameless sadness o'er me roll.
Yes, yes, we know that we can jest,
We know, we know that we can smile!
But there's a something in this breast,
To which thy light words bring no rest,
And thy gay smiles no anodyne.
Give me thy hand, and hush awhile,
And turn those limpid eyes on mine,
And let me read there, love! thy inmost soul.

Alas! is even love too weak
To unlock the heart, and let it speak?
Are even lovers powerless to reveal
To one another what indeed they feel?
I knew the mass of men conceal'd
Their thoughts, for fear that if reveal'd
They would by other men be met
With blank indifference, or with blame reproved;

I knew they lived and moved
Trick'd in disguises, alien to the rest
Of men, and alien to themselves—and yet
The same heart beats in every human breast!
But we, my love!—doth a like spell benumb
Our hearts, our voices?—must we too be dumb?

Ah! well for us, if even we,
Even for a moment, can get free
Our heart, and have our lips unchain'd;
For that which seals them hath been deep-ordain'd!
Fate, which foresaw
How frivolous a baby man would be—
By what distractions he would be possess'd,
How he would pour himself in every strife,
And well-nigh change his own identity—
That it might keep from his capricious play
His genuine self, and force him to obey
Even in his own despite his being's law,
Bade through the deep recesses of our breast
The unregarded river of our life
Pursue with indiscernible flow its way;
And that we should not see
The buried stream, and seem to be
Eddying at large in blind uncertainty,
Though driving on with it eternally.

But often, in the world's most crowded streets,
And often, in the din of strife,
There rises an unspeakable desire
After the knowledge of our buried life;
A thirst to spend our fire and restless force
In tracking out our true, original course;
A longing to inquire
Into the mystery of this heart which beats
So wild, so deep in us—to know
Whence our lives come and where they go.
And many a man in his own breast then delves,
But deep enough, alas! none ever mines.
And we have been on many thousand lines,
And we have shown, on each, spirit and power;
But hardly have we, for one little hour,

Been on our own line, have we been ourselves—
Hardly had skill to utter one of all
The nameless feelings that course through our breast,
But they course on for ever unexpress'd.
And long we try in vain to speak and act
Our hidden self, and what we say and do
Is eloquent, is well—but 'tis not true!
And then we will no more be rack'd
With inward striving, and demand
Of all the thousand nothings of the hour
Their stupefying power;
Ah yes, and they benumb us at our call!
Yet still, from time to time, vague and forlorn,
From the soul's subterranean depth upborne
As from an infinitely distant land,
Come airs, and floating echoes, and convey
A melancholy into all our day.
Only—but this is rare—
When a belov'ed hand is laid in ours,
When, jaded with the rush and glare
Of the interminable hours,
Our eyes can in another's eyes read clear,
When our world-deafen'd ear
Is by the tones of a loved voice caress'd—
A bolt is shot back somewhere in our breast,
And a lost pulse of feeling stirs again.
The eye sinks inward, and the heart lies plain,
And what we mean, we say, and what we would, we know.
A man becomes aware of his life's flow,
And hears its winding murmur; and he sees
The meadows where it glides, the sun, the breeze.

And there arrives a lull in the hot race
Wherein he doth for ever chase
That flying and elusive shadow, rest.
An air of coolness plays upon his face,
And an unwonted calm pervades his breast.
And then he thinks he knows
The hills where his life rose,
And the sea where it goes.

Meeting At Night
Robert Browning

I

The grey sea and the long black land;
And the yellow half-moon large and low;
And the startled little waves that leap
In fiery ringlets from their sleep,
As I gain the cove with pushing prow,
And quench its speed i' the slushy sand.

II

Then a mile of warm sea-scented beach;
Three fields to cross till a farm appears;
A tap at the pane, the quick sharp scratch
And blue spurt of a lighted match,
And a voice less loud, thro' its joys and fears,
Than the two hearts beating each to each!

Never the Time and the Place
Robert Browning

Never the time and the place
    And the loved one all together!
This path—how soft to pace!
    This May—what magic weather!
Where is the loved one's face?
In a dream that loved one's face meets mine,
    But the house is narrow, the place is bleak
Where, outside, rain and wind combine
    With a furtive ear, if I strive to speak,
    With a hostile eye at my flushing cheek,
With a malice that marks each word, each sign!
O enemy sly and serpentine,
Uncoil thee from the waking man!
    Do I hold the Past
    Thus firm and fast
Yet doubt if the Future hold I can?

This path so soft to pace shall lead
Thro' the magic of May to herself indeed!
Or narrow if needs the house must be,
Outside are the storms and strangers: we
Oh, close, safe, warm sleep I and she,—
I and she!

Ca' The Yowes To The Knowes

Robert Burns

Ca' the yowes to the knowes,
  Ca' them where the heather grows
  Ca' them where the burnie rows,
    My bonnie dearie.

  Hark! the mavis' evening sang
  Sounding Cluden's woods amang,
  Then a-fauldin let us gang,
    My bonnie dearie.

  We'll gae down by Cluden side,
  Thro' the hazels spreading wide,
  O'er the waves that sweetly glide
    To the moon sae clearly.

  Yonder Cluden's silent towers,
  Where at moonshine midnight hours,
  O'er the dewy-bending flowers,
    Fairies dance sae cheery.

  Ghaist nor bogle shalt thou fear;
  Thou 'rt to love and Heaven sae dear,
  Nocht of ill may come thee near,
    My bonnie dearie.

  Fair and lovely as thou art,
  Thou hast stown my very heart;
  I can die—but canna part,
    My bonnie dearie.

COURTSHIP

Jamie, Come Try Me

Robert Burns

Jamie, come try me,
    Jamie, come try me!
If thou would win my love,
    Jamie, come try me!
If thou should ask my love,
    Could I deny thee ?
If thou would win my love,
    Jamie, come try me!
If thou should kiss me, love,
    Wha' could espy thee ?
If thou wad be my love,
    Jamie, come try me!

Sally In Our Alley

Henry Carey

Of all the girls that are so smart
    There's none like pretty Sally;
She is the darling of my heart,
    And she lives in our alley.
There is no lady in the land
    Is half so sweet as Sally;
She is the darling of my heart,
    And she lives in our alley.

Her father he makes cabbage-nets,
    And through the streets does cry 'em;
Her mother she sells laces long
    To such as please as buy 'em;
But sure such folks could ne'er beget
    So sweet a girl as Sally!
She is the darling of my heart,
    And she lives in our alley.

When she is by, I leave my work,
    I love her so sincerely;
My master comes like any Turk,

And bangs me most severely:
But let him bang his bellyful,
    I'll bear it all for Sally'
She is the darling of my heart,
    And she lives in our alley.

Of all the days that's in the week
    I dearly love but one day -
And that's the day that comes betwixt
    A Saturday and Monday;
For then I'm dressed all in my best
    To walk abroad with Sally;
She is the darling of my heart,
    And she lives in our alley.

My master carries me to church,
    And often am I blamed
Because I leave him in the lurch
    As soon as text is named;
I leave the church in sermon-time
    And slink away to Sally;
She is the darling of my heart,
    And she lives in our alley.

When Christmas comes about again,
    O, then I shall have money;
I'll hoard it up, and box it all,
    I'll give it to my honey:
I would it were ten thousand pound,
    I'd give it all to Sally;
She is the darling of my heart,
    And she lives in our alley.

My master and the neighbours all,
    Make game of me and Sally,
And, but for her, I'd better be
    A slave and row a galley;
But when my seven long years are out,
    O, then I'll marry Sally;
O, then we'll wed, and then we'll bed
    But not in our alley!

The Change
Paul Laurence Dunbar

Love used to carry a bow, you know,
But now he carries a taper;
It is either a length of wax aglow,
Or a twist of lighted paper.

I pondered a little about the scamp,
And then I decided to follow
His wandering journey to field and camp,
Up hill, down dale or hollow.

I dogged the rollicking, gay, young blade
In every species of weather;
Till, leading me straight to the home of a maid
He left us there together.

And then I saw it, oh, sweet surprise,
The taper it set a-burning
The love-light brimming my lady's eyes,
And my heart with the fire of yearning.

Ripest Apples
Traditional, Irish

Madam I am come to court you
If so be you'd let me in
Sit you down, you're kindly welcome
Then perhaps you'll call again
Madam I've got gold and silver
Madam I've got house and land
Madam I've a world of pleasure
All to be at your command
I don't value your gold and silver
I don't value your house and land
I don't value your worlds of pleasure
All I want is a handsome man
Why do you dive so deep in beauty
It's a flower will soon decay

You pick it on a summer's morning
Before the evening it fades away
Ripest apples are soonest rotten
Hottest love is soonest cold
Young men's words are soon forgotten
Pretty maid, don't be too bold
After cowslips there come roses
After night there comes day
After false love comes a true love
So our time will pass away.

*S*ONG

Paul Laurence Dunbar

Bird of my lady's bower,
Sing her a song;
Tell her that every hour,
All the day long,
Thoughts of her come to me,
Filling my brain
With the warm ecstasy
Of love's refrain.

Little bird! happy bird! Being so near,
Where e'en her slightest word
Thou mayest hear,
Seeing her glancing eyes,
Sheen of her hair,
Thou art in paradise,
—Would I were there.
I am so far away,
Thou art so near;
Plead with her, birdling gay,
Plead with my dear.
Rich be thy recompense,
Fine be thy fee,
If through thine eloquence
She hearken me.

HASELBURY GIRL

Traditional, Irish

As I was going to Haselbury, all on one market day
I met a little Haselbury girl, her business being that way
Her business being to market; with butter, cheese and eggs
And we both jogged on together, my boys
Sing Fal-the-ral-looral-i-day
As we were jogging along the road, chatting side by side
I spied this pretty fair maid's garter come untied
And fearing she should lose it, I unto her did say
My love, your garter is coming untied
Sing Fal-the-ral-looral-i-day
Now if you tie it up for me, rewarded you shall be
Then if I tie it up for you, come under yonder tree
Whilst tying up her garter, such a wonderful sight did I see
My hand did slip right up to her hip
Sing Fal-the-ral-looral-i-day
Now since you've had your way to-day, pray tell to me your name
Likewise your occupation, from where and whence you came
My name is Jack the Rover, from Dub-i-lin Town I do come
And I live alongside of the Ups and Downs
Sing Fal-the-ral-looral-i-day
Returning home from the market, her butter it being all sold
And a-losing of her maidenhead, it made her blood run cold
O it's gone, it's gone, so let it go, it's gone to the lad I adore
And he lives alongside of the Ups and Downs
And I'll never see him any more.

THE NIGHT PIECE, TO JULIA

Robert Herrick

Her eyes the glow-worm lend thee,
The shooting stars attend thee;
And the elves also,
Whose little eyes glow
Like the sparks of fire, befriend thee.

No Will-o'-th'-Wisp mislight thee,
Nor snake or slow-worm bite thee;

But on, on thy way,
Not making a stay,
Since ghost there's none to affright thee.

Let not the dark thee cumber;
What though the moon does slumber?
The stars of the night
Will lend thee their light,
Like tapers clear without number.

Then Julia let me woo thee,
Thus, thus to come unto me;
And when I shall meet
Thy silv'ry feet,
My soul I'll pour into thee.

THE WOOING
Paul Laurence Dunbar

A youth went faring up and down,
Alack and well-a-day.
He fared him to the market town,
Alack and well-a-day.

And there he met a maiden fair,
With hazel eyes and auburn hair;
His heart went from him then and there,
Alack and well-a-day.

She posies sold right merrily,
Alack and well-a-day;
But not a flower was fair as she,
Alack and well-a-day.

He bought a rose and sighed a sigh,
"Ah, dearest maiden, would that I
Might dare the seller too to buy!"
Alack and well-a-day.

She tossed her head, the coy coquette,
Alack and well-a-day.
"I'm not, sir, in the market yet,"
Alack and well-a-day.

"Your love must cool upon a shelf;
Tho' much I sell for gold and pelf,
I'm yet too young to sell myself,"
Alack and well-a-day.

The youth was filled with sorrow sore,
Alack and well-a-day;
And looked he at the maid once more,
Alack and well-a-day.

Then loud he cried, "Fair maiden, if
Too young to sell, now as I live,
You're not too young yourself to give,"
Alack and well-a-day.

The little maid cast down her eyes,
Alack and well-a-day,
And many a flush began to rise,
Alack and well-a-day.

"Why, since you are so bold," she said,
"I doubt not you are highly bred,
So take me!" and the twain were wed,
Alack and well-a-day.

DRINKING WITH SOMEONE IN THE MOUNTAINS
Li Po

As the two of us drink
together, while mountain
flowers blossom beside, we
down one cup after the other
until I am drunk and sleepy
so that you better go!
Tomorrow if you feel like it
do come and bring your lute
along with you!

Johnny and Mollie

Anonymous, American

Johnny: Oh, Mollie, Oh Mollie, would you take it unkind
  For me to sit by you and tell you my mind?
  For my mind is to marry and never to part
  For the first time I saw you, you wounded my heart.

Mollie: Yes, you may be seated and say what you will
  For I've time a-plenty, will listen, be still;
  The subject of marriage means much in my life
  Should I need a husband and you want a wife.

Johnny: Oh Mollie, consider for you sure understand
  That love now is speaking, O heed her command;
  We will ramble together in ways of true love
  Until life is past, then renew it above.

Mollie: Put your horse in the stable and feed him some hay,
  Come and seat yourself by me so long as you may,
  For who would be hasty in matters like this,
  Repent at our leisure, the true object miss?

Johnny: My horse is not hungry and won't eat your hay,
  So fare you well, Mollie, I'll be on my way.
  You take all things lightly, my heart like a toy
  Toss about like a plaything and count it a joy.

Mollie: You really surprise me, for all this is new,
  I need time for thought and consider your view.
  I will marry for love or not wed at all,
  My mate will be waiting and answer my call.

Johnny: A meeting is a pleasure but parting is grief,
  An inconstant lover is worse than a thief,
  For a thief can but rob you and take all you have
  But an inconstant lover can lead to the grave.

Mollie: My heart you have wounded, but wounds they will heal,
  And this changes all things, you know how l feel,
  When you fall from your high horse and could happy be ,
  So whatever happens, just remember me.

Johnny: The grave it will rob you and turn you to dust,
   So where's a fair lady, a young man to trust?
   A cuckoo's a pretty bird and sings as she flies,
   Yes she brings us glad tidings and tells us no lies.

Mollie: Now don't be presumptuous, all things have two sides,
   There's nothing worth while if it's never been tried.
   I know what you have said in some cases is true
   But my love for you, Johnny, will sure change your view!

*O*H MISTRESS MINE

Traditional, English

O mistress mine, where are you roaming?
O stay and hear your true love's coming
That can sing both high and low.
   Trip no further, pretty sweeting,
   Journeys end in lovers meeting
   Ev'ry wise man's son doth know.
What is love? 'tis not hereafter
Present mirth hath present laughter,
What's to come is still unsure.
   In delay there lies no plenty
   Then come kiss me, sweet and twenty
   Youth's stuff will not endure.

*S*EVEN DAFFODILS

Traditional, American

Haven't got a mansion, haven't any land
Not one paper dollar to crumple in my hand
But I can show you morning on a thousand hills
And kiss you and give you seven daffodils
Haven't got a fortune to buy you pretty things
But I can give you moonbeams for necklaces and rings
But I can show you morning on a thousand hills
And kiss you and give you seven daffodils
Seven golden daffodils shining in the sun
Light our way to evening when the day is done
And I can give you music and a crust of bread
A pillow of piney bows to rest your head.

Sally Goodin

Traditional, American

Had a piece of pie an' I had a piece of puddin',
An' I give it all away just to see my Sally Goodin.
Had a piece of pie an' I had a piece of puddin',
An' I give it all away just to see my Sally Goodin.
Well, I looked down the road an' I see my Sally comin',
An' I thought to my soul that I'd kill myself a-runnin'.
Well, I looked down the road an' I see my Sally comin',
An' I thought to my soul that I'd kill myself a-runnin'.
Love a 'tater pie an' I love an apple puddin ,
An' I love a little gal that they call Sally Goodin.
An' I dropped the 'tater pie an' I left the appie puddin',
But I went across the mountain to see my Sally Goodin.
Sally is my dooxy an' Sally is my daisy,
When Sally says she hates me I think I'm goin crazy.
Little dog'll bark an' the big dog'll bite you,
Little gal'll court you an' big gal'll fight you.
Rainin' an' a-pourin' an' the creek's runnin' muddy,
An' I'm so dam' drunk I can't stand steady,
I'm goin up the mountain an' marry little Sally,
Raise corn on the hillside an' the devil in the valley.

Madam, Withouten Many Words

Sir Thomas Wyatt

Madam, withouten many words,
    Once, I am sure, ye will or no;
And if ye will, then leave your bourds
    And use your wit and show it so,

And with a beck ye shall me call;
    And if of one that burneth alway
Ye have any pity at all,
    Answer him fair with yea or nay.

If it be yea, I shall be fain;
    If it be nay, friends as before;
Ye shall another man obtain,
    And I mine own and yours no more.

THE PASSIONATE SHEPHERD TO HIS LOVE

Christopher Marlowe

Come live with me and be my love,
And we will all the pleasures prove
That valleys, groves, hills, and fields,
Woods, or steepy mountain yields.

And we will sit upon the rocks,
Seeing the shepherds feed their flocks,
By shallow rivers to whose falls
Melodious birds sing madrigals.

And I will make thee beds of roses
And a thousand fragrant posies,
A cap of flowers, and a kirtle
Embroidered all with leaves of myrtle;

A gown made of the finest wool
Which from our pretty lambs we pull;
Fair lined slippers for the cold,
With buckles of the purest gold;

A belt of straw and ivy buds,
With coral clasps and amber studs:
And if these pleasures may thee move,
Come live with me, and be my love.

The shepherds' swains shall dance and sing
For thy delight each May morning:
If these delights thy mind may move,
Then live with me and be my love.

THE NYMPH'S REPLY TO THE SHEPHERD

Sir Walter Raleigh

If all the world and love were young,
And truth in every shepherd's tongue,
These pretty pleasures might me move
To live with thee and be thy love.

Time drives the flocks from field to fold
When rivers rage and rocks grow cold,
And Philomel becometh dumb;
The rest complains of cares to come.

The flowers do fade, and wanton fields
To wayward winter reckoning yields;
A honey tongue, a heart of gall,
Is fancy's spring, but sorrow's fall.

Thy gowns, thy shoes, thy beds of roses,
Thy cap, thy kirtle, and thy posies
Soon break, soon wither, soon forgotten-
In folly ripe, in reason rotten.

Thy belt of straw and ivy buds,
Thy coral clasps and amber studs,
All these in me no means can move
To come to thee and be thy love.

But could youth last and love still breed,
Had joys no date nor age no need,
Then these delights my mind might move
To live with thee and be thy love.

Romance
Robert Louis Stevenson

I will make brooches and toys for your delight
Of birdsong at morning and starshine at night.
I will make a palace fit for you and me
Of green days in forests and blue days at sea.

I will make my kitchen and you shall keep your room
Where white flows the river and bright blows the broom,
And you shall wash your linen and keep your body white
In rainfall at morning and dewfall at night.

And this shall be for music when no one else is near,
The fine song for singing, the rare song to hear!
That only I remember, that only you admire,
Of the broad road that stretches and the roadside fire.

A Valentine
Matilda Betham-Edwards

What shall I send my sweet today,
When all the woods attune in love?
And I would show the lark and dove,
That I can love as well as they.
I'll send a locket full of hair, -
But no, for it might chance to lie
Too near her heart, and I should die
Of love's sweet envy to be there.
A violet is sweet to give, -
Ah, stay! she'd touch it with her lips,
And, after such complete eclipse,
How could my soul consent to live?
I'll send a kiss, for that would be
The quickest sent, the lightest borne,
And well I know tomorrow morn
She'll send it back again to me.
Go, happy winds; ah, do not stay,
Enamoured of my lady's cheek,
But hasten home, and I'll bespeak
Your services another day!

From "The Rubaiyat"
Omar Khayyam

Ah, my Belov'd fill the Cup that clears
To-day Past Regrets and Future Fears:
To-morrow!—Why, To-morrow I may be
Myself with Yesterday's Sev'n Thousand Years.

Nora: A Serenade
Paul Laurence Dunbar

Ah, Nora, my Nora, the light fades away,
While Night like a spirit steals up o'er the hills;
The thrush from his tree where he chanted all day,
No longer his music in ecstasy trills.

Then, Nora, be near me; thy presence doth cheer me,
Thine eye hath a gleam that is truer than gold.
I cannot but love thee; so do not reprove me,
If the strength of my passion should make me too bold.

Nora, pride of my heart,—
Rosy cheeks, cherry lips, sparkling with glee,—
Wake from thy slumbers, wherever thou art;
Wake from thy slumbers to me.

Ah, Nora, my Nora, there's love in the air,—
It stirs in the numbers that thrill in my brain;
Oh, sweet, sweet is love with its mingling of care,
Though joy travels only a step before pain.

Be roused from thy slumbers and list to my numbers;
My heart is poured out in this song unto thee.
Oh, be thou not cruel, thou treasure, thou jewel;
Turn thine ear to my pleading and hearken to me.

Child's Talk In April
Christina Rossetti

I wish you were a pleasant wren,
And I your small accepted mate;
How we'd look down on toilsome men!
We'd rise and go to bed at eight
Or it may be not quite so late.
Then you should see the nest I'd build,
The wondrous nest for you and me;
The outside rough perhaps, but filled
With wool and down; ah, you should see
The cosy nest that it would be.
We'd have our change of hope and fear,
Small quarrels, reconcilements sweet:
I'd perch by you to chirp and cheer,
Or hop about on active feet,
And fetch you dainty bits to eat.
We'd be so happy by the day,
So safe and happy through the night,
We both should feel, and I should say,

It's all one season of delight,
And we'll make merry whilst we may,
Perhaps some day there'd be an egg
When spring had blossomed from the snow:
I'd stand triumphant on one leg;
Like chanticleer I'd almost crow
To let our little neighbors know.
Next you should sit and I would sing
Through lengthening days of sunny spring;
Till, if you wearied of the task,
I'd sit; and you should spread your wing
From bough to bough; I'd sit and bask
Fancy the breaking of the shell,
The chirp, the chickens wet and bare,
The untried proud paternal swell;
And you with housewife-matron air
Enacting choicer bills of fare.
Fancy the embryo coats of down,
The gradual feathers soft and sleek;
Till clothed and strong from tail to crown,
With virgin warblings in their beak,
They too go forth to soar and seek.
So would it last an April through
And early summer fresh with dew,
Then should we part and live as twain:
Love-time would bring me back to you
And build our happy nest again.

ℐHE OWL AND THE PUSSY-CAT
Edward Lear

The Owl and the Pussy-Cat went to sea
In a beautiful pea-green boat.
They took some honey, and plenty of money,
Wrapped up in a five pound note.
The Owl looked up to the stars above,
And sang to a small guitar,
"O lovely Pussy! O Pussy, my love,
What a beautiful Pussy you are,

You are,
You are!
What a beautiful Pussy you are!"

Pussy said to the Owl, "You elegant fowl!
How charmingly sweet you sing!
O let us be married! Too long we have tarried:
But what shall we do for a ring?"
They sailed away for a year and a day,
To the land where the Bong-Tree grows,
And there in a wood a Piggy-wig stood,
With a ring at the end of his nose,
His nose,
His nose,
With a ring at the end of his nose.

"Dear Pig, are you willing to sell for one shilling
Your ring?" Said the Piggy, "I will."
So they took it away, and were married next day
By the Turkey who lives on the hill.
They dined on mince, and slices of quince,
Which they ate with a runcible spoon;
And hand in hand, on the edge of the sand,
They danced by the light of the moon,
The moon,
The moon,
They danced by the light of the moon.

PASSION AND LOVE
Paul Laurence Dunbar

A maiden wept and, as a comforter,
Came one who cried, "I love thee," and he seized
Her in his arms and kissed her with hot breath,
That dried the tears upon her flaming cheeks.
While evermore his boldly blazing eye
Burned into hers; but she uncomforted
Shrank from his arms and only wept the more.

Then one came and gazed mutely in her face
With wide and wistful eyes; but still aloof
He held himself; as with a reverent fear,
As one who knows some sacred presence nigh.
And as she wept he mingled tear with tear,
That cheered her soul like dew a dusty flower,
—Until she smiled, approached, and touched his hand!

What Is To Come

William Ernest Henley

What is to come we know not. But we know
That what has been was good—
was good to show,Better to hide, and best of all to bear.
We are the masters of the days that were;
We have lived, we have loved, we have suffered.even so
.Shall we not take the ebb who had the flow?Life was our friend?
Now, if it be our foe—Dear, though it spoil and break us!—
need we careWhat is to come?
Let the great winds their worst and wildest blow,
Or the gold weather round us mellow slow;
We have fulfilled ourselves, and we can dare
And we can conquer, though we may not share
In the rich quiet of the afterglowWhat is to come.

Invitation To Love

Paul Laurence Dunbar

Come when the nights are bright with stars
Or when the moon is mellow;
Come when the sun his golden bars
Drops on the hay-field yellow.

Come in the twilight soft and gray,
Come in the night or come in the day,
Come, O Love, whene'er you may,
And you are welcome, welcome.

You are sweet, O Love, dear Love,
You are soft as the nesting dove.

Come to my heart and bring it rest
As the bird flies home to its welcome nest.

Come when my heart is full of grief
Or when my heart is merry;
Come with the falling of the leaf
Or with the redd'ning cherry,

Come when the year's first blossom blows,
Come when the summer gleams and glows,
Come with the winter's drifting snows,
And you are welcome, welcome.

Aedh Gives His Beloved Certain Rhymes
William Butler Yeats

Fasten your hair with a golden pin,
And bind up every wandering tress;
I bade my heart build these poor rhymes:
It worked at them, day out, day in,
Building a sorrowful loveliness
Out of the battles of old times.
You need but lift a pearl-pale hand,
And bind up your long hair and sigh;
And all men's hearts must burn and beat;
And candle-like foam on the dim sand,
And stars climbing the dew-dropping sky,
Live but to light your passing feet.

Thomas The Rhymer
Anonymous

True Thomas lay on Huntly bank;
  A ferly he spied wi' his ee;
And there he saw a lady bright
  Come riding down by the Eildon Tree.
Her shirt was o' the grass-green silk,
  Her mantle o' the velvet fine;
At ilka tett of her horse's mane
  Hung fifty sil'er bells and nine.

True Thomas he pulled off his cap
    And louted low down to his knee:"
All hail, thou mighty Queen of Heaven!
    For thy peer on earth I never did see."
"O no, O no Thomas," she said,
    "That name does not belong to me;
"I am but the Queen of fair Elfland,
    That am hither come to visit thee."
"Play and speak, Thomas," she said,
    "Play and speak along wi' me;
And if ye dare to kiss my lips,
    Sure of your body I will be."
"Betide me weal, betide me woe,
    That fate shall never daunten me.
"Then he has kissed her rosy lips,
    All underneath the Eildon Tree.
"Now you must go wi' me," she said,
    "True Thomas you must go wi' me;
And you must serve me seven years
    Through weal or woe, as may chance to be.
"She mounted on her milk-white steed;
    She's taken True Thomas up behind;
And ay whene'er her bridle rung,
    The steed flew swifter than the wind.
On they rode on and farther on;
    The steed went swifter than the wind,
Until they reached a desert wide,
    And living land was left behind.
"Light down, light down now, True Thomas,
    And lean your head upon my knee.
Abide and rest a little space,
    And I will show you frelies three."
"O see ye not yon narrow road,
    So thick beset with thorns and briars?
That is the path of righteousness,
    Though after it but few inquires."
"And see you that braid, braid road
    That lies across that lily lawn?
That is the path of wickedness,

Though some call it the road to heaven."
"And see not ye that bonny road
That winds about the ferny brae?
That is the road to fair Elfland
    Where you and I this night must go."
"But Thomas you must hold your tongue,
    Whatever ye may hear or see;
For if you speak word in Elfenland,
    Ye'll ne'er get back to your ain country
."O they rode on and further on,
    And they waded through rivers above the knee,
And they heard neither sun nor moon,
    But they heard the roaring of the sea.
It was dark, dark night and there was no starlight,
    And they waded through red blude to the knee,
For a' the blude that's shed on earth
    Runs through the springs o' that country.
Soon they came onto a garden green,
    And she pulled an apple from a tree.
"Take this for thy wages, True Thomas,
    It will give thee the tongue that ne'er can lie."
"My tongue is mine own," True Thomas said;
    "A goodly gift ye would give to me!
I neither feared to buy or sell
    At fair or tryst where I may be."
"I feared neither speak to prince or peer,
    Nor ask of grace from fair lady."
"Now hold thy peace," the lady said,
    "For as I say, so must it be.
"He has gotten a coat of the even cloth,
    And a pair of shoes of velvet green;
And till seven years were gone and past,
    True Thomas on earth was never seen.

$\mathcal{Q}$uote
Benjamin Disraeli

The magic of first love is our ignorance that it can ever end.

Saucy Sailor

Anonymous

"Come my own one, come my fair one,
Come now unto me, Could you fancy a poor sailor lad
Who has just come from sea?" "You are ragged love, you are dirty love,
And your clothes smell much of tar So be gone you saucy sailor lad,
So be gone you Jack Tar." "If I am ragged love and I am dirty love,
And my clothes smell much of tar, I have silver in my pocket love
And gold in great store."And then when she heard him say so
On her bended knees she fell, "I will mary my dear Henry
For I love a sailor lad so well." "Do you think that I am foolish love,
Do you think that I am mad, For to wed a poor country girl
Where no fortune's to be had? I will cross the briny ocean,
I will whistle and sing, And since you have refused the offer love
Some other girl shall wear the ring. I am frolicsome, I am easy,
Good tempered and free, And I don't give a single pin my boys
What the world thinks of me."

Love's Philosophy

Percy Bysshe Shelley

The fountains mingle with the river,
And the rivers with the ocean;
The winds of heaven mix for ever
With a sweet emotion;
Nothing in the world is single;
All things, by a law divine,
In one another's being mingle—
Why not I with thine?

Young Young Love

Andrew Marvell

Come little Infant, Love me now,
While thine unsuspected years
Clear thine aged Fathers brow
From cold Jealousie and Fears.

Pretty surely 'twere to see
By young Love old Time beguil'd:

While our Sportings are 'as free
As the Nurses with the Child.

Common Beauties stay fifteen;
Such as yours should swifter move;
Whole fair Blossoms are too green
Yet for lust, but not for Love.

Love as much the snowy Lamb
Or the wanton Kid does prize,
As the lusty Bull or Ram,
For his morning Sacrifice.

Now then love me: time may take
Thee before thy time away:
Of this Need wee'l Virtue make,
And learn Love before we may.

So we win of doubtful Fate;
And, if good she to us meant,
We that Good shall antedate,
Or, if ill, that Ill prevent.

Thus as Kingdomes, frustrating
Other Titles to their Crown,
In the cradle crown their King,
So all Forraign Claims to drown.

So, to make all Rivals vain,
Now I crown thee with my Love:
Crown me with thy Love again,
And we both shall Monarchs prove.

Quote

George Bernard Shaw

First love is only a little foolishness and a lot of curiosity.

Sonnet 83

William Shakespeare

I saw that you did painting need,
And therefore to your fair no painting set,
I found (or thought I found) you did exceed,
That barren tender of a poet's debt:
And therefore have I slept in your report,
That you your self being extant well might show,
How far a modern quill doth come too short,
Speaking of worth, what worth in you doth grow.
This silence for my sin you did impute,
Which shall be most my glory being dumb,
For I impair not beauty being mute,
When others would give life, and bring a tomb.
    There lives more life in one of your fair eyes,
    Than both your poets can in praise devise.

Have Me

Carl Sandburg

Have me in the blue and the sun.
Have me on the open sea and the mountains.
When I go into the grass of the sea floor, I will go alone.
This is where I came from—the chlorine and the salt are blood and bones.
It is here the nostrils rush the air to the lungs.
It is here oxygen clamors to be let in.
And here in the root grass of the sea floor I will go alone.
Love goes far.
Here love ends.
Have me in the blue and the sun.

Sonnet 84

William Shakespeare

Who is it that says most, which can say more,
Than this rich praise, that you alone, are you?
In whose confine immured is the store,
Which should example where your equal grew.
Lean penury within that pen doth dwell,

That to his subject lends not some small glory,
But he that writes of you, if he can tell,
That you are you, so dignifies his story.
Let him but copy what in you is writ,
Not making worse what nature made so clear,
And such a counterpart shall fame his wit,
Making his style admired every where.
     You to your beauteous blessings add a curse,
     Being fond on praise, which makes your praises worse.

Sonnet 85

William Shakespeare

My tongue-tied muse in manners holds her still,
While comments of your praise richly compiled,
Reserve their character with golden quill,
And precious phrase by all the Muses filed.
I think good thoughts, whilst other write good words,
And like unlettered clerk still cry Amen,
To every hymn that able spirit affords,
In polished form of well refined pen.
Hearing you praised, I say 'tis so, 'tis true,
And to the most of praise add something more,
But that is in my thought, whose love to you
(Though words come hindmost) holds his rank before,
     Then others, for the breath of words respect,
     Me for my dumb thoughts, speaking in effect.

Sonnet 140

William Shakespeare

Be wise as thou art cruel, do not press
My tongue-tied patience with too much disdain:
Lest sorrow lend me words and words express,
The manner of my pity-wanting pain.
If I might teach thee wit better it were,
Though not to love, yet love to tell me so,
As testy sick men when their deaths be near,
No news but health from their physicians know.
For if I should despair I should grow mad,

And in my madness might speak ill of thee,
Now this ill-wresting world is grown so bad,
Mad slanderers by mad ears believed be.
That I may not be so, nor thou belied,
Bear thine eyes straight, though thy proud heart go wide.

Duncan Gray

Robert Burns

Duncan Gray came here to woo,
Ha, ha, the wooin o't!
On blythe Yule night when we were fou,
Ha, ha, the wooin o't!
Maggie coost her head fu high,
Look'd asklent and unco skeigh,
Gart poor Duncan stand abeigh;
Ha, ha, the wooin o't!

Duncan fleech'd, and Duncan pray'd,
Ha, ha, the wooin o't!
Meg was deaf as Ailsa Craig,
Ha, ha, the wooin o't!
Duncan sigh'd baith out and in,
Grat his een baith bleer't and blin',
Spak o' lowpin owre a linn;
Ha, ha, the wooin o't!

Time and chance are but a tide,
Ha, ha, the wooin o't!
Slighted love is sair to bide,
Ha, ha, the wooin o't!
"Shall I, like a fool," quoth he,
"For a haughty hizzie die?
She may gae to—France for me!"—
Ha, ha, the wooin o't!

How it comes let doctors tell,
Ha, ha, the wooin o't!
Meg grew sick as he grew hale,
Ha, ha, the wooin o't!
Something in her bosom wrings,
For relief a sigh she brings;

And O! her een, they spak sic things
  Ha, ha, the wooin o't!

Duncan was a lad o' grace,
  Ha, ha, the wooin o't!
Maggie's was a piteous case,
  Ha, ha, the wooin o't!
Duncan could na be her death,
Swelling pity smoor'd his wrath;
Now they're crouse and cantie baith;
  Ha, ha, the wooin o't!

Mary Morrison
Robert Burns

O Mary, at thy window be,
  It is the wish'd, the trysted hour!
Those smiles and glances let me see,
  That makes the miser's treasure poor:
How blythely wad I bide the stoure,
  A weary slave frae sun to sun,
Could I the rich reward secure,
  The lovely Mary Morrison.

Yestreen when to the trembling string
  The dance gaed thro' the lighted ha'
To thee my fancy took its wing,
  I sat, but neither heard nor saw:
Tho' this was fair, and that was braw,
  And yon the toast of a' the town,
I sigh'd, and said amang them a',
  "Ye are na Mary Morrison."

O Mary, canst thou wreck his peace,
  Wha for thy sake wad gladly die?
Or canst thou break that heart of his,
  Whase only faut is loving thee?
If love for love thou wilt na gie
  At least be pity to me shown:
A thought ungentle canna be
  The thought o' Mary Morrison.

Last May A Braw Wooer

Robert Burns

Last May a braw wooer cam down the lang glen,
And sair wi' his love he did deave me;
I said there was naething I hated like men:
The deuce gae wi 'm to believe me, believe me,
The deuce gae wi 'm to believe me.

He spak o' the darts in my bonie black een,
And vow'd for my love he was diein;
I said he might die when he liked for Jean:
The Lord forgie me for liein, for liein,
The Lord forgie me for liein!

A weel-stocked mailen, himsel for the laird,
And marriage aff-hand, were his proffers:
I never loot on that I ken'd it, or car'd,
But thought I might hae waur offers, waur offers,
But thought I might hae waur offers.

But what wad ye think? in a fortnight or less,
 (The deil tak his taste to gae near her!)
He up the lang loan to my black cousin Bess,
Guess ye how, the jad! I could bear her.
 Guess ye how, the jad! I could bear her, could bear her

But a' the niest week I fretted wi' care,
I gaed to the tryste o' Dalgarnock,
And wha but my fine fickle lover was there,
I glowr'd as I'd seen a warlock, a warlock.
I glowr'd as I'd seen a warlock.

But owre my left shoulder I gae him a blink,
Lest neibors might say I was saucy;
My wooer he caper'd as he'd been in drink,
And vow'd I was his dear lassie, dear lassie,
And vow'd I was his dear lassie.

I spier'd for my cousin fu' couthy and sweet,
Gin she had recover'd her hearin,
And how her new shoon fit her auld shachl't feet-

But, heavens! how he fell a swearin, a swearin,
But, heavens! how he fell a swearin.

He begg'd, for gudesake, I wad be his wife,
Or else I wad kill him wi' sorrow:
So e'en to preserve the poor body in life,
I think I maun wed him to-morrow, to-morrow,
I think I maun wed him to-morrow.

Love

Samuel Taylor Coleridge

All thoughts, all passions, all delights,
Whatever stirs this mortal frame,
All are but ministers of Love,
And feed his sacred flame.

Oft in my waking dreams do I
Live o'er again that happy hour,
When midway on the mount I lay,
Beside the ruined tower.

The moonshine, stealing o'er the scene
Had blended with the lights of eve;
And she was there, my hope, my joy,
My own dear Genevieve!

She leant against the arm'ed man,
The statue of the arm'ed knight;
She stood and listened to my lay,
Amid the lingering light.

Few sorrows hath she of her own,
My hope! my joy! my Genevieve!
She loves me best, whene'er I sing
The songs that make her grieve.

I played a soft and doleful air,
I sang an old and moving story—
An old rude song, that suited well
That ruin wild and hoary.

She listened with a flitting blush,
With downcast eyes and modest grace;
For well she knew, I could not choose
But gaze upon her face.

I told her of the Knight that wore
Upon his shield a burning brand;
And that for ten long years he wooed
The Lady of the Land.

I told her how he pined: and ah!
The deep, the low, the pleading tone
With which I sang another's love,
Interpreted my own.

She listened with a flitting blush,
With downcast eyes, and modest grace;
And she forgave me, that I gazed
Too fondly on her face!

But when I told the cruel scorn
That crazed that bold and lovely Knight,
And that he crossed the mountain-woods,
Nor rested day nor night;

That sometimes from the savage den,
And sometimes from the darksome shade,
And sometimes starting up at once
In green and sunny glade,—

There came and looked him in the face
An angel beautiful and bright;
And that he knew it was a Fiend,
This miserable Knight!

And that unknowing what he did,
He leaped amid a murderous band,
And saved from outrage worse than death
The Lady of the Land!

And how she wept, and clasped his knees;
And how she tended him in vain—
And ever strove to expiate
The scorn that crazed his brain;—

And that she nursed him in a cave;
And how his madness went away,
When on the yellow forest-leaves
A dying man he lay;—

His dying words—but when I reached
That tenderest strain of all the ditty,
My faltering voice and pausing harp
Disturbed her soul with pity!

All impulses of soul and sense
Had thrilled my guileless Genevieve;
The music and the doleful tale,
The rich and balmy eve;

And hopes, and fears that kindle hope,
An undistinguishable throng,
And gentle wishes long subdued,
Subdued and cherished long!

She wept with pity and delight,
She blushed with love, and virgin-shame;
And like the murmur of a dream,
I heard her breathe my name.

Her bosom heaved—she stepped aside,
As conscious of my look she stepped—
Then suddenly, with timorous eye
She fled to me and wept.

She half enclosed me with her arms,
She pressed me with a meek embrace;
And bending back her head, looked up,
And gazed upon my face.

Twas partly love, and partly fear,
And partly 'twas a bashful art,
That I might rather feel, than see,
The swelling of her heart.

I calmed her fears, and she was calm,
And told her love with virgin pride;
And so I won my Genevieve,
My bright and beauteous Bride.

Canzo

Bernard de Ventadour

When Fresh Grass-Blades and Leaves Appear
And flowers bud the branching plants,
And the nightingale most loud and clear
Uplifts its voice and song descants,
I joy in it, and in the flowered air
And take joy in my self and lady fair;
All round I'm wrapped with joy and girl indeed,
But this is a joy all other joys exceed.

Alas! I waste from thought so drear!
In so oft troubled circumstance:
And thieves could carry me off from here
And I know naught they do, perchance
For God's sake, Love! you find my fortress bare,
With few friends and no other lord to dare.
Why don't you urge my lady to such speed,
Before I am destroyed by longing need?

I marvel how I persevere
To hide my love from cognizance.
When I behold my lady near,
Such good dwells in her lovely glance
That I can hardly keep from running there.
So were it not for fear, I'd vouch I ne'er
Saw figure, better cut and broideried
For love, be so severe and slow to lead.

So much I cherish and hold her dear,
So much I dread and serve her commands,
I dare not plead my self from fear,
Nor send nor beg aught of her hands.
But of my hurt and sorrow she's aware,
And when she please, does prize and realm declare,
And when she please, my patience I must heed,
So censure on her may not be decreed.

If I knew sorcery's tricks and gear,
My enemy a child would prance,

So he would never spy our cheer
Nor speak no harm to our romance.
And then I know I'd see her past compare,
And her lovely eyes and color fresh and rare,
And kiss her mouth all ways in such a greed
That for a month my marks there one could read.

I fain would find her lone and sheer,
In sleep, or feigning such a trance,
So I might steal a sweet souvenir,
As I get not that much by demands.
By God, we do but little with love, I swear!
Time flies, my lady, and we lose our best share!
We must converse with signals secret keyed,
And should our daring not, tricks may succeed!

Well must one blame the lady austere,
Who stays her lover and nothing grants,
For talk of love trough many a year
Annoys and seems from guile to chance;
For one can love and act at love elsewhere,
And sweetly lit if none may witness bear.
Dear lady, if but my worth for love you'll cede,
From lying's grasp I'll be forever freed.

Messenger, go, and think me not low breed
If to my lady I'm afraid to speed.

The Conquest Of Love

Jean Racine

I know that to the winds my reason is cast!
But since I have begun to speak at last,
I must go on and unto thee declare
A secret that I can no longer bear
In silence. Here before thee in distress
Thou seest a prince, of most rash haughtiness
A signal instance. I who in my pride
Was rebel against love, and who defied
His captive chains—I who would oft deplore
The shipwreck of weak mortals, from the shore

Thinking always to view the storm—ah, now,
Subjected to the universal law,
Do I behold myself swept far away
From every mooring. In one moment's fray
Was my presumptuous confidence o'erthrown.
This spirit doth finally a sovereign own.
For nearly six months, shamed and in despair,
Bearing the fatal arrow everywhere
That wounds me, I have struggled against thee
Vainly, and 'gainst myself. Present, I flee;
Absent, I seek thee. Even in the deeps
Of forests doth thine image haunt my steps,
Following; and to mine eyes alike the light
Of day recalleth and the shades of night
That loveliness I shun. All things combine
To make Hippolytus, despite him, thine.
My every effort fruitless proves; in vain
My every effort fruitless proves; in vain
I seek to find my former self again.
My bow, my javelin, my chariot,
All weary me, and I remember not
The art which Neptune gave. The only noise
The woods hear is my sighings, and this voice
Mine idle coursers grow forgetful of.
It may be that so badly told a love
Will make thee, hearing me, to blush with shame
At having won it. Crude indeed and lame
The speech that tenders thee my heart, and I
How strange a captive for how sweet a tie!
Yet thou shouldst find mine offering hence more dear.
Remember that I speak a tongue I ne'er
Have learned. Disdain not my ill-uttered plea,
Which would not have been made, except to thee.

DESIRE

The Travail Of Passion
William Butler Yeats

When the flaming lute-thronged angelic door is wide;
When an immortal passion breathes in mortal clay;
Our hearts endure the scourge, the plaited thorns, the way
Crowded with bitter faces, the wounds in palm and side,
The hyssop-heavy sponge, the flowers by Kidron stream:
We will bend down and loosen our hair over you,
That it may drop faint perfume, and be heavy with dew,
Lilies of death-pale hope, roses of passionate dream.

Sonnet 45
William Shakespeare

The other two, slight air, and purging fire,
Are both with thee, wherever I abide,
The first my thought, the other my desire,
These present-absent with swift motion slide.
For when these quicker elements are gone
In tender embassy of love to thee,
My life being made of four, with two alone,
Sinks down to death, oppressed with melancholy.
Until life's composition be recured,
By those swift messengers returned from thee,
Who even but now come back again assured,
Of thy fair health, recounting it to me.
    This told, I joy, but then no longer glad,
    I send them back again and straight grow sad.

Sonnet 51
William Shakespeare

Thus can my love excuse the slow offence,
Of my dull bearer, when from thee I speed,
From where thou art, why should I haste me thence?
Till I return of posting is no need.
O what excuse will my poor beast then find,
When swift extremity can seem but slow?

Then should I spur though mounted on the wind,
In winged speed no motion shall I know,
Then can no horse with my desire keep pace,
Therefore desire (of perfect'st love being made)
Shall neigh (no dull flesh) in his fiery race,
But love, for love, thus shall excuse my jade,
    Since from thee going, he went wilful-slow,
    Towards thee I'll run, and give him leave to go.

Sonnet 131

William Shakespeare

Thou art as tyrannous, so as thou art,
As those whose beauties proudly make them cruel;
For well thou know'st to my dear doting heart
Thou art the fairest and most precious jewel.
Yet in good faith some say that thee behold,
Thy face hath not the power to make love groan;
To say they err, I dare not be so bold,
Although I swear it to my self alone.
And to be sure that is not false I swear,
A thousand groans but thinking on thy face,
One on another's neck do witness bear
Thy black is fairest in my judgment's place.
    In nothing art thou black save in thy deeds,
    And thence this slander as I think proceeds.

Sonnet 153

William Shakespeare

Cupid laid by his brand and fell asleep,
A maid of Dian's this advantage found,
And his love-kindling fire did quickly steep
In a cold valley-fountain of that ground:
Which borrowed from this holy fire of Love,
A dateless lively heat still to endure,
And grew a seeting bath which yet men prove,
Against strange maladies a sovereign cure:
But at my mistress' eye Love's brand new-fired,

The boy for trial needs would touch my breast,
I sick withal the help of bath desired,
And thither hied a sad distempered guest.
But found no cure, the bath for my help lies,
Where Cupid got new fire; my mistress' eyes.

Sonnet 154
William Shakespeare

The little Love-god lying once asleep,
Laid by his side his heart-inflaming brand,
Whilst many nymphs that vowed chaste life to keep,
Came tripping by, but in her maiden hand,
The fairest votary took up that fire,
Which many legions of true hearts had warmed,
And so the general of hot desire,
Was sleeping by a virgin hand disarmed.
This brand she quenched in a cool well by,
Which from Love's fire took heat perpetual,
Growing a bath and healthful remedy,
For men discased, but I my mistress' thrall,
Came there for cure and this by that I prove,
Love's fire heats water, water cools not love.

The Touch
Rene Vivien

The trees have kept some lingering sun in their branches,
Veiled like a woman, evoking another time,
The twilight passes, weeping. My fingers climb,
Trembling, provocative, the line of your haunches.
My ingenious fingers wait when they have found
The petal flesh beneath the robe they part.
How curious, complex, the touch, this subtle art—
As the dream of fragrance, the miracle of sound.
I follow slowly the graceful contours of your hips,
The curves of your shoulders, your neck, your unappeased breasts.
In your white voluptuousness my desire rests,
Swooning, refusing itself the kisses of your lips.

To Celia

Ben Jonson

Drink to me only with thine eyes,
And I will pledge thee with mine;
Or leave a kiss but in the cup,
And I'll not look for wine.
The thirst that from the soul doth rise,
Doth ask a drink divine:
But might I of Jove's nectar sup,
I would not change for thine.

I sent thee late a rosy wreath,
Not so much honoring thee,
As giving it a hope, that there
It could not withered be.
But thou thereon did'st only breathe,
And sent'st it back to me;
Since when it grow and smells, I swear,
Not of itself, but thee.

I Dreamed

Lady Kasa

I dreamed I held
A sword against my flesh.
What does it mean?
It means I shall see you soon.

Three Poems

Anonymous, Japanese

They say there is
A still pool even in the middle of
The rushing whirlpool—
Why is there none in the whirlpool of my love?

If only, when one heard
That Old Age was coming
One could bolt the door,
Answer "not at home"
And refuse to meet him!

Shall we make love
Indoors
On this night when the moon has begun to shine
Over the rushes
Of Inami Moor?

$\mathcal{A}$RDOR

Gamliel Bradford

Others make verses of grace.
    Mine are all muscle and sinew.
Others can picture your face.
    But I all the tumult within you.
Others can give you delight,
    And delight I confess is worth giving.
But my songs must tickle and bite
    And burn with the ardor of living

$\mathcal{M}$Y LOVE SWAYS, DANCING

Moses Ibn Ezra

My Love sways, dancing, like the myrtle tree,
The masses of her curls, disheveled, see!
She kills me with her darts, intoxicates
My burning blood, and will not set me free.

Within the aromatic garden come,
And slowly in its shadows let it roam,
The foliage be the turban for our brows,
And the green branches o'er our heads a dome.

All pain thou with the goblet shall assuage,
The wine-cup heals the sharpest pangs that rage,
Let others crave inheritance of wealth,
Joy be our portion and our heritage.

Drink in the garden, friend, anigh the rose,
Richer than spice's breath the soft air blows.
If it should cease a little traitor then,
A zephyr light its secret would disclose.

*T*HIS LOVE BEGAN AS GRATITUDE

Ellen Bass

This love began as gratitude,
the natural response
to being dragged from the fire. Faint,
consumed with smoke, I had inhaled
ash so long my lungs were paper bags,
seared, about to crumble.

Your mouth was wet.
I drank you like a future.
Your hands raised a sweat
along my spine, tracing my ribs.
Your breath misted me like a meadow before dawn.
Dew clung to my belly.
And the grasses parched between my thighs
grew succulent, blossomed dense as clover.

I learned the folds of your desire,
the underground spring whch gushed
like laughter. I found your hidden life—
bobcat, cougar—I learned to tempt her out,
to coax her, luxurious, slow,
to circle in that damp field until she bounded,
muscles rippling with stunning urgency.

You were steady as monsoons. You
would not relent. I trusted you.
You lapped me like waves,
cresting me, foamy and roaring,
the taffeta swish of bubbles dissolving.

I opened my heart like an astonished mouth.

Night after night, we are immersed in this salt sea.
We emerge dripping, briny,
like ancient life, re-created.
We stream with possibility.

$\mathcal{D}$ID NOT
Thomas Moore

'Twas a new feeling—something more
Than we had dared to own before,
    Which then we hid not;
We saw it in each other's eye,
And wished, in every half-breathed sigh,
    To speak, but did not.

She felt my lips' impassioned touch -
'Twas the first time I dared so much,
    And yet she chide not;
But whispered o'er my burning brow,
"Oh, do you doubt I love you now?"
    Sweet soul! I did not.

Warmly I felt her bosom Thrill,
I pressed it closer, closer still,
    Though gently bid not;
Till-oh! the world hath seldom heard
Of lovers, who so nearly erred,
    And yet, who did not.

$\mathcal{D}$OING, A FILTHY PLEASURE IS
Petronius Arbiter

Doing, a filthy pleasure is, and short;
And done, we straight repent us of the sport:
Let us not then rush blindly on unto it,
Like lustful beasts, that only know to do it:
For lust will languish, and that heat decay,
But thus, thus, keepeing endless Holy-day,
Let us together closely lie, and kiss,
There is no labour, nor no shame in this;
This hath pleased, doth please, and long will please; never
Can this decay, but is beginning ever.

*T*o His Mistress Going To Bed

John Donne

Come, Madam, come, all rest my powers defy,
Until I labour, I in labour lie.
The foe oft-times, having the foe in sight,
Is tired with standing, though they never fight.
Off with that girdle, like heaven's zone glistering
But a far fairer world encompassing.
Unpin that spangled breast-plate, which you wear
That th' eyes of busy fools may be stopped there:
Unlace yourself, for that harmonious chime
Tells me from you that now 'tis your bed time.
Off with that happy busk, whom I envy
That still can be, and still can stand so nigh.
Your gown's going off such beauteous state reveals
As when from flowery meads th' hills shadow steals.
Off with your wiry coronet and show
The hairy diadem which on you doth grow.
Off with those shoes: and then safely tread
In this love's hallowed temple, this soft bed.
In such white robes heaven's angels used to be
Received by me; thou Angel bring'st with thee
A heaven like Mahomet's Paradis; and though
Ill spirits walk in white, we easily know
By this these Angels from an evil sprite:
They set out hairs, but these the flesh upright.
Licence my roving hands, and let them go
behind, before, above,between, below.
Oh my America, my new found land,
My kingdom, safeliest when with one man manned,
My mine of precious stones, my Empery,
How blessed am I in this discovering thee.

Elegy 5

Ovid

In summer's heat and mid-time of the day
To rest my limbs upon a bed I lay,
One window shut, the other open stood,
Which gave such light, as twinkles in a wood,
Like twilight glimpse at setting of the sun,
Or night being past, and yet not day begun.
Such light to shamefast maidens must be shown,
Where thy must sport, and seem to be unknown.
Then came Corinna in a long loose gown,
Her white neck hid with tresses hanging down:
Resembling fair Semiramis going to bed
Or Lays of a thousand wooers sped.
I snatched her gown, being thin, the harm was small,
Yet strived she to be covered there withal.
And striving thus as one that would be cast,
Betrayed herself, and yielded at the last.
Stark naked as she stood before mine eye,
Not one wen in her body could I spy.
What arms and shoulders did I touch and see,
How apt her breasts were to be pressed by me.
How smooth a belly under her waist saw I?
How large a leg, and what a lusty thigh?
To leave the rest, all liked me passing well,
I clinged her naked body, down she fell,
Judge you the rest, being tired she bade me kiss,
Jove send me more such afternoons as this.

I Gently Touched Her Hand

Anonymous

I gently touched her hand: she gave
A look that did my soul enslave;
I pressed her rebel lips in vain:
They rose up to be pressed again.
    Thus happy, I no farther meant,
    Than to be pleased and innocent.
On her soft breasts my hand I laid,
And a quick, light impression made;

They with a kindly warmth did glow,
And swelled, and seemed to overflow.
    Yet, trust me, I no farther meant,
    Than to be pleased and innocent.

On her eyes my eyes did stay:
O'er her smooth limbs my hands did stray;
Each sense was ravished with delight,
And my soul stood prepared for flight.
    Blame me not if at last I meant
    More to be pleased than innocent

To The Fair Clarinda

Aphra Behn

Who made love to me,
Imagin'd more than woman.
Fair lovely Maid, or if that Title be
Too weak, too Feminine for Nobler thee,
Permit a Name that more Approaches Truth:
And let me call thee, Lovely Charming Youth.
This last will justifie my soft complaint,
While that may serve to lessen my constraint;
And without Blushes I the Youth persue,
When so much beauteous Woman is in view.
Against thy Charms we struggle but in vain
With thy deluding Form thou giv'st us pain,
While the bright Nymph betrays us to the Swain.
In pity to our Sex sure thou wer't sent,
That we might Love, and yet be Innocent:
For sure no Crime with thee we can commit;
Or if we shou'd-thy Form excuses it.
For who, that gathers fairest Flowers believes
A Snake lies hid beneath the Fragrant Leaves.
Though beauteous Wonder of a different kind,
Soft Cloris with the dear Alexis join'd;
When e'er the Manly part of thee, wou'd plead
Though tempts us with the Image of the Maid,
While we the noblest Passions do extend
The Love to Hermes, Aphrodite the Friend.

The Dream

Aphra Behn

All trembling in my arms Aminta lay,
Defending of the bliss I strove to take;
Raising my rapture by her kind delay,
Her force so charming was and weak.
The soft resistance did betray the grant,
While I pressed on the heaven of my desires;
Her rising breasts with nimbler motions pant;
Her dying eyes assume new fires.
Now to the height of languishment she grows,
And still her looks new charms put on;
–Now the last mystery of Love she knows,
We sigh, and kiss: I waked, and all was done.
`Twas but a dream, yet by my heart I knew,
Which still was panting, part of it was true:
Oh how I strove the rest to have believed;
Ashamed and angry to be undeceived!

Liaison

D. H. Lawrence

A big bud of moon hangs out of the twilight,
Star-spiders spinning their thread
Hang high suspended, without respite
Watching us overhead.
Come then under the trees, where the leaf-cloths
Curtain us in so dark
That here we're safe from even the ermin-moth's
Flitting remark.
Here in this swarthy, secret tent,
Where black boughs flap the ground,
You shall draw the thorn from my discontent,
Surgeon me sound.
This rare, rich night! For in here
Under the yew-tree tent
The darkness is loveliest where I could sear
You like frankincense into scent.
Here not even the stars can spy us,

Not even the white moths write
With their little pale signs on the wall, to try us
And set us affright.
Kiss but then the dust from off my lips,
But draw the turgid pain
From my breast to your bosom, eclipse
My soul again.
Waste me not, I beg you, waste
Not the inner night:
Taste, oh taste and let me taste
The core of delight.

Mystery

D. H. Lawrence

Now I am all
One bowl of kisses,
Such as the tall
Slim votaresses
Of Egypt filled
For a God's excesses.
I lift to you
My bowl of kisses,
And through the temple's
Blue recesses
Cry out to you
In wild caresses.
And to my lips'
Bright crimson rim
The passion slips,
And down my slim
White body drips
The shining hymn.

And still before
The altar I
Exult the bowl
Brimful, and cry
To you to stoop
And drink, Most High.
Oh drink me up
That I may be
Within your cup
Like a mystery,
Like wine that is still
In ecstasy.
Glimmering still
In ecstasy,
Commingled wines
Of you and me
In one fulfill
The mystery.

Now Sleeps The Crimson Petal

Alfred Lord Tennyson

Now sleeps the crimson petal, now the white;
Now waves the cypress in the palace walk;
Now winks the gold fin in the porphyry font:

The fire-fly wakens: waken thou with me.
Now droops the milk-white peacock like a ghost,
And like a ghost she glimmers on to me.
Now lies the earth all Danae to the stars,
And all thy heart lies open unto me.
Now slides the silent meteor on, and leaves
A shining furrow, as thy thoughts in me.
Now folds the lily all her sweetness up,
And slips into the bosom of the lake:
So fold thyself, my dearest, thou, and slip
Into my bosom and be lost in me.

Song

John Dryden

Whilst Alexis lay pressed
    In her arms he loved best,
With his hands round her neck,
    And his head on her breast,
He found the fierce pleasure too hasty to stay,
And his soul in the tempest just flying away.

When Celia saw this,
With a sigh and a kiss,
She cried, "Oh, my dear, I am robbed of my bliss;
'Tis unkind to your love, and unfaithfully done,
To leave me behind you, and die all alone."

Thus entranced they did lie,
Till Alexis did try
To recover new breath, that again he might die:
Then often they died; but the more they did so,
The nymph died more quick, and the shepherd more slow.

To A Young Lover

Amur Mu'izzi

O thou whose cheeks are the Pleiades and whose lips are coral,
Thy Pleiades are the torment of the heart, thy coral is the food of the soul.
In chase of those Pleiades my back hath become like the sjy,
For love of that coral my eyes have become like the sea.

Methinks, thy down is a smoke thro' which are seen rose-leaves,
Methinks, thy tresses are a cloud in which is hidden the sun—
A smoke that hath set my stack on fire,
A cloud that hath loosed from mine eyes the rain.

Thine eye, by wounding my heart, hath made me helpless;
Thy tress, by ravishing my soul, hath made me distraught.
If thine eye pierces my heart, tis right, for thou art my soul's desire.

In peace, the banquet-hall without thy countenance is not lighted;
In war, the battle-field without thy statue is not arrayed.
The banquet-hall without thy countenance is the sky without the moon;
The battle-field without thy stature is the garden without the cypress.

My body is in pain from thine eye full of enchantments,
My heart is in sorrow from thy tresses full of guile —
A pain that thy sight turns in a moment to pleasure,
A sorrow that thy speech turns into an instant to joy.

Thy face is a tulip for delicacy and pinkness,
Thy teeth are pearls for brightness and purity.
I never heard of pearls in honey-laden coral,
I never heard of tulips amidst musk-shedding hyacinths.

*G*OOD GOD, WHAT A NIGHT THAT WAS
Petronius Arbiter

Good God, what a night that was,
The bed was so soft, and how we clung,
Burning together, lying this way and that,
Our uncontrollable passions
Flowing through our mouths.
If I could only die that way,
I'd say goodbye to the business of living.

*E*ROTIC PASSION
Bhartrihari

I do indeed speak without bias;
this is acknowledged as truth among men.
nothing enthralls us like an ample-hipped woman;
nothing else cause such pain.

O wordly existence, the path
that leads beyond your bounds
would be less treacherous
were it not for intoxicating glances
waylaying us at every turn.

Surely the moon does not rise in her face,
or a pair of lotuses rest in her eyes,
or gold compose her body's flesh.
Yet, duped by poets' hyperbole, even a sage,
a pondering man worships the body of woman—
a mere concoction of skin and flesh and bones.

In this vapid, mundane world,
wise men take two courses:
they spend some time with minds
submerged in the fluid elixir of wisdom,
the rest with tender woman
whose breasts and hips enjoy the pleasure
of hiding men's eager hands
in their laps of ample flesh.

Spells cannot cure it, nor drugs confound it,
nor ritual magic deal it destruction—
passion, like an epileptic fit, attacks man's limbs
to inflict the torment of frenzied derangement.

Heavy rains keep lovers
trapped in their mansions—
in the shivering cold a lord
is embraced by his long-eyed mistress
and winds bearing cool mists
sooth their fatigue after loveplay
Even a dreary day is fair
for men who lie in love's arms.

Cut off all envy, examine the matter,
tell us decisively, you noble men,
which we ought to attend upon:
the sloping sides of wilderness mountains
or the buttocks of women abounding in passion?

At first she rebuffs me,
then in a mood born of dalliance, passion is roused;
slowly her body falls languid, and composure is shed,
leaving her bold enough to indulge in games of love
played by her limb's abandoned gesture—
a gentlewoman's pleasure is my delight.

Nutting Girl

Traditional, English

Now come all you jovial fellows, come listen to my song
It is a little ditty and it won't detail you long
It's of a fair young damsel, and she lived down in Kent
Arose one summer's morning, and she a-nutting went
 With my fal-lal to my ral-tal-lal
 Whack-fol-the-dear-ol-day
 And what few nuts that poor girl had
 She threw them all away.
It's of a brisk young farmer, was ploughing of his land
He called unto his horses, to bid them gently stand
As he sit down upon his plough, all for a song to sing
His voice was so melodious, it made the valleys ring
It's of this fair young damsel, she was nutting in the wood
His voice was so melodious, it charmed her as she stood
In that lonely wood, she could no longer stay
And what few nuts she had, poor girl, she threw them all away
She then came to young Johnny, as he sit on his plough
She said: "Young man I really feel I cannot tell you how"
She took her to some shady broom, and there he laid her down
Said she: "Young man, I think I feel the world
Go round and round"
He went back to his horses to finish off his song
He said: "My pretty fair maid, your mother will think you long"
But she flung her arms all round his neck
As they went o'er the plain
And she said: "My dear, I should like to see
The world go round again"
Now, come all you young women, take warning by my song
If you should a-nutting go, don't stay from home too long
For if you should stay too late, to hear the ploughboy sing
You might have a young farmer to nurse up in the spring.

One Hour Mama

Ida Cox

I've always heard that haste makes waste
So I believe in taking my time
The highest mountain can't be raced
It's something you must slowly climb
I want a slow and easy man
He needn't ever take the lead
'Cause I work on that long term plan
And I ain't a lookin' for no speed
I'm a one hour mama so no one minute papa
Ain't the kind of man for me
Set your 'larm clock papa, one hour that's proper
Then love me like I like to be
I don't want no lame excuses 'bout my lovin' bein' so good
That you couldn't wait no longer
Now I hope I'm understood
I'm a one hour mama so no one minute papa
Ain't the kind of man for me
I can't stand no greenhorn lover
Like rookie going to war
With a load of big artillery
But he don't know what it's for
He got to bring me ref'rence
With a long pedigree
And must prove he's got endurance
Or he don't mean snap to me
I'm a one hour mama so no one minute papa
Ain't the kind of man for me
I can't stand no crowing rooster
What just likes a hit or two
Action is the only kind of booster
Of just what my man can do
I don't want no imitation
My requirements ain't no joke
'Cause I got pure indignation
For a guy what's lost his stroke
I'm a one hour mama so no one minute papa
Ain't the kind of man for me.
Set your 'larm clock papa one hour, that's proper

Then love me like I like to be
I may want love for an hour
Then decide to make it two
Takes an hour 'fore I get started
Maybe three before I'm through
I'm a one hour mama so no one minute papa
Ain't the kind of man for me

THE MOWER

Anonymous

As I went out one morning on the fourteenth of July
I met a maid and I asked her age and she gave me this reply:
"I have a little meadow, I've kept for you in store
And it's only due, I should tell you true, it never was mowed before"
She said: "Me handsome young man, if a mower that you be
I give you good employment, so come along with me"
Well it was me good employment to wander up and down
With me tearing scythe all to contrive to mow her meadow down.
Now me courage being undaunted, I stepped out on the ground
And with me tearing scythe I then did strive to mow her meadow down
I mowed from nine till dinnertime, it was far beyond my skill
I was obliged to yield and to quit the field and the grass was growing still
Now the mower she kissed and did protest, this fair maid bein' so young
Her little eyes they glittered like to the rising sun
She said: "I'll strive to sharpen your scythe, so set it in me hand
And then perhaps you will return again to mow me meadow land."

OVALTINE

Unknown, British

Uncle George and Auntie Mabel
Passed out at the breakfast table.
Little children, take fair warning
Do not try it in the morning.
    Ovaltine has set them right
    Now they do it morn and night,
    And Uncle George is planning soon
    To try it in the afternoon...
Hark the herald angels sing:
Ovaltine is damn good thing!

Supper Isna Ready

Traditional, Scots

Roseberry to his lady says,
"My hinnie an' my succour, O
Shall we do the thing you ken
Or shall we take our supper?"
Wi' modest grace, sae fu' o' grace
Replied the bonnie lady,
"My noble lord, do as you please
But supper isna ready."

Orgie

Madison Julius Cawein

On nights like this, when bayou and lagoon
Dream in the moonlight's mystic radiance,
I seem to walk like one deep in a trance
With old-world myths born of the mist and moon.

Lascivious eyes and mouths of sensual rose
Smile into mine; and breasts of luring light,
And tresses streaming golden to the night,
Persuade me onward where the forest glows.

And then it seems along the haunted hills
There falls a flutter as of beautiful feet,
As if tempestuous troops of Maenads meet
To drain deep bowls and shout and have their wills.

And then I feel her limbs will be revealed
Like some great snow-white moth among the trees;
Her vampire beauty, waiting there to seize
And dance me downward where my doom is sealed.

Song To Amarantha, That She Would Dishevel Her Hair

Richard Lovelace

Amarantha sweet and fair
Ah braid no more that shining hair!
As my curious hand or eye
Hovering round thee let it fly.

Let it fly as unconfin'd
As its calm ravisher, the wind,
Who hath left his darling th'East,
To wanton o'er that spicy nest.

Ev'ry tress must be confest
But neatly tangled at the best;
Like a clue of golden thread,
Most excellently ravelled.

Do not then wind up that light
In ribands, and o'er-cloud in night;
Like the sun in's early ray,
But shake your head and scatter day.

See 'tis broke! Within this grove
The bower, and the walks of love,
Weary lie we down and rest,
And fan each other's panting breast.

Here we'll strip and cool our fire
In cream below, in milk-baths higher:
And when all wells are drawn dry,
I'll drink a tear out of thine eye,

Which our very joys shall leave
That sorrows thus we can deceive;
Or our very sorrows weep,
That joys so ripe, so little keep.

$\mathcal{T}$HE CLINGING KISS

Fenton Johnson

The earth awhirl, Sweetheart, I wander far
Adown the crowded street,
Upon my burning lips
The clinging kiss.

A thousand years
May sear this life of mine,
But in my memory
I hold one treasure dear, The clinging kiss.

A thousand caravans
May bear a wealth untold,
The stones of India
Will pale beside my gem,
The clinging kiss.

O wondrous love,
That burns to ash my heart,
Give back to me that hour
She placed upon my lips
The clinging kiss.

My Beloved's Body

Anonymous, Egyptian

Her necklace is made of buds.
Her bones are delicate reeds.
She wears a signet ring
and has a lotus
in her hand. I kiss her before
everyone that they
all may see my love.
She enraptures my heart, and when
she sees me, I am refreshed.

Sonnet XII

Sappho

Now o'er the tessellated pavement strew
Fresh saffron, steep'd in essence of the rose,
While down yon agate column gently flows
A glitt'ring streamlet of ambrosial dew!
My Phaon smiles! the rich carnation's hue,
On his flush'd cheek in conscious lustre glows,
While o'er his breast enamour'd Venus throws
Her starry mantle of celestial blue!
Breathe soft, ye dulcet flutes, among the trees
Where clust'ring boughs with golden citron twine;
While slow vibrations, dying on the breeze,
Shall soothe his soul with harmony divine!
Then let my form his yielding fancy seize,
And all his fondest wishes, blend with mine.

$\int$ONNET 128
William Shakespeare

How oft , when thou, my music, music play'st
Upon that blessed wood whose motion sounds
With thy sweet fingers when thou gently sway'st
The wiry concord that mine ear confounds,
Do I envy those jacks that nimble leap
To kiss the tender inward of thy hand,
Whilst my poor lips which should that harvest reap,
At the wood's boldness by thee blushing stand.
To be so tickled, they would change their state
And situation with those dancing chips
O'er whom thy fingers walk with gentle gait,
Making dead wood more blest than living lips.
    Since saucy jacks so happy are in this,
    Give them thy fingers, me thy lips to kiss.

$\mathcal{T}$HE CROSSING

Anonymous, Egyptian

My God, my lotus, my love
the north wind is blowing.
How pleasant to reach the river!
  breath
    flower...
My heart longs to go down
to bathe before you
to show you my loveliness
in a tunic of expensive
royal linen, drenched
in oil, my hair
braided in plaits like reeds.
I'll enter the river with you
and come out carrying
a red fish for you
splendid in my fingers.
I'll offer it to you
as I behold your beauty.
O my hero, my love,
come and behold me.

SQUEAL

Heather McHugh

She rides the last few minutes
hard, pressing her heels
in the stirrups, keeping
what she can concealed, a stone
hidden in a fist. But she's grown
too big, the room too cramped,
the body too well lit
with wet. A man has got a hand
in her again, he wants to pick
her pocket, leave her flat.

The room begins to heave, the white
elastic walls of senses, wow,
the words well up, the skin
begins to give and give until the sheet-
rock splits, the last uncommon
syllable is leaking from her lips:
her body breaks in two. Spectators
grin. The sex is speakable.
The secret's out.

DREAMER

George Syvester Viereck

He dreams.
The scented breath of June
Fans his bare limbs.
He softly sighs,
And still more softly smiles.

His eyes
Through closed lids gaze into the moon.
Now the boy's arms enfold the air,
His pulses quicken with delight:
For through the casements of the night
A dream-girl floats with burnished hair.
The gold of silken locks is spread
Above him like a coverlet.

His lips, now curved with passion, fret
The milk-white down where lies his head.
Can maid of flesh be half so sweet?
She knows no fear.
She asks no gain,
Nor of her roses winds a chain
For Love to drag with weary feet.
And now her phantom hands caress

His youth.
Her kisses fall like rain.
And stabs of pleasure kin to pain
Perturb his rose-pink nakedness.
His breath comes fast.

Desire shakes
His blood.
In amorous eclipse
The whole world lies between the hips
Of love.
He moans.
He swoons.
He wakes.

THE MASTER
Emily Dickinson

He fumbles at your spirit
As players at the keys
Before they drop full music on;
He stuns you by degrees,
Prepares your brittle substance
For the ethereal blow,
By fainter hammers, further heard,
Then nearer, then so slow
Your breath has time to straighten,
Your brain to bubble cool,—
Deals one imperial thunderbolt
That scalps your naked soul.

ATRIMONY

MARRIAGE

Raymond Carver

In our cabin we eat breaded oysters and fries
with lemon cookies for dessert, as the marriage
of Kitty and Levin unfolds on Public TV.
The man in the trailer up the hill, our neighbor,
has just gotten out of jail again.
This morning he drove into the yard with his wife
in a big yellow car, radio blaring.
His wife turned off the radio while he parked,
and together they walked slowly
to their trailer without saying anything.
It was early morning, birds were out.
Later, he propped open the door
with a chair to let in spring air and light.

It's Easter Sunday night,
and Kitty and Levin are married at last.
It's enough to bring tears to the eyes, that marriage
and all the lives it touched. We go on
eating oysters, watching television
remarking on the fine clothes and amazing grace
of the people caught up in this story, some of them
straining under the pressures of adultery,
separation from loved ones, and the destruction
they know lies in store just after
the next cruel turn of circumstance, and then the next.

A dog barks. I get up to check the door.
Behind the curtains are trailers and a muddy
parking area with cars. The moon sails west
as I watch, armed to the teeth, hunting
for my children. My neighbor,
liquored up now, starts his big car, races
the engine, and heads out again, filled
with confidence. The radio wails,
beats something out. When he has gone
there are only the little ponds of silver water
that shiver and can't understand their being here.

Two Sleepy People
Hoagy Carmichael & Frank Loesser

Here we are, out of cigarettes
Holding hands and yawning, look how late it gets
Two sleepy people by dawn's early light
And too much in love to say goodnight.

Here we are, in the cozy chair
Picking on a wishbone, from the Frigidaire
Two sleepy people with nothing to say
And too much in love to break away.

Do you remember the nights we used to linger in the hall?
(Your father didn't like me at all)
Do you remember the reason why we married in the Fall?
To rent this little nest, and get a bit of rest.

Well, here we are, just about the same
Foggy little fellow, dizzy little dame
Two sleepy people by dawn's early light
And too much in love to say goodnight.

A Dedication To My Wife
T.S. Eliot

To whom I owe the leaping delight
That quickens my senses in our wakingtime
And the rhythm that governs the repose of our sleepingtime,
    The breathing in unison

Of lovers whose bodies smell of each other
Who think the same thoughts without the need of speech
And babble the same speech without the need of meaning.

No peevish winter shall chill
No sullen tropic sun shall wither
The roses in the rose-garden which is ours and ours only

But this dedication is forf others to read:
These are private words addressed to you in public.

This Marriage
Jalál u'ddín Rumi

May these vows and this marriage be blessed.
May it be sweet milk,
this marriage, like wine and halvah.
May this marriage offer fruit and shade
like the date palm.
May this marriage be full of laughter,
our every day a day in paradise.
May this marriage be a sign of compassion,
a seal of happiness here and hereafter.
May this marriage have a fair face and a good name,
an omen as welcome as the moon in a clear blue sky.
I am out of words to describe
how spirit mingles in this marriage.

Bridget Flynn
Traditional, Irish

I've a nice little house and a cow or two with grass
I've a plant garden running by my door
I've a shelter for the hens and a stable for the ass
Now what could a man want more?

I don't know, maybe so
But a bachelor's life is easy and it's free
I'm the last to complain, but I'm living all alone
Sure nobody's looking after me

Me father often tells me I should go and have a try
To find a girl that owns a bit of land
And I know the way he says it, there is someone on his mind
And my mother has the whole thing planned

I don't know, maybe so
It would mollify them so to agree
Now there's little Bridget Flynn, sure it's her I'd like to win
But she never has an eye for me

Now there's a little girl who is worth her weight in gold
And that's a decent dowry, don't you see
And I mean to go and ask her just as soon as I get home
If she'll come and have an eye for me

Will she go, I don't know
But I'd love to have her sitting on my knee
And I'd sing like a thrush in the hawthorn bush
If she'd come and have an eye for me

*A*PPOMATTOX

Ai

The bus was full the rainy afternoon
we sat across the aisle from one another
and unashamed, I stared at you.
You had a choirboy's face,
tempered by the promise of sin.
I thought you were a pretty man,
the kind who was too dangerous
for anything but friendship.
When I got off, I was surprised
to find you matching my stride
through the pools of standing water.
One block, two blocks,
upstairs to my apartment.
I still remember the slow, sweet time
before the foreplay ended.
We never spoke.
We kept our separate war and peace to ourselves,
until one day, you broke the spell.
I'm James, you said
and I told you the imtimacy of names
was still too much to ask of me,
but you insisted,
and we lost the game of keeping thngs simple
and plain as a Shaker hatbox,
where we could store our past
poor failures at loving.

I don't want to see you anymore, I said, one day
as you were leaving,
but suddenly, I wanted to suck your fingertips
and twist those long strands of your hair
in my hands until you begged me
to make love to you again,
so I pulled you back inside.
I wish the floor had opened up
and swallowed me,
but here we are five years from then,
locked in our wedded misery.
Sex without responsibility could have saved us
from disaster,
but now it's too late,
now love's a letter stamped "return to sender,"
stamped "surrender" on delivery.

*H*ER BRIGHT SMILE HAUNTS ME STILL

Traditional, American

It's been a year since last we met
We may never meet again
I have struggled to forget,
But the struggle was in vain.
For her voice lives in the breeze,
Her spirit comes at will.
In the midnight on the seas
Her bright smile haunts me still.

    In the midnight on the seas
    Her bright smile haunts me still.

I have sailed a falling sky
And I've charted hazard's paths
I have seen the storm arise
Like a giant in his wrath.
Every danger I have known
That a reckless life can fill,
Though her presence is now flown

Her bright smile haunts me still.

Though her presence is now flown
Her bright smile haunts me still.

At the first sweet dawn of light
When I gaze upon the deep,
Her form still greets my sight
While the stars their vigil keep.
When I close my aching eyes
Sweet dreams my memory fill.
And from sleep when I arise
Her bright smile haunts me still.

And from sleep when I arise
Her bright smile haunts me still.

*P*OEM IN PRAISE OF MY HUSBAND (TAOS)
Diane Di Prima

I supose it hasn't been easy living with me either,
with my piques, and ups and downs, my need for privacy
leo pride and weeping in bed when you're trying to sleep
and you, interrupting me in the middle of a thousand poems
did I call the insurance people? the time you stopped a poem
in the middle of our drive over the nebraska hills and
into colorado, odetta singing, the whole world singing in me
the triumph of our revolution in the air
me about to get that down, and you
you saying something about the carburetor
so that it all went away

but we cling to each other
as if each thought the other was the raft
and he adrift alone, as in this mud house
not big enough, the walls dusting down around us, a fine dust rain
counteracting the good, high air, and stuffing our nostrils
we hang our pictures of the several worlds:
new york collage, and san francisco posters,
set out our japanese dishes, chinese knives

hammer small indian marriage cloths into the adobe
we stumble thru silence into each other's gut

blundering thru from one long place to the next
like kids who snuck out to play on a boat at night
and the boat slipped from its moorings, and they look at the stars
about which they know nothing, to find out
where they are going

Sonnet 116

William Shakespeare

Let me not to the marriage of true minds
Admit impediments, love is not love
Which alters when it alteration finds,
Or bends with the remover to remove.
O, no, it is an ever-fixed mark
That looks on tempests and is never shaken;
It is the star to every wand'ring bark,
Whose worth's unknown, although his height be taken.
Love's not Time's fool, though rosy lips and cheeks
Within his bending sickle's compass come;
Love alters not with his brief hours and weeks,
But bears it out even to the edge of doom:
    If this be error and upon me proved,
    I never writ, nor no man ever loved.

Beautiful, Beautiful Brown Eyes

Traditional, American

"Willie, oh Willie, I love you
Love you with all my heart;
Tomorrow we might have been married,
But liquor has kept us apart."

    Beautiful, beautiful brown eyes,
    Beautiful, beautiful brown eyes,
    Beautiful, beautiful brown eyes,
    I'll never love blue eyes again.

"Seven long years l've been married,
l wish l was single again;
A woman never knows of her troubles
Until she has married a man."
Down to the barroom he staggered,
Staggered and fell at the door;
The last words that he ever uttered,
"'l'll never get drunk any more.'"

$\mathscr{I}$'D RATHER MAKE COFFEE THAN LOVE

Anonymous

Tho' he brought her sweet candy, a flower, a dove
She preferred making pots of hot coffee to love.
Though from Everest he plucked her a star from above
 he preferred making coffee to love.

> And her outspoken credo was "Damn the libido!
> I'd rather make coffee than love."

She would even brew scrapings from overdone toast
She would open her arms to Sumatran French Roast
Her cafe au lait was the lait she loved most
"I'm Queen of the Bean," was her boast.
He'd have given her Cuba for one litle kiss
A Vesuvio brewer, accounts with the Swiss
When he married her, thinking that thus he'd find bliss
She preferred making coffee to love.

$\mathscr{A}$ LETTER TO HER HUSBAND

Anne Bradstreet

Absent upon Public Employment
My head, my heart, mine eyes, my life, nay more,
My joy, my magazine, of earthly store,
If two be one, as surely thou and I,
How stayest thou there, whilst I at Ipswich lie?
So many steps, head from the heart to sever,
If but a neck, soon should we be together.

I, like the Earth this season, mourn in black,
My Sun is gone so far in's zodiac,
Whom whilst I 'joyed, nor storms, nor frost I felt,
His warmth such fridged colds did cause to melt.
My chilled limbs now numbed lie forlorn;
Return; return, sweet Sol, from Capricorn;
In this dead time, alas, what can I more
Than view those fruits which through thy heart I bore?
Which sweet contentment yield me for a space,
True living pictures of their father's face.
O strange effect! now thou art southward gone,
I weary grow the tedious day so long;
But when thou northward to me shalt return,
I wish my Sun may never set, but burn
Within the Cancer of my glowing breast,
The welcome house of him my dearest guest.
Where ever, ever stay, and go not thence,
Till nature's sad decree shall call the hence;
Flesh of thy flesh, bone of thy bone,
I here, thou there, yet both but one.

To My Dear And Loving Husband
Anne Bradstreet

If ever two were one then surely we.
If ever man were loved by wife, then thee;
If ever wife were happy in a man,
Compare with me, ye women, if you can.
I prize thy love more than whole mines of gold
Or all the riches that the East doth hold.
My love is such that rivers cannot quench,
Nor aught but love from thee give recompense.
Thy love is such I can no way repay,
The heavens reward thee manifold, I pray.
Then while we live, in love let's so perservere
That when we live no more, we may live ever.

THE MILKMAID'S EPITHALAMIUM
Thomas Randolf

Joy to the bridegroom and the bride
That lie by one another's side!
O fie upon the virgin beds,
No loss is gain but maidenheads.
Love quickly send tthe time may be
Then I shall dear my rosemary!

I long to simper at a feast,
To dance, and kiss, and do the rest.
When I shall wed, and bedded be
O then the qualm comes over me,
And tells the sweetness of a theme
that I ne'er knew but in a dream.

You ladies have the blessed nights,
I pine in hope of such delights.
And silly damsel only can
Milk the cows' teats and think on man:
And sigh and wish to taste and prove
The wholesome sillabub of love.

Make haste, at once twin-brother bear;
And leave new matter for a star.
Women and ships are never shown
So fair as when their sails be blown.
then when the midwife hears your moan,
I'll sigh for grief that I have none.

And you, dear knight, whose every kiss
Reaps the full crop of Cupid's bliss,
Now you have found, confess and tell
That single sheets do make up hell.
And then so charitable be
To get a man to pity me.

TWO WIVES
D. H. Lawrence

I

Into the shadow-white chamber silts the white
Flux of another dawn. The wind that all night
Long has waited restless, suddenly wafts
A whirl like snow from the plum-trees and the pear,
Till petals heaped between the window-shafts,
In a drift die there.
A nurse in white, at the dawning, flower-foamed pane
Draws down the blinds, whose shadows scarcely stain
The white rugs on the floor, nor the silent bed
That rides the room like a frozen berg, its crest
Finally ridged with the austere line of the dead;

Stretched out at rest.
Less than a year the fourfold feet had pressed
The peaceful floor, when fell the sword on their rest.
Yet soon, too soon, she had him home again
With wounds between them, and suffering like a guest
That will not go. Now suddenly going, the pain;
Leaves an empty breast.

II

A tall woman, with her long white gown aflow
As she strode her limbs amongst it, once more
She hastened towards the room. Did she know
As she listened in silence outside the silent door?
Entering, she saw him in outline, raised on a pyre;
Awaiting the fire.
Upraised on the bed, with feet erect as a bow,
Like the prow of a boat, his head laid back like the stern
Of a ship that stands in a shadowy sea of snow
With frozen rigging, she saw him; she drooped like a fern
Refolding, she slipped to the floor as a ghost-white peony slips;
When the thread clips.
Soft she lay as a shed flower fallen, nor heard
The ominous entry, nor saw the other love,
The dark, the grave-eyed mistress who thus dared
At such an hour to lay her claim, above
A stricken wife, so sunk in oblivion, bowed;
With misery, no more proud.

III

The stranger's hair was shorn like a lad's dark poll
And pale her ivory face: her eyes would fail
In silence when she looked: for all the whole
Darkness of failure was in them, without avail.
Dark in indomitable failure, she who had lost;
Now claimed the host,
She softly passed the sorrowful flower shed
In blonde and white on the floor, nor even turned
Her head aside, but straight towards the bed
Moved with slow feet, and her eyes' flame steadily burned.

She looked at him as he lay with banded cheek,
And she started to speak
Softly: "I knew it would come to this," she said,
"I knew that some day, soon, I should find you thus.
So I did not fight you. You went your way instead
Of coming mine—and of the two of us
I died the first, I, in the after-life;
Am now your wife.

IV

"'Twas I whose fingers did draw up the young
Plant of your body: to me you looked e'er sprung
The secret of the moon within your eyes!
My mouth you met before your fine red mouth
Was set to song—and never your song denies
My love, till you went south.
'Twas I who placed the bloom of manhood on
Your youthful smoothness: I fleeced where fleece was none
Your fervent limbs with flickers and tendrils of new
Knowledge; I set your heart to its stronger beat;
I put my strength upon you and I threw
My life at your feet."
But I whom the years had reared to be your bride,
Who for years was sun for your shivering, shade for your sweat,
Who for one strange year was as a bride to you—you set me aside
With all the old, sweet things of our youth;—and never yet
Have I ceased to grieve that I was not great enough
To defeat your baser stuff."

V

"But you are given back again to me
Who have kept intact for you your virginity.
Who for the rest of life walk out of care,
Indifferent here of myself, since I am gone
Where you are gone, and you and I out there
Walk now as one.
Your widow am I, and only I. I dream
God bows his head and grants me this supreme
Pure look of your last dead face, whence now is gone

The mobility, the panther's gambolling,
And all your being is given to me, so none
Can mock my struggling.
And now at last I kiss your perfect face,
Perfecting now our unfinished, first embrace.
Your young hushed look that then saw God ablaze
In every bush, is given you back, and we
Are met at length to finish our rest of days
In a unity."

Old and New

Anonymous, Chinese

She went up the mountain to pluck wild herbs;
She came down the mountain and met her former husband.
She knelt down and asked her former husband
"What do you find your new wife like?"
"My new wife, although her talk is clever,
Cannot charm me as my old wife could.
In beauty of face there is not much to choose,
But in usefulness they are not at all alike.
My new wife comes in from the road to meet me;
My old wife always came down from her tower.
My new wife weaves fancy silks;
My old wife was good at plain weaving.
Of fancy silk one can weave a strip a day;
Of plain weaving more than fifty feet.
Putting her silks by the side of your weaving,
I see that the new will not compare with the old."

A Love Song

D. H. Lawrence

Reject me not if I should say to you
I do forget the sounding of your voice,
I do forget your eyes that searching through
The mists perceive our marriage, and rejoice.
Yet, when the apple-blossom opens wide
Under the pallid moonlight's fingering,

I see your blanched face at my breast, and hide
My eyes from diligent work, malingering.
Ah, then, upon my bedroom I do draw
The blind to hide the garden, where the moon
Enjoys the open blossoms as they straw
Their beauty for his taking, boon for boon.
And I do lift my aching arms to you,
And I do lift my anguished, avid breast,
And I do weep for very pain of you,
And fling myself at the doors of sleep, for rest.
And I do toss through the troubled night for you,
Dreaming your yielded mouth is given to mine,
Feeling your strong breast carry me on into
The peace where sleep is stronger even than wine.

MARRIAGE A-LA-MODE

John Dryden

Why should a foolish marriage vow,
Which long ago was made,
Oblige us to each other now
When passion is decay'd?
We lov'd, and we lov'd, as long as we could,
Till our love was lov'd out in us both:
But our marriage is dead, when the pleasure is fled:
'Twas pleasure first made it an oath.

If I have pleasures for a friend,
And farther love in store,
What wrong has he whose joys did end,
And who could give no more?
'Tis a madness that he should be jealous of me,
Or that I should bar him of another:
For all we can gain is to give ourselves pain,
When neither can hinder the other.

The Wife's Appeal

Grace Greenwood

I'm thinking, Charles, 'tis just a year,
Or will be, very soon,
Since first you told me of your love,
One glorious day in June.

All nature seemed to share our bliss,
—The skies hung warm above,
The winds from opening roses bore
The very breath of love!

We sought the still, deep forest shades,
Within whose leafy gloom
Few ardent sunbeams stole to kiss
The young buds into bloom;

The birds caught up our tones of love,
In songs not half so sweet,
And earth's green carpet, violet-flowered,
It scarcely felt our feet!

Ah, apropos of carpets, Charles,
I looked at some to-day,
Which you will purchase,—won't you, dear,
Before our next soiree?

And then remember you how lost
In love's delicious dream,
We long stood silently beside
A gently gliding stream?

'Twas Nature's mirror,—when your gaze
No longer I could bear,
I modestly cast down my eyes,
Yet but to meet it there!

And apropos of mirrors, love,
The dear gift of your mother
Is quite old-fashioned,—and to-day
I ordered home another.

Ah, well do I remember, Charles,
When first your arm stole round me,
—You little dreamed how long your soul
In golden chains had bound me!

And apropos of chains, my own,
At Allen's shop last week
I saw the sweetest love, so rich,
So tasteful and unique!
The workmanship is most superb,

The gold most fine and pure,
—I quite long, Charles, to see that chain
Suspend your miniature!
I 've heard sad news while you were out,

— My nerves are much affected,
—You know the navy officer
I once for you rejected;
Driven to despair by your success,

Made desperate by my score,
He went to sea,—
and has been lost
In passing round Cape Horn!

Ah, apropos of capes, my love,
I saw one in Broadway,
Of lace as fine as though 'twere wove
Of moonlight, by a fay!

You'll purchase the exquisite thing?
'T will suit your taste completely;
Above the heart that loves you, Charles,
'Twill rise and fall so sweetly!

To His Wife

Ch'in Chia

Solemn, solemn the coachman gets ready to go;
"Chiang, chiang" the harness bells ring.
At break of dawn I must start on my long journey;
At cock-crow I must gird my belt.
I turn back and look at the empty room;
For a moment I almost think I see you there.
One parting, but ten thousand regrets;
As I take my seat, my heart is unquiet.
What shall I do to tell you all my thoughts?
How can I let you know all my love?
Precious hairpins make the head to shine
And bright mirrors can reflect beauty.
Fragrant herbs banish evil smells
And the scholar's lute has a clear note.
The man in the Book of Songs who was given a quince
Wanted to pay it back with precious stones.
When I think of all the things you have done for me,
How ashamed I am to have done so little for you!
Although I know that it is a poor return,
All I can give you is this description of my feelings.

The Anniversary

John Donne

All Kings, and all their favourites,
    All glory of honours, beauties, wits,
The sun itself, which makes times, as they pass,
Is elder by year now than it was
When thou and I first one another saw:
All other things to their destruction draw,
    Only our love hath no decay;
This no tomorrow hath, nor yesterday,
Running it never runs from us away,
But truly keeps his first, last, everlasting day.

    Two graves must hide thine and my corse;
    If one might, death were no divorce.

Alas, as well as other Princes, we
(Who Prince enough in one another be)
Must leave at last in death these eyes and ears,
Oft fed with true oaths, and with sweet salt tears;
But souls where nothing dwells but love
(All other thoughts being inmates) then shall prove
When bodies to their graves, souls from their graves remove.

And then we shall be throughly blessed;
But we no more than all the rest.
Here upon earth we're Kings, and none but we
Can be such Kings, not of such subjects be;
Who is so safe as we: where none can do
Treason to us, except one of us two.
True and false fears let us refrain,
Let us love nobly, and live, and add again
Years and years unto years, till we attain
To write threescore: this is the second of our reign.

THE BANKS OF INVERARY

Traditional, Scots

'Twas on a summer's morning, alone as I did pass
On the banks of Inverary I met a com-e-ly lass.
Her hair hung over her shoulders, her eyes like stars did shine,
On the banks of Inverary I wish'd her heart was mine.
I did embrace this fair maid as fast as e'er I could,
Her hair hung over her shoulders most like to threads of gold;
Her hair hung over her shoulders, her tears like drops of dew -
"On the banks of Inverary I'm glad to meet with you."
"Leave off, my handsome young man, do not embrace me so,
For after so much kissing there comes a dreadful woe,
And if my poor heart should be ensnared and I beguil'd by thee,
On the banks of Inverary I shall walk alone," said she.
I said, "My handsome fair maid, the truth to you I'll tell,
On the banks of Inverary twelve maidens I've beguil'd;
But I will not begin to-night, my charmer," then said he,
"On the banks of Inverary I've found my wife," said he.
So he set this handsome fair maid on horseback very high,

"Unto some parson we will go and there the knot will tie,
And then we will sing songs of love until the day we die;
On the banks of Inverary where no-one there is nigh."

$\mathcal{G}$OOD NIGHT IRENE
Leadbelly

Last Saturday night, I got married,
Me and my wife settled down.
Now me and my wife are parted,
I'm gonna take another stroll downtown.
Sometimes I live in the country,
sometimes I live in town.
Sometimes I take a great notion,
To jump into the river and drown.
I love Irene, God knows I do,
I'll love her till the seas run dry
But if Irene should turn me down,
I'd take the morphine and die.
Stop rambling, stop your gambling
Stop staying out late at night,
Go home to your wife and your family
Stay there by your fireside bright.

$\mathcal{M}$ARRIED AND SINGLE LIFE
Traditional, American

Come all ye young people and listen to me
I'm going to tell you my sad destiny,
I'm a man by experience whose favor is won
Love has been the ruin of many a man.
If you go to get married, don't hasten it on
And don't you get married till you're full twenty-one
And don't you get married till you find your love set,
Then marry some good girl your love won't forget.
Come all you young gentlemen who want to be smart
Don't place your affections on a smiling sweetheart.
She's dancing before you some favors to gain,

Then turns her back on you with scorn and disdain.
When a man's married he ain't his own man,
He must rove through the country and live as he can.
He's lost that sweet apparel, the flowers of life,
For selling his freedom to buy him a wife.
But when a man's single he can live at his ease,
He can rove through the country and do as he please
He can rove through the country and live at his will
Kiss Polly, kiss Betsy, and he is the same still.
Just pour out another bowl, boys, we'll drink bumpers round
We'll drink to the poorest, if they're to be found;
We'll drink to the single with the greatest success,
Likewise to the married and wish them no less.

*A*MONG THE BLUE FLOWERS AND THE YELLOW

Traditional, Scots

"Oh, Willie, my son, what makes ye so sad?"
As the sun shines over the valley
"I lie sorely sick for the love of a maid."
Among the blue flow'rs and the yellow.
"Oh, is she an heiress or lady fine?
That she winna take nae pity on thee?"
Oh, Willie, my son, lay doon in your bed.
And I will go tell her that my young son is dead."
And the lady came doon frae her castle sae high
Not knowing her Willie would sicken and die.
As she looked into the coffin and pall
He pulled her doon by him and lay her ni'est the wall.
"Though all of your kin were aboot yon bower
Ye shall no be a maiden one single hour.
For a maid ye came here wi' oot a convoy
And ye shall return wi' a horse and a boy.
Ye came here a maiden sae meek and sae mild
But ye shall gae hame a wedded wife wi' a child."

Love

Ralph Waldo Emerson

The introduction to this felicity is in a private and tender relation
of one to one, which is the enchantment of human life; which, like certain
divine rage and enthusiasm, seizes on one man at one period and works a
revolution in his mind's and body; unites him to his race, pledges him
to the domestic and civic relations, carries him with new sympathy into nature,
enhances the power of the senses, adds to his character heroic and scared attributes,
establishes marriage and gives permanence to human society.

Lines Written By Ellen Louisa Tucker Shortly Before Her Marriage To Mr. Emerson (Ralph Waldo)

Ellen Louisa Tucker

Love scatters oil
On Life's dark sea,
Sweetens its toil—
Our helmsman he.

Around him hover
Odorous clouds;
Under this cover
His arrows he shrouds.

The cloud was around me,
I knew not why
Such sweetness crowned me,
While Time shot by.

No pain was within,
But calm delight,
Like a world without sin,
Or a day without night.
The shafts of the god
Were tipped with down,
For they drew no blood,
And they knit no frown.

I knew of them not
Until Cupid laughed loud,
And saying "You're caught!"
Flew off in the cloud.

O then I awoke,
And I lived but to sigh,
Till a clear voice spoke,
—And my tears are dry.

WEDDING HYMN

Sidney Lanier

Thou God, whose high, eternal Love
Is the only blue sky of our life,
Clear all the Heaven that bends above
The life-road of this man and wife.
May these two lives be but one note
In the world's strange-sounding harmony,
Whose sacred music e'er shall float
Through every discord up to Thee.
As when from separate stars two beams
Unite to form one tender ray:
As when two sweet but shadowy dreams
Explain each other in the day:
So may these two dear hearts one light
Emit, and each interpret each.
Let an angel come and dwell to-night
In this dear double-heart, and teach

DOMESTIC HAPPINESS

Fitz-Greene Halleck

"...he only bliss
Of Paradise that has survived the fall."
—Cowper
"Beside the nuptial curtain bright,"
The Bard of Eden sings,
"Young Love his constant lamp will light,
And wave his purple wings."
But rain-drops from the clouds of care
May bid that lamp be dim,
And the boy Love will pout and swear
'Tis then no place for him.

So mused the lovely Mrs. Dash;
'Tis wrong to mention names;
When for her surly husband's cash
She urged in vain her claims.

"I want a little money, dear,
For Vandervoort and Flandin,
Their bill, which now has run a year,
To-morrow mean to hand in."

"More?" cried the husband, half asleep,
"You'll drive me to despair."
The lady was too proud to weep,
And too polite to swear.
She bit her lip for very spite,
He felt a storm was brewing,
And dreamed of nothing else all night
But brokers, banks, and ruin.

He thought her pretty once, but dreams
Have sure a wondrous power,
For to his eye the lady seems
Quite altered since that hour—
And Love, who on their bridal eve,
Had promised long to stay,
Forgot his promise—took French leave—
And bore his lamp away.

THE BACHELOR

Lucretia Maria Davidson (*Written in her fifteenth year.*)

To the world (whose dread laugh he would tremble to hear,
From whose scorn he would shrink with a cowardly fear),
The old bachelor proudly and boldly will say,
Single lives are the longest, single lives are most gay.

To the ladies, with pride, he will always declare,
That the links in love's chain are strife, trouble, and care;
That a wife is a torment, and he will have none,
But at pleasure will roam through the wide world alone.

And let him pass on, in his sulky of state;
O say, who would envy that mortal his fate?
To brave all the ills of life's tempest alone,
Not a heart to respond the warm notes of his own.

His joys undivided no longer will please;
The warm tide of his heart through inaction will freeze:
—His sorrows concealed, and unanswered his sighs,
The old bachelor curses his folly, and dies.

Pass on, then, proud lone one, pass on to thy fate;
Thy sentence is scaled, thy repentance too late;
Like an arrow, which leaves not a trace on the wind,
No mark of thy pathway shall linger behind.

Not a sweet voice shall murmur its sighs o'er thy tomb;
Not a fair hand shall teach thy lone pillow to bloom;
Not a kind tear shall water thy dark, lonely bed;
By the living 't was scorned, 'tis refused to the dead.

Upon The Death Of Sir Albert Morton's Wife
Sir Henry Wotton

He first deceased; she for a little tried
To live without him, liked it not, and died.

To His Wife
Decimus Magnus Ausonius

Love, let us live as we have lived, nor lose
    The little names that were the first night's grace,
And never come the day that sees us old,
    I still your lad, and you my little lass.
Let me be older than old Nestor's years,
    And you the Sibyl, if we heed it not.
What should we know, we two, of ripe old age?
    We'll have its richness, and the years forgot.

To Her Husband, At The Wedding
Kaga no Chiyo

The persimmon, lo!
No one can tell till he tastes it!
Marriage is even so.

Lament For Her Absent Lord
Lady Surrey

Good ladies, you that have your pleasure in exile,
Step in your foot, come take a place, and mourn with me a while,
And such as by their lords do set but little price,
Let them sit still: it skills them not what chance come on the dice.
But ye whom Love hath bound by order of desire
To love your lords, whose good desserts none other would require:
Come you yet once again, and set your foot by mine,
Whose woeful plight and sorrows great no tongue may well define.
My love and lord, alas, in whom consists my wealth,
Hath fortune sent to pass the seas in hazard of his health.
That I was wont for to embrace, contented mind's,
Is now amid the foaming floods at pleasure of the winds.
There God him well preserve, and safely me him send,
Without which hope, my life alas were shortly at an end.
Whose absence yet, although my hope doth tell me plain,
With short return he comes anon, yet ceaseth not my pain.
The fearful dreams I have, oft times they grieve me so,
That then I wake and stand in doubt, if they be true, or no.
Sometime the roaring seas, me seems, they grow so high,
That my sweet lord in danger great, alas, doth often lie.
Another time the same doth tell me, he is come;
And playing, where I shall him find with T., his little son.
So forth I go apace to see that liefsome sight,
And with a kiss me thinks I say: "Now welcome home, my knight;
Welcome my sweet, alas, the stay of my welfare;
Thy presence bringeth forth a truce betwixt me and my care."
Then lively doth he look, and salveth me again,
And saith: "My dear, how is it now that you have all this pain?"
Wherewith the heavy cares that heap'd are in my breast,
Break forth, and me dischargeth clean of all my huge unrest.
But when I me awake and find it but a dream,
The anguish of my former woe beginneth more extreme,
And me tormenteth so, that uneath may I find
Some hidden where, to steal the grief of my unquiet mind.
Thus every way you see with absence how I burn;
And for my wound no cure there is but hope of good return;

Save when I feel, by sour how sweet is felt the more,
It doth abate some of my pains that I abode before.
And then unto myself I say: "When that we two shall meet,
But little time shall seem this pain, that joy shall be so sweet."
Ye winds, I you convert in chiefest of your rage,
That you my lord me safely send, my sorrows to assuage;
And that I may not long abide in such excess,
Do your good will to cure a wight that liveth in distress.

Love And A Question
Robert Frost

A Stranger came to the door at eve,
And he spoke to the bridegroom fair.
He bore a green-white stick in his hand,
And, for all burden, care.
He asked with the eyes more than the lips
For a shelter for the night,
And he turned and looked at the road afar
Without a window light.

The bridegroom came forth into the porch
With, "Let us look at the sky,
And question what of the night to be,
Stranger, you and I."
The woodbine leaves littered the yard,
The woodbine berries were blue,
Autumn, yes, winter was in the wind;
"Stranger, I wish I knew."

Within, the bride in the dusk alone
Bent over the open fire,
Her face rose-red with the glowing coal
And the thought of the heart's desire.

An Old Man To His Sleeping Young Bride

Ella Wheeler Wilcox

As when the old moon lighted by the tender
And radiant crescent of the new is seen,
And for a moment's space suggests the splendor
Of what in its full prime it once has been,

So on my waning years you cast the glory
Of youth and pleasure, for a little hour;
And life again seems like an unread story,
And joy and hope both stir me with their power.

Can blooming June be fond of bleak December?
I dare not wait to hear my heart reply.
I will forget the question—and remember
Alone the priceless feast spread for mine eye,

That radiant hair that flows across the pillows,
Like shimmering sunbeams over drifts of snow;
Those heaving breasts, like undulating billows,
Whose dangers or delights but Love can know,

That crimson mouth from which sly Cupid borrowed
The pattern for his bow, nor asked consent;
That smooth, unruffled brow which has not sorrowed—
All these are mine; should I not be content?

Yet are these treasures mine, or only lent me?
And, who shall claim them when I pass away?
Oh, jealous Fate, to torture and torment me
With thoughts like these in my too fleeting day!

For while I gained the prize which all were seeking,
And won you with the ardor of my quest,
The bitter truth I know without your speaking—
You only let me love you at the best.

E'en while I lean and count my riches over,
And view with gloating eyes your priceless charms,
I know somewhere there dwells the unnamed lover
Who yet shall clasp you, willing, in his arms.

And while my hands stray through your clustering tresses,
And while my lips are pressed upon your own,
This unseen lover waits for such caresses
As my poor hungering clay has never known,

And when some day, between you and your duty
A green grave lies, his love shall make you glad,
And you shall crown him with your splendid beauty—
Ah, God! ah, God! 'tis this way men go mad!

CONTENT

Madison Cawein

When I behold how some pursue
Fame, that is Care's embodiment
Or fortune, whose false face looks true,
—An humble home with sweet content
Is all I ask for me and you.

An humble home, where pigeons coo,
Whose path leads under breezy lines
Of frosty-berried cedars to
A gate, one mass of trumpet-vines,
Is all I ask for me and you.

A garden, which all summer through,
The roses old make redolent,
And morning-glories, gay of hue,
And tansy, with its homely scent,
Is all I ask for me and you.

An orchard, that the pippins strew,
From whose bruised gold the juices spring;
A vineyard, where the grapes hang blue,
Wine-big and ripe for vintaging,
Is all I ask for me and you.

A lane that leads to some far view
Of forest or of fallow-land,
Bloomed o'er with rose and meadow-rue,
Each with a bee in its hot hand,
Is all I ask for me and you.

At morn, a pathway deep with dew,
And birds to vary time and tune;
At eve, a sunset avenue,
And whippoorwills that haunt the moon,
Is all I ask for me and you.

Dear heart, with wants so small and few,
And faith, that's better far than gold,
A lowly friend, a child or two,
To care for us when we are old,
Is all I ask for me and you.

Wedded
Emily Dickinson

A solemn thing it was, I said,
A woman white to be,
And wear, if God should count me fit,
Her hallowed mystery.

A timid thing to drop a life
Into the purple well,
Too plummetless that it come back
Eternity until.

A Song
Paul Laurence Dunbar

On a summer's day as I sat by a stream,
A dainty maid came by,
And she blessed my sight like a rosy dream,
And left me there to sigh, to sigh,
And left me there to sigh, to sigh.

On another day as I sat by the stream,
This maiden paused a while,
Then I made me bold as I told my dream,
She heard it with a smile, a smile,
She heard it with a smile, a smile.

Oh, the months have fled and the autumn's red,
The maid no more goes by;
For my dream came true and the maid I wed,
And now no more I sigh, I sigh,
And now no more I sigh.

EULALIE
Edgar Allan Poe

I dwelt alone
    In a world of moan,
   And my soul was a stagnant tide,
Till the fair and gentle Eulalie became my blushing bride-
Till the yellow-haired young Eulalie became my smiling bride.

    Ah, less—less bright
    The stars of the night
Than the eyes of the radiant girl!
    That the vapor can make
   With the moon-tints of purple and pearl,
Can vie with the modest Eulalie's most unregarded curl—
Can compare with the bright-eyed Eulalie's most humble and careless curl.

    Now Doubt—now Pain
    Come never again,
  For her soul gives me sigh for sigh,
    And all day long
    Shines, bright and strong,
  Astarte within the sky,
While ever to her dear Eulalie upturns her matron eye—
While ever to her young Eulalie upturns her violet eye.

PUTTING IN THE SEED
Robert Frost

You come to fetch me from my work to-night
When supper's on the table, and we'll see
If I can leave off burying the white
Soft petals fallen from the apple tree.
 (Soft petals, yes, but not so barren quite,
Mingled with these, smooth bean and wrinkled pea;)
And go along with you ere you lose sight
Of what you came for and become like me,
Slave to a springtime passion for the earth.
How Love burns through the Putting in the Seed

On through the watching for that early birth
When, just as the soil tarnishes with weed,
The sturdy seedling with arched body comes
Shouldering its way and shedding the earth crumbs.

Truly Great

W. H. Davies

My walls outside must have some flowers,
My walls within must have some books;
A house that's small; a garden large,
And in it leafy nooks.

A little gold that's sure each week;
That comes not from my living kind,
But from a dead man in his grave,
Who cannot change his mind.

A lovely wife, and gentle too;
Contented that no eyes but mine
Can see her many charms, nor voice
To call her beauty fine.

Where she would in that stone cage live,
A self-made prisoner, with me;
While many a wild bird sang around,
On gate, on bush, on tree.

And she sometimes to answer them,
In her far sweeter voice than all;
Till birds, that loved to look on leaves,
Will doat on a stone wall.

With this small house, this garden large,
This little gold, this lovely mate,
With health in body, peace in heart—
Show me a man more great.

At The Wedding March

Gerard Manley Hopkins

God with honour hang your head,
Groom, and grace you, bride, your bed
With lissome scions, sweet scions,
Out of hallowed bodies bred.
Each be other's comfort kind:
Deep, deeper than divined,
Divine charity, dear charity,
Fast you ever, fast bind.
Then let the March tread our ears:
I to him turn with tears
Who to wedlock, his wonder wedlock,
Deals triumph and immortal years.

The Good-Morrow

John Donne

I wonder by my troth, what thou and I
Did, till we lov'd? Were we not wean'd till then,
But suck'd on country pleasures, childishly?
Or snorted we in the seven sleepers' den?
'Twas so; but this, all pleasures fancies be.
If ever any beauty I did see,
Which I desir'd, and got, 'twas but a dream of thee.

And now good morrow to our waking souls,
Which watch not one another out of fear;
For love, all love of other sights controls,
And makes one little room, an everywhere.
Let sea-discoverers to new worlds have gone,
Let maps to other, worlds on worlds have shown,
Let us possess one world, each hath one, and is one.

My face in thine eye, thine in mine appears,
And true plain hearts do in the faces rest;
Where can we find two better hemispheres,
Without sharp north, without declining west?
Whatever dies, was not mix'd equally;
If our two loves be one, or, thou and I
Love so alike, that none do slacken, none can die.

FIDELITY AND INFIDELITY

Love And Life

John Wilmot, *Second Earl of Rochester*

All my past life is mine no more,
The flying hours are gone,
Like transitory dreams giv'n o'er,
Whose images are kept in store
By memory alone.
The time that is to come is not;
How can it then be mine?
The present moment's all my lot;
And that, as fast as it is got,
Phyllis, is only thine.
Then talk not of inconstancy,
False hearts, and broken vows;
If I, by miracle, can be
This live-long minute true to thee,
'Tis all that Heav'n allows.

Song

John Donne

Go and catch a falling star,
        with child a mandrake root,
Tell me where all past years are,
        Or who cleft the Devil's foot,
Teach me to hear mermaids singing,
Or to keep off envy's stinging,
        And find
        What wind
Serves to advance an honest mind.

If thou beest born to strange sights,
        Things invisible to see,
Ride ten thousand days and nights,
        Till age snow white hairs on thee,
Thou, when thou return'st, wilt tell me
All strange wonders that befell thee,
        And swear
        No where

Lives a woman true, and fair.
If thou find'st one, let me know,
        Such a pilgrimage were sweet;
Yet do not, I would not go,
        Though at next door we might meet;
Though she were true when you met her,
And last till you write your letter,
        Yet she
        Will be
False, ere I come, to two, or three.

$\mathcal{A}$s I Roved Out

Traditional Irish Folk Song

As I roved out on a bright May morning
To view the meadows and flowers gay
Whom should I spy but my own true lover
As she sat under yon willow tree
I took off my hat and I did salute her
I did salute her most courageously
When she turned around well the tears fell from her
Sayin' "False young man, you have deluded me
A diamond ring I owned I gave you
A diamond ring to wear on your right hand
But the vows you made, love, you went and broke them
And married the lassie that had the land."
"If I'd married the lassie that had the land, my love
It's that I'll rue till the day I die
When misfortune falls sure no man can shun it
I was blindfolded I'll ne'er deny."
Now at nights when I go to my bed of slumber
The thoughts of my true love run in my mind
When I turned around to embrace my darling
Instead of gold sure it's brass I find
And I wish the Queen would call home her army
From the West Indies, Amerikay and Spain
And every man to his wedded woman
In hopes that you and I will meet again.

For My Lover, Returning To His Wife

Anne Sexton

She is all there.
She was melted carefully down for you
and cast up from your childhood,
cast up from your one hundred favorite aggies.

She has always been there, my darling.
She is, in fact, exquisite.
Fireworks in the dull middle of February
and as real as a cast-iron pot.

Let's face it, I have been a momentary.
A luxury. A bright red sloop in the harbor.
My hair rising like smoke from the car window.
Littleneck clams out of season.

She is more than that. She is your have to have,
has grown you your practical your tropical growth.
This is not an experiment. She is all harmony.
She sees to oars and oarlocks for the dinghy,

has placed wild flowers at the window at breakfast,
sat by the potter's wheel at midday,
set forth three children under the moon,
three cherubs drawn by Michelangelo,

done this with her legs spread out
in the terrible months in the chapel.
If you glance up, the children are there
like delicate balloons resting on the ceiling.

She has also carried each one down the hall
after supper, their heads privately bent,
two legs protesting, person to person,
her face flushed with a song and their little sleep.

I give you back your heart.
I give you permission—

for the fuse inside her, throbbing
angrily in the dirt, for the bitch in her

and the burying of her wound—
for the burying of her small red wound alive—

for the pale flickering flare under her ribs,
for the drunken sailor who waits in her left pulse,
for the mother's knee, for the stockings,
for the garter belts, for the call—

the curious call
when you will burrow in arms and breasts
and tug at the orange ribbon in her hair
and answer the call, the curious call.

She is so naked and singular.
She is the sum of yourself and your dream.
Climb her like a monument, step after step.
She is solid.

As for me, I am a watercolor.
I wash off.

*S*ONG: TO MY INCONSTANT MISTRESS
Thomas Carew

When thou, poor excommunicate
From all the joys of love, shalt see
The full reward and glorious fate
Which my strong faith shall purchase me,
Then curse thine own inconstancy.
A fairer hand than thine shall cure
That heart, which thy false oaths did wound;
And to my soul, a soul more pureThan thine shall by
Love's hand be bound, And both with equal glory crown'd.
Then shalt thou weep, entreat, complain
To Love, as I did once to thee;
When all thy tears shall be as vain
As mine were then, for thou shalt be
Damn'd for thy false apostasy.

Song
Robert Burns

O whistle, and I'll come to ye, my lad,
O whistle, and I'll come to ye my lad;
Tho' father, and mother, and a' should gae mad,
  Thy Jeanie will venture wi' he, my lad.

But warily tent, fwhen ye come to court me,
And come nae unless the back-yett be a-jee;
Syne up the back-style and let naebody see,
  And come as ye were na comin to me -
  And come as ye were no comin to me. -
   O whistle etc.

At kirk, or at market whene'er ye meet me,
Gang by me as tho—that ye car'd nae a fie;
But steal me ablink o' your bonie black e'e,
  Yet look as ye were na lookin at me -
  Yet look as ye were na lookin at me. -
   O whistle etc.

Ay vow and protest that ye care na for me,
And whyles ye may lightly my beauty a wee;
But court nae anither, tho' jokin ye be,
  For fear that she wyle your fancy frae me -
  For fear that she wyle your fancy frae me. -

Non Sum Qualis Eram Bonae Sub Regno Cynarae
("I am not quite as I was under the rule of the beautiful Cynara")
Ernest Dowson

Last night, ah, yesternight, betwixt her lips and mine
  There fell thy shadow, Cynara! Thy breath was shed
Upon my soul between the kisses and the wine;
  And I was desolate and sick of an old passion,
   Yea, I was desolate and bowed my head:
I have been faithful to thee, Cynara! In my fashion.

All night upon mine heart I felt her warm heart beat,
  Night-long within mine arms in love and sleep she lay;
Surely the kisses of her bought red mouth were sweet;

But I was desolate and sick of an old passion,
    When I awoke and found the dawn was gray:
I have been faithful to thee, Cynara! In my fashion.

I have forgot much, Cynara! Gone with the wind,
    Flung roses, roses riotously with the throng,
Dancing, to put thy pale, lost lilies out of mind;
    But I was desolate and sick of an old passion,
        Yea, all the time, because the dance was long:
I have been faithful to thee, Cynara! In my fashion.

I cried for madder music and for stronger wine,
    But when the feast is finished and the lamps expire,
Then falls thy shadow, Cynara! The night is thine,
    And I am desolate and sick of an old passion,
        Yea hungry for the lips of my desire:
I have been faithful to thee, Cynara! In my fashion.

THE HANDS OF THE BETROTHED

D. H. Lawrence

Her tawny eyes are onyx of thoughtlessness,
Hardened they are like gems in ancient modesty;
Yea, and her mouth's prudent and crude caress
Means even less than her many words to me.
Though her kiss betrays me also this, this only
Consolation, that in her lips her blood at climax clips
Two wild, dumb paws in anguish on the lonely
Fruit of my heart, ere down, rebuked, it slips.
I know from her hardened lips that still her heart is
Hungry for me, yet if I put my hand in her breast
She puts me away, like a saleswoman whose mart is
Endangered by the pilferer on his quest.
But her hands are still the woman, the large, strong hands
Heavier than mine, yet like leverets caught in steel
When I hold them; my still soul understands
Their dumb confession of what her sort must feel.
For never her hands come nigh me but they lift
Like heavy birds from the morning stubble, to settle
Upon me like sleeping birds, like birds that shift
Uneasily in their sleep, disturbing my mettle.

How caressingly she lays her hand on my knee,
How strangely she tries to disown it, as it sinks
In my flesh and bone and forages into me,
How it stirs like a subtle stoat, whatever she thinks!
And often I see her clench her fingers tight
And thrust her fists suppressed in the folds of her skirt;
And sometimes, how she grasps her arms with her bright
Big hands, as if surely her arms did hurt.
And I have seen her stand all unaware
Pressing her spread hands over her breasts, as she
Would crush their mounds on her heart, to kill in there
The pain that is her simple ache for me.
Her strong hands take my part, the part of a man
To her; she crushes them into her bosom deep
Where I should lie, and with her own strong span
Closes her arms, that should fold me in sleep.
Ah, and she puts her hands upon the wall,
Presses them there, and kisses her bright hands,
Then lets her black hair loose, the darkness fall
About her from her maiden-folded bands.
And sits in her own dark night of her bitter hair
Dreaming—God knows of what, for to me she's the same
Betrothed young lady who loves me, and takes care
Of her womanly virtue and of my good name.

*D*OVER BEACH
Matthew Arnold

The sea is calm tonight.
The tide is full, the moon lies fair
Upon the straits;— on the French coast the light
Gleams and is gone; the cliffs of England stand,
Glimmering and vast, out in the tranquil bay.
Come to the window, sweet is the night-air!
Only, from the long line of spray
Where the sea meets the moon-blanched land,
Listen! you hear the grating roar
Of pebbles which the waves draw back, and fling,

At their return, up the high strand,
Begin, and cease, and then again begin,
With tremulous cadence slow, and bring
The eternal note of sadness in.

Sophocles long ago
Heard it on the Aegean, and it brought
Into his mind the turbid ebb and flow
Of human misery; we
Find also in the sound a thought,
Hearing it by this distant northern sea.

The Sea of Faith
Was once, too, at the full, and round earth's shore
Lay like the folds of a bright girdle furled.
But now I only hear
Its melancholy, long, withdrawing roar,
Retreating, to the breath
Of the night-wind, down the vast edges drear
And naked shingles of the world.

Ah, love, let us be true
To one another! for the world, which seems
To be before us like a land of dreams,
So various, so beautiful, so new,
Hath really neither joy, nor love, nor light,
Nor certitude, nor peace, nor help for pain;
And we are here as on a darkling plain
Swept with confused alarms of struggle and flight,
Where ignorant armies clash by night.

The Hunt Is Up

Traditional, English

The hunt is up, the hunt is up
And now it is almost day
And he that's abed with another man's wife
It's time to get him away

GREEN BUSHES

Traditional, English

As I was a walking one morning in May
To hear the birds whistle and see the lambkins play
I espied a young damsel, so sweetly sang she
Down by the green bushes where she chanced to meet me
"Oh why are you loitering here, pretty maid?"
"I am waiting for my true love, " softly she said
"Shall I be your true love and will you agree
Down by the green bushes to tarry with me?
I will give you fine beavers and fine silken gowns
I will give you smart petticoats flounced to the ground
I will give you fine jewels and live just for thee
If you'll leave your own true love and marry with me"
"I want none of your beavers or fine silken hose
For I'm not so poor as to marry for clothes
But if you be constant and true unto me
I'll leave my own true love and marry with thee
Come let us be going, kind sir, if you please
Come let us be going from under these trees
For yonder is coming, my true love I see
Down by the green bushes where he thinks to meet me"
And when he came there and found she was gone
He looked very foolish and cried quite forlorn
"She's gone with a lover and forsaken me
And left the green bushes where she vowed to meet me"

TO HIS MISTRESS

Ovid

Your husband will be with us at the treat;
May that be the last supper he shall eat.
And am poor I, a guest invited there,
Only to see, while he may touch the Fair?
To see you kiss and hug your nauseous Lord,
While his lewd hand descends below the board?
Now wonder not that Hippodamia's charms,
At such a sight, the Centaurs urged to arms;
That in a rage they threw their cups aside,

Assailed the bridegroom, and would force the bride.
I am not half a horse (I would I were):
Yet hardly can from you my hands forbear.
Take then my counsel; which, observed, may be
Of some importance both to you and me.
Be sure to come before your man be there;
There's nothing can be done; but come how'er.
Sit next him (that belongs to decency);
But tread upon my foot in passing by.
Read in my looks what silently they speak,
And slyly, with your eyes, your answer make.
My right-hand to his fellow shall complain;
And on the back a letter shall design;
Besides a note that shall be writ in wine.
When'er you think upon our last embrace,
With your forefinger gently touch your face.
If any word of mine offend my dear,
Pull, with your hand, the velvet of your ear.
If you are please with what I do or say,
Handle your rings, or with your fingers play.
As suppliants use at altars, hold the board,
When'er you wish the Devil may take your Lord.
When he fills for you, never touch the cup;
But bid th' officious cuckold drink it up.
The waiter on those services employ.
Drink you, and I will snatch it from the boy:
Watching the part where your sweet mouth hath been,
And thence, with eager lips, will suck it in.
If he, with clownish manners, thinks it fit
To taste, and offer you the nasty bit,
Reject his greasy kindness, and restore
Th' unsavory morsel he had chewed before
Nor let his arms embrace your neck, nor rest
Your tender cheek upon his hairy breast.
Let not his hand within your bosom stray,
And rudely with your pretty bubbies play.
But above all, let him no kiss receive;
that's an offence I never can forgive.
Do not, O do not that sweet mouth resign,
Lest I rise up in arms, and cry, 'Tis mine.

I shall thrust in betwixt, and void of fear
The manifest adulterer will appear.
These things are plain to sight; but more I doubt
What you conceal beneath your petticoat.
Take not his leg between your tender thighs,
Nor, with your hand, provoke my foe to rise.
How many love-inventions I deplore,
Which I, myself, have practised all before!
How oft have I been forced the robe to lift
In company to make a homely shift
For a bare bout, ill huddled o'er in haste,
While o'er my side the Fair her mantle cast.
You to your husband shall not be so kind;
But, lest you should, your mantle leave behind.
Encourage him to tope; but kiss him not,
Nor mix one drop of water in his pot.
If he be fuddled well, and snores apace
then we may take advice from Time and Place.
When all depart, when compliments are loud,
Be sure to mix among the thickest crowd.
There I will be, and there we cannot miss,
Perhaps to grubble, or at least to kiss.
Alas, what length of labour I employ,
Just to secure a short and transient joy!
For night must part us; and when night is come,
Tucked underneath his arms he leads you home.
He locks you in; I follow to the door,
His fortune envy, and my own deplore.
He kisses you, he more than kisses too;
Th' outrageous cuckold thinks it all his due.
But, add not to his joy, by your consent,
And let it not be given, but only lent.
Return no kiss, nor move in any sort;
Make it a dull and malignant sport.
Had I my wish, he should no pleasure take,
But slubber o'er your business for my sake.
And what e'er Fortune shall this night befall,
Coax me tomorrow, by forswearing all.

THE SCRUTINY

Richard Lovelace

Why should you swear I am foresworn,
Since thine I vowed to be?
Lady it is already morn,
And 'twas last night I swore to thee
That fond impossibility.

Have I not loved thee much and long,
A tedious twelve hours' space?
I must all other Beauties wrong,
And rob thee of a new embrace;
Could I still dote upon thy face.

Not, but all joy in thy brown hair,
By others may be found;
But I must search the black and fair
Like skillful mineralists that sound
For treasure in un-plowed-up ground.

Then, if when I have loved my round.
Thou provest the pleasant she;
With spoils of meaner Beauties crowned,
I laden will return to thee,
Ev'n sated with variety.

OH, NO JOHN

Traduitional, English

On yonder hill there stands a maiden
Who she is I do not know;
I shall court her, for her beauty,
She must answer yes or no,
    Oh, Oh, no John,
    No John, No John, No.
Madam, on thy face is beauty
On thy lips wild roses grow,
Madam, I would be thy lover,
Madam, answer yes or no,
Madam, on thy face is beauty,

At thy bosom lilies grow,
In your bedroom there is pleasure,
Shall I view it? Yes or no.
Madam, I will give you jewels
I will make you rich and free;
I will give you silk and satins
Madam, if you lie with me.
"My husband is a Spanish captain,
Went to sea a month ago.
First he kissed me, then he left me,
Bade me always answer 'No!'"
Madam, may I tie your garter
Just an inch above your knee?
If my hand should slip a little farther,
Would you think it ill of me?
My love and I went to bed together,
There we lay till the cocks did crow;
Open your arms my dearest darling,
Open your arms and let me go.

$\mathcal{A}$s I Walked Out

Traditional, Scots

As I walked out on an evening so clear,
A young man lamented for the loss of his dear;
And as he lamented, full sore did he cry,
Saying, "Alas, I'm tormented, for love I must die.
My dear and my jewel, my honey," said he,
"Will you let me gang wi' you a sweetheart to be?
And my dear and my jewel, my honey," said he,
"Will you let me gang wi' you a sweetheart to be?"
"Were I to say yea, I would say 'gainst my mind,
And for to say no, you would think I was unkind
For to sit and say nothing, you would say I was dumb,
So take that for your answer and go as you come."
"Oh, pox take you, Sally, for you are unkind.
You pulled the lily, left the red rose behind,
But the lily will yellow, and the time will come soon,
When the red rose will flourish in the sweet month of June."
"Oh, some court for beauty, but beauty soon fades,

Others marry for riches, get bold saucy jades,
But if I ever marry, as plain as you may see,
The wee lass that's loyal is the darling for me."

*F*INE KNACKS FOR LADIES

Anonymous

Fine knacks for ladies, cheap, choice, brave and new!
Good pennyworths-but money cannot move:
I keep a fair but for the fair to view;
A beggar may be liberal of love.
Though all my wares be trash, the heart is true,
    The heart is true.

Great gifts are guiles and look for gifts again;
My trifles come as treasures from my mind.
It is a precious jewel to be plain;
Sometimes in shell the orient'st pearls we find.
Of others take a sheaf, of me a grain!
    Of me a grain!

Within this pack pins, points, laces, and gloves,
And divers toys fitting a country fair;
But in my heart, where duty serves and loves,
Turtles and twins, court's brood, a heavenly pair.
Happy the heart that thinks of no removes!
    Of no removes!

*S*ONNET 105

William Shakespeare

Let not my love be called idolatry,
Nor my belove'd as an idol show,
Since all alike my songs and praises be
To one, of one, still such, and ever so.
Kind is my love today, tomorrow kind,
Still constant in a wondrous excellence
Therefore my verse, to constancy confined,
One thing expressing, leaves out difference.
Fair, kind, and true is all my argument,

Fair, kind, and true, varying to other words;
And in this change is my invention spent,
Three themes in one, which wondrous scope affords.
    Fair, kind, and true, have often lived alone,
    Which three till now never kept seat in one.

$\mathscr{I}$T WAS DEEP APRIL
Michael Field

It was deep April, and the morn
Shakespeare was born;
The world was on us, pressing sore;
My love and I took hands and swore,
Against the world, to be
Poets and lovers evermore,
To laugh and dream on Lethe's shore,
To sing to Charon in his boat,
Heartening the timid souls afloat;
Of judgement never to take heed,
But to those fast-locked souls to speed,
    Who never from Apollo fled,
    Who spent no hour among the dead;
    Continually
    With them to dwell,
    Indifferent to heaven and hell.

$\mathscr{S}$ONNET 138
William Shakespeare

When my love swears that she is made of truth,
I do believe her though I know she lies,
That she might think me some untutored youth,
Unlearned in the world's false subtleties.
Thus vainly thinking that she thinks me young,
Although she knows my days are past the best,
Simply I credit her false-speaking tongue
On both sides thus is simple truth suppressed.
But wherefore says she not she is unjust?
And wherefore say not I that I am old?

O, love's best habit is in seeming trust,
And age in love, loves not to have years told.
Therefore I lie with her, and she with me,
And in our faults by lies we flattered be.

Sonnet 53

William Shakespeare

What is your substance, whereof are you made,
That millions of strange shadows on you tend?
Since every one hath, every one, one shade,
And you, but one, can every shadow lend.
Describe Adonis and the counterfeit,
Is poorly imitated after you;
On Helen's cheek all art of beauty set,
And you in Grecian tires are painted new.
Speak of the spring, and foison of the year;
The one doth shadow of your beauty show,
The other as your bounty doth appear,
And you in every blessed shape we know.
In all external grace you have some part,
But you like none, none you, for constant heart.

Guilt

John Betjeman

The clock is frozen in the tower,
The thickening fog with sooty smell
Has blanketed the motor power
Which turns the London streets to hell;
And footsteps with their lonely sound
Intensify the silence round.

I haven't hope. I haven't faith.
I live two lives and sometimes three.
The lives I live make life a death
For those who have to live with me.
Knowing the virtues that I lack,
I pat myself upon the back.

With breastplate of self-righteousness
And shoes of smugness on my feet,
Before the urge in me grows less
I hurry off to make retreat,
For somewhere, somewhere, burns a light
To lead me out into the night.

It glitters icy, thin and plain,
And leads me down to Waterloo—
Into a warm electric train
Which travels sorry Surrey through
And crystal-hung the clumps of pine
Stand deadly still beside the line.

What Should I Say

Thomas Wyatt

What should I say,
　Since faith is dead,
And truth away
　From you is fled?
　Should I be led
　With doubleness?
　Nay, nay, Mistress!

I promised you,
　And you promised me,
To be as true
　As I would be;
　But since I see
　Your double heart,
　Farewell my part!

Though for to take
　It is not my mind,
But to forsake,
　I am not blind,
　And as I find,
　So will I trust.
　Farewell, unjust!

Can ye say nay
　But you said
That I always
　Should be obeyed?
　And thus betrayed
　Or that I wist
　Farewell, unkist!

Sapphic Stanzas

Alexander Radishchev

Icy cold the night was, in heaven the vrilliant
Stars were shining, silently flowed the waters,
Gently blew the night-wind, and gently whispered
　　Leaves of white poplars.

Vows of deathless constancy thou didst utter;
Sweet the pledge the goddess of darkness gave me;
Roared the blasts of winter, but once and all those
　　Vows were forgotten.

Why those rash vows? O it were surely better
Far if thou hadst always been cruel, less would
I have suffered. Thou with thy false words lured me
　　Down to destruction.

Cruel art thou, destiny; take my lf but
Only keep her constancy still unspotted.
Happy mayst thou be if thou canst be only
　　Happy without love.

*O*h, When I Was In Love With You

A.E. Houseman

Oh, when I was in love with you,
    Then I was clean and brave,
And miles around the wonder grew
    How well did I behave.
And now the fancy passes by,
    And nothing will remain,
And miles around they 'll say that I
    Am quite myself again.

VII

e e cummings

O Distinct Lady of my unkempt adoration if
I have made a fragile curtain
  song under the window of your soul it is not like any songs
(the singers the others they have been faithful
    to many things and which die i have been sometimes true to
  Nothing and which lives
    they were fond of the handsome moon
    never spoke ill of the pretty stars
    and to the serene the complicated
  and the obvious
  they were faithful and which i despise, frankly
    admitting i have been true only to the noise of worms in the eligible day under the
    unaccountable sun)
Distinct Lady swiftly take my fragile certain song that we may watch together
    how behind the doomed exact smile of life's placid obscure palpable carnival
    where to a normal
melody of probable violins dance the square virtues with the oblong sins perfectly
    gesticulate the accurate
    strenuous lips of incorruptible
  Nothing
under the ample sun, under the insufficient day under the noise of worms

Sonnet 41

William Shakespeare

Those pretty wrongs that liberty commits,
When I am sometime absent from thy heart,
Thy beauty and thy years full well befits,
For still temptation follows where thou art.
Gentle thou art, and therefore to be won;
Beauteous thou art, therefore to be assailed;
And when a woman woos, what woman's son
Will sourly leave her tills he have prevailed?
Ay me, but yet thou mightst my seat forbear,
And chide thy beauty, and thy straying youth,
Who lead thee in their riot even there
Where thou art forced to break a twofold truth:
    Hers, by thy beauty tempting her to thee,
    Thine, by thy beauty being false to me.

Daphnis and Chloe

Andrew Marvell

Daphnis must from Chloe part:
Now is come the dismal Hour
That must all his Hopes devour,
All his Labour, all his Art.
Nature, her own Sexes foe,
Long had taught her to be coy:
But she neither knew t' enjoy,
Nor yet let her Lover go.
But, with this sad News surpriz'd,
Soon she let that Niceness fall;
 And would gladly yield to all,
So it had his stay compriz'd.

Nature so her self does use
To lay by her wonted State,
Left the World should separate;
Sudden Parting closer glews.
He, well read in all the wayes
By which men their Siege maintain,

Knew not that the Fort to gain
Better 'twas the siege to raise.
But he came so full possest
With the Grief of Parting thence,
That he had not so much Sence
As to see he might be blest.
Till Love in her Language breath'd
Words she never spake before;
But then Legacies no more
To a dying Man bequeath'd.
For, Alas, the time was spent,
Now the latest minut's run
When poor Daphnis is undone,
Between Joy and Sorrow rent.
At that Why, that Stay my Dear,
His disorder'd Locks he tare;
And with rouling Eyes did glare,
And his cruel Fate forswear.

As the Soul of one scarce dead,
With the shrieks of Friends aghast,
Looks distracted back in hast,
And then streight again is fled.
So did wretched Daphnis look,
Frighting her he loved most.
At the last, this Lovers Ghost
Thus his Leave resolved took.
Are my Hell and Heaven
Joyn'd More to torture him that dies?
Could departure not suffice,
But that you must then grow kind?
Ah my Chloe how have I
Such a wretched minute found,
When thy Favours should me wound
More than all thy Cruelty?
So to the condemned Wight
The delicious Cup we fill;
And allow him all he will,
For his last and short Delight.
But I will not now begin

Such a Debt unto my Foe;
Nor to my Departure owe
What my Presence could not win.

Absence is too much alone:
Better 'tis to go in peace,
Than my Losses to increase
By a late Fruition.
Why should I enrich my Fate?
'Tis a Vanity to wear,
For my Executioner, Jewels of so high a rate.
Rather I away will pine
In a manly stubborness
Than be fatted up express
For the Canibal to dine.
Whilst this grief does thee disarm,
All th' Enjoyment of our Love
But the ravishment would prove
Of a Body dead while warm.
And I parting should appear
Like the Gourmand Hebrew dead,
While he Quailes and Manna fed,
And does through the Desert err.
Or the Witch that midnight wakes
For the Fern, whose magick Weed
In one minute casts the Seed.
And invisible him makes.

Gentler times for Love are ment:
Who for parting pleasure strain
Gather Roses in the rain,
Wet themselves and spoil their Sent.
Farewel therefore all the fruit
Which I could from Love receive:
Joy will not with Sorrow weave,
Nor will I this Grief pollute.
Fate I come, as dark, as sad,
As thy Malice could desire;
Yet bring with me all the Fire
That Love in his Torches had.

At these words away he broke;
As who long has praying ly'n,
To his Heads-man makes the Sign,
And receives the parting stroke.
But hence Virgins all beware.
Last night he with Phlogis slept;
This night for Dorinda kept;
And but rid to take the Air.
Yet he does himself excuse;
Nor indeed without a Cause.
For, according to the Lawes,
Why did Chloe once refuse?

*T*HE SAILOR'S WIFE SPEAKS
Don Marquis

Ye are dead, they say, but ye swore, ye swore,
Ye would come to me back from the sea!
From out of the sea and the night, ye cried,
Nor the crawling weed nor the dragging tide
Could hold ye fast from me:
—Come, ah, come to me!
Three spells I have laid on the rising sun
And three on the waning moon
Are ye held in the bonds of the night or the day
Ye must loosen your bonds and away, away!
Ye must come where I wait ye, soon
Ah, soon! soon! soon!
Three times I have cast my words to the wind,
And thrice to the climbing sea;
If ye drift or dream with the clouds or foam
Ye must drift again home, ye must drift again home
Wraith, ye are free, ye are free;
Ghost, ye are free, ye are free!
Are the coasts of death so fair, so fair?
But I wait ye here on the shore!
It is I that ye hear in the calling wind
I have stared through the dark till my soul is blind!
O lover of mine, ye swore, Lover of mine, ye swore!

$\mathcal{G}$OING AWAY, COMING BACK

Amber Coverdale Sumrall

Driving Laguna Canyon after midnight
we do not talk for a long time, though it has
been months since we were last together.
Sadness rides with us and the waning moon,
Finally you speak of your father
dead now three years. How you've never cried
for him, the only man you loved.
I say nothing. My white bird dead three days,
the one who flew to my fingers
her songs like falling water. Already
I have wept for much more than her passing.
The Big Dipper lies on its side in the winter sky,
its handle points below the horizon. Everything
is changing its shape or position. Going away.
Coming back. We hide our losses only to find them
years later, like downed limbs blocking our way.
Grief, the old bear that slumbers in us.

We stop for cigarettes, tequila, fill the hours
before dawn with all the necessary stories.
Who you're seeing. Why I'm still married.
A surplus of words to keep our bodies apart,
the dark cave of our mouths. The lovers
we once were look back from our eyes.
In the morning we read the Sunday Times,
watch your neighbors leave for Mass.
Next door someone sinks nails into wood,
a woman sings arias as she prepares chorizo.
I cannot sleep alone in your bed,
you on the couch doing what is right.
When I close my eyes the shy brown-skinned boy
in your kitchen photograph enters the room,
the one who has not yet learned to hold
so much inside. When I take him in my arms
touch becomes unbearable, as if small bones
are breaking just beneath the surface of my skin.

Loves Alchemy

John Donne

Some that have deeper digg'd love's mine than I,
Say, where his centric happiness doth lie;
I have lov'd, and got, and told,
But should I love, get, tell, till I were old,
I should not find that hidden mystery.
Oh, 'tis imposture all!
And as no chemic yet th'elixir got,
But glorifies his pregnant pot
If by the way to him befall
Some odoriferous thing, or medicinal,
So, lovers dream a rich and long delight,
But get a winter-seeming summer's night.

Our ease, our thrift, our honour, and our day,
Shall we for this vain bubble's shadow pay?
Ends love in this, that my man
Can be as happy'as I can, if he can
Endure the short scorn of a bridegroom's play?
That loving wretch that swears
Tis not the bodies marry, but the minds,
Which he in her angelic finds,
Would swear as justly that he hears,
In that day's rude hoarse minstrelsy, the spheres.
Hope not for mind in women; at their best
Sweetness and wit, they'are but mummy, possess'd.

Wishes To His (Supposed) Mistress

Richard Crashaw

Who e'er she be
That not impossible she
That shall command my heart and me;

Where'er she lie,
Lock'd up from mortal eye
In shady leaves of destiny;

Till that ripe birth
Of studied fate stand forth
And teach her fair steps to our earth;

Till that divine
Idea take a shrine
Of crystal flesh, through which to shine;

Meet you her, my wishes,
Bespeak her to my blisses,
And be ye call'd my absent kisses.

I wish her beauty
That owes not all his duty
To gaudy tire, or glist'ring shoe-ty.

Something more than
Taffeta or tissue can,
Or rampant feather, or rich fan.

More than the spoil
Of shop, or silkworm's toil,
Or a bought blush, or a set smile.

A face that's best
By its own beauty drest,
And can alone command the rest.

A face made up
Out of no other shop
Than what nature's white hand sets ope.

A cheek where youth,
And blood, with pen of truth
Write, what the reader sweetly ru'th.

A cheek where grows
More than a morning rose,
Which to no box his being owes.

Lips, where all day
A lover's kiss may play,
Yet carry nothing thence away.

Looks that oppress
Their richest tires, but dress
And clothe their simplest nakedness.

Eyes, that displaces
The neighbour diamond, and outfaces
That sunshine, by their own sweet graces.

Tresses, that wear
Jewels but to declare
How much themselves more precious are.

Whose native ray
Can tame the wanton day
Of gems, that in their bright shades play.

Each ruby there,
Or pearl that dare appear,
Be its own blush, be its own tear.

A well-tam'd heart,
For whose more noble smart
Love may be long choosing a dart.

Eyes, that bestow
Full quivers on Love's bow,
Yet pay less arrows than they owe.

Smiles, that can warm
The blood, yet teach a charm,
That chastity shall take no harm.

Blushes, that bin
The burnish of no sin,
Nor flames of aught too hot within.

Joys, that confess
Virtue their mistress,
And have no other head to dress.

Fears, fond and flight
As the coy bride's when night
First does the longing lover right.

Tears, quickly fled,
And vain, as those are shed
For a dying maidenhead.

Days, that need borrow
No part of their good morrow
From a forespent night of sorrow.

Days, that in spite
Of darkness, by the light
Of a clear mind are day all night.

Nights, sweet as they,
Made short by lovers' play,
Yet long by th' absence of the day.

Life, that dares send
A challenge to his end,
And when it comes say, "Welcome friend."

Sidneian showers
Of sweet discourse, whose powers
Can crown old Winter's head with flowers.

Soft silken hours,
Open suns, shady bowers,
'Bove all, nothing within that lours.

Whate'er delight
Can make Day's forehead bright,
Or give down to the wings of Night.

In her whole frame
Have nature all the name,
Art and ornament the shame.

Her flattery,
Picture and poesy,
Her counsel her own virtue be.

I wish, her store
Of worth may leave her poor
Of wishes, and I wish—no more.

Now if time knows
That her whose radiant brows
Weave them a garland of my vows,

Her whose just bays
My future hopes can raise,
A trophy to her present praise;

Her that dares be
What these lines wish to see:
I seek no further, it is she.

'Tis she, and here,
Lo, I unclothe and clear
My wishes' cloudy character.

May she enjoy it,
Whose merit dare apply it,
But modesty dares still deny it.

Such worth as this is
Shall fix my flying wishes,
And determine them to kisses.

Let her full glory,
My fancies, fly before ye;
Be ye my fictions; but her story.

To My Inconstant Mistress

Thomas Carew

When thou, poor excommunicate
From all the joys of love, shalt see
The full reward and glorious fate
Which my strong faith shall purchase me,
Then curse thine own inconstancy.

A fairer hand than thine shall cure
That heart, which thy false oaths did wound;
And to my soul, a soul more pure
Than thine shall by Love's hand be bound,
And both with equal glory crown'd.

Then shalt thou weep, entreat, complain
To Love, as I did once to thee;
When all thy tears shall be as vain
As mine were then, for thou shalt be
Damn'd for thy false apostasy.

$\mathcal{M}$ANON LESCAUT
Abbe Prevost

We sat down side by side. I took her hands in mine. Ah Manon! said I, gazing at her with sad eyes, I had not a thought of the black treachery with which you repaid my love. It was easy for you to deceive a heart of which you were absolute sovereign, and whose whole happiness was set in pleasing and obeying you. Tell me, have you found any since as tender and as submssive? No, no. Nature will hardly have made another of the same temper. Tell me at least if you have sometimes regretted it? What am I to count on in this return of tenderness that brings you here to comfort me? I see only too well that you are lovelier than ever: but in the name of all the grief that I have suffered from you, tell me, lovely Manon, if you will be more faithful?

She made answer, telling me such touching things of her repentance, and bound herself to constancy with so many vows and protestations, that she softened me beyond my saying. Dearest Manon, I cried, profanely lingering the language of Love anad Theology, you are too adorable for a created thing. I feel my heart swept by an overpowering delight.

PARTING

The Chilterns

Rupert Brooke

Your hands, my dear, adorable,
Your lips of tenderness
—Oh, I've loved you faithfully and well,
Three years, or a bit less.
It wasn't a success.

Thank God, that's done! and I'll take the road,
Quit of my youth and you,
The Roman road to Wendover
By Tring and Lilley Hoo,
As a free man may do.

For youth goes over, the joys that fly,
The tears that follow fast;
And the dirtiest things we do must lie
Forgotten at the last;
Even love goes past.
What's left behind I shall not find,
The splendor and the pain;
The splash of sun, the shouting wind,
And the brave sting of rain,
I may not meet again.

But the years, that take the best away,
Give something in the end;
And a better friend than love have they,
For none to mar or mend,
That have themselves to friend.

I shall desire and I shall find
The best of my desires;
The autumn road, the mellow wind
That soothes the darkening shires.
And laughter, and inn-fires.

White mist about the black hedgerows,
The slumbering Midland plain,
The silence where the clover grows,

And the dead leaves in the lane,
Certainly, these remain.

And I shall find some girl perhaps,
And a better one than you,
With eyes as wise, but kindlier,
With lips as soft, but true.
And I daresay she will do.

The Maid's Lament
William Savage Landor

I loved him not; and yet, now he is gone,
I feel I am alone.
I check'd him while he spoke; yet, could he speak,
Alas! I would not check.
For reasons not to love him once I sought,
And wearied all my thought
To vex myself and him: I now would give
My love could he but live
Who lately lived for me, and, when he found
'Twas vain, in holy ground
He hid his face amid the shades of death!
I waste for him my breath
Who wasted his for me! but mine returns,
And this torn bosom burns
With stifling heat, heaving it up in sleep,
And waking me to weep
Tears that had melted his soft heart: for years
Wept he as bitter tears!
Merciful God! such was his latest prayer,
These may she never share.
Quieter is his breath, his breast more cold,
Than daisies in the mould,
Where childern spell, athwart the churchyard gate,
His name and life's brief date.
Pray for him, gentle souls, whoe'er you be,
And oh! pray too for me!

*G*ETTING OUT
Cleopatra Mathis

That year we hardly slept, waking like inmates
who beat the walls. Every night
another refusal, the silent work
of tightening the heart.
Exhausted, we gave up; escaped
to the apartment pool, swimming those laps
Until the first light relieved us.

Days were different: FM and full-blast
blues, hours of guitar "you gonna miss me
when I'm gone." Think of how you tried
to pack up and go, for weeks stumbling
over piles of clothing, the unstrung tennis rackets.
Finally locked into blame, we paced
that short hall, heaving words like furniture.

I have the last unshredded pictures
of our matching eyes and hair. We've kept
to separate sides of the map,
still I'm startled by men who look like you.
And in the yearly letter, you're sure to say
you're happy now. Yet I think of the lawyer's bewilderment
when we cried, the last day. Taking hands
we walked apart, until our arms stretched between us.
We held on tight, and let go.

*S*O WE'LL GO NO MORE A-ROVING
Lord Byron (George Gordon)

1. So we'll go no more a-roving
    So late into the night,
Though the heart be still as loving,
    And the moon be still as bright.

2. For the sword outwears its sheath,
    And the soul wears out the breast,
And the heart must pause to breathe,
    And Love itself have rest.

3. Though the night was made for loving,
      And the day returns too soon,
Yet we'll go no more a-roving
      By the light of the moon.

*A*FTER THE QUARREL
Paul Laurence Dunbar

So we, who've supped the self-same cup,
To-night must lay our friendship by;
Your wrath has burned your judgment up,
Hot breath has blown the ashes high.

You say that you are wronged— ah, well,
I count that friendship poor, at best
A bauble, a mere bagatelle,
That cannot stand so slight a test.

I fain would still have been your friend,
And talked and laughed and loved with you
But since it must, why, let it end; The false but dies,
'Tis not the true.

So we are favored, you and I,
Who only want the living truth.
It was not good to nurse the lie;
'Tis well it died in harmless youth.

I go from you to-night to sleep.
Why, what's the odds? why should I grieve?
I have no fund of tears to weep
For happenings that undeceive.

The days shall come, the days shall go
Just as they came and went before.
The sun shall shine, the streams shall flow
Though you and I are friends no more.

And in the volume of my years,
Where all my thoughts and acts shall be,
The page whereon your name appears
Shall be forever sealed to me.

Not that I hate you over-much,
'Tis less of hate than love defied;
Howe'er, our hands no more shall touch,
We'll go our ways, the world is wide.

$\mathscr{D}$ISDAIN RETURNED
Thomas Carew

He that loves a rosy cheek,
Or a coral lip admires,
Or from star-like eyes doth seek
Fuel to maintain his fires;
As old Time makes these decay,
So his flames must waste away.

But a smooth and steadfast mind,
Gentle thoughts and calm desires,
Hearts with equal love combin'd,
Kindle never-dying fires.
Where these are not, I despise
Lovely cheeks, or lips, or eyes.

No tears, Celia, now shall win
My resolv'd heart to return;
I have search'd thy soul within,
And find nought, but pride, and scorn;
I have learn'd thy arts, and now
Can disdain as much as thou.
Some power, in my revenge, convey
That love to her I cast away.

$\mathscr{P}$ARTED LOVERS
Yehuda Halevi

Wherefore, O fair one, dost withold thy messengers
From the lover whose frame is filled with the pains of thee?...
If parting be decreed for the two of us,
Stand yet a little while I gaze upon thy face...
By the life of love, remember the days of thy longing,
As I rememeber the nights of my delight.
As thine image passeth into my dreams,

Between me and thee roar the waves of a sea of tears
And I cannot pass over unto thee.
But O, if thy steps shoud draw nigh to cross—
Then would its waters be divided at the touch of thy foot.
Would that after my death unto mine ears should come
The sound of the golden bells upon my skirts!
Or shouldst thou be asking how fareth thy beloved,
I from the depths of the tomb
Would ask of thy love and welfare.
Verily, to the shedding of mine heart's blood
There be two witnesses, thy cheeks and thy lips.
How sayest thou it is not true, since these be my witnesses
For my blood, and that thine have shed it?
Why dearest thou my death, whilst I but desire
To add years unto the tears of thy life?
Though thou dost rob my slumber in the night of my longing,
Would I not give the sleep of mine eyes unto thy eyelids?...
Yea, betwen the bitter and the sweet standeth my heart —
The gall of parting, and the honey of thy kisses.
After thy words have beaten out my heart into plates,
Thine hands have cut it into shreds.
It is the likeness of rubies over pearls
What time I behold thy lips over thy teeth.
The sun is on thy face and thou spreadest out the night
Over his radiance with the clouds of thy locks.
Fine silk and broidered work are the covering of thine eyes.
The adornment of maidens is the work of human hands,
But thou - majesty and sweetness are thine adornment...
My sweet wild honey is between thy lips,
My spikenard and my myrrh between they breasts...
In the fioeld of the daughters of delight, the sheaves of love
Make obesiance unto thy sheaf...
I cannot hear thy voice, but I hear
Upon the secret places of my heart, the sound of thy steps.
On the day when thou wilt revive
The victims whom love for thee hath slain—on the day when the dead
    shall live anew,
Then turn again to my soul to restore it to my body; for on the day
Of thy departure, when thou wentest forth, it went out after thee...
Return, so our God shall restore thee to the haven
Of thy desire, and to the land of thy true belonging.

Sonnet XIX

Anna Seward

Farewell, false Friend!—our scenes of kindness close!
To cordial looks, to sunny smiles farewell!
To sweet consolings, that can grief expel,
And every joy soft sympathy bestows!
For alter'd looks, where truth no longer glows,
Thou hast prepared my heart;—and it was well
To bid thy pen th' unlook'd—for story tell,
Falsehood avow'd, that shame, nor sorrow knows.
O! when we meet,—(to meet we're destin'd, try
To avoid it as thou may'st) on either brow,
Nor in the stealing consciousness of eye,
Be seen the slightest trace of what, or how
We once were to each other;—nor one sigh
Flatter with weak regret a broken vow!

Parting

Emily Dickinson

My life closed twice before its close;
It yet remains to see
If Immortality unveil
A third event to me,
So huge, so hopeless to conceive,
As these that twice befell.
Parting is all we know of heaven,
And all we need of hell.

Go From My Window

Traditional, English

Go from my window, love, go;
Go from my window my dear.
The wind and rain
Will drive you back again
You cannot be lodged here.
Go from my window, love, go;
Go from my window my dear.

The wind is in the west
And the cuckoo's in the nest
You cannot be lodged here.
Go from my window, love, go;
Go from my window my dear.
The devil's in the man
And he cannot understand
That he cannot be lodged here.

Green Grow The Lilacs

Traditional, American

Green grow the lilacs, all sparkling with dew
I'm lonely, my darling, since parting with you;
But by our next meeting I'll hope to prove true
And change the green lilacs to the Red, White and Blue.

I once had a sweetheart, but now I have none
She's gone and she's left me, I care not for one
Since she's gone and left me, contented I'll be,
For she loves another one better than me.

I passed my love's window, both early and late
The look that she gave me, it makes my heart ache;
Oh, the look that she gave me was painful to see,
For she loves another one better than me.

I wrote my love letters in rosy red lines,
She sent me an answer all twisted with twine
Saying,"Keep your love letters and I will keep mine
Just you write to your love and I'll write to mine."

Fare Thee Well My Own True Love

Traditional, English

Farewell to Prince's Landing Stage
River Mersey, fare thee well
I am bound for California
A place I know right well

So fare thee well, my own true love
When I return united we will be
It's not the leaving of Liverpool that's grieving me
But my darling when I think of thee

I'm bound off for California
By the way of stormy Cape Horn
And I'm bound to write you a letter, love
When I am homeward bound

I have signed on a Yankee Clipper ship
Davy Crockett is her name

And Burgess is the Captain of her
And they say she's a floating Hell

I have shipped with Burgess once before
And I think I know him well
If a man's a seaman, he can get along
If not, then he's sure in Hell

Farewell to lower Frederick Street
Ensign Terrace and Park Lane
For I think it will be a long, long time
Before I see you again

Oh the sun is on the harbor, love
And I wish I could remain
For I know it will be a long, long time
Till I see you again

A Farewell

Harriet Monroe

Good-bye! — no, do not grieve that it is over,
The perfect hour;
That the winged joy, sweet honey-loving rover, Flits from the flower.
Grieve not — it is the law. Love will be flying —
Yes, love and all.
Glad was the living — blessed be the dying.
Let the leaves fall.

Go And Leave Me

Traditional, English and Irish

Once I loved with fond affection
All his thoughts they were of me
Until a dark girl did persuade him
Now he thinks no more of me
One hour he's happy with another
One that has great gold in store
While I poor girl am left broken-hearted
I'm left alone because I'm poor

So go and leave me if you wish, love
Never let me cross your mind
For if you think I'm so unworthy
Go and leave me I don't mind
Many's the day, love, with you I've rambled
Many was the night that with you I've spent
For I always thought you were mine forever
But now I know you were only lent
Here's the ring, love, which first you gave me
When our hearts they were entwined
Give it to that dark-haired lady
She'll never know that it once was mine
Many's the night, love, as you lie sleeping
Dreaming in your sweet repose
While I young girl lie broken-hearted
Listening to the wind that blows
Fare thee well friends and kind relations
Farewell to you, you false young man
'Tis you that has caused me pain and suffering
Never to return again

After

Lizette Woodward Reese

Oh, the littles that remain!
Scent of mint out in the lane;
Flare of window; sound of bees;
—These, but these.

Three times sitting down to bread;
One time climbing up to bed;
Table-setting o'er and o'er;
Drying herbs for winter's store;

This thing; that thing;
— nothing more.
But just now out in the lane,
Oh, the scent of mint was plain!

PRETTY SARA

Traditional, English

Down in some lone valley, in some lonesome place
Where the wild birds do whistle and their notes do increase
Farewell pretty Sara, I'll bid you adieu
And I'll dream of pretty Sara where ever I go
My love, she won't have me, so I understand
She wants a freeholder and I have no land
I can no maintain her with silver and gold
Nor buy all the fine things that a big house can hold
If I were a merchant and could write a fine hand
I'd write my love a letter so she'd understand
But I'll wander by the river where the waters o'erflow
And I'll dream of pretty Sara where ever I go

FAREWELL TO THE MUSE

Sir Walter Scott

Enchantress, farewell, who so oft hast decoy'd me,
At the close of the evening through woodlands to roam,
Where the forester, 'lated, with wonder espied me
Explore the wild scenes he was quitting for home.
Farewell and take with thee thy numbers wild speaking
The language alternate of rapture and woe:
Oh! none but some lover, whose heartstrings are breaking
The pang that I feel at our parting can know.
Each joy thou couldst double, and when there came sorrow,
Or pale disappointment to darken my way,
What voice was like thine, that could sing of tomorrow,
Till forgot in the strain was the grief of today!
But when friends drop around us in life's weary waning,
The grief, Queen of Numbers, thou canst not assuage;
Nor the gradual estrangement of those yet remaining,
The languor of pain, and the chillness of age.
'Twas thou that once taught me, accents bewailing,
To sing how a warrior I lay stretch'd on the plain,
And a maiden hung o'er him with aid unavailing,
And held to his lips the cold goblet in vain ;
As vain thy enchantments, O Queen of wild Numbers

To a bard when the reign of his fancy is o'er,
And the quick pulse of feeling in apathy slumbers—
Farewell, then, Enchantress

De L'Amour
Stendhal

She leaves you because she is too sure of you. You killed fear, and the little doubts of happy love can no longer be born; disquiet her and, above all, keep yourself from the absurdity of making protestations.

Red River Valley
James Kerrigan

From this valley they say you are going
We will miss your bright eyes and sweet smile
For they say you are taking the sunshine
That has brightened our path for a while.
    Come and sit by my side if you love me
    Do not hasten to bid me adieu
    But remember the Red River Valley
    And the cowboy who loved you so true.
Won't you think of the valley you're leaving
Oh how lonely, how sad it will be?
Oh think of the fond heart you're breaking
And the grief you are causing to me
As you go to your home by the ocean
May you never forget those sweet hours
That we spent in the Red River Valley
And the love we exchanged 'mid the flowers

I'll meet thee no more!

Isolation: To Marguerite
Sir Matthew Arnold

We were apart; yet, day by day,
I bade my heart more constant be.
I bade it keep the world away,
And grow a home for only thee;
Nor fear'd but thy love likewise grew,

Like mine, each day, more tried, more true.

The fault was grave! I might have known,
What far too soon, alas! I learn'd—
The heart can bind itself alone,
And faith may oft be unreturn'd.
Self-sway'd our feelings ebb and swell—
Thou lov'st no more;—Farewell! Farewell!

Farewell!—and thou, thou lonely heart,
Which never yet without remorse
Even for a moment didst depart
From thy remote and spher`ed course
To haunt the place where passions reign—
Back to thy solitude again!

Back! with the conscious thrill of shame
Which Luna felt, that summer-night,
Flash through her pure immortal frame,
When she forsook the starry height
To hang over Endymion's sleep
Upon the pine-grown Latmian steep.

Yet she, chaste queen, had never proved
How vain a thing is mortal love,
Wandering in Heaven, far removed.
But thou hast long had place to prove
This truth—to prove, and make thine own:
"Thou hast been, shalt be, art, alone."

Or, if not quite alone, yet they
Which touch thee are unmating things—
Ocean and clouds and night and day;
Lorn autumns and triumphant springs;
And life, and others' joy and pain,
And love, if love, of happier men.

Of happier men—for they, at least,
Have dream'd two human hearts might blend
In one, and were through faith released
From isolation without end
Prolong'd; nor knew, although not less
Alone than tho

When We Two Parted
Lord Byron (George Gordon)

When we two parted
In silence and tears,
Half broken-hearted
To sever for years,
Pale grew thy cheek and cold,
Colder thy kiss;
Truly that hour foretold
Sorrow to this.

The dew of the morning
Sunk chill on my brow—
It felt like the warning
Of what I feel now.
Thy vows are all broken,
And light is thy fame;
I hear thy name spoken,
And share in its shame.

They name thee before me,
A knell to mine ear;
A shudder comes o'er me—
Why wert thou so dear?
They know not I knew thee,
Who knew thee too well:—
Long, long shall I rue thee,
Too deeply to tell.

In secret we met—
In silence I grieve
That thy heart could forget,
Thy spirit deceive.
If I should meet thee
After long years,
How should I greet thee?—
With silence and tears.

June
Amy Levy

Last June I saw your face three times,
Three times I touched your hand;
Now, as before, May month is o'er,
And June is in the land.

O many Junes shall come and go,
Flower-footed o'er the mead;
O many Junes for me, to whom
Is length of days decreed.

There shall be sunlight, scent of rose,
Warm mist of Summer rain;
Only this change—I shall not look
Upon your face again.

Sonnet 90

William Shakespeare

Then hate me when thou wilt, if ever, now;
Now, while the world is bent my deeds to cross,
Join with the spite of fortune, make me bow,
And do not drop in for an after-loss:
Ah, do not, when my heart hath 'scaped this sorrow,
Come in the rearward of a conquered woe;
Give not a windy night a rainy morrow,
To linger out a purposed overthrow.
If thou wilt leave me, do not leave me last,
When other petty griefs have done their spite,
But in the onset come so shall I taste
At first the very worst of fortune's might,
    And other strains of woe, which now seem woe,
    Compared with loss of thee will not seem so.

I, Being Born A Woman

Edna St. Vincent Millay

I, being born a woman and distressed
By all the needs and notions of my kind,
Am urged by your propinquity to find
Your person fair, and feel a certain zest
To bear your body's weight upon my breast:
So subtly is the fume of life designed,
To clarify the pulse and cloud the mind,
And leave me once again undone, possessed.
Think not for this, however, the poor treason
Of my stout blood against my staggering brain,
I shall remember you with love, or season
My scorn with pity,—let me make it plain:
I find this frenzy insufficient reason
For conversation when we meet again.

Song

Edwin Arnold

Nay! If thou must depart, thou shalt depart;
But why so soon—oh, heart-blood of my heart?
Go then! Yet—going—turn and stay thy feet,
That I may once more see that face so sweet.
Once more—if never more; for swift days go
As hastening waters from their fountains flow;
And whether yet again shall meeting be
Who knows? Who knows? Ah! turn once more to me.

Sonnet 87

William Shakespeare

Farewell, thou art too dear for my possessing,
And like enough thou know'st thy estimate.
The charter of thy worth gives thee releasing;
My bonds in thee are all determinate.
For how do I hold thee but by thy granting,
And for that riches where is my deserving?
The cause of this fair gift in me is wanting,
And so my patent back again is swerving.
Thyself thou gav'st, thy own worth then not knowing,
Or me, to whom thou gav'st it, else mistaking;
So thy great gift upon misprision growing,
Comes home again, on better judgement making.
 Thus have I had thee as a dream doth flatter,
 In sleep a king, but waking no such matter.

A Song Of Separation

Lizette Woodward Reese

The long, stripped days, the nights void of a kiss,
The streets wherein not any step I take
Brings sound or sight of you, though my heart break,
Yea, the round year—were not my trouble this,
It would be yours, beloved; one must miss
Honey for gall, and one go unbereft;

One must be taken and the other left:
I praise God that my bitter is your bliss.
Out of this thought, as out some reed apace,
I draw a faltering music for relief,
Yet sweet enough to make, from door to door,
My empty house a habitable place.
My tears break off: I will have naught of grief,
For I remember you do weep no more.

FLOWER OR LOVE

Oscar Wilde

Sweet, I blame you not, for mine the fault was,
Had I not been made of common clay
I had climbed the higher heights unclimbed yet,
Seen the fuller air, the larger day.

From the wildness of my wasted passion I had
Struck a better, clearer song,
Lit some lighter light of freer freedom, battled
With some Hydra-headed wrong.

Had my lips been smitten into music by the
Kisses that but made them bleed,
You had walked with Bice and the angels on
That verdant and enamelled mead.

I had trod the road which Dante treading saw
The suns of seven circles shine,
Ay! perchance had seen the heavens opening, as
They opened to the Florentine.

And the mighty nations would have crowned me,
Who am crownless now and without name,
And some orient dawn had found me kneeling
On the threshold of the House of Fame

I had sat within that marble circle where the
Oldest bard is as the young,
And the pipe is ever dropping honey, and the
Lyre's strings are ever strung.

Keats had lifted up his hymeneal curls from out
The poppy-seeded wine,
With ambrosial mouth had kissed my forehead,
Clasped the hand of noble love in mine.

And at springtime, when the apple-blossoms
Brush the burnished bosom of the dove,
Two young lovers lying in an orchard would
Have read the story of our love.

Would have read the legend of my passion,
Known the bitter secret of my heart,
Kissed as we have kissed, but never parted as
We two are fated now to part.

For the crimson flower of our life is eaten by
The canker-worm of truth,
And no hand can gather up the fallen withered
Petals of the rose of youth.

Yet I am not sorry that I loved you- ah! what
Else had I a boy to do,—
For the hungry teeth of time devour, and the
Silent-footed years pursue.

Rudderless, we drift athwart a tempest, and
When once the storm of youth is past,
Without lyre, without lute or chorus, Death a
Silent pilot comes at last.

And within the grave there is no pleasure, for
The blind-worm battens on the root,
And Desire shudders into ashes, and the tree of
Passion bears no fruit.

Ah! what else had I to do but love you, God's
Own mother was less dear to me,
And less dear the Cytheraean rising like an
Argent lily from the sea.

I have made my choice, have lived my poems,
And, though youth is gone in wasted days,
I have found the lover's crown of myrtle
Better than the poet's crown of bays.

Why Can't I Leave You?

Ai

You stand behind the old black mare,
dressed as always in that red shirt,
stained from sweat, the crying of the armpits,
that will not stop for anything,
stroking her rump, while the barley goes unplanted.
I pick up my suitcase and set it down,
as I try to leave you again.
I smooth the hair back from your forehead.
I think with your laziness and the drought too,
you'll be neding my help more than ever.
You take my hands, I nod
and go to the house to unpack,
having found reason to stay.

I undress, then put on my white lace slip
for you to take off, because you like that
and when you come in, you pull down the straps
and I unbutton your shirt.
I know we can't give each other any more
or any less than what we have.
There is safety in that, so much
that I can never get past the packing,
the begging you to please, if I can't make you happy,
come close between my thighs
and let me laugh for you from my second mouth.

The Last Lover

Lizette Woodward Reese

It is so late!
Down all our days are set
November and the snows;
Yet now, when we are ready to forget,
For both has blown a rose.
Right well we know nor you nor I can make
A blaze of one lean spark;
And it were all in vain for us to take

This candle to the dark.
Now what, in truth, the fitting word to say,
And what the proper fate,
For growing red on a November day,
For being a rose so late?
Oh, must we pluck it, sweet though come to dust,
A moment hold it fast?
Or leave it to the gathering of the gust?
—A rose, but at the last!

Sonnet 139
William Shakespeare

O, call not me to justify the wrong
That thy unkindness lays upon my heart;
Wound me not with thine eye but with thy tongue;
Use power with power, and slay me not by art.
Tell me thou lov'st elsewhere; but in my sight,
Dear heart, forbear to glance thine eye aside;
What need'st thou wound with cunning when thy might
Is more than my o'erpressed defence can bide?
Let me excuse thee; ah, my love well knows
Her pretty looks have been mine enemies,
And therefore from my face she turns my foes,
That they elsewhere might dart their injuries.
    Yet do not so; but since I am near slain,
    Kill me outright with looks and rid my pain.

Gone In Good Sooth
Edna St. Vincent Millay

Gone in good sooth you are; not even in dream
You come. As if the strictures of the light,
Laid on our glances to their disesteem,
Extended even to shadows and the night,
Extended even beyond that drowsy sill
Along whose galleries open to the skies
All maskers move unchallenged and at will,
Visor in hand or hooded to the eyes.
To that pavilion the green sea in flood

Cuts in, and the slow dancers dance in foam.
I find again the pink camellia-bud
On the wide step, beside a silver comb...
But it is scentless; up the marble stair
I mount with pain, knowing you are not there.

They Flee From Me

Thomas Wyatt

They flee from me, that sometime did me seek,
With naked foot stalking in my chamber.
I have seen them, gentle, tame, and meek,
That now are wild, and do not remember
That sometime they put themselves in danger
To take bread at my hand; and now they range,
Busily seeking with a continual change.

Thanked be Fortune it hath been otherwise,
Twenty times better; but once in special,
In thin array, after a pleasant guise,
When her loose gown from her shoulders did fall,
And she me caught in her arms long and small,
And therewith I sweetly did me kiss
And softly said, "Dear heart, how like you this?"

It was no dream, I lay broad waking.
But all is turned, thorough my gentleness,
Into a strange fashion of forsaking;
And I have leave to go, of her goodness,
And she also to use newfangleness.
But since that I so kindely am served,
I fain would know what she hath deserved.

Sonnet 36

William Shakespeare

Let me confess that we two must be twain,
Although our undivided loves are one.
So shall those blots that do with me remain,
Without thy help, by me be borne alone.

In our two loves there is but one respect,
Though in our lives a separable spite,
Which though it alter not love's sole effect,
Yet doth it steal sweet hours from love's delight.
I may not evermore acknowledge thee,
Lest my bewailed guilt should do thee shame;
Nor thou with public kindness honour me,
Unless thou take that honour from thy name.
    But do not so; I love thee in such sort
    As thou being mine, mine is thy good report.

I Shall Go Back
Edna St. Vincent Millay

I shall go back again to the bleak shore
And build a little shanty on the sand
In such a way that the extremest band
Of brittle seaweed shall escape my door
But by a yard or two; and nevermore
Shall I return to take you by the hand.
I shall be gone to what I understand,
And happier than I ever was before.
The love that stood a moment in your eyes,
The words that lay a moment on your tongue,
Are one with all that in a moment dies,
A little under-said and over-sung.
But I shall find the sullen rocks and skies
Unchanged from what they were when I was young.

*H*er Voice
Oscar Wilde

The wild bee reels from bough to bough
    With his furry coat and his gauzy wing.
    Now in a lily-cup, and now
    Setting a jacinth bell a-swing,
    In his wandering;
    Sit closer love: it was here I trow
    I made that vow,

Swore that two lives should be like one
As long as the sea-gull loved the sea,
As long as the sunflower sought the sun,—
It shall be, I said, for eternity
    'Twixt you and me!
Dear friend, those times are over and done,
    Love's web is spun.
Look upward where the poplar trees
Sway and sway in the summer air,
Here in the valley never a breeze
Scatters the thistledown, but there
    Great winds blow fair
From the mighty murmuring mystical seas,
    And the wave-lashed leas.
Look upward where the white gull screams,
What does it see that we do not see?
Is that a star? or the lamp that gleams
On some outward voyaging argosy,—
    Ah! can it be
We have lived our lives in a land of dreams!
    How sad it seems.
Sweet, there is nothing left to say
But this, that love is never lost,
Keen winter stabs the breasts of May
Whose crimson roses burst his frost,
    Ships tempest-tossed
Will find a harbour in some bay,
    And so we may.
And there is nothing left to do
But to kiss once again, and part,
Nay, there is nothing we should rue,
I have my beauty,—you your Art,
    Nay, do not start,
One world was not enough for two
    Like me and you.

VIII

Emily Dickinson

A murmur in the trees to note,
Not loud enough for wind;
A star not far enough to seek,
Nor near enough to find;
A long, long yellow on the lawn,
A hubbub as of feet;
Not audible, as ours to us,
But dapperer, more sweet;
A hurrying home of little men
To houses unperceived,—
All this, and more, if I should tell,
Would never be believed.
Of robins in the trundle bed
How many I espy
Whose nightgowns could not hide the wings,
Although I heard them try!
But then I promised ne'er to tell;
How could I break my word?
So go your way and I 'll go mine,—
No fear you 'll miss the road.

Sonnet

Edna St. Vincent Millay

If to be left were to be left alone,
And lock the door, and find one's self again,
Drag forth and dust Penates of one's own,
That in a corner all too long have lain;
Read Brahms, read Chaucer, set the chessmen out
In classic problem, stretch the shrunken mind
Back to its stature on the rack of thought—
Loss might be said to leave its boon behind.
But fruitless conversation and the exchange
With callow wits of bearded cons and pros
Enlist the neutral daylight, and derange
A will too sick to battle for repose.
Neither with you nor with myself, I spend
Loud days that have no meaning and no end.

You Thought That I Was That Type

Anna Akhmatova

You thought that I was that type:
    that you could forget me, and
    that I'd plead and weep and throw myself
    under the hooves of a bay mare,
    or that I'd ask the sorcerers
    for some magic potion made from roots
    and send you a terrible gift: my precious
    perfumed hankerchief.
Damn you! I will not grant
your cursed soul
vicarious tears or a single glance.
And I swear to you by the garden of the angels,
I swear by the miracle-working ikon,
and by the fire and smoke of our nights:
I will never come back to you

Auld Lang Syne

Robert Burns

Should auld acquaintance be forgot,
    And never brought to min'?
Should auld acquaintance be forgot,
    And days o' lang syne?

For auld lang syne, my dear,
    For auld lang syne,
We'll tak a cup o' kindness yet,
    For auld lang syne.

We twa hae run about the braes;
    And pow'w the gowans fine;
But we've wandered mony a weary foot
    Sin' auld lang syne.

For auld lang syne, my dear,
    For auld lang syne,
We'll tak a cup o' kindness yet,
    For auld lang syne.

We twa hae paidl't i' the burn,
    Frae mornin' sun till dine;
But seas between us braid hae roared
    Sin' auld lang syne.

For auld lang syne, my dear,
    For auld lang syne,
We'll tak a cup o' kindness yet,
    For auld lang syne.

And here's a hand, my trusty fiere,
    And gie's a hand o' thine;
And we'll tak a right guid willie-waught
    For auld lang syne.

For auld lang syne, my dear,
    For auld lang syne,
We'll tak a cup o' kindness yet,
    For auld lang syne.

And surely ye'll be your pint-stoup,
    And surely I'll be mine,
And we'll tak a cup o' kindness yet,
    For auld lang syne.

For auld lang syne, my dear,
    For auld lang syne,
We'll tak a cup o' kindness yet,
    For auld lang syne.

ℰNDING

Emily Dickinson

That is solemn we have ended,—
    Be it but a play,
Or a glee among the garrets,
    Or a holiday,
Or a leaving home; or later,
    Parting with a world
We have understood, for better
    Still it be unfurled.

Farewell, Ungrateful Traitor!

John Dryden

Farewell, ungrateful traitor!
Farewell, my perjur'd swain!
Let never injur'd woman
Believe a man again.
The pleasure of possessing
Surpasses all expressing,
But 'tis too short a blessing,
And love too long a pain.

'Tis easy to deceive us
In pity of your pain,
But when we love, you leave us
To rail at you in vain.
Before we have descried it,
There is no joy beside it,
But she that once has tried it
Will never love again.

The passion you pretended
Was only to obtain,
But once the charm is ended,
The charmer you disdain.
Your love by ours we measure
Till we have lost our treasure,
But dying is a pleasure
When living is a pain.

Consecration

Emily Dickinson

Proud of my broken heart since thou didst break it,
Proud of the pain I did not feel till thee,
Proud of my night since thou with moons dost slake it,
Not to partake thy passion, my humility

XX
Emily Dickinson

Could I but ride indefinite,
As doth the meadow-bee,
And visit only where I liked,
And no man visit me,
And flirt all day with buttercups,
And marry whom I may,
And dwell a little everywhere,
Or better, run away
With no police to follow,
Or chase me if I do,
Till I should jump peninsulas
To get away from you,—
I said, but just to be a bee
Upon a raft of air,
And row in nowhere all day long,
And anchor off the bar,—
What liberty! So captives deem
Who tight in dungeons are.

A VALEDICTION: OF WEEPING
John Donne

Let me pour forth
My tears before thy face whilst I stay here,
For thy face coins them, and thy stamp they bear,
And by this mintage they are something worth,
  For thus they be
  Pregnant of thee;
Fruits of much grief they are, emblems of more;
When a tear falls, that Thon falls which it bore,
So thou and I are nothing then, when on a diverse shore.

  On a round ball
A workman that hath copies by, can lay
An Europe, Afric, and an Asia,
And quickly make that, which was nothing, all,
  So doth each tear
  Which thee doth wear,

A globe, yea world, by that impression grow,
Till thy tears mix'd with mine do overflow
This world; by waters sent from thee, my heaven dissolved so.

O more than moon,
Draw not up seas to drown me in thy sphere,
Weep me not dead, in thine arms, but forbear
To teach the sea what it may do too soon;
Let not the wind
Example find,
To do me more harm than it purposeth;
Since thou and I sigh one another's breath,
Whoe'er sighs most is cruellest, and hastes the other's death.

ℛELUCTANCE

Robert Frost

Out through the fields and the woods
And over the walls I have wended;
I have climbed the hills of view
And looked at the world, and descended;
I have come by the highway home,
And lo, it is ended.
The leaves are all dead on the ground,
Save those that the oak is keeping
To ravel them one by one
And let them go scraping and creeping
Out over the crusted snow,
When others are sleeping.
And the dead leaves lie huddled and still,
No longer blown hither and thither;
The last lone aster is gone;
The flowers of the witch-hazel wither;
The heart is still aching to seek,
But the feet question "Whither?"
Ah, when to the heart of man
Was it ever less than a treason
To go with the drift of things,
To yield with a grace to reason,
And bow and accept the end
Of a love or a season?

The Lover Is Near

Johann Wolfgang Von Goethe

I think of you with sudden splendor
    Glows from the sea,
I think of you when moon's reflected glimmer
    Rests on the brook.
I see you on the road where dust is rising
    Far from my glance,
In darkest night when travelling feet are trembling
    On narrow trail.
I hear you in the hollow roar of billows
    Heaving to break,
I seek the silent glade to stand and listen
    When all is mute.
I am with you, no distance keeps your image
    Far from my side.
The sun is set, I wait the rise of starlight,
    Starlight and—you!

Joy and Dream

Johann Wolfgang Von Goethe

You often have in dreams, I know,
    Seen us unto the altar go,
And you as wife and I as man.
And often I would wake and shower
Upon your mouth, in guardless hour,
    As many kisses as one can.

The purest joy that once was ours,
    The full delight of golden hours,
Fled, as Time flees, for all our bliss.
Of what avail are joys that die?
Like dreams the warmest kisses fly,
    And every joy but as one kiss.

SONNET 26

William Shakespeare

Lord of my love, to whom in vassalage
Thy merit hath my duty strongly knit;
To thee I send this written embassage
To witness duty, not to show my wit.
Duty so great, which wit so poor as mine
May make seem bare, in wanting words to show it;
But that I hope some good conceit of thine
In thy soul's thought (all naked) will bestow it:
Till whatsoever star that guides my moving,
Points on me graciously with fair aspect,
And puts apparel on my tattered loving,
To show me worthy of thy sweet respect,
    Then may I dare to boast how I do love thee,
    Till then, not show my head where thou mayst prove me.

SONNET 38

William Shakespeare

How can my muse want subject to invent
While thou dost breathe that pour'st into my verse,
Thine own sweet argument, too excellent,
For every vulgar paper to rehearse?
O give thy self the thanks if aught in me,
Worthy perusal stand against thy sight,
For who's so dumb that cannot write to thee,
When thou thy self dost give invention light?
Be thou the tenth Muse, ten times more in worth
Than those old nine which rhymers invocate,
And he that calls on thee, let him bring forth
Eternal numbers to outlive long date.
    If my slight muse do please these curious days,
    The pain be mine, but thine shall be the praise.

Sonnet 102

William Shakespeare

My love is strengthened though more weak in seeming,
I love not less, though less the show appear,
That love is merchandized, whose rich esteeming,
The owner's tongue doth publish every where.
Our love was new, and then but in the spring,
When I was wont to greet it with my lays,
As Philomel in summer's front doth sing,
And stops her pipe in growth of riper days:
Not that the summer is less pleasant now
Than when her mournful hymns did hush the night,
But that wild music burthens every bough,
And sweets grown common lose their dear delight.
    Therefore like her, I sometime hold my tongue:
    Because I would not dull you with my song.

We Met On Roads Of Laughter

Charles Divine

We met on roads of laughter,
    Both careless at the start,
But other roads came after
    And wound around my heart.

There are roads a wise man misses,
    And roads where fools will try
To say farewell with kisses,
    Touch love and say goodbye.

We met on roads of laughter;—
    Now wistful roads depart,
For I must hurry after
    To overtake my heart.

Absence

Comte DeBussy Rabutin

Absence is to love what wind is to fire;
it extinguishes the small, it enkindles the great.

SONNET 11

William Shakespeare

Since I left you, mine eye is in my mind,
And that which governs me to go about,
Doth part his function, and is partly blind,
Seems seeing, but effectually is out:
For it no form delivers to the heart
Of bird, of flower, or shape which it doth latch,
Of his quick objects hath the mind no part,
Nor his own vision holds what it doth catch:
For if it see the rud'st or gentlest sight,
The most sweet favour or deformed'st creature,
The mountain, or the sea, the day, or night:
The crow, or dove, it shapes them to your feature.
    Incapable of more, replete with you,
    My most true mind thus maketh mine untrue.

THE LAND OF YESTERDAY

Don Marquis

And I would seek the country town
Amid green meadows nestled down
If I could only find the way
Back to the Land of Yesterday!
How I would thrust the miles aside,
Rush up the quiet lane, and then,
Just where her roses laughed in pride,
Find her among the flowers again.
I'd slip in silently and wait
Until she saw me by the gate,
And then…read through a blur of tears
Quick pardon for the selfish years.
This time, this time, I would not wait
For that brief wire that said, Too late!—
If I could only find the way Into the Land of Yesterday.

I wonder if her roses yet
Lift up their heads and laugh with pride,
And if her phlox and mignonette
Have heart to blossom by their side;

I wonder if the dear old lane
Still chirps with robins after rain,
And if the birds and banded bees
Still rob her early cherry-trees…
I wonder, if I went there now,
How everything would seem, and how—
But no! not now; there is no way
Back to the Land of Yesterday.

*A*WAY

Walter De La Mare

There is no sorrow
Time heals never;
No loss, betrayal,
Beyond repair.
Balm for the soul, then,
Though grave shall sever
Lover from loved
And all they share.
See, the sweet sun shines,
The shower is over;
Flowers preen their beauty,
The day how fair!
Brood not too closely
On love or duty;
Friends long forgotten
May wait you where
Life with death
Brings all to an issue;
None will long mourn for you,
Pray for you, miss you,
Your place left vacant,
You not there.

SONNET

John Masefield

Flesh, I have knocked at many a dusty door,
Gone down full many a midnight lane,
Probed in old walls and felt along the floor,
Pressed in blind hope the lighted window-pane,
But useless all, though sometimes when the moon
Was full in heaven and the sea was full,
Along my body's alleys came a tune
Played in the tavern by the Beautiful.
Then for an instant I have felt at point
To find and seize her, whosoe'er she be,
Whether some saint whose glory doth anoint
Those whom she loves, or but a part of me,
Or something that the things not understood
Make for their uses out of flesh and blood.

SONNET 66

William Shakespeare

Tired with all these for restful death I cry,
As to behold desert a beggar born,
And needy nothing trimmed in jollity,
And purest faith unhappily forsworn,
And gilded honour shamefully misplaced,
And maiden virtue rudely strumpeted,
And right perfection wrongfully disgraced,
And strength by limping sway disabled
And art made tongue-tied by authority,
And folly (doctor-like) controlling skill,
And simple truth miscalled simplicity,
And captive good attending captain ill.
    Tired with all these, from these would I be gone,
    Save that to die, I leave my love alone.

MODERN LOVE
George Meredith

Thus piteously Love closed what he begat:
    The union of this ever-diverse pair!
    These two were rapid falcons in a snare,
    Condemned to do the flitting of the bat.
    Lovers beneath the singing sky of May,
    They wandered once; clear as the dew on flowers:
    But they fed not on the advancing hours:
    Their hearts held cravings for the buried day.
    Then each applied to each that fatal knife,
    Deep questioning, which probes to endless dole.
    Ah, what a dusty answer gets the soul
    When hot for certainties in this our life!—
    In tragic hints here see what evermore
    Moves dark as yonder midnight ocean's force,
    Thundering like ramping hosts of warrior horse,
    To throw that faint thin line upon the shore!

IT WAS A' FOR OUR RIGHTFUL KING
Robert Burns

    It was a' for our rightful king
      That we left fair Scotland's strand;
    It was a' for our rightful king
      We e'er saw Irish land,
       My dear,
      We e'er saw Irish land.
    Now a' is done that men can do,
      And a' is done in vain!
    My love, and native land, fareweel!
      For I maun cross the main,
       My dear,
      For I maun cross the main.

    He turn'd him right and round about,
      Upon the Irish shore,
    He gave his bridle-reins a shake,

With, Adieu for evermore,
  My dear!
And adieu for evermore!

The soldier frae the war returns,
  And the merchant frae the main.
But I hae parted frae my love,
  Never to meet again,
    My dear,
  Never to meet again.

When day is gone and night is come,
  And a' folk bound to sleep,
I think on him that's far awa
  The lee-lang night, and weep,
    My dear,
  The lee-lang night, and weep.

LONGINGS AND YEARNINGS

*Y*OU DON'T KNOW ME
Eddy Arnold & Cindy Walker

You give your hand to me and then you say hello
And I can hardly speak my heart is beating so
And anyone can tell you think you know me well
But you don't know me

No you don't know the one who dreams of you at night
And longs to kiss your lips and longs to hold you tight
Oh I'm just a friend that's all I've ever been
'Cause you don't know me

For I never knew the art of making love
Though my heart aches with love for you
Afraid and shy I let my chance go by
The chance that you might love me too

No I never knew

You give your hand to me and then you say good-bye
I watch you walk away in my heart I cry
You'll never never know the one who loves you so
'Cause you don't know me

*L*ONGING
Paul Laurence Dunbar

If you could sit with me beside the sea to-day,
And whisper with me sweetest dreamings o'er and o'er;
I think I should not find the clouds so dim and gray,
And not so loud the waves complaining at the shore.

If you could sit with me upon the shore to-day,
And hold my hand in yours as in the days of old,
I think I should not mind the chill baptismal spray,
Nor find my hand and heart and all the world so cold.

If you could walk with me upon the Strand to-day,
And tell me that my longing love had won your own,
I think all my sad thoughts would then be put away,
And I could give back laughter for the Ocean's moan!

Isolation: To Marguerite

Sir Matthew Arnold

We were apart; yet, day by day,
I bade my heart more constant be.
I bade it keep the world away,
And grow a home for only thee;
Nor fear'd but thy love likewise grew,
Like mine, each day, more tried, more true.

The fault was grave! I might have known,
What far too soon, alas! I learn'd—
The heart can bind itself alone,
And faith may oft be unreturn'd.
Self-sway'd our feelings ebb and swell—
Thou lov'st no more;—Farewell! Farewell!

Farewell!—and thou, thou lonely heart,
Which never yet without remorse
Even for a moment didst depart
From thy remote and spher'ed course
To haunt the place where passions reign—
Back to thy solitude again!

Back! with the conscious thrill of shame
Which Luna felt, that summer-night,
Flash through her pure immortal frame,
When she forsook the starry height
To hang over Endymion's sleep
Upon the pine-grown Latmian steep.

Yet she, chaste queen, had never proved
How vain a thing is mortal love,
Wandering in Heaven, far removed.
But thou hast long had place to prove
This truth—to prove, and make thine own:
"Thou hast been, shalt be, art, alone."

Or, if not quite alone, yet they
Which touch thee are unmating things—
Ocean and clouds and night and day;
Lorn autumns and triumphant springs;
And life, and others' joy and pain,
And love, if love, of happier men.

Of happier men—for they, at least,
Have dream'd two human hearts might blend
In one, and were through faith released
From isolation without end
Prolong'd; nor knew, although not less
Alone than thou, their loneliness.

A Drinking Song

W. B. Yeats

Wine comes in at the mouth
And love comes in at the eyes;
That's all we know for truth
Before we grow old and die.
I lift the glass to my mouth,
I look at you, and I sigh.

Night Of Love

Paul Laurence Dunbar

The moon has left the sky, love,
The stars are hiding now,
And frowning on the world, love,
Night bares her sable brow.

The snow is on the ground, love,
And cold and keen the air is.
I'm singing here to you, love;
You're dreaming there in Paris.

But this is Nature's law, love,
Though just it may not seem,
That men should wake to sing, love;
While maidens sleep and dream.

Them care may not molest, love,
Nor stir them from their slumbers,
Though midnight find the swain, love.
Still halting o'er his numbers.

I watch the rosy dawn, love,
Come stealing up the east,
While all things round rejoice, love,
That Night her reign has ceased.

The lark will soon be heard, love,
And on his way be winging;
When Nature's poets wake, love,
Why should a man be singing?

I Hid My Love

John Clare

I hid my love when young till I
Couldn't bear the buzzing of a fly;
I hid my love to my despite
Till I could not bear to look at light:
I dare not gaze upon her face
But left her memory in each place;
Where'er I saw a wild flower lie
I kissed and bade my love good-bye.

I met her in the greenest dells,
Where dewdrops pearl the wood bluebells;
The lost breeze kissed her bright blue eye,
The bee kissed and went singing by,
A sunbeam found a passage there,
A gold chain round her neck so fair;
As secret as the wild bee's song
She lay there all the summer long.

I hid my love in field and town
Till e'en the breeze would knock me down;
The bees seemed singing ballads o'er,
The fly's bass turned a lion's roar;
And even silence found a tongue,
To haunt me all the summer long;
The riddle nature could not prove
Was nothing else but secret love.

DESIRE

Jennifer Tseng

this desire
is a kind of sleeping,
a kind of forgetting,
a lost childhood.
I see myself as a skin cave
dark, without details
you and I are there having tea
stirring the tea with our bones
each with our own bones

I would drink your reflection
but I cannot find the cup
I cannot find my hands.

To _____

Elizabeth Barrett Browning

Mine is a wayward lay;
And, if its echoing rhymes I try to string,
    Proveth a truant thing,
Whenso some names I love, send it away!
    For then, eyes swimming o'er,
And clasped hands, and smiles in fondness meant,
    Are much more eloquent —
So it had fain begone, and speak no more!
    Yet shall it come again,
Ah, friend belov'd! if so thy wishes be,
    And, with wild melody,

I will, upon thine ear, cadence my strain —
    Cadence my simple line,
Unfashion'd by the cunning hand of Art,
    But coming from my heart,
To tell the message of its love to thine!
    As ocean shells, when taken
From Ocean's bed, will faithfully repeat
    Her ancient music sweet—
Ev'n so these words, true to my heart, shall waken!
    Oh! while our bark is seen,
Our little bark of kindly, social love,
    Down life's clear stream to move
Toward the summer shores, where all is green—
    So long thy name shall bring,
Echoes of joy unto the grateful gales,
    And thousand tender tales,
To freshen the fond hearts that round thee cling!
    Hast thou not look'd upon
The flowerets of the field in lowly dress?
    Blame not my simpleness—
Think only of my love!— my song is gone.

ALBERTA

Traditional Blues

Alberta, let your hair hang low.
Alberta, let your hair hang low,
I'll give you more gold than your apron can hold
If you'll only let your hair hang low.
Alberta, what's on your mind?
Alberta, what's on your mind?
You keep me worried, you keep me bothered all the time
Alberta, what's on your mind?
Alberta, don' you treat me unkind
Alberta, don' you treat me unkind
My heart feel so sad, 'cause I want you so bad.
Alberta, don' you treat me unkind.
Alberta, let your hair hang low

To Rosamond
Geoffrey Chaucer

Madame, ye been of alle beautee shrine
As fer as cercled is the mapemounde:
For as the crystal glorious ye shine,
And like ruby been youre cheekes rounde.
Therwith ye been so merye and so jocounde
That at a revel whan that I see you daunce
It is an oinement unto my wounde,
Though ye to me ne do no daliaunce.

For though I weepe of teres ful a tine,
Yit may that wo myn herte nat confounde;
Youre semy vois, that ye so smale outtwine,
Maketh my thought in joye and blis habounde:
So curteisly I go with love bounde
That to myself I saye in my penaunce,
"Suffiseth me to love you, Rosemounde,
Though ye to me ne do no daliaunce."

Was nevere pik waiwed in galauntine
As I in love am waiwed and ywounde,
For which ful ofte I of myself divine
That I am trewe Tristam the secounde;
My love may not refreide nor affounde;
I brenne ay in amorous plesaunce:
Do what you list, I wol youre thral be founde,
Though ye to me ne do no daliaunce.

Cruel War
Traditional

The cruel war is raging, Johnny has to fight.
I long to be with him from morning 'till night.
I want to be with him, it grieves my heart so
Won't you let me come with you? No, my love, no.
Tomorrow is Sunday, Monday is the day
That your captain will call you and you must obey
Your captain will call you, it grieves my heart so

Won't you let me come with you? No, my love, no.
I'll tie back my hair, men's clothing I'll put on.
I'll pass for your comrade as we march along.
I'll pass for your comrade, no one will ever know
Won't you let me come with you? No, my love, no.
Oh Johnny, oh Johnny, I feel you are unkind
I love you far better than all of mankind
I love you far better than words can e'er express
Won't you let me come with you? Yes, my love, yes.

Wishes To His (Supposed) Mistress

Sir Thomas Crashaw

Who e'er she be
That not impossible she
That shall command my heart and me;

Wher e'er she lie,
Lock'd up from mortal eye
In shady leaves of destiny;

Till that ripe birth
Of studied fate stand forth
And teach her fair steps to our earth;

Till that divine
Idea take a shrine
Of crystal flesh, through which to shine;

Meet you her, my wishes,
Bespeak her to my blisses,
And be ye call'd my absent kisses.

I wish her beauty
That owes not all his duty
To gaudy tire, or glist'ring shoe-ty.

Something more than
Taffeta or tissue can,
Or rampant feather, or rich fan.

More than the spoil
Of shop, or silkworm's toil,
Or a bought blush, or a set smile.

A face that's best
By its own beauty drest,
And can alone command the rest.

A face made up
Out of no other shop
Than what nature's white hand sets ope.

A cheek where youth,
And blood, with pen of truth
Write, what the reader sweetly ru'th.

A cheek where grows
More than a morning rose,
Which to no box his being owes.

Lips, where all day
A lover's kiss may play,
Yet carry nothing thence away.

Looks that oppress
Their richest tires, but dress
And clothe their simplest nakedness.

Eyes, that displaces
The neighbour diamond, and outfaces
That sunshine, by their own sweet graces.

Tresses, that wear
Jewels but to declare
How much themselves more precious are.

Whose native ray
Can tame the wanton day
Of gems, that in their bright shades play.

Each ruby there,
Or pearl that dare appear,
Be its own blush, be its own tear.

A well-tam'd heart,
For whose more noble smart
Love may be long choosing a dart.

Eyes, that bestow
Full quivers on Love's bow,
Yet pay less arrows than they owe.

Smiles, that can warm
The blood, yet teach a charm,
That chastity shall take no harm.

Blushes, that bin
The burnish of no sin,
Nor flames of aught too hot within.

Joys, that confess
Virtue their mistress,
And have no other head to dress.

Fears, fond and flight
As the coy bride's when night
First does the longing lover right.

Tears, quickly fled,
And vain, as those are shed
For a dying maidenhead.

Days, that need borrow
No part of their good morrow
From a forespent night of sorrow.

Days, that in spite
Of darkness, by the light
Of a clear mind are day all night.

Nights, sweet as they,
Made short by lovers' play,
Yet long by th' absence of the day.

Life, that dares send
A challenge to his end,
And when it comes say, "Welcome friend."

Sidneian showers
Of sweet discourse, whose powers
Can crown old Winter's head with flowers.

Soft silken hours,
Open suns, shady bowers, '
Bove all, nothing within that lours.

Whate'er delight
Can make Day's forehead bright,
Or give down to the wings of Night.

In her whole frame
Have nature all the name,
Art and ornament the shame.

Her flattery,
Picture and poesy,
Her counsel her own virtue be.

I wish, her store
Of worth may leave her poor
Of wishes, and I wish—no more.

Now if time knows
That her whose radiant brows
Weave them a garland of my vows,

Her whose just bays
My future hopes can raise,
A trophy to her present praise;

Her that dares be
What these lines wish to see:
I seek no further, it is she.

'Tis she, and here,
Lo, I unclothe and clear
My wishes' cloudy character.

May she enjoy it,
Whose merit dare apply it,
But modesty dares still deny it.

Such worth as this is
Shall fix my flying wishes,
And determine them to kisses.

Let her full glory,
My fancies, fly before ye;
Be ye my fictions; but her story.

REPROACH
Firdusi

Were it mine to repose for one night on thy bosom,
My head, thus exalted, would reach to the skies;
In Mercury's fingers the pen I would shatter;
The crown of the Sun I would grasp as my prize.
O'er the ninth sphere of heaven my soul would be flying
And Saturn's proud head 'neath my feet would be lying,
Yet I'd pity poor lovers sore wounded and dying,
Were thy beauty mine own, or thy lips, or thine eyes.

THE LOVELY DELIGHTFUL SONG OF THY SISTER
Anonymous, Egyptian

My Beloved brother, my heart burneth for thy love.
I say to thee, "Behold what I do!"
I am come to catch with my trap in my hand and my cage.
All the birds of Punt settle upon Egypt, anointed with myrrh.
The one that cometh first taketh my worm.
Its odor comes from Punt, its claws are full of myrrh.

How I long for thee,
That we might take it out together!
I alone with thee, that thou might hear
The shrill cry of my myrrh-anointed one.

How good it were if thou shouldst be with me
When I set the trap!
How lovely it is to go to the meadow
Unto him who is beloved.

The voice of the goose caught on its worm crieth out,
But love of thee holdeth me back
So that I cannot release it.

I will take away my nets.
"How then," my mother will say,
To whom I go each evening laden with birds,
"Hast thou set no traps today?"

Thy love hath carried me off.
I see sweet cake and it is as salt,
And mead, which is sweet in the mouth,
Is like the gall of birds.
The breath of thy nostrils is that alone
Which maketh my heart to live.
I have found that Amon is given to me thereby
For ever and ever.

THE LIPS OF THE ONE I LOVE

Hafiz

The lips of the one I love are my perpetual pleasure:
The Lord be praised, for my heart's desire is attained.

O Fate, cherish my darling close to your breast:
Present now the golden wine-cup, now the rubies of those lips.

They talk scandal about us, and say we are drunks -
The silly old men, the elders lost in their error.
But we have done penance on the pious man's behalf,
And ask God's pardon for what the religious do.

O my dear, how can I speak of being apart from you?
The eyes know a hundred tears, and the soul has a hundred sighs.

I'd not have even an infidel suffer the torment your beauty has caused
To the cypress which envies your body, and the moon that's outshone
    by your face.

Desire for your lips has stolen from Hafiz's thought
His evening lectionary, and reciting the Book at dawn.

ON HIS LOVE

Daqiqi

O would that in the world there were no night,
That I may ne'er be parted from her lips!
No scorpion-sting would sink deep in my heart
    But for her scorpions coils of darkest hair.
    If 'neath her lip no starry dimple shone,
    I would not linger with the stars till day;

And if she were not cast in beauty's mould,
My soul would not be moulded of her love.
If I must live without my Well-belov'd,
Oh God! I would there were no life for me.

Ode

Walter Davison

At her fair hands how have I grace entreated,
With prayers oft repeated,
Yet still my love is thwarted:
Heart, let her go, for she'll not be converted.
   Say, shall she go?
   O! no, no, no, no, no.
She is most fair, though she be marble hearted.

How often have my sighs declared mine anguish,
Wherein I daily languish,
Yet doth she still procure it:
Heart, let her go, for I cannot endure it.
   Say, shall she go?
   O! no, no, no, no, no.
She gave the wound,. and she alone must cure it.

The trickling tears, that down my cheeks have flowed,
My love have often showed;
Yet still unkind I prove her:
Heart, let her go, for nought I do can move her.
   Say, shall she go?
   O! no, no, no, no, no.
Though me she hate, I cannot choose but love her.

But shall I still a true affection owe her,
Which prayers, sighs, tears do show her;
And shall she still disdain me?
Heart, let her go, if they no grace can gain me.
   Say, shall she go?
   O! no, no, no, no.
She made me hers, and hers she will retain me.

But if the love that hath, and still doth burn me,
No love at length return me,

Out of my thoughts I'll set her:
Heart, let her go, oh heart, I pray thee let her.
    Say, shall she go?
    O! no, no, no, no, no.
Fixed in the heart, how can the heart forget her?

But if I weep and sigh, and often wail me,
Till tears, sighs, prayers fail me,
Shall yet my love persevere?
Heart, let her go, if she will right thee let her.
    Say, shall she go?
    O! no, no, no, no, no.
Tears, sighs, prayers, fail, but true love lasteth ever.

ON THE ROAD TO THE SEA

Charlotte Mew

We passed each other, turned and stopped for half an hour, then went our way,
I who make other women smile did not make you—
But no man can move mountains in a day.
So this hard thing is yet to do.
But first I want your life—before I die I want to see
The world that lies behind the strangeness of your eyes,
There is nothing gay or green there for my gathering, it may be,
Yet on brown fields there lies
A haunting purple bloom: is there not something in grey skies
And in grey sea?
I want what world there is behind your eyes,
I want your life and you will not give it me.
Now, if I look, I see you walking down the years,
Young, and through August fields—a face, a thought, a swinging dream
perched on a stile—;
I would have liked (so vile we are!) to have taught you tears
But most to have made you smile.
To-day is not enough or yesterday: God sees it all—
Your length on sunny lawns, the wakeful rainy nights—; tell me—;
(how vain to ask), but it is not a question—just a call—;
Show me then, only your notched inches climbing up the garden wall,
I like you best when you are small.

Is this a stupid thing to say
Not having spent with you one day?
No matter; I shall never touch your hair
Or hear the little tick behind your breast,
Still it is there,
And as a flying bird
Brushes the branches where it may not rest
I have brushed your hand and heard
The child in you: I like that best
So small, so dark, so sweet; and were you also then too grave and wise?
Always I think. Then put your far off little hand in mine;—
Oh! let it rest;
I will not stare into the early world beyond the opening eyes,
Or vex or scare what I love best.
But I want your life before mine bleeds away—
Here—not in heavenly hereafters—soon,—
I want your smile this very afternoon,
(The last of all my vices, pleasant people used to say,
I wanted and I sometimes got—the Moon!)
You know, at dusk, the last bird's cry,
And round the house the flap of the bat's low flight,
Trees that go black against the sky
And then—how soon the night!
No shadow of you on any bright road again,
And at the darkening end of this—what voice? whose kiss? As if you'd say!
It is not I who have walked with you, it will not be I who take away
Peace, peace, my little handful of the gleaner's grain
From your reaped fields at the shut of day.
Peace! Would you not rather die
Reeling,—with all the cannons at your ear?
So, at least, would I,
And I may not be here
To-night, to-morrow morning or next year.
Still I will let you keep your life a little while,
See dear?
I have made you smile.

*T*EASE

D. H. Lawrence

I will give you all my keys,
You shall be my chatelaine,
You shall enter as you please,
As you please shall go again.

When I hear you jingling through
All the chambers of my soul,
How I sit and laugh at you
In your vain housekeeping role.

Jealous of the smallest cover,
Angry at the simpler door;
Well, you anxious, inquisitive lover,
Are you pleased with what's in store?

You have fingered all my treasures,
Have you not, most curiously,
Handled all my tools and measures
And masculine machinery?

Over every single beauty
You have had your little rapture;
You have slain, as was your duty,
Every sin-mouse you could capture.

Still you are not satisfied,
Still you tremble faint reproach;
Challenge me I keep aside
Secrets that you may not broach.

Maybe yes, and maybe no,
Maybe there are secret places,
Altars barbarous below,
Elsewhere halls of high disgraces.

Maybe yes, and maybe no,
You may have it as you please,
Since I choose to keep you so,
Suppliant on your curious knees.

Beautiful Dreamer

Stephen Foster

Beautiful dreamer, awake unto me
Starlight and dewdrops are waiting for thee
Sounds of the rude world heard in the day
Lulled by the moonlight have all passed away.

Beautiful dreamer, queen of my song,
Gone are the cares of life's busy throng
List while I woo thee with soft melody
Beautiful dreamer, awake unto me!
Beautiful dreamer, awake unto me.

The Ecstasy

John Donne

Where, like a pillow on a bed,
    A pregnant bank swelled up, to rest
The violet's reclining head,
    Sat we two, one another's best.

Our hands were firmly cemented
    With a fast balm, which thence did spring;
Our eye-beams twisted, and did thread
    Our eyes upon one double string;

So to entergraft our hands, as yet
    Was all our means to make us one.
And pictures on our eyes to get
    Was all our propagation.

As 'twixt two equal armies, Fate
    Suspends uncertain victory,
Our souls (which to advance their state
    Were gone out) hung 'twixt her and me.

And whilst our souls negotiate there,
    We like sepulchral statues lay;
All day the same our postures were,
    And we said nothing all the day.

If any, so by love refined
      That the soul's language understood,
And by good love were grown all mind,
      Within convenient distance stood,

He (though he knew not which soul spake,
      Because both meant, both spake the same)
Might thence a new concoction take,
      And part far purer than he came.

This ecstasy doth unperplex
      (We said) and tell us what we love,
We see by this, it was not sex,
      We see, we say not what did move:

But as all several souls contain
      Mixture of things, they know not what,
Love these mixed souls doth mix again,
      And makes both one, each this and that.

A single violet transplant,
      The strength, the colour, and the size,
(All which before was poor and scant)
      Redoubles still, and multiplies.

When love with one another
      so interinanimates two souls,
That abler soul, which thence doth flow,
      Defects of loneliness controls.

We then, who are this new soul, know
      Of what we are composed, and made,
For the atomies of which we grow
      Are souls, whom no change can invade.

But, O alas! so long, so far
      Our bodies why do we forbear?
They are ours, though they are not we; we are
      The intelligences, they the sphere.

We owe them thanks, because they thus
      Did us, to us, at first convey
Yielded their forces, sense, to us,
Nor are dross to us, but allay.

On man heaven's influence works not so,
    But that it first imprints the air;
So soul into the soul may flow,
    Though it to body first repair.

As our blood labours to beget
    Spirits, as like souls as it can;
Because such fingers need to knit
    That subtle knot, which makes us man;

So must pure lovers' souls descend
    To affections, and to faculties,
Which sense may reach and apprehend,
    Else a great Prince in prison lies.

To our bodies turn we then, that so
    Weak men on love revealed may look;
Love's mysteries in souls do grow,
    But yet the body is his book.

And if some lover, such as we,
    Have heard this dialogue of one,
Let him still mark us, he shall see
    Small change, when we're to bodies gone.

THINE EYES STILL SHINED

Ralph Waldo Emerson

Thine eyes still shined for me, though far
I lonely roved the land or sea:
As I behold yon evening star,
Which yet beholds not me.
This morn I climbed the misty hill
And roamed the pastures through;
How danced thy form before my path
Amidst the deep-eyed dew!
When the redbird spread his sable wing,
And showed his side of flame;
When the rosebud ripened to the rose,
In both I read thy name.

East Virginia

Traditional, American

I was born in East Virginia
North Carolina I did roam
There I met a pretty fair maiden
Her name and age I do not know
Her hair it was of a brightsome color
And her lips of a ruby red
On her breast she wore white lilies
There I longed to lay my head
Well in my heart you are my darling
And at my door you're welcome in
At my gate I'll meet you my darling
If your love I could only win

I'd rather be in some dark holler
Where the sun refused to shine
Than to see you another man's darling
And to know that you'll never be mine
Well in the night I'm dreaming about you
In the day I find no rest
Just the thought of you my darling
Sends aching pains all through my breast
Well when I'm dead and in my coffin
With my feet turned toward the sun
Come and sit beside me darling
Come and think on the way you done.

The Rose Is Not The Rose

Hafiz

The rose is not the rose unless thou see;
Without good wine, spring is not spring to me.

Without thy tulip cheek, the gracious air
Of gardens and of meadows is not fair.

Thy rosy limbs, unless I may embrace,
Lose for my longing eyes full half their grace;

Nor does thy scarlet mouth with honey drip
Unless I taste its honey, lip to lip.

Vainly the cypress in the zephyr sways,
Unless the nightingale be there to praise.

Nothing the mind imagines can be fair,
Except the picture that it makes of her.

Surely good wine is good, and green the end
Of gardens old — but not without the Friend.

Hafiz, the metal of thy soul is base;
Stamp not upon it the Beloved's face.

*L*IFE'S TRADES
Emily Dickinson

It 's such a little thing to weep,
So short a thing to sigh;
And yet by trades the size of these
We men and women die!

*L*OST JOY
Emily Dickinson

I had a daily bliss
I half indifferent viewed,
Till sudden I perceived it stir,—
It grew as I pursued,
Till when, around a crag,
It wasted from my sight,
Enlarged beyond my utmost scope,
I learned its sweetness right.

*T*O ONE
Gustaf Munch-Petersen

—You I dare not love—
your great soft embracing love
spreads like oil
on the restless sea of my youth—

—while I am still intoxicated, asleep
between your swaying limbs
your smile and empty
my quiver of arrow —

—you I do not want to love—
I want to see the sun through breaking seas—
—to the harsh music of my bow-string
I will go out to hunt life—

Before Day

Siegfried Sassoon

Come in this hour to set my spirit free
When earth is no more mine though night goes out,
And stretching forth these arms I cannot be
Lord of winged sunrise and dim Arcady:
When fieldward boys far off with clack and shout
From orchards scare the birds in sudden rout,
Come, ere my heart grows cold and full of doubt,
In the still summer dawns that waken me.
When the first lark goes up to look for day
And morning glimmers out of dreams, come then
Out of the songless valleys, over grey
Wide misty lands to bring me on my way:
For I am lone, a dweller among men
Hungered for what my heart shall never say.

What Kind Of Mistress He Would Have

Robert Herrick

Be the mistress of my choice,
Clean in manners, clear in voice;
Be she witty, more than wise,
Pure enough, though not precise;
Be she showing in her dress,
Like a civil wilderness,
That the curious may detect
Order in a sweet neglect;
Be she rolling in her eye,
Tempting all the passers by;
And each ringlet of her hair,
An enchantment, or a snare,
For to catch the lookers on;
But herself held fast by none.
Let her Lucrece all day be,
Then in the night, to me.
Be she such, as neither will
Famish me, nor overfill.

If You Could Come

Katharine Lee Bates

My love, my love, if you could come once more
    From your high place,
I would not question you for heavenly lore,
But, silent, take the comfort of your face.
I would not ask you if those golden spheres
    In love rejoice,
If only our stained star hath sin and tears,
But fill my famished hearing with your voice.
One touch of you were worth a thousand creeds.
    My wound is numb
Through toil-pressed, but all night long it bleeds
In aching dreams, and still you cannot come.

Song

William Congreve

Pious Selinda goes to prayers,
    If I but ask the favour;
And yet the tender fool's in tears,
    When she believes I'll leave her.

Would I were free from this restraint,
    Or else had hopes to win her;
Would she could make of me a saint,
    Or I of her a sinner.

Lingering Clouds

T'ao Ch'ien

How fair, the lingering clouds!
How misty, the seasonal rain!
Darkness fills the universe,
Blurring the level pathway.
I sit quietly in the eastern study,
Drinking spring wine alone.
My good friends are far away.
Scratching my head, I long for them.
How fair, the lingering clouds!

How misty, the seasonal rain!
Darkness fills the universe;
The land becomes a river.
I have wine! I have wine!
Leisurely I drink by the eastern window.
I yearn to speak to my friends,
But no boats or carts come.
The branches of the trees in the eastern
        garden
Are again burgeoning.
With their fresh beauty, they compete
To attract my love.
As the saying goes,
Time is short.
How can we find time to sit together
And talk of our lives?
Fluttering, the flying birds
Rest on the branches of my garden tree.
Scratching their feathers, they sit
And harmonize sweetly.
I have many friends
But I think most of you.
I want to talk with you, but you are not
        to be found.
How I resent it!

Song

John Brainard

The rocks, the rocks, among the rocks
My only lover lives;
To me the plain, to me the main,
Nor fear nor pleasure gives.

I love not in the sunny day
To weed and till the ground,
While my wild lover far away,
Hunts with his lazy hound.

Nor would I be a sailor's wife,

Too far from me is he;
For I must toil, and I must strive,
While he is on the sea.
Give me a lover to my cheek,
A husband to my arms,
Nor would I other dowry seek,
Than hills and rocky farms.

The meadow's calms, the ocean's shocks,
Each ruins or deceives;
The rocks, the rocks, among the rocks,
My only lover lives.

*W*OMAN!

John Keats

Woman! when I behold thee flippant, vain,
      Inconstant, childish, proud, and full of fancies;
  Without that modest softening that enhances
The downcast eye, repentant of the pain
That its mild light creates to heal again:
  E'en then, elate, my spirit leaps, and prances,
      E'en then my soul with exultation dances
For that to love, so long, I've dormant lain:
But when I see thee meek, and kind, and tender,
  Heavens! how desperately do I adore
Thy winning graces—to be thy defender
      I hotly burn—to be a Calidore—
A very Red Cross Knight—a stout Leander—
  Might I be loved by thee like these of yore.
Light feet, dark violet eyes, and parted hair;
  Soft dimpled hands, white neck, and creamy breast,
  Are things on which the dazzled senses rest
Till the fond, fixed eyes, forget they stare.
From such fine pictures, heavens! I cannot dare
  To turn my admiration, though unpossess'd
  They be of what is worthy,—though not drest
In lovely modesty, and virtues rare.
Yet these I leave as thoughtless as a lark;
  These lures I straight forget—e'en ere I dine,

Or thrice my palate moisten: but when I mark
    Such charms with mild intelligences shine,
My ear is open like a greedy shark,
    To catch the tunings of a voice divine.
Ah! who can e'er forget so fair a being?
    Who can forget her half retiring sweets?
    God! she is like a milk-white lamb that bleats
For man's protection. Surely the All-seeing,
Who joys to see us with his gifts agreeing,
    Will never give him pinions, who intreats
    Such innocence to ruin,—who vilely cheats
A dove-like bosom. In truth there is no freeing
One's thoughts from such a beauty; when I hear
    A lay that once I saw her hand awake,
Her form seems floating palpable, and near;
    Had I e'er seen her from an arbour take
A dewy flower, oft would that hand appear,
    And o'er my eyes the trembling moisture shake.

The Fair Singer

Andrew Marvell

To make a final conquest of all me,
Love did compose so sweet an Enemy,
In whom both Beauties to my death agree,
Joyning themselves in fatal Harmony;
That while she with her Eyes my Heart does bind,
She with her Voice might captivate my Mind.
I could have fled from One but singly fair:
My dis-intangled Soul it self might save,
Breaking the curled trammels of her hair.
But how should I avoid to be her Slave,
Whose subtile Art invisibly can wreath
My Fetters of the very Air I breath?
It had been easie fighting in some plain,
Where Victory might hang in equal choice.
But all resistance against her is vain,
Who has th' advantage both of Eyes and Voice.
And all my Forces needs must be undone,
She having gained both the Wind and Sun.

Londonberry Air

Traditional, Irish

Would God I were the tender apple blossom
That floats and falls from off the twisted bough,
To lie and faint within you silken bosom,
Within your silken bosom as that does now!
    Or would I were a little burnish'd apple
    For you to pluck me, gliding by so cold,
    While sun and shade you robe of lawn will dapple,
    Your robe of lawn, and you hair's spun gold.
Yea, would to God I were among the roses
That lean to kiss you as you float between,
While on the lowest branch a bud uncloses,
A bud uncloses, to touch you, queen.
    Nay, since you will not love, would I were growing,
    A happy daisy, in the garden path;
    That so your silver foot might press me going,
    Might press me going even unto death.

Special Pleading

Sidney Lanier

Time, hurry my Love to me:
Haste, haste! Lov'st not good company?
Here's but a heart-break sandy waste
'Twixt Now and Then.
Why, killing haste
Were best, dear Time, for thee, for thee!
Oh, would that I might divine
Thy name beyond the zodiac sign
Wherefrom our times-to-come descend.
He called thee
Sometime.
Change it, friend:
Now-time sounds so much more fine!
Sweet Sometime, fly fast to me:
Poor Now-time sits in the Lonesome-tree
And broods as gray as any dove,
And calls,

When wilt thou come, O Love?
And pleads across the waste to thee.
Good Moment, that giv'st him me,
Wast ever in love?
Maybe, maybe
Thou'lt be this heavenly velvet time
When Day and Night as rhyme and rhyme
Set lip to lip dusk-modestly;
Or haply some noon afar,
—O life's top bud, mixt rose and star,
How ever can thine utmost sweet
Be star-consummate, rose-complete,
Till thy rich reds full opened are?
Well, be it dusk-time or noon-time,
I ask but one small boon, Time:
Come thou in night, come thou in day,
I care not, I care not: have thine own way,
But only, but only, come soon, Time.

You Smiled, You Spoke, And I Believed
Walter Savage Landor

You smiled, you spoke, and I believed,
By every word and smile deceived.
Another man would hope no more;
Nor hope I what I hoped before:
But let not this last wish be vain;
Deceive, deceive me once again!

Parted
Siegfried Sassoon

Sleepless I listen to the surge and drone
And drifting roar of the town's undertone;
Till through quiet falling rain I hear the bells
Tolling and chiming their brief tune that tells
Day's midnight end. And from the day that's over
No flashes of delight I can recover;
But only dreary winter streets, and faces
Of people moving in loud clanging places:
And I in my loneliness, longing for you...
For all I did to-day, and all I'll do
To-morrow, in this city of intense
Arteried activities that throb and strive,
Is but a beating down of that suspense
Which holds me from your arms.

I am alive
Only that I may find you at the end
Of these slow-striking hours I toil to spend,
Putting each one behind me, knowing but this—
That all my days are turning toward your kiss;
That all expectancy awaits the deep
Consoling passion of your eyes, that keep
Their radiance for my coming, and their peace
For when I find in you my love's release.

All Things Are Quite Silent

Traditional, English

All things are quite silent, each mortal at rest,
When me and my love got snug in one nest,
When a bold set of ruffians they entered our cave,
And they forced my dear jewel to plough the salt wave.
I begged hard for my sailor as though I begged for life.
They'd not listen to me although a fond wife,
Saying: "The king he wants sailors, to the sea he must go,"
And they've left me lamenting in sorrow and woe.
Through green fields and meadows we ofttimes did walk,
And sweet conversation of love we have talked,
With the birds in the woodland so sweetly did sing,
And the lovely thrushes' voices made the valleys to ring.
Although my love's gone I will not be cast down.
Who knows but my sailor may once more return ?
And will make me amends for all trouble and strife,
And my true love and I might live happy for life.

Seeds Of Love

Traditional, English

I sowed the seeds of love
I sowed them in the springtime
Gathered them up in the morning so soon
While small birds sweetly sing
My garden was planted well
With flowers everywhere
I had not the liberty to choose for myself
The flower I held most dear
The gardener standing by
Three flowers he gave to me
He gave me the violet, the lily and the pink
But I refused all three
The violet I did not like
Because it fades so soon
The lily and the pink I did overthink
And vowed I would wait til June
For in June is the red, red rose
And that's the flower for me
Ofttimes have I plucked that red rosy bush
And gained a willow tree
Now the willow tree may twist
And the willow tree may twine
I wish I was lying in that young woman's
arms
That once held this heart of mine

Lonesome Dove

Traditional, American

So far away from friends and home
There's one so dear to me
There's one forever in my mind
And that fair one is she
Come back, come back, my own true love
And stay awhile with me
For if ever I had a friend on this earth
You have been a friend to me
Hush up, hush up, my own true love
For I hate to hear you cry
For the best of friends on earth must part
And so must you and I

Don't you see that lonesome dove
That flies from pine to pine
She's mourning for her own true love
Just like I mourn for mine
O don't you see the crow fly high
She turns both black and white
If ever I prove false to you
The day will turn to night
O take this ring I will to thee
And wear it on your right hand
And think of my poor aching heart
When I'm in a foreign land

Westron Wynd

Traditional, English

Westron wynd, when wilt thou blow
The smalle rain down can rain
Christ yf my love were in my arms
And I yn my bed again

An Argument

Thomas Moore

I've oft been told by learned friars,
    That wishing and the crime are one,
And Heaven punishes desires
    As much as if the deed were done.

If wishing damns us, you and I
    Are damned to all our heart's content;
Come, then, at least we may enjoy
    Some pleasure for our punishment.

If I Could Be With You

Henry Creamer & Jimmy Johnson

I'm so blue, I don't know what to do
All day long I'm pining just for you
I did wrong when I let you go away
For now I grieve about you night and day
I'm unhappy and dissatisfied
But I'd be happy if I had you by my side

All dressed up, but still nowhere to go
How I wish that I could see a show
Here I wait with no one to call me Dear
The one I love is many miles from here
Central give me One-Two-Three-Four-J
Oh won't you listen little sweetie while I say

If I could be with you I'd love you strong
If I could be with you I'd love you long
I want you to know I wouldn't go
Until I told you honey why I love you so
If I could be with you one hour tonight
If I was free to do the things I might
I'm telling you true
I'd be anything but blue
If I could be with you
If I could be with you

Sonnet VI

Sappho

Is it to love, to fix the tender gaze,
 To hide the timid blush, and steal away;
 To shun the busy world, and waste the day
In some rude mountain's solitary maze?
Is it to chant one name in ceaseless lays,
 To hear no words that other tongues can say,
 To watch the pale moon's melancholy ray,
To chide in fondness, and in folly praise?
 Is it to pour th' involuntary sigh,
To dream of bliss, and wake new pangs to prove;
 To talk, in fancy, with the speaking eye,
Then start with jealousy, and wildly rove;
 Is it to loathe the light, and wish to die?
For these I feel,—and feel that they are Love.

Absence

Duc de la Rochefoucauld

Absence lesssens half-hearted passions, and increases great ones,
as the wind puts out candles and yet stirs up the fire.

MOTHER, I CANNOT MIND MY WHEEL
Sappho

Mother, I cannot mind my wheel;
My fingers ache, my lips are dry;
Oh! if you felt the pain I feel!
But oh, whoever felt as I!

LOVE'S PHILOSOPHY
Percy Bysshe Shelley

The fountains mingle with the river,
And the rivers with the Ocean,
The winds of Heaven mix for ever
With a sweet emotion;
Nothing in the world is single;
All things by laws divine
In one spirit meet and mingle.
Why not I with thine?

See the mountains kiss high Heaven
And the waves clasp one another;
No sister flower would be forgiven
If it disdained its brother;
And the sunlight clasps the earth
And the moonbeams kiss the sea;
What is all this sweet work worth
If thou not kiss me?

SONNET XXVIII
Sappho

Weak is the sophistry, and vain the art
    That whispers patience to the mind's despair!
    That bids reflection bathe the wounds of care,
While Hope, with pleasing phantoms, soothes their smart.
For mem'ry still, reluctant to depart
    From the dear spot, once rich in prospects fair,
    Bids the fond soul enamour'd there,
And its least charm is grateful to the heart!
    He never lov'd, who could not muse and sigh,
Spangling the sacred turf with frequent tears,
    Where the small rivulet, that ripples by,
Recalls the scenes of past and happier years,
    When, on its banks he watch'd the speaking eye,
And one sweet smile o'erpaid an age of fears!

𝒥 Sing Thee With The Stock-Dove's Throat
Michael Field

I sing thee with the stock-dove's throat,
Warm, crooning, superstitious note,
That on its dearie so doth dote
It falls to sorrow,
And from the fair, white swans afloat
A dirge must borrow.
In thee I have such deep content,
I can but murmur a lament;
It is as though my heart were rent
By thy perfection,
And all my passion's torrent spent
In recollection.

𝑀y Darling
Michael Field

At this, my darling, thou did'st stray
A few feet to the rushy bed,
When a great fear and passion shook
My heart lest haply thou wert dead;
It grew so still about the brook,
As if a soul were drawn away.
My darling! Nay, our very breath
Nor light nor darkness shall divide;
Queen Dawn shall find us on one bed,
Nor must thou flutter from my side
An instant, lest I feel the dread,
At this, the immanence of death.

𝒻rom "The Rubaiyat"
Omar Khayyam

Ah, Love! could you and I with Him conspire
To grasp this sorry Scheme of Things entire,
Would not we shatter it to bits—and then
Re-mould it nearer to the Heart's Desire!

I Love Him
Barry Cornwall

I love him, I dream of him,
I sing of him by day;
And all the night I hear him talk,—
And yet he's far away.

There's beauty in the morning,
There's swetness in the May,
There's music in the running stream;
And yet he's far away.

I love him, I trust in him;
He trustesth me always:
And so the time flies hopefully,
Although he's far away.

A Hope Carol
Christina Rossetti

A night was near, a Day was near,
Between a day and night
I heard sweet voices calling clear,
Calling me:
I heard a whirr of wing on wing,
But could not see the sight;
I long to see my birds that sing,
I long to see.
Below the stars, beyond the moon,
Between the night and day
I heard a rising falling tune
Calling me:

I long to see the pipes and strings
Whereon such minstrels play;
I long to see each face that sings,
I long to see.
To-day or may be not to-day,
To-night or not to-night,
All voices that command or pray
Calling me,
Shall kindle in my soul such fire
And in my eyes such light
That I shall see that heart's desire
I long to see.

While I Walked
Lady Murasaki Shibiku

While I walked in the moonlight
I thought someone rushed past:
but clouds rolled over the sky;
I heard only the sigh of the wind.

To_____

Sidney Lanier

The Day was dying; his breath
Wavered away in a hectic gleam;
And I said, if Life's a dream, and Death
And Love and all are dreams—I'll dream.

A mist came over the bay
Like as a dream would over an eye.
The mist was white and the dream was grey
And both contained a human cry,

The burden whereof was "Love,"
And it filled both mist and dream with pain,
And the hills below and the skies above
Were touched and uttered it back again.

The mist broke: down the rift
A kind ray shot from a holy star.
Then my dream did waver and break and lift—
Through it, O Love, shone thy face, afar.

So Boyhood sets: comes Youth,
A painful night of mists and dreams;
That broods till Love's exquisite truth,
The star of a morn-clear manhood, beams.

Sonnet 97

William Shakespeare

How like a winter hath my absence been
From thee, the pleasure of the fleeting year!
What freezings have I felt, what dark days seen,
What old December's bareness everywhere!
And yet this time removed was summer's time,
The teeming autumn big with rich increase,
Bearing the wanton burden of the prime,
Like widowed wombs after their lords' decease.
Yet this abundant issue seemed to me
But hope of orphans, and unfathered fruit;

For summer and his pleasures wait on thee,
And thou away, the very birds are mute,
Or, if they sing, 'tis with so dull a cheer,
That leaves look pale, dreading the winter's near.

Sonnet XVII.
Sappho

Love steals unheeded o'er the tranquil mind,
As Summer breezes fan the sleeping main,
Slow through each fibre creeps the subtle pain,
'Till closely round the yielding bosom twin'd.
Vain is the hope the magic to unbind,
The potent mischief riots in the brain,
Grasps ev'ry thought, and burns in ev'ry vein,
'Till in the heart the Tyrant lives enshrin'd.
Oh! Victor strong! bending the vanquish'd frame;
Sweet is the thraldom that thou bid'st us prove!
And sacred is the tear thy victims claim,
For blest are those whom sighs of sorrow move!
Then nymphs beware how ye profane my name,
Nor blame my weakness, till like me ye love!

Sonnet 75
William Shakespeare

So are you to my thoughts as food to life,
Or as sweet-seasoned showers are to the ground;
And for the peace of you I hold such strife
As 'twixt a miser and his wealth is found;
Now proud as an enjoyer, and anon
Doubting the filching age will steal his treasure;
Now counting best to be with you alone,
Then bettered that the world may see my pleasure;
Sometime all full with feasting on your sight,
And by and by clean starved for a look,
Possessing or pursuing no delight
Save what is had or must from you be took.
Thus do I pine and surfeit day by day,
Or gluttoning on all, or all away.

Autumn

Christina Rossetti

I dwell alone——I dwell alone, alone,
Whilst full my river flows down to the sea,
Gilded with flashing boats
That bring no friend to me:
O love-songs, gurgling from a hundred throats,
O love-pangs, let me be.
Fair fall the freighted boats which gold and stone
And spices bear to sea:
Slim, gleaming maidens swell their mellow notes,
Love-promising, entreating——
Ah! sweet, but fleeting——
Beneath the shivering, snow-white sails.
Hush! the wind flags and fails——
Hush! they will lie becalmed in sight of strand——
Sight of my strand, where I do dwell alone;
Their songs wake singing echoes in my land——
They cannot hear me moan.
One latest, solitary swallow flies
Across the sea, rough autumn-tempest tost,
Poor bird, shall it be lost?
Dropped down into this uncongenial sea,
With no kind eyes
To watch it while it dies,
Unguessed, uncared for, free:
Set free at last,
The short pang past,
In sleep, in death, in dreamless sleep locked fast.
Mine avenue is all a growth of oaks,
Some rent by thunder strokes,
Some rustling leaves and acorns in the breeze;
Fair fall my fertile trees,
That rear their goodly heads, and live at ease.
A spider's web blocks all mine avenue;
He catches down and foolish painted flies
That spider wary and wise.
Each morn it hangs a rainbow strung with dew

Betwixt boughs green with sap,
So fair, few creatures guess it is a trap:
I will not mar the web,
Though sad I am to see the small lives ebb.
It shakes——my trees shake——for a wind is roused
In cavern where it housed:
Each white and quivering sail,
Of boats among the water leaves
Hollows and strains in the full-throated gale:
Each maiden sings again——
Each languid maiden, whom the calm
Had lulled to sleep with rest and spice and balm
Miles down my river to the sea
They float and wane,
Long miles away from me.
Perhaps they say: "She grieves,
Uplifted, like a beacon, on her tower."
Perhaps they say: "One hour
More, and we dance among the golden sheaves."
Perhaps they say: "One hour
More, and we stand,
Face to face, hand in hand;
Make haste, O slack gale, to the looked-for land!"
My trees are not in flower,
I have no bower,
And gusty creaks my tower,
And lonesome, very lonesome, is my strand.

*W*ITCH-WIFE

Edna St. Vincent Millay

She is neither pink nor pale,
    And she never will be all mine;
She learned her hands in a fairy-tale,
    And her mouth on a valentine.

She has more hair than she needs;
    In the sun 'tis a woe to me!
And her voice is a string of colored beads,
    Or steps leading into the sea.

She loves me all that she can,
    And her ways to my ways resign;
But she was not made for any man,
    And she never will be all mine.

SONNET 61
William Shakespeare

Is it thy will thy image should keep open
My heavy eyelids to the weary night?
Dost thou desire my slumbers should be broken
While shadows like to thee do mock my sight?
Is it thy spirit that thou send'st from thee
So far from home into my deeds to pry,
To find out shames and idle hours in me,
The scope and tenure of thy jealousy?
O no, thy love though much, is not so great.
It is my love that keeps mine eye awake,
Mine own true love that doth my rest defeat,
To play the watchman ever for thy sake.
    For thee watch I, whilst thou dost wake elsewhere,
    From me far off, with others all too near.

SONNET VIII
Sappho

Why, through each aching vein, with lazy pace
Thus steals the languid fountain of my heart,
While, from its source, each wild convulsive start
Tears the scorch'd roses from my burning face?
In vain, O Lesbian Vales! your charms I trace;
Vain is the poet's theme, the sculptor's art;
No more the Lyre its magic can impart,
Though wak'd to sound, with more than mortal grace!
Go, tuneful maids, go bid my Phaon prove
That passion mocks the empty boast of fame;
Tell him no joys are sweet, but joys of love,
Melting the soul, and thrilling all the frame!
Oh! may th' ecstatic thought in bosom move,
And sighs of rapture, fan the blush of shame!

Two Poems

Anonymous, Japanese

I wait and he does not come.
What difference does it make
If the nightingale sings,
When the flowering branch
Is broken?

Wing by wing the wild geese fly,
Silhouetted against high white clouds
So clearly I can count them
In the autumn night, under the moon

Sonnet 47

William Shakespeare

Betwixt mine eye and heart a league is took,
And each doth good turns now unto the other,
When that mine eye is famished for a look,
Or heart in love with sighs himself doth smother,
With my love's picture then my eye doth feast,
And to the painted banquet bids my heart.
Another time mine eye is my heart's guest
And in his thoughts of love doth share a part.
So either by thy picture or my love,
Thyself away, art present still with me,
For thou not farther than my thoughts canst move,
And I am still with them, and they with thee;
 Or if thy sleep, thy picture in my sight
 Awakes my heart to heart's and eye's delight.

Sonnet XXXVI.

Sappho

Lead me, Sicilian Maids, to haunted bow'rs,
 While yon pale moon displays her faintest beams
 O'er blasted woodlands, and enchanted streams,
Whose banks infect the breeze with pois'nous flow'rs.
Ah! lead me, where the barren mountain tow'rs,
 Where no sounds echo, but the night-owl's screams,
 Where some lone spirit of the desert gleams,
And lurid horrors wing the fateful hours!
 Now goaded frenzy grasps my shrinking brain,

Her touch absorbs the crystal fount of woe!
My blood rolls burning through each gasping vein;
Away, lost Lyre! unless thou can'st bestow
A charm, to lull that agonizing pain,
Which those who never lov'd, can never know!

Two Poems
Sosei Hoshi

Only because she said
"I will come to you soon,"
I have waited for her
a long month, and now
the moon rises at dawn.

You bring no joy, but strange regret,
O song of nightingale:
a memory of what did not exist —
the pale lover I never knew.

Sonnet 43
William Shakespeare

When most I wink, then do mine eyes best see,
For all the day they view things unrespected,
But when I sleep, in dreams they look on thee
And darkly bright, are bright in dark directed.
Then thou whose shadow shadows doth make bright,
How would thy shadow's form, form happy show
To the clear day with thy much clearer light,
When to unseeing eyes thy shade shines so!
How would, I say, mine eyes be blessed made,
By looking on thee in the living day,
When in dead night thy fair imperfect shade
Through heavy sleep on sightless eyes doth stay!
    All days are nights to see till I see thee,
    And nights bright days when dreams do show thee me.

Sonnet 147
William Shakespeare

My love is as a fever, longing still
For that which longer nurseth the disease,
Feeding on that which doth preserve the ill,

Th' uncertain sickly appetite to please.
My reason the physician to my love,
Angry that his prescriptions are not kept,
Hath left me, and I desperate now approve
Desire is death, which physic did except.
Past cure I am, now reason is past care,
And frantic-mad with evermore unrest;
My thoughts and my discourse as mad men's are,
At random from the truth vainly expressed:
    For I have sworn thee fair, and thought thee bright,
    Who art as black as hell, as dark as night.

Sonnet LXXXIX
Petrarch

Fleeing the prison where Love made me wait
So many years, only his whim to please,
Ladies, it would be tedious to relate
How the new freedom deepened my unease.
The heart was telling me that such a task
It could not bear; then I saw him go by,
The betrayer, in such deceptive mask,
That would have seduced one wiser than I.
Hence often sighing behind him I said:
—Ah me! the yoke, the fetters and the chains
Were sweeter than to go without your reins.
Unlucky, that too late I knew my ill!
How painfully I try to free my will
From the pitfall that I myself have laid.

An Ancient Gesture
Edna St. Vincent Millay

I thought, as I wiped my eyes on the corner of my apron:
Penelope did this too.
And more than once: you can't keep weaving all day
And undoing it all through the night;
Your arms get tired, and the back of your neck gets tight;
And along towards morning, when you think it will never be light,

And your husband has been gone, and you don't know where, for years.
Suddenly you burst into tears;
There is simply nothing else to do.

And I thought, as I wiped my eyes on the corner of my apron:
This is an ancient gesture, authentic, antique,
In the very best tradition, classic, Greek;
Ulysses did this too.
But only as a gesture,—a gesture which implied
To the assembled throng that he was much too moved to speak.
He learned it from Penelope...
Penelope, who really cried.

FLOWER-GATHERING
Robert Frost

I left you in the morning,
And in the morning glow
You walked a way beside me
To make me sad to go.
Do you know me in the gloaming,
Gaunt and dusty gray with roaming?
Are you dumb because you know me not,
Or dumb because you know?

All for me? And not a question
For the faded flowers gay
That could take me from beside you
For the ages of a day?
They are yours, and be the measure
Of their worth for you to treasure,
The measure of the little while
That I've been long away.

THE PIANO
Paul Verlaine

The piano, kissed by hands not sure nor strong,
   Shines dimly in the rose-grey evening air,
The while a well-remembered charming song,
   Whose wavering wings its half-heard whispers bear,
With fearful-seeming pauses here and there,
Steal round the chamber that was Hers so long.

What is this sudden strain that brings repose
   In lingering cadence on my languid eyes?
What means the playful air, that floats and flows?
Why seeks it me, the tune that softly rose,
And on the way towards the window dies,
Half-open on the little garden-close?

The Crossing

Anonymous, Egyptian

Your love is as longed for
as honey mixed with oil
on the limbs of noblemen,
as linen on bodies of gods,
as incense to the nose.

It's like a mandragora
held in a man's hand.
It's like dates a man
mixes into his beer.
It's like salt a man
adds to his daily bread.

We will be together
even in the days
of the peace of old age.
I will be with you
every day to set
before you food as though
I were a serving maid
attendant upon her master.

That Love At Length

Edna St. Vincent Millay

That Love at length should find me out and bring
This fierce and trivial brow into the dustIs,
after all, I must confess, but just;
There is a subtle beauty in the thing,
A wry perfection; wherefore now let sing
All voices how into my heart was thrust,
Unwelcome as Death's own, Love's bitter crust,
All criers proclaim it, and all steeples ring.
This being done, there let the matter rest;
What more remains is neither here nor there.
That you requite me not is plain to see;
Myself your slave herein have I confessed.
Thus far, indeed, the world may mock at me,
But if I suffer, it is my own affair.

And If At Last

Louise Labé

And if at last he drew me to his side
In hot embrace, for whom I waste away;
And if this sick necessity to stay
With him forever so were satisfied;
And if he held me so and sighed, O love,
Let us be true, let such fatality
Join us as neither hurricane nor sea
Nor subtler turbulence shall ever move;
And if I held him bound upon my breast,
Frantic and ardent, as the ivies cling
About the mighty bough; and death should spring
Upon me: I should offer all my breath
Upon his lips at last, and sink to rest.
Knowing in life no lovelier thing than death.

Serenade (For Music)

Oscar Wilde

The western wind is blowing fair
      Across the dark Aegean sea,
  And at the secret marble stair
      My Tyrian galley waits for thee.
Come down! the purple sail is spread,
      The watchman sleeps within the town,
O leave thy lily-flowered bed,
      O Lady mine come down, come down!
She will not come, I know her well,
      Of lover's vows she hath no care,   10
And little good a man can tell
      Of one so cruel and so fair.
True love is but a woman's toy,
      They never know the lover's pain,
And I who loved as loves a boy
      Must love in vain, must love in vain.
O noble pilot tell me true

Is that the sheen of golden hair?
Or is it but the tangled dew
    That binds the passion-flowers there?   20
Good sailor come and tell me now
    Is that my Lady's lily hand?
Or is it but the gleaming prow,
    Or is it but the silver sand?
No! no! 'tis not the tangled dew,
    'Tis not the silver-fretted sand,
It is my own dear Lady true
    With golden hair and lily hand!
O noble pilot steer for Troy,
    Good sailor ply the labouring oar,   30
This is the Queen of life and joy
    Whom we must bear from Grecian shore!
The waning sky grows faint and blue,
    It wants an hour still of day,
Aboard! aboard! my gallant crew,
    O Lady mine away! away!
O noble pilot steer for Troy,
    Good sailor ply the labouring oar,
O loved as only loves a boy!
    O loved for ever evermore!

BUT IN THE WINE-PRESSES THE HUMAN GRAPES SING NOT NOR DANCE
William Blake

But in the Wine-presses the human grapes sing not nor dance:
They howl and writhe in shoals of torment, in fierce flames consuming,
In chains of iron and in dungeons circled with ceaseless fires,
In pits and dens and shades of death, in shapes of torment and woe:
The plates and screws and racks and saws and cords and fires and cisterns
The cruel joys of Luvah's Daughters, lacerating with knives
And whips their victims, and the deadly sport of Luvah's Sons.

They dance around the dying and they drink the howl and groan,
They catch the shrieks in cups of gold, they hand them to one another:
These are the sports of love, and these the sweet delights of amorous play,
Tears of the grape, the death sweat of the cluster, the last sigh
Of the mild youth who listens to the luring songs of Luvah.

Ardor
Gamliel Bradford

Others make verses of grace.
　Mine are all muscle and sinew.
Others can picture your face.
　But I all the tumult within you.

Others can give you delight,
And delight I confess is worth giving.
But my songs must tickle and bite
And burn with the ardor of living.

Venus Americana
George Sylvester Viereck

Tannhaeuser speaks:
Time's famished mouth is choked with sands,
But I, thy knight, have made no gain,
Save tribulations of the hands,
And fierce caresses of the brain.

Once more the Magic Mound is rent,
My feet, but not for Rome, depart
From hectic lusts that die unspent,
The sterile orchids of thy heart.

Ten thousand years and lovers tire
Even the gods. They wrought such change
That the Greek wine of thy desire
Has turned to absinthe, drugged and strange.

Thou art a captive of thy spleen
Within thy golden House of Mirth,
Borne in a shimmering limousine,
Thy small feet never touch the earth.

Fear and earth-strange nerve fibres pull
Thy heart-strings by an unseen wire
From the fruition of love's full
Delight. Thy brain alone is fire.

But though thy body's loveliness
Pin man's heart like a butterfly,
I shall not sell my soul for less
Than love for love, than eye for eye.

Such pleasure as Prince Paris had
To whom thy pulses sang out sweet,
And many a brown Sicilian lad—
The ungirt loin, the sun-kissed feet!

My love's too dear a thing, I ween,
To thrill an empty mood of thine,
Drowned like that pearl the dusky queen
Dissolved in dark Egyptian wine.

Neurotic Venus, from thy cave
Come into God's air, salt and fresh,
Or snatch from some Hellenic grave
The splendid courage of the flesh!

The Dreame
John Donne

Image of her whom I love, more than she,
Whose faire impression in my faithfull heart,
Makes me her Medall, and makes her love mee,
As Kings do coynes, to which their stamps impart
The value: goe, and take my heart from hence,
Which now is growne too great and good for me:
Honours oppresse weake spirits, and our sense
Strong objects dull; the more, the lesse wee see.
When you are gone, and Reason gone with you,
Then Fantasie is Queene and Soule, and all;
She can present joyes meaner than you do;
Convenient and more proportional. So, if I dreame
I have you, I have you,
For, all our joyes are but fantasticall.
And so I 'scape the paine, for paine is true;
And sleep which locks up sense, doth lock out all.
After such a fruition I shall wake,
And, but to the waking nothing shall repent;
And shall to love more thankful Sonnets make,
Than if more honour, teares, and paines were spent.
But dearest heart, and dearer image stay;
Alas, true joyes at best are dreame enough;
Though you stay here you passe too fast away:
For even at first lifes Taper is a snuffe.
Fill'd with her love, may I rather be grown
Mad with much heart, than idiot with none.

Dreams
Emily Dickinson

Let me not mar that perfect dream
By an auroral stain,
But so adjust my daily night
That it will come again.

Lyrics Of Love, Lyric One

Fenton Johnson

When in Slumberland the dreams go forth
To my heart a darling maiden comes,
Stardust are her eyes, her lips love flame,
And an angel tune she softly hums.

Never 'neath the dwelling place of God,
Never by the lake or by the sea,
Was a man so blest as I am blest
With the love that Clara gives to me.

Oh, my heart will burn for ages long
From a fever that will never die,
For in Slumber land an elfin rogue
Poured his magic lotion on my eye.

To Citriodora

Philip Henry Savage

I turn and see you passing in the street
When you are not. I take another way,
Lest missing you the fragrance of the day
Exhale, and I know not that it is sweet.

And marking you I follow, and when we meet
Love laughs to see how sudden I am gay;
Sweetens the air with fragrance like a spray
Of sweet verbena, and bids my heart to beat.

Love laughs; and girls that take you by the hand,
Know that a sweet thing has befallen them;
And women give their hearts into your heart.
There is, I think, no man in all the land
But would be glad to touch your garment's hem.
And I, I love you with a love apart.

IV

Emily Dickinson

We cover thee, sweet face.
Not that we tire of thee,
But that thyself fatigue of us;
Remember, as thou flee,
We follow thee until
Thou notice us no more,

And then, reluctant, turn away
To con thee o'er and o'er,
And blame the scanty love
We were content to show,
Augmented, sweet, a hundred fold
If thou would'st take it now.

*F*OILED SLEEP

Baronness Marie-Madeleine Von Puttkamer

Ah me! I cannot sleep at night;
And when I shut my eyes, forsooth,
I cannot banish from my sight
The vision of her slender youth.
She stands before me lover-wise,
Her naked beauty fair and slim,
She smiles upon me, and her eyes
With over fierce desire grow dim.

Slowly she leans to me. I meet
The passion of her gaze anew,
And then her laughter, clear and sweet,
Thrills all the hollow silence through.
O, siren, with the mocking tongue!
O beauty, lily-sweet and white!
I see her, slim and fair and young.
And ah! I cannot sleep tonight.

*T*o_____

Edgar Allan Poe

The bowers whereat, in dreams, I see
    The wantonest singing birds,
Are lips-and all thy melody
    Of lip-begotten words-

Thine eyes, in Heaven of heart enshrined,
    Then desolately fall,
O God! on my funereal mind
    Like starlight on a pall-

Thy heart- thy heart!- I wake and sigh,
    And sleep to dream till day
Of the truth that gold can never buy—
    Of the baubles that it may.

$\mathcal{I}$F

Paul Laurence Dunbar

If life were but a dream, my Love,
And death the waking time;
If day had not a beam, my Love,
And night had not a rhyme,
—A barren, barren world were this
Without one saving gleam;
I'd only ask that with a kiss
You'd wake me from the dream.

If dreaming were the sum of days,
And loving were the bane;
If battling for a wreath of bays
Could soothe a heart in pain,
—I'd scorn the meed of battle's might,
All other aims above
I'd choose the human's higher right,
To suffer and to love!

$\mathcal{L}$ONGING

Emily Dickinson

I envy seas whereon he rides,
I envy spokes of wheels
Of chariots that him convey,
I envy speechless hills
That gaze upon his journey;
How easy all can see
What is forbidden utterly
As heaven, unto me!
I envy nests of sparrows
That dot his distant eaves,
The wealthy fly upon his pane,
The happy, happy leaves
That just abroad his window
Have summer's leave to be,
The earrings of Pisarro
Could not obtain for me.
I envy light that wakes him,
And bells that boldly ring
To tell him it is noon abroad,—
Myself his noon could bring,
Yet interdict my blossom
And abrogate my bee,
Lest noon in everlasting night
Drop Gabriel and me.

Waiting, Afield At Dusk
Robert Frost

What things for dream there are when spectre-like,
Moving among tall haycocks lightly piled,
I enter alone upon the stubble field,
From which the laborers' voices late have died,
And in the antiphony of afterglow
And rising full moon, sit me down
Upon the full moon's side of the first haycock
And lose myself amid so many alike.
I dream upon the opposing lights of the hour,
Preventing shadow until the moon prevail;
I dream upon the night-hawks peopling heaven,
Each circling each with vague unearthly cry,
Or plunging headlong with fierce twang afar;
And on the bat's mute antics, who would seem
Dimly to have made out my secret place,
Only to lose it when he pirouettes,
And seek it endlessly with purblind haste;
On the last swallow's sweep; and on the rasp
In the abyss of odor and rustle at my back,
That, silenced by my advent, finds once more,
After an interval, his instrument,
And tries once—twice—and thrice if I be there;
And on the worn book of old-golden song
I brought not here to read, it seems, but hold
And freshen in this air of withering sweetness;
But on the memory of one absent most,
For whom these lines when they shall greet her eye.

Sonnet 6
William Shakespeare

Then let not winter's ragged hand deface,
In thee thy summer ere thou be distilled:
Make sweet some vial; treasure thou some place,
With beauty's treasure ere it be self-killed:
That use is not forbidden usury,
Which happies those that pay the willing loan;

That's for thy self to breed another thee,
Or ten times happier be it ten for one,
Ten times thy self were happier than thou art,
If ten of thine ten times refigured thee:
Then what could death do if thou shouldst depart,
Leaving thee living in posterity?
> Be not self-willed for thou art much too fair,
> To be death's conquest and make worms thine heir.

Sonnet 17

William Shakespeare

Who will believe my verse in time to come
If it were filled with your most high deserts?
Though yet heaven knows it is but as a tomb
Which hides your life, and shows not half your parts:
If I could write the beauty of your eyes,
And in fresh numbers number all your graces,
The age to come would say this poet lies,
Such heavenly touches ne'er touched earthly faces.
So should my papers (yellowed with their age)
Be scorned, like old men of less truth than tongue,
And your true rights be termed a poet's rage,
And stretched metre of an antique song.
> But were some child of yours alive that time,
> You should live twice in it, and in my rhyme.

Sonnet 31

William Shakespeare

Thy bosom is endeared with all hearts,
Which I by lacking have supposed dead,
And there reigns love and all love's loving parts,
And all those friends which I thought buried.
How many a holy and obsequious tear
Hath dear religious love stol'n from mine eye,
As interest of the dead, which now appear,
But things removed that hidden in thee lie.
Thou art the grave where buried love doth live,

Hung with the trophies of my lovers gone,
Who all their parts of me to thee did give,
That due of many, now is thine alone.
　　Their images I loved, I view in thee,
　　And thou (all they) hast all the all of me.

Sonnet 63

William Shakespeare

Against my love shall be as I am now
With Time's injurious hand crushed and o'erworn,
When hours have drained his blood and filled his brow
With lines and wrinkles, when his youthful morn
Hath travelled on to age's steepy night,
And all those beauties whereof now he's king
Are vanishing, or vanished out of sight,
Stealing away the treasure of his spring:
For such a time do I now fortify
Against confounding age's cruel knife,
That he shall never cut from memory
My sweet love's beauty, though my lover's life.
　　His beauty shall in these black lines be seen,
　　And they shall live, and he in them still green.

Sonnet 71

William Shakespeare

No longer mourn for me when I am dead,
Than you shall hear the surly sullen bell
Give warning to the world that I am fled
From this vile world with vilest worms to dwell:
Nay if you read this line, remember not,
The hand that writ it, for I love you so,
That I in your sweet thoughts would be forgot,
If thinking on me then should make you woe.
O if (I say) you look upon this verse,
When I (perhaps) compounded am with clay,
Do not so much as my poor name rehearse;
But let your love even with my life decay.
　　Lest the wise world should look into your moan,
　　And mock you with me after I am gone.

Sonnet 107

William Shakespeare

Not mine own fears, nor the prophetic soul,
Of the wide world, dreaming on things to come,
Can yet the lease of my true love control,
Supposed as forfeit to a confined doom.
The mortal moon hath her eclipse endured,
And the sad augurs mock their own presage,
Incertainties now crown themselves assured,
And peace proclaims olives of endless age.
Now with the drops of this most balmy time,
My love looks fresh, and death to me subscribes,
Since spite of him I'll live in this poor rhyme,
While he insults o'er dull and speechless tribes.
    And thou in this shalt find thy monument,
    When tyrants' crests and tombs of brass are spent.

Believe Me,
If All Those Endearing Young Charms

Thomas Moore

Believe me, if all those endearing young charms,
Which I gaze on so fondly to-day,
Were to change by to-morrow, and fleet in my arms,
Live fairy-gifts fading away,
Thou wouldst still be adored, as this moment thou art,
Let thy loveliness fade as it will,
And around the dear ruin each wish of my heart
Would entwine itself verdantly still.
It is not while beauty and youth are thine own,
And thy cheeks unprofaned by a tear,
That the fervor and faith of a soul may be known,
To which time will but make thee more dear!
No, the heart that has truly loved never forgets,
But as truly loves on to the close,
As the sunflower turns on her god when he sets
The same look which she turned when he rose!

'Tis The Last Rose Of Summer

Thomnas Moore

'Tis the last rose of Summer,
Left blooming alone;
All her lovely companions
Are faded and gone;
No flower of her kindred,
No rosebud is nigh,
To reflect back her blushes,
Or give sigh for sigh!
I'll not leave thee, thou lone one,
To pine on the stem;
Since the lovely are sleeping,
Go sleep thou with them.
Thus kindly I scatter

Thy leaves o'er the bed
Where thy
mates of the garden
Lie scentless and dead.
So soon may I follow,
When friendships decay,
And from Love's shining circle
The gems drop away!
When true hearts lie withered,
And fond ones are flown,
Oh! who would inhabit
This bleak world alone?

Self-Confidence

Sharon Mesmer

I have forsaken thoughts of watching clocks,
and groping blindly for phones at ungodly hours.
It is time now to search for shopkeepers,
proudly unrolling red and white canopies.
Time to sit on the fire escape in the red fog
and not blubber,
so that my tongue becomes thick as bubble gum,
and I pull frantically in my half-sleep to free it.
Something must be done.
My former intention was to be a movie star,
but you say I was born in the wrong era:
I should have been thirty-five years old in the Fifties,
with stiff blonde hair stouter than a muscleman,
and gotten picked up in bars by gas station attendants
while applying lipstick,
a shade called "Rich Girl Red,"
and reapplying it again and again.
I was also born in the wrong country:
I should have smoked Gitanes,
clutched a bottle of Chanel,

opened a slim gold compact
and loosened your thin tie on crowded downtown streets,
as you ran your thumb across your lips...

My glove is in the garden.
Get it!
There's a fire on the floor.
Now find it!
Please come in wearing your black beret and camel coat,
I really don't care where you bought it.

Pajaro Valley, Early Spring (for Ed)
Amber Coverdale Sumrall

In the orchard blackbirds fly close
to the ground, their wings burnished
by morning sun. Heat ripples above
wild mustard, blurs the landscape.
Not a single leaf is visible on rows
of apple trees, only their hard green buds.
I sit in a field of tall grasses
wondering if there will come a time when
our bodies lose their familiar pull,
when our hearts refuse to rekindle.
A time in which we may as well be dead.

Tonight I will be hundreds of miles south
of this valley, in a place that holds
most of our history. You will look at me
and open your arms. I will walk into
the light and dark of your eyes.
A country without map or direction.

A kestrel waits in the empty branches
for the smallest movement. What could it teach
me of patience if I were willing to stay?
In the warming earth, moles forage among
twisted roots. They know it is time to surface.
Time to risk the keen eye and swift descent,
the sudden black shadow they will never even see.

To Marguerite: Continued
Matthew Arnold

Yes! in the sea of life enisled,
With echoing straits between us thrown,
Dotting the shoreless watery wild,
We mortal millions live alone.
The islands feel the enclasping flow,
And then their endless bounds they know.

But when the moon their hollows lights,
And they are swept by balms of spring,
And in their glens, on starry nights,
The nightingales divinely sing;
And lovely notes, from shore to shore,
Across the sounds and channels pour—

Oh! then a longing like despair
Is to their farthest caverns sent;
For surely once, they feel, we were
Parts of a single continent!
Now round us spreads the watery plain—
Oh might our marges meet again!

Who order'd, that their longing's fire
Should be, as soon as kindled, cool'd?
Who renders vain their deep desire?—
A God, a God their severance ruled!
And bade betwixt their shores to be
The unplumb'd, salt, estranging sea.

Love In A Life
Robert Browning

I

Room after room,
I hunt the house through
We inhabit together.
Heart, fear nothing, for, heart, thou shalt find her—
Next time, herself!—not the trouble behind her
Left in the curtain, the couch's perfume!
As she brushed it, the cornice-wreath blossomed anew:
Yon looking-glass gleamed at the wave of her feather.

II

Yet the day wears,
And door succeeds door;
I try the fresh fortune—
Range the wide house from the wing to the centre.
Still the same chance! she goes out as I enter.
Spend my whole day in the quest,—who cares?
But 'tis twilight, you see,—with such suites to explore,
Such closets to search, such alcoves to importune!

Roses Rising

Rene Viviewn

My brunette with the golden eyes, your ivory body, your amber
Has left bright reflections in the room
Above the garden.
The clear midnight sky, under my closed lids,
Still shines…I am drunk from so many roses
Redder than wine.
Leaving their garden, the roses have followed me....
I drink their brief breath, I breathe their life.
All of them are here.
It's a miracle…The stars have risen,
Hastily, across the wide windows
Where the melted gold pours.
Now, among the roses and the stars,
You, here in my room, loosening your robe,
And your nakedness glistens
Your unspeakable gaze rests on my eyes....
Without stars and without flowers, I dream the impossible
In the cold night.

Slumber Song

Siegfried Sassoon

Sleep; and my song shall build about your bed
A paradise of dimness. You shall feel
The folding of tired wings; and peace will dwell
Throned in your silence: and one hour shall hold
Summer, and midnight, and immensity
Lulled to forgetfulness. For, where you dream,
The stately gloom of foliage shall embower
Your slumbering thought with tapestries of blue.
And there shall be no memory of the sky,
Nor sunlight with its cruelty of swords.
But, to your soul that sinks from deep to deep
Through drowned and glimmering colour, Time shall be
Only slow rhythmic swaying; and your breath;
And roses in the darkness; and my love.

Undine

Rene Vivien

Your laughter is light, your caress deep,
Your cold kisses love the harm they do;
Your eyes—blue lotus waves
And the water lilies are less pure than your face..
You flee, a fluid parting,
Your hair falls in gentle tangles;
Your voice—a treacherous tide;
Your arms—supple reeds.
Long river reeds, their embrace
Enlaces, chokes, strangles savagely,
Deep in the waves, an agony
Extinguished in a night drift.

Valley Song

Carl Sandburg

Your eyes and the valley are memories.
Your eyes fire and the valley a bowl.
It was here a moonrise crept over the timberline.
It was here we turned the coffee cups upside down.
And your eyes and the moon swept the valley.
I will see you again to-morrow.
I will see you again in a million years.
I will never know your dark eyes again.
These are three ghosts I keep.
These are three sumach-red dogs I run with.
All of it wraps and knots to a riddle:
I have the moon, the timberline, and you.
All three are gone—and I keep all three.

Sonnet 39

William Shakespeare

O how thy worth with manners may I sing,
When thou art all the better part of me?
What can mine own praise to mine own self bring:
And what is't but mine own when I praise thee?
Even for this, let us divided live,

And our dear love lose name of single one,
That by this separation I may give:
That due to thee which thou deserv'st alone:
O absence what a torment wouldst thou prove,
Were it not thy sour leisure gave sweet leave,
To entertain the time with thoughts of love,
Which time and thoughts so sweetly doth deceive.
    And that thou teachest how to make one twain,
    By praising him here who doth hence remain.

Sonnet 44

William Shakespeare

If the dull substance of my flesh were thought,
Injurious distance should not stop my way,
For then despite of space I would be brought,
From limits far remote, where thou dost stay,
No matter then although my foot did stand
Upon the farthest earth removed from thee,
For nimble thought can jump both sea and land,
As soon as think the place where he would be.
But ah, thought kills me that I am not thought
To leap large lengths of miles when thou art gone,
But that so much of earth and water wrought,
I must attend, time's leisure with my moan.
    Receiving nought by elements so slow,
    But heavy tears, badges of either's woe

Sonnet 48

William Shakespeare

How careful was I when I took my way,
Each trifle under truest bars to thrust,
That to my use it might unused stay
From hands of falsehood, in sure wards of trust!
But thou, to whom my jewels trifles are,
Most worthy comfort, now my greatest grief,
Thou best of dearest, and mine only care,
Art left the prey of every vulgar thief.
Thee have I not locked up in any chest,
Save where thou art not, though I feel thou art,

Within the gentle closure of my breast,
From whence at pleasure thou mayst come and part,
And even thence thou wilt be stol'n I fear,
For truth proves thievish for a prize so dear.

Sonnet 52

William Shakespeare

So am I as the rich whose blessed key,
Can bring him to his sweet up-locked treasure,
The which he will not every hour survey,
For blunting the fine point of seldom pleasure.
Therefore are feasts so solemn and so rare,
Since seldom coming in that long year set,
Like stones of worth they thinly placed are,
Or captain jewels in the carcanet.
So is the time that keeps you as my chest
Or as the wardrobe which the robe doth hide,
To make some special instant special-blest,
By new unfolding his imprisoned pride.
    Blessed are you whose worthiness gives scope,
    Being had to triumph, being lacked to hope.

Sonnet 58

William Shakespeare

That god forbid, that made me first your slave,
I should in thought control your times of pleasure,
Or at your hand th' account of hours to crave,
Being your vassal bound to stay your leisure.
O let me suffer (being at your beck)
Th' imprisoned absence of your liberty,
And patience tame to sufferance bide each check,
Without accusing you of injury.
Be where you list, your charter is so strong,
That you your self may privilage your time
To what you will, to you it doth belong,
Your self to pardon of self-doing crime.
    I am to wait, though waiting so be hell,
    Not blame your pleasure be it ill or well.

Sonnet 59

William Shakespeare

If there be nothing new, but that which is,
Hath been before, how are our brains beguiled,
Which labouring for invention bear amis
The second burthen of a former child!
O that record could with a backward look,
Even of five hundred courses of the sun,
Show me your image in some antique book,
Since mind at first in character was done.
That I might see what the old world could say,
To this composed wonder of your frame,
Whether we are mended, or whether better they,
Or whether revolution be the same.
    O sure I am the wits of former days,
    To subjects worse have given admiring praise.

Sonnet 77

William Shakespeare

Thy glass will show thee how thy beauties wear,
Thy dial how thy precious minutes waste,
These vacant leaves thy mind's imprint will bear,
And of this book, this learning mayst thou taste.
The wrinkles which thy glass will truly show,
Of mouthed graves will give thee memory,
Thou by thy dial's shady stealth mayst know,
Time's thievish progress to eternity.
Look what thy memory cannot contain,
Commit to these waste blanks, and thou shalt find
Those children nursed, delivered from thy brain,
To take a new acquaintance of thy mind.
    These offices, so oft as thou wilt look,
    Shall profit thee, and much enrich thy book.

Sonnet 98

William Shakespeare

From you have I been absent in the spring,
When proud-pied April (dressed in all his trim)
Hath put a spirit of youth in every thing:
That heavy Saturn laughed and leaped with him.
Yet nor the lays of birds, nor the sweet smell
Of different flowers in odour and in hue,
Could make me any summer's story tell:
Or from their proud lap pluck them where they grew:
Nor did I wonder at the lily's white,
Nor praise the deep vermilion in the rose,
They were but sweet, but figures of delight:
Drawn after you, you pattern of all those.
    Yet seemed it winter still, and you away,
    As with your shadow I with these did play.

Sonnet 120

William Shakespeare

That you were once unkind befriends me now,
And for that sorrow, which I then did feel,
Needs must I under my transgression bow,
Unless my nerves were brass or hammered steel.
For if you were by my unkindness shaken
As I by yours, y'have passed a hell of time,
And I a tyrant have no leisure taken
To weigh how once I suffered in your crime.
O that our night of woe might have remembered
My deepest sense, how hard true sorrow hits,
And soon to you, as you to me then tendered
The humble salve, which wounded bosoms fits!
    But that your trespass now becomes a fee,
    Mine ransoms yours, and yours must ransom me.

Sonnet 135

William Shakespeare

Whoever hath her wish, thou hast thy will,
And 'Will' to boot, and 'Will' in over-plus,
More than enough am I that vex thee still,
To thy sweet will making addition thus.
Wilt thou whose will is large and spacious,
Not once vouchsafe to hide my will in thine?
Shall will in others seem right gracious,
And in my will no fair acceptance shine?
The sea all water, yet receives rain still,
And in abundance addeth to his store,
So thou being rich in will add to thy will
One will of mine to make thy large will more.
    Let no unkind, no fair beseechers kill,
    Think all but one, and me in that one 'Will.'

Sonnet 136

William Shakespeare

If thy soul check thee that I come so near,
Swear to thy blind soul that I was thy 'Will',
And will thy soul knows is admitted there,
Thus far for love, my love-suit sweet fulfil.
'Will', will fulfil the treasure of thy love,
Ay, fill it full with wills, and my will one,
In things of great receipt with case we prove,
Among a number one is reckoned none.
Then in the number let me pass untold,
Though in thy store's account I one must be,
For nothing hold me, so it please thee hold,
That nothing me, a something sweet to thee.
    Make but my name thy love, and love that still,
    And then thou lov'st me for my name is Will.

Sonnet 151

William Shakespeare

Love is too young to know what conscience is,
Yet who knows not conscience is born of love?
Then gentle cheater urge not my amiss,
Lest guilty of my faults thy sweet self prove.
For thou betraying me, I do betray
My nobler part to my gross body's treason,
My soul doth tell my body that he may,
Triumph in love, flesh stays no farther reason,
But rising at thy name doth point out thee,
As his triumphant prize, proud of this pride,
He is contented thy poor drudge to be,
To stand in thy affairs, fall by thy side.
    No want of conscience hold it that I call,
    Her love, for whose dear love I rise and fall.

The Living Flame Of Love

St. John of the Cross

O Living flame of love
That, burning, dost assail
My inmost soul with tenderness untold,
Since thour dost freely move
Deign to consume the veil
Which sunders this sweet converse that
    we hold.

O burn that searest never!
O wound of deep delight!
O gentle hand! O touch of love supernal
That quick'nest life for ever,
Putt'st all my woes to flight,
And, slaying, changest death to life eternal!

And O, ye lamps of fire,
In whose resplendent light
The deepest caverns where the senses meet,
Erst steep'd in darkness dire,
blaze with new glories bright
And to the lov'd one give both light
    and heat!

How tender is the love
Thou wak'nest in my breast
When thou, alone and secretly, art there!
Whispering of things above,
Most glorious and most blest,
How delicate the love thou mak'st me bear!

THE RELIC

John Donne

When my grave is broke up again
Some second guest to entertain,
For graves have learn'd that woman head,
To be to more than one a bed)
And he that digs it, spies
A bracelet of bright hair about the bone,
Will he not let's alone,
And think that there a loving couple lies,
Who thought that this device might be some way
To make their souls, at the last busy day,
Meet at this grave, and make a little stay?

If this fall in a time, or land,
Where mis-devotion doth command,
Then he, that digs us up, will bring
Us to the bishop, and the king,
To make us relics; then
Thou shalt be a Mary Magdalen, and I
A something else thereby;
All women shall adore us, and some men;
And since at such time miracles are sought,
I would have that age by this paper taught
What miracles we harmless lovers wrought.

First, we lov'd well and faithfully,
Yet knew not what we lov'd, nor why;
Difference of sex no more we knew
Than our guardian angels do;
Coming and going, we
Perchance might kiss, but not between those meals;
Our hands ne'er touch'd the seals
Which nature, injur'd by late law, sets free;
These miracles we did, but now alas,
All measure, and all language, I should pass,
Should I tell what a miracle she was.

The Flaming Heart (excerpt)

Richard Crashaw

O heart, the equal poise of love's both parts,
Big alike with wounds and darts,
Live in these conquering leaves; live all the same,
And walk through all tongues one triumphant flame;
Live here, great heart, and love and die and kill,
And bleed and wound, and yield and conquer still.
Let this immortal life, where'er it comes,
Walk in a crowd of loves and martyrdoms;
Let mystic deaths wait on 't, and wise souls be
The love-slain witnesses of this life of thee.
O sweet incendiary! show here thy art,
Upon this carcass of a hard cold heart,
Let all thy scatter'd shafts of light, that play
Among the leaves of thy large books of day,
Combin'd against this breast, at once break in
And take away from me my self and sin;
This gracious robbery shall thy bounty be,
And my best fortunes such fair spoils of me.
O thou undaunted daughter of desires!
By all thy dow'r of lights and fires,
By all the eagle in thee, all the dove,
By all thy lives and deaths of love,
By thy large draughts of intellectual day,
And by thy thirsts of love more large than they,
By all thy brim-fill'd bowls of fierce desire,
By thy last morning's draught of liquid fire,
By the full kingdom of that final kiss
That seiz'd thy parting soul and seal'd thee his,
By all the heav'ns thou hast in him,
Fair sister of the seraphim!
By all of him we have in thee,
Leave nothing of my self in me:
Let me so read thy life that I
Unto all life of mine may die.

Constancy To An Ideal Object
Samuel Taylor Coleridge

Since all that beat about in Nature's range,
Or veer or vanish; why should'st thou remain
The only constant in a world of change,
O yearning Thought! that liv'st but in the brain?
Call to the Hours, that in the distance play,
The faery people of the future day—
Fond Thought! not one of all that shining swarm
Will breathe on thee with life-enkindling breath,
Till when, like strangers shelt'ring from a storm,
Hope and Despair meet in the porch of Death!
Yet still thou haunt'st me; and though well I see,
She is not thou, and only thou are she,
Still, still as though some dear embodied Good,
Some living Love before my eyes there stood
With answering look a ready ear to lend,
I mourn to thee and say—"Ah! loveliest friend!
That this the meed of all my toils might be,
To have a home, an English home, and thee!"
Vain repetition! Home and Thou are one.
The peacefull'st cot, the moon shall shine upon,
Lulled by the thrush and wakened by the lark,
Without thee were but a becalm{'e}d bark,
Whose Helmsman on an ocean waste and wide
Sits mute and pale his mouldering helm beside.

And art thou nothing? Such thou art, as when
The woodman winding westward up the glen
At wintry dawn, where o'er the sheep-track's maze
The viewless snow-mist weaves a glist'ning haze,
Sees full before him, gliding without tread,
An image with a glory round its head;
The enamoured rustic worships its fair hues,
Nor knows he makes the shadow, he pursues!

LOVE EVERLASTING

Rhyme LXXXI (Eternal Love)

Gustavo Adolfo Becquer

The sun could cast an eternal shadow,
And the sea could run dry in but a chime;
The earth's axis could break
Like crystal fine.
Anything could happen! Death enswathing
Could cover me with it's mournful attire;
But in me your love's flame
Could never expire.

All Around My Hat (I Will Wear The Green Willow)

Traditional English Folk Song

My love she was fair, and my love she was kind
And cruel the judge and jury that sentenced her away
For thieving was a thing that she never was inclined to
They sent my love across the sea ten thousand miles away.

All around my hat, I will wear the green willow
All around my hat for a year and a day
And if anyone should question me the reason for my wearing it
I'll tell them that my own true love is ten thousand miles away.

I bought my love a golden ring to wear upon her finger
A token of our own true love and to remember me
And when she returns again, we never will be parted
We'll marry and be happy for ever and a day.

Seven, seven long years my love and I are parted
Seven, seven long years my love is bound to stay
Seven long years I'll love my love and never be false-hearted
And never sigh or sorrow while she's far, far away.

Some young men there are who are preciously deceitful,
A-coaxin' of the fair young maids they mean to lead astray
As soon as they deceive them, so cruelly they leave them
I'll love my love forever though she's far, far away.

Sonnet 65

William Shakespeare

Since brass, nor stone, nor earth, nor boundless sea,
But sad mortality o'ersways their power,
How with this rage shall beauty hold a plea,
Whose action is no stronger than a flower?
O, how shall summer's honey breath hold out,
Against the wrackful siege of batt'ring days,
When rocks impregnable are not so stout,
Nor gates of steel so strong but Time decays?
O fearful meditation, where alack,
Shall Time's best jewel from Time's chest lie hid?
Or what strong hand can hold his swift foot back,
Or who his spoil of beauty can forbid?
    O, none, unless this miracle have might,
    That in black ink my love may still shine bright.

Danny Boy

Traditional, Irish

Oh Danny boy, the pipes, the pipes are calling
From glen to glen, and down the mountain side
The summer's gone, and all the flowers are dying
'Tis you, 'tis you must go and I must bide.
But come you back when summer's in the meadow
Or when the valley's hushed and white with snow
'Tis I'll be there in sunshine or in shadow
Oh Danny boy, oh Danny boy, I love you so.
And if you come, when all the flowers are dying
And I am dead, as dead I well may be
You'll come and find the place where I am lying
And kneel and say an "Ave" there for me.
And I shall hear, tho' soft you tread above me
And all my dreams will warm and sweeter be
If you'll not fail to tell me that you love me
I simply sleep in peace until you come to me.

The Bailiff Of Islington's Daughter

Anonymous, Traditional English Folk Song

There was a youth and a well belov-ed youth
And he was the Squire's son.
He loved the bailiff's daughter dear
That lived in Islington.
But she was coy and would not believe
That he did love her so,
Nor would she at any time
Any countenance to him show.
And when his friends did understand
His fond and foolish pride
They sent him up to far London
An apprentice for to bind.
Seven long years went rolling by
And ne'er did his true love see.
Many a tear have I shed for her sake
When little she thought of me.
The maids of Islington went forth
Went forth to sport and play,
All but the bailiff's daughter dear.
She secretly stole away.
And as she went along the road,
The weather being hot and dry,
She sat down on a shady bank.
Her true love came riding by.
She sprang up with color so bright
And seized his bridle rein,
"One penny, one penny, kind sir," she said,
"T'would ease me of much pain."
"Before I give you a penny, sweetheart,
Pray tell me where you were born."
"At Islington, kind sir," said she,
"Where I have had many a scorn."
"Before I give you a penny, sweetheart,
Pray tell me whether you know
The bailiff's daughter of Islington."
"She's dead, sir, long ago."

"If she be dead, then take my horse,
My saddle and bridle also,
And I will go to some far land
Where no one me shall know."
"Oh, stay, oh, stay, you goodly youth,
She's standing by your side.
She is not dead but alive and well
And ready to be your bride."
"Depart sorrow and welcome joy,
Many thousand times and more,
For now I have my own true love
Whom I thought I would see no more "

Sonnet 109

William Shakespeare

O, never say that I was false of heart,
Though absence seemed my flame to qualify.
As easy might I from myself depart
As from my soul, which in thy breast doth lie.
That is my home of love; if I have ranged,
Like him that travels I return again,
Just to the time, not with the time exchanged,
So that myself bring water for my stain,
Never believe, though in my nature reigned
All frailties that besiege all kinds of blood,
That it could so preposterously be stained
To leave for nothing all thy sum of good:
    For nothing this wide universe I call
    Save thou my rose; in it thou art my all.

Black Is The Color Of My True Love's Hair

Anonymous, Traditional English

Black is the color of my true love's hair
Her lips are like some rosy fair
The purest eyes and the neatest hands
I love the ground whereon she stands
I go to the Clyde for to mourn and weep

But satisfied I never can sleep
I'll write to you in a few short lines
I'll suffer death ten thousand times
I know my love and well she knows
I love the grass whereon she goes
If she on earth no more I see
My life will quickly fade away
A winter's past and the leaves are green
The time has past that we have seen
But still I hope the time will come
When you and I will be as one
Black is the color of my true love's hair
Her lips are like some rosy fair
The purest eyes and the neatest hands
I love the ground whereon she stands.

WHEN MY BLUE MOON TURNS TO GOLD AGAIN

Traditional, American

When my blue moon turns to gold again
When the rainbow turns the clouds away
When my blue moon turns to gold again
You'll be back in my arms to stay

Memories that linger in my heart
Memories that make my heart grow cold
But someday they'll live again sweetheart
And my blue moon again will turn to gold

The lips that used to thrill me so
Your kisses were meant for only me
In my dreams they live again sweetheart
But my blue moon is just a memory

The castles we used to build together
Were the sweetest stories ever told
Maybe we will live them all again
And my blue moon again will turn to gold

Discipline

D. H. Lawrence

It is stormy, and raindrops cling like silver bees to the pane,
The thin sycamores in the playground are swinging with flattened leaves;
The heads of the boys move dimly through a yellow gloom that stains
The class; over them all the dark net of my discipline weaves.
It is no good, dear, gentleness and forbearance, I endured too long:
I have pushed my hands in the dark soil, under the flower of my soul
And the gentle leaves, and have felt where the roots are strong
Fixed in the darkness, grappling for the deep soil's little control.
And there is the dark, my darling, where the roots are entangled and fight
Each one for its hold on the oblivious darkness, I know that there
In the night where we first have being, before we rise on the light,
We are not brothers, my darling, we fight and we do not spare.
And in the original dark the roots cannot keep, cannot know
Any communion whatever, but they bind themselves on to the dark,
And drawing the darkness together, crush from it a twilight, a slow
Burning that breaks at last into leaves and a flower's bright spark.
I came to the boys with love, my dear, but they turned on me;
I came with gentleness, with my heart 'twixt my hands like a bowl,
Like a loving-cup, like a grail, but they spilt it triumphantly
And tried to break the vessel, and to violate my soul.
But what have I to do with the boys, deep down in my soul, my love?
I throw from out of the darkness my self like a flower into sight,
Like a flower from out of the night-time, I lift my face, and those
Who will may warm their hands at me, comfort this night.
But whosoever would pluck apart my flowering shall burn their hands,
So flowers are tender folk, and roots can only hide,
Yet my flowerings of love are a fire, and the scarlet brands
Of my love are roses to look at, but flames to chide.
But comfort me, my love, now the fires are low,
Now I am broken to earth like a winter destroyed, and all
Myself but a knowledge of roots, of roots in the dark that throw
A net on the undersoil, which lies passive beneath their thrall.
But comfort me, for henceforth my love is yours alone,
To you alone will I offer the bowl, to you will I give
My essence only, but love me, and I will atone
To you for my general loving, atone as long as I live.

Lovers' Infiniteness
John Donne

If yet I have not all thy love,
Dear, I shall never have it all;
I cannot breathe one other sigh, to move,
Nor can intreat one other tear to fall;
And all my treasure, which should purchase thee—
Sighs, tears, and oaths, and letters—I have spent.
Yet no more can be due to me,
Than at the bargain made was meant;
If then thy gift of love were partial,
That some to me, some should to others fall,
Dear, I shall never have thee all.

Or if then thou gavest me all,
All was but all, which thou hadst then;
But if in thy heart, since, there be or shall
New love created be, by other men,
Which have their stocks entire, and can in tears,
In sighs, in oaths, and letters, outbid me,
This new love may beget new fears,
For this love was not vow'd by thee.
And yet it was, thy gift being general;
The ground, thy heart, is mine; whatever shall
Grow there, dear, I should have it all.

Yet I would not have all yet,
He that hath all can have no more;
And since my love doth every day admit
New growth, thou shouldst have new rewards in store;
Thou canst not every day give me thy heart,
If thou canst give it, then thou never gavest it;
Love's riddles are, that though thy heart depart,
It stays at home, and thou with losing savest it;
But we will have a way more liberal,
Than changing hearts, to join them; so we shall
Be one, and one another's all.

Life In A Love

Robert Browning

Escape me?
Never—
Beloved!
While I am I, and you are you,
So long as the world contains us both,
Me the loving and you the loth,
While the one eludes, must the other pursue.
My life is a fault at last, I fear:
It seems too much like a fate, indeed!
Though I do my best I shall scarce succeed.
But what if I fail of my purpose here?
It is but to keep the nerves at strain,
To dry one's eyes and laugh at a fall,
And, baffled, get up and begin again,—
So the chase takes up one's life, that's all.
While, look but once from your farthest bound
At me so deep in the dust and dark,
No sooner the old hope goes to ground
Than a new one, straight to the self-same mark,
I shape me—
Ever
Removed!

To Asra

Samuel Taylor Coleridge

Are there two things, of all which men possess,
That are so like each other and so near,
As mutual Love seems like to Happiness?
Dear Asra, woman beyond utterance dear!
This Love which ever welling at my heart,
Now in its living fount doth heave and fall,
Now overflowing pours thro' every part
Of all my frame, and fills and changes all,
Like vernal waters springing up through snow,
This Love that seeming great beyond the power
Of growth, yet seemeth ever more to grow,

Could I transmute the whole to one rich Dower
Of Happy Life, and give it all to Thee,
Thy lot, methinks, were Heaven, thy age, Eternity!

THE DREAM

Grace Greenwood

Last night, my love, I dreamed of thee,
Yet 'twas no dream Elysian:
Draw closer to my breast, dear Blanche,
The while I tell the vision.

Methought that I had left thee long,
And, home in haste returning,
My heart, lip, cheek, with love and joy
And wild impatience burning,

—I called thee through the silent house;
But here, at last, I found thee,
Where, deathly still and ghostly white,
The curtains fell around thee.

Dead! —dead thou wert! Cold lay that form,
In rarest beauty moulded,
And meekly, o'er thy still, white breast
The snowy hands were folded.

Methought thy couch was fitly strewn
With many a fragrant blossom;
Fresh violets thy fingers clasped,
And rose-buds decked thy bosom:

But thine eyes, so like young violets,
Might smile upon me never
—And the rose-bloom from thy cheek and lip
Had fled away for ever!

I raised thee lovingly, thy head
Against my bosom leaning,
And called thy name, and spoke to thee
In words of tenderest meaning.

I sought to warm thee at my breast,
My arms close round thee flinging;
To breathe my life into thy lips,
With kisses fond and clinging.

O hour of fearful agony!
In vain my frenzied pleading!
Thy dear voice hushed, thy kind eye closed,
My lonely grief unheeding!

Pale wert thou as the lily-buds
Twined 'mid thy raven tresses,
And cold thy lip and still thy heart
To all my wild caresses!

I woke, amid the autumn night,
To hear the rain descending,
And roar of waves and howl of winds
In stormy concert blending.

But, O, my waking joy was morn,
From heaven's own portals flowing!
And the summer of thy living love
Was round about me glowing!

I woke,—ah, blessedness! —to feel
Thy white arms round me wreathing,
—To hear, amid the lonely night,
Thy calm and gentle breathing!

I bent above thy rest till morn,
With many a whispered blessing;
Soft, timid kisses on thy lips
And blue-veined eyelids pressing.

While thus, from slumber's shadowy realm,
Thy truant soul recalling,
Thou couldst not know whence sprang the tears
Upon thy forehead falling.

And, O, thine eyes' sweet wonderment,
When thou didst ope them slowly,
To mark mine own bent on thy face
In rapture deep and holy!

Thou couldst not know, till I had told
That dream of fearful warning,
How much of heaven was in my words,
—"God bless thee, love,—good morning!"

To Anthea, Who May Command Him Anything

Robert Herrick

Bid me to live, and I will live
Thy protestant to be;
Or bid me love, and I will give
A loving heart to thee.

A heart as soft, a heart as kind,
A heart as sound and free,
As in the whole world thou canst find,
That heart I'll give to thee.

Bid that heart stay, and it will stay,
To honour thy decree;
Or bid it languish quite away,
And 't shall do so for thee.

Bid me to weep, and I will weep,
While I have eyes to see;
And having none, yet I will keep
A heart to weep for thee.

Bid me despair, and I'll despair,
Under that cypress tree;
Or bid me die, and I will dare
E'en death, to die for thee.

Thou art my life, my love, my heart,
The very eyes of me;
And hast command of every part,
To live and die for thee.

To—In Absence

Grace Greenwood

When first we met, beloved, rememberest thou
How all my nature was athirst and faint?
My soul's high powers lay wasting still and slow,
While my sad heart sighed forth its ceaseless plaint.

For frowning pride life's summer waves did lock
Away from light, —their restless murmuring hushed;
But thou didst smite the cold, defying rock,
And full and fast the living waters gushed!

O, what a summer glory life put on!
What morning freshness those swift waters gave,
That leaped from darkness forth into the sun,
And mirrored heaven in every smallest wave!

The cloud that darkened long our sky of love,
And flung a shadow o'er life's Eden bloom,
Hath deepened into night, around, above,
—But night beneficent and void of gloom,

—The dews of peace and faith's sweet quiet bringing,
And memory's starlight, as joy's sunlight fades,
While, like the nightingale's melodious singing,
The voice of Hope steals out amid the shades.

Now it hath come and gone, the shadowed day,
The time of farewells that beheld us part,
I miss thy presence from my side alway,
—Thy smile's sweet comfort raining on my heart.

Yes, we are parted.
Now I call thy name,
And listen long, but no dear voice replies:
I miss thine earnest praise, thy gentle blame,
And the mute blessing of thy loving eyes.

Yet no, not parted.
Still in life and power
Thy spirit cometh over wild and wave,
Is ever near me in the trial-hour,
A ready help, a presence strong and brave.

Thy love breathes o'er me in the winds of heaven,
Floats to me on the tides of morning light,
Descends upon me in the calms of even,
And fills with music all the dreamy night.

It falleth as a robe of pride around me,
A royal vesture rich. with purple gleams,
—It is the glory wherewith life hath crowned me,
The large fulfilment of my soul's long dreams!

It is a paling; and drowning notes of sadness,
It is a great light shutting out all gloom,
It is a fountain of perpetual gladness,
It is a garden of perpetual bloom.

But to thy nature pride and power belong,
And death-defying courage; what to thee,
With thy great life, thy spirit high and strong,
May my one love in all its fulness be?

An inward joy, sharp e'en to pain, yet dear
As thy soul's life, —a warmth, a light serene,
—A low, deep voice which none save thou may hear,
—A living presence, constant, though unseen.

Yet shalt thou fold it closer to thy breast,
In the dark days, when other loves depart,
And when thou liest down for the long rest,
Then, O beloved, 'twill sleep upon thy heart!

The Good Morrow

John Donne

I wonder by me troth, what thou and I
    Did, till we loved? Were we not weaned till then?
But sucked on country pleasures, childishly?
    Or snorted we i' the seven sleepers' den?
'Twas so; But this, all pleasures fancies be.
If ever any beauty I did see,
Which I desired, and got, 'twas but a dream of thee.

And now good morrow to our waking souls,
    Which watch not one another out of fear;
For love, all love of other sights controls,
    And makes one little room, and everywhere.
Let sea-discoverers to new worlds have gone,
Let maps to others, worlds on worlds have shown,
Let us possess our world, each hath one, and is one.

My face in thine eye, thine in mine appears,
    And true plain hearts do in the faces rest,
    Without sharp North, without declining West?
Whatever dies, was not mixed equally;
If for two loves be one, or, thou and I
Love so alike, that none do slacken, none can die.

To My Excellent Lucasia, On Our Friendship
Katherine Fowler Philips

I did not live until this time
    Crown'd my felicity,
When I could say without a crime,
    I am not thine, but thee.
This carcass breath'd, and walk't, and slept,
    So that the world believe'd
There was a soul the motions kept;
    But they were all deceiv'd.
For as a watch by art is wound
    To motion, such was mine:
But never had Orinda found
    A soul till she found thine;
Which now inspires, cures and supplies,
    And guides my darkened breast:
For thou art all that I can prize,
    My joy, my life, my rest.
No bridegroom's nor crown-conqueror's mirth
    To mine compar'd can be:
They have but pieces of the earth,
    I've all the world in thee.
Then let our flames still light and shine,
    And no false fear control,
As innocent as our design,
    Immortal as our soul.

Do You Remember Me? Or Are You Proud?
William Savage Landor

"Do you remember me? or are you proud?"
Lightly advancing thro' her star-trimm'd crowd,
Ianthe said, and lookt into my eyes,
"A yes, a yes, to both: for Memory
Where you but once have been must ever be,
And at your voice Pride from his throne must rise."

Bright Star

John Keats

Bright star! would I were steadfast as thou art—
    Not in lone splendour hung aloft the night,
And watching, with eternal lids apart,
    Like Nature's patient sleepless Eremite,
The moving waters at their priestlike task
    Of pure ablution round earth's human shores,
Or gazing on the new soft fallen mask
    Of snow upon the mountains and the moors—
No—yet still steadfast, still unchangeable,
    Pillow'd upon my fair love's ripening breast,
To feel for ever its soft fall and swell,
    Awake for ever in a sweet unrest,
Still, still to hear her tender-taken breath,
    And so live ever—or else swoon to death.

A Song Of Eternity In Time

Sidney Lanier

Once, at night, in the manor wood
My Love and I long silent stood,
Amazed that any heavens could
Decree to part us, bitterly repining.

My Love, in aimless love and grief,
Reached forth and drew aside a leaf
That just above us played the thief
And stole our starlight that for us was shining.

A star that had remarked her pain
Shone straightway down that leafy lane,
And wrought his image, mirror-plain,
Within a tear that on her lash hung gleaming.

"Thus Time," I cried, " is but a tear
Some one hath wept 'twixt hope and fear,
Yet in his little lucent sphere
Our star of stars, Eternity, is beaming"

Lorena

Traditional, American

The years creep slowly by, Lorena,
The snow is on the grass again;
The sun's low down the sky, Lorena,
The frost gleams where the flowers have been.
>But the heart throbs on as warmly now
>As when the summer days were nigh;
>Oh, the sun can never dip so low
>A-down affection's cloudless sky.
A hundred months have passed, Lorena,
Since last I held that hand in mine,
And felt the pulse beat fast, Lorena,
Though mine beat faster far than thine.
>A hundred months—'twas flowery May,
>When up the hilly slope we climbed,
>To watch the dying of the day
>And hear the distant church bells chime.
We loved each other then, Lorena,
More than we ever dared to tell;
And what we might have been, Lorena,
Had but our loving prospered well!
>But then, 'tis past; the years have gone,
>I'll not call up their shadowy forms;
>I'll say to them, "Lost years, sleep on,
>Sleep on, nor heed life's pelting storms."
The story of the past, Lorena,
Alas! I care not to repeat;
The hopes that could not last, Lorena,
They lived, but only lived to cheat.
>I would not cause e'en one regret _
>To rankle in your bosom now —
>"For if we try we may forget,"
>Were words of thine long years ago.
Yes, these were words of thine, Lorena—
They are within my memory yet.
They touched some tender chords, Lorena,
Which thrill and tremble with regret.

'Twas not the woman's heart which spoke—
Thy heart was always true to me;
A duty stern and piercing broke
The tie which linked my soul with thee.
It matters little now, Lorena,
The past is in the eternal past;
Our hearts will soon lie low, Lorena,
Life's tide is ebbing out so fast.
There is a future, oh, thank God!
Of life this is so small a part—
'Tis dust to dust beneath the sod.
But there, up there, 'tis heart to heart.

The Widower

John Brainard

O doth it walk—that spirit bright and pure,
And may it disembodied, ever come
Back to this earth? I do not, dare not hope,
A reappearance of that kindest eye,

Or of that smoothest cheek or sweetest voice,
—But can she see my tears, when I, alone,
Weep by her grave? and may she leave the throng
Where angels minister and saints adore,

To visit this sad earth!
When, as the nights
Of fireside winter gather chilly round,
I kiss our little child, and lay me down

Upon a widowed pillow, doth she leave
Those glorious, holy, heavenly essences,
Those sacred perfumes round the throne on high,
To keep a watch on me? and upon ours?

—Her I did love, and I was loved again,
—And had it been my mortal lot, instead,
I would, were I accepted, ask my God,
For one more look upon my wife and child.

At The Foot Of Yonder Mountain

Anonymous, American

At the foot of yonder mountain there runs a clear stream,
At the foot of yonder mountain there lives a fair queen;
She's handsome, she's proper, and her ways are complete.
I ask no better pasttime than to be with my sweet.
But why she won't have me I well understand;
She wants some freeholder and I have no land.
I cannot maintain her on silver and gold,
And all the other fine things that my love's house should hold.
Oh I wish I were a penman and could write a fine hand!
I would write my love a letter from this distant land.
I'd send it by the waters just for to let her know
That I think of pretty Mary wherever I go.
Oh I wish I were a bird and had wings and could fly,
It's to my love's dwelling this night I'd draw nigh.
I'd sit in her window all night long and cry
That for love of pretty Mary I gladly would die.

Plaisir D'amour

Traditional, Canadian

The joys of love are but a moment long
The pain of love endures the whole life long
Your eyes kissed mine, I saw the love in them shine
You brought me heaven right there when your eyes kissed mine
My love loves me, a world of wonder I see
A rainbow shines thru my window; my love loves me
And now he's gone like a dream that fades in the dawn
But the words stay locked in my heartstrings; my love loves me
Plaisir d'amour ne dure qu'on moment
Chagrin d'amour dure toute la vie
J'ai toute quitte pour l'ingrate Sylvie
Elle me quit et me prend un autre amour
Tant qur cette eau coutera doucement
Vera a ruisseau qui bord la prairie
Je t'amerai, me repetait Sylvie
Mais l'eau coute encore elle a change portant

Banks Of The Condamine

Anonymous, Australian

"Oh hark! The dogs are barking, I can no longer stay
The men have all gone mustering," I heard the publican say
And I must be off in the morning, love, before the sun does shine
To meet the contract shearers on the banks of the Condamine."
"Oh Willie, dearest Willie, don't leave me here to mourn
Don't make me curse and rue the day that ever I was born
For parting with you Willie is like parting with me life
So stay and be a selector, love, and I will be your wife."
"Oh Nancy, dearest Nancy, you know that I must go
Old Hallerand is expecting me, his shearing for to do
But while I'm on the bogs, me love, I'll think of you with pride
And our shears they will go freely when I'm on the whippin' side."
"Oh I'll cut off my yellow hair and go along with you
I'll dress myself in men's attire and be a shearer too
I'll cook and count your tally, love while, ringer, you will shine?
And I'll wash your greasy moleskins on the banks of the Condamine."
"Oh Nancy, dearest Nancy, you know that can't be so
The boss has given order, love, no woman shall do so
And your delicate constitution's not equal unto mine
To eat the ramstack mutton on the banks of the Condamine.
But when the shearing's over, love, I'll make you me wife
I'll take up a selection and I'll settle down for life
And when the day's work's over, love, and the evening's clear and fine
I'll tell of them sandy cobblers on the banks of the Condamine."

Absence

Percy Bysshe Shelley

Music, when soft voices die,
Vibrates in the memory;
Odors, when sweet violets sicken,
Live within the scent they quicken.

Rose leaves, when the rose is dead,
Are heaped for the beloved's bed;
And so thy thoughts, when thou art gone,
Love itself shall slumber on.

Since First I Saw Your Face

Thomas Ford

Since first I saw your face
I resolv'd to honour and reknown ye,
If now I be disdained
I wish my heart had never known ye.
    What! I that lov'd and you that lik'd
    Shall be begin to wrangle?
    No, no, no, my heart is fast
    And cannot disentangle.
If I admire or praise you too much
That fault you may forgive me.
Or if my hands had stray'd a touch
Then justly might you leave me.

I ask'd you leave, you bade me love
Is't now a time to chide me?
No, no, no, I'll love you still
What fortune e'er betide me.
The sun, whose beams most glorious are
Rejecteth no beholder;
And your sweet beauty, past compare,
Made my poor eyes the bolder.
    Where beauty moves and wit delights
    And signs of kindness find me
    There, oh there, where'er I go
    I'll leave my heart behind me.

Love Me Little, Love Me Long

Anonymous, British

Love me little, love me long,
Is the burden of my song.
Love that is too hot and strong
    Burneth soon to waste.
Still, I would not have thee cold,
Not too backward, nor too bold;
Love that lasteth till 'tis old
    Fadeth not in haste.

If thou lovest me too much,
It will not prove as true as touch;
Love me little, more than such,
    For I fear the end.
I am little well content,
And a little from thee sent
Is enough, with true intent
    To be steadfast friend.

Say thou lov'st me while thou live;
I to my love will give,
Never dreaming to deceive
    While that life endures.

Nay, and after death, in sooth,
I to thee will keep my truth,
As now, when in my May of youth;
    This my love asssures.

Constant love is moderate ever,
And it will through life persevere;
Give me that, with true endeavor
    I will it restore.
A suit of durance let it be,
For all weathers that for me,
For the land or for the sea,
    Lasting evermore.

Winter's cold or summer's heat,
Autumn's tempests on it beat,
It can never know defeat,
    Never can rebel.
Such the love that I would gain,
Such the love, I tell thee plain,
Thou must give, or woo in vain;
    So to thee, farewell!

Slumber-Song
Siegfried Sassoon

Sleep, and my song shall build about your bed
A paradise of dimness. You shall feel
The folding of tired wings; and peace will dwell
Throned in your silence: and one hour shall hold
Summer, and midnight, and immensity
Lulled to forgetfulness. For, where you dream,
The stately gloom of foliage shall embower
Your slumbering thought with tapestries of blue.
And there shall be no memory of the sky,
Nor sunlight with its cruelty of swords.
But, to your soul that sinks from deep to deep
Through drowned and glimmering colour, Time shall be
Only slow rhythmic swaying; and your breath;
And roses in the darkness; and my love.

To_____
Percy Bysshe Shelley

One word is too often profaned
 For me to profane it;
One feeling too falsely disdained
For thee to disdain it;
One hope is too like despair
For prudence to smother;
And pity from thee more dear
Than that from another.

I can give not what men call love:
But wilt thou accept not
The worship the heart lifts above
And the heavens reject not,
The desire of the moth for the star,
Of the night for the morrow,
The devotion to something afar
From the fear of our sorrow?

REMEMBRANCE
Emily Brontë

Cold in the earth, and the deep snow piled above thee!
Far, far removed, cold in the dreary grave!
Have I forgot, my Only Love, to love thee,
Severed at last by Time's all-wearing wave?

Now, when alone, do my thoughts no longer hover
Over the mountains, on that northern shore;
Resting their wings where heath and fern-leaves cover
Thy noble heart for ever, ever more?

Cold in the earth, and fifteen wild Decembers
From those brown hills have melted into spring-
Faithful indeed is the spirit that remembers
After such years of change and suffering!

Sweet Love of youth, forgive if I forget thee
While the World's tide is bearing me along:
Other desires and other hopes beset me,
Hopes which obscure but cannot do thee wrong.

No later light has lightened up my heaven,
No second morn has ever shone for me:
All my life's bliss from thy dear life was given-
All my life's bliss is in the grave with thee.

But when the days of golden dreams had perished
And even Despair was powerless to destroy,
Then did I learn how existence could be cherished,
Strengthened and fed without the aid of joy;

Then did I check the tears of useless passion,
Weaned my young soul from yearning after thine;
Sternly denied its burning wish to hasten
Down to that tomb already more than mine!

And even yet, I dare not let it languish,
Dare not indulge in Memory's rapturous pain;
Once drinking deep of that divinest anguish,
How could I seek the empty world again?

As A Perfume

Arthur Symons

As a perfume doth remain
In the folds where it hath lain,
So the thought of you, remaining
Deeply folded in my brain,
Will not leave me: all things leave me:
You remain.

Other thoughts may come and go,
Other moments I may know
That shall waft me, in their going,
As a breath blown to and fro,
Fragrant memories: fragrant memories
Come and go.

Only thoughts of you remain
In my heart where they have lain,
Perfumed thoughts of you, remaining,
A hid sweetness, in my brain.
Other leave me: all things leave me:
You remain.

Will He

Lady Horikawa

Will he love me forever?
There's no way I can tell.
Since sunrise my thoughts
have been as disheveled
as my black hair.

There Is A Lady Sweet And Kind

Anonymous

There is a lady sweet and kind,
Was never a face so pleased my mind;
I did but see her passing by,
And yet I love her till I die.

Her gesture, motion and her smiles,
Her wit, her voice, my heart beguiles,
Beguiles my heart, I know not why,
And yet I love her till I die.

Her free behavior, winning looks,
Will make a lawyer burn his books.
I touched her not, alas, not I,
And yet I love her till I die.

Had I her fast betwixt mine arms,
Judge you that think such sports were harms,
Were't any harm? No, no, fie, fie!
For I will love her till I die.

Should I remain confin'd there,
So long as Phoebus in his sphere,
I to request, she to deny,
Yet would I love her till I die.

Cupid is wing'd and doth range;
Her country so my love doth change,
But change she earth, or change she sky,
Yet will I love her till I die.

XLIV

Emily Dickinson

If I may have it when it 's dead
I will contented be;
If just as soon as breath is out
It shall belong to me,
Until they lock it in the grave,
'T is bliss I cannot weigh,
For though they lock thee in the grave,
Myself can hold the key.
Think of it, lover! I and thee
Permitted face to face to be;
After a life, a death we 'll say,—
For death was that, and this is thee.

Love Me

Fenton Johnson

Love me, love me evermore,
Oh, my honey! Oh, my honey!
Love me till the Judgment Day,
Oh, my honey! Oh, my honey!
When the angel sounds the call
Hold my hand and hold it long
I will guide thee o'er the tide
To the Throne of God Himself,
Oh, my honey! Oh, my honey!

Love me, love me evermore,
Oh, my honey! Oh, my honey!
Love me through the ages long,
Oh, my honey! Oh, my honey!
Kiss my brow when life is cold
And a-down the stream I float,
Lift me from the ways of earth
To the warmth of God Himself,
Oh, my honey! Oh, my honey!

Love me, love me evermore,
Oh, my honey! Oh, my honey!
Love me till the stream runs dry,
Oh, my honey! Oh, my honey!
Thrice a thousand times to die
Would be like a day with God
If that dying would bring thee
To my heart a single hour,
Oh, my honey! Oh, my honey!

Love

Emily Dickinson

Love is anterior to life,
Posterior to death,
Initial of creation, and
The exponent of breath.

L'ENVOI

Fenton Johnson

The dreamer nods, and honeyed sleep
His eyelids woo; his day is done.
No more the vision burns his soul,
But lives within his memory.

Her shadow mantle Evening drops;
The bee is drowsy on the vine;
From heart of rose the pollen drips,
And dripping blinds the fairy's eye.

Across the surging tide of Night
Comes reasonant the voice of God
"Oh Love! —True love is best of all;
It lives…it lives beyond the years."

SONNET 116

William Shakespeare

Let me not to the marriage of true minds
Admit impediments. Love is not love
Which alters when it alteration finds,
Or bends with the remover to remove:
O no! it is an ever-fixed mark
That looks on tempests and is never shaken;
It is the star to every wandering bark,
Whose worth's unknown, although his height be taken.
Love's not Time's fool, though rosy lips and cheeks
Within his bending sickle's compass come:
Love alters not with his brief hours and weeks,
But bears it out even to the edge of doom.
    If this be error and upon me proved,
    I never writ, nor no man ever loved.

Sonnet 55

William Shakespeare

Not marble, nor the gilded monuments
Of princes, shall outlive this powerful rhyme,
But you shall shine more bright in these contents
Than unswept stone, besmeared with sluttish time.
When wasteful war shall statues overturn,
And broils root out the work of masonry,
Nor Mars his sword, nor war's quick fire shall burn
The living record of your memory.
'Gainst death, and all-oblivious enmity
Shall you pace forth; your praise shall still find room
Even in the eyes of all posterity
That wear this world out to the ending doom.
    So, till the judgment that yourself arise,
    You live in this, and dwell in lovers' eyes.

Song Of A Second April

Edna St. Vincent Millay

April this year, not otherwise
Than April of a year ago
Is full of whispers, full of sighs,
Dazzling mud and dingy snow;
Hepaticas that pleased you so
Are here again, and butterflies.

There rings a hammering all day,
And shingles lie about the doors;
From orchards near and far away
The gray wood-pecker taps and bores,
And men are merry at their chores,
And children earnest at their play.

The larger streams run still and deep;
Noisy and swift the small brooks run.
Among the mullein stalks the sheep
Go up the hillside in the sun
Pensively; only you are gone,
You that alone I cared to keep.

Song From Chartivel

Marie de France

Hath any loved you well, down there,
    Summer or winter through?
Down there, have you found any fair
    Laid in the grave with you?
Is death's long kiss a richer kiss
    Than mine was wont to be-
Or have you gone to some far bliss
    And quite forgotten me?

What soft enamoring of sleep
    Hath you in some soft way?
What charmed death holdeth you with deep
    Strange lure by night and day?
A little space below the grass,
    Out of the sun and shade;
But worlds away from me, alas,
    Down there where you are laid.

My brightest waved and wasted gold,
    What is it now to thee-
Whether the rose-red life I hold
    Or white death holdeth me?
Down there you love the grave's own green,
    And evermore you rave
Of some sweet seraph you have seen
    Or dreamt of in the grave.

There you shall lie as you have lain,
    Though in the world above,
Another live your life again,
    Loving again your love:

Is it not sweet beneath the palm?
    Is it not warm day rife
With some long mystic golden calm
    Better than love and life?

The broad quaint odorous leaves like hands
    Weaving the fair day through,
Weave sleep no burnished bird withstands,
    While death weaves sleep for you;
And many a strange rich breathing sound
    Ravishes morn and noon:
And in that place you must have found
    Death a delicious swoon-

Hold me no longer for a word
    I used to say or sing:
Ah, long ago you must have heard
    So many a sweeter thing:
For rich earth must have reached your heart
    And turned the faith to flowers;
And warm wind stolen, part by part,
    Your soul through faithless hours.

And many a soft seed must have won
    Soil of some yeilding thought,
To bring a bloom up to the sun
    That else had ne'er been brought;
And, doubtless, many a passionate hue
    Hath made that place more fair,
Making some passionate part of you
    Faithless to me down there.

*R*OSES

Pierre de Ronsard

As one sees on the branch in the month of May the rose
In her beautiful youth, in the dawn of her flower,
When the break of day softens her life with the shower,
Make jealous the sky of the damask bloom she shows:
Grace lingers in her leaf and love sleeping glows
But, broken by the rain or the sun's oppressive power,
Languishing she dies, and all her petals throws,
Thus in thy first youth, in thy awakening fair
When thy beauty was honnored by lips of Earth and Air,
Atropos has killed thee and dust thy form reposes.
O take, take for obsequies my tears, these poor showers,
This vase filled with milk, this basket strewn with flowers,
That in death as in life thy body may be roses.

A CARRION

Charles Baudelaire

Remember now, my Love, what piteous thing
    We saw on a summer's gracious day:
By the roadway a hideous carrion, quivering
    On a clean bed of pebbly clay,

Her legs flexed in the air like a courtesan,
    Burning and sweating venomously,
Calmly exposed it belly, ironic and wan,
    Clamorous with foul ecstasy.

The sun bore down upon this rottenness
    As if to roast it with gold fire,
And render back to Nature her own largess
    A hundredfold of her desire.

Heaven observed the vaunting carcass there
    Blooming with the richness of a flower;
And that almighty stink which corpses wear
    Choked you with sleepy power!

The flies swarmed on that putrid vulva, then
    A black tumbling rout would seethe
Of maggots, thick like a torrent in a glen,
    Over those rags that lived and seemed to breathe.

They darted down and rose up like a wave
    Or buzzed impetuously as before;
One would have thought the corpse was held a slave
    To living by the life it bore!

This world had music, its own swift emotion
    Like water and the wind running,
Or corn that a winnower rhythmic motion
    Fans with fiery cunning.

All forms receded, as in a dream were still,
    Where white visions vaguely start
From the sketch of a painter's long-neglected idyl;
    Into a perfect art!

Behind the rocks a restless bitch looked on,
    Regarding us with jealous eyes,
Waiting to tear from the livid skeleton
    Her loosed morsel quick with flies.

And even you will come to this foul shame,
    This ultimate infection,
Star of my eyes, my being's inner flame,
    My angel and my passion!

Yes: such you shall be, O queen of heavenly grace,
    Beyond the last sacrament,
When through your bones the flowers and sucking grass
    Weave their rank cerement.

Speak, then, my Beauty, to this dire putrescence,
    To the worm that shall kiss your proud estate,
That I have kept the divine form and the essence
    Of my festered loves inviolate!

Song

Gil Vicente

If thou art sleeping, maiden,
    Awake and open thy door.
'Tis the break of day, and we must away
    O'er meadow, and mount, and moor.

Wait not to find thy slippers,
    But come with thy naked feet;
We shall have to pass through the dewy grass
    And waters wide and fleet.

To _____

Fitz-Greene Halleck

The world is bright before thee,
Its summer flowers are thine,
Its calm blue sky is o'er thee,
Thy bosom
Pleasure's shrine;
And thine the sunbeam given
To Nature's morning hour,
Pure, warm, as when from heaven
It burst on Eden's bower.

There is a song of sorrow,
The death-dirge of the gay,
That tells, ere dawn of morrow,
These charms may melt away,
That sun's bright beam be shaded,
That sky be blue no more,
The summer flowers be faded,
And youth's warm promise o'er.

Believe it not—though lonely
Thy evening home may be;
Though Beauty's bark can only
Float on a summer sea;
Though Time thy bloom is stealing,
There's still beyond his art
The wild-flower wreath of feeling,
The sunbeam of the heart.

The Night Piece, To Julia

Robert Herrick

Her eyes the glowworm lend thee;
The shooting stars attend thee;
 And the elves also
 Whoses little eyes glow
Like the sparks of fire, befriend thee.

No will-o'-the-wisp mislight thee;
Nor snake or slowworm bite thee;
 But on thy way,
 Not making a stay,
Since ghost there's none to affright thee.

Let not the dark thee cumber;
What though the moon does slumber?
 The stars of the night
 Will lend thee their light,
Like tapers clear without number.

Then, Julia, let me woo thee,
Thus, thus to come unto me;
 And when I shall meet
 Thy silvery feet,
My soul I'll pour into thee.

Promised Land

Ahmet Hasim

Let it play with your hair, this gentle breeze
Blowing from the seven seas.
If only you knew
How lovely you are the way you gaze at the edge of the night
Steeped in the grief of exile and longing, in sorrow.
Neither you
Nor I
Nor the dusk that gathers in your beauty
Nor the blue sea.
That safe harbour for the distress that assaults the brain-
We spurn the generation which knows nothing of the soul's pain.
Mankind today
Brands you merely a fresh slender woman
And me just an old fool.
That wretched appetite, that filthy sight
Can find no meaning in you or me
Nor a tender grief in the night
Nor the sullen tremor of secrecy and disdain
On the calm sea.
You and I

And the sea
And the night that seems to gather silently,
Without trembling, the fragrance of your soul,
Far away
Torn asunder from the land where blue shadows hold sway,
We are forever doomed to this exile here.
That land?
Stretches along the chaste regions of imagination, and
A blue nightfall
Reposes there for all;
At its outer edges, the sea
Pours the calm of sleep on each soul...
There, women are lovely, tender, nocturnal, pure.
Over their eyes your sadness hovers,
They are all sisters or lovers:
The tearful kisses on their lips can cure,
And the indigo quiet of their inquiring eyes
Can soothe the heart's suffering.
Their souls are violets
Distilled from the night of despair,
In a ceaseless search for silence and repose.
The dim glare from the moon's sorrows
Finds haven in their immaculate hands.
Ah, they are so frail-
The mute anguish they share,
The night deep in thought, the ailing sea ...
They all resemble each other there.
That land
Is on which imaginary continent, and
Dimmed by what distant river?
Is it a land of illusions- or real,
A utopia bound to remain unknown forever?
I do not know... All I know is
You and I and the blue sea
And the dusk that vibrates in me
The strings of inspiration and agony,
Far away
Torn asunder from the land where blue shadows hold sway
We are forever doomed to this exile here.

MY BETTER HALF

Ike Muila and Isabella Motadinyane

My better half
Love nest well
in hard times
bad times
together
in difficulties
Cool drinks
both of us
down the bottom
Of hardship
had times
Mafanya life
Money there
Money here
In good times
buy a cool drink
both of us
Joburg our home
Our stable
Window pane
drink it cool
My better half
We build a home
On top of a rock
Our Joburg home
In hard times
in difficulties together
Come rain come
thou thunder storms
My better half
Thou shall never wither

The Rough Man
Pir Sultan Abdal

The rough man entered the lover's garden
It is woods now, my beautiful one, it is woods,
Gathering roses, he has broken their stems
They are dry now, my beautiful one, they are dry
In this square our hide is stretched
Blessed be, we saw our friend off to God
One day, too, black dust must cover us
We will rot, my beautiful one, we will rot
He himself reads and He also writes
God's holy hand has closed her crescent eyebrows
Your peers are wandering in Paradise
They are free, my beautiful one, they are free
Whatever religion you are, I'll worship it too
I will be torn off with you even the Day of Judgement
Bend for once, let me kiss you on your white neck
Just stay there for a moment, my beautiful one, just stay there
I'm Pir Sultan Abdal, I start from the root
I eat the kernel and throw out the evil weed
And weave from a thousand flowers to one hive honey
I am an honest bee, my beautiful one, an honest bee.

Numen Lumen
Emily Dickinson

I live with him, I see his face;
I go no more away
For visitor, or sundown;
Death's single privacy,
The only one forestalling mine,
And that by right that he
Presents a claim invisible,
No wedlock granted me.

I live with him, I hear his voice,
I stand alive to-day
To witness to the certainty
Of immortality
Taught me by Time,—the lower way,
Conviction every day,—
That life like this is endless,
Be judgment what it may.

Heloise To Abelard: A Sonnet
Elizabeth Oakes Smith

Must I not love thee? When the heart would leap,
With all its thrilling pulses, unto thee,
Must it be staid? Is not the spirit free?
Can human bonds or bars its essence keep?
Or drugs and banes hold love in deathful sleep?
Love thee I must-yet I content will be,
Like the pale victim who, on bended knee,
Presents the chalice, which his blook must steep,
And prostrate on the altar falls to die.
So let me kneel, a guiltless votary sink,
Prayer on my lips, and love within my heart-
Thus from these willing eyes recede the sky-
Thus let these sighs my ebbing life-blood drink,
May I but love thee still, but feel how dear thou art?

Love's Growth
John Donne

I scarce believe my love to be so pure
    As I had thought it was,
    Because it doth endure
Vicissitude, and season, as the grass;
Methinks I lied all winter, when I swore
My love was infinite, if spring make' it more.

But if medicine, love, which cures all sorrow
With more, not only be no quintessence,
But mixed of all stuffs paining soul or sense,
And of the sun his working vigor borrow,
Love's not so pure, and abstract, as they use
To say, which have no mistress but their muse,
But as all else, being elemented too,
Love sometimes would contemplate, sometimes do.

And yet no greater, but more eminent,
    Love by the spring is grown;
    As, in the firmament,

Stars by the sun are not enlarged, but shown,
Gentle love deeds, as blossoms on a bough,
From love's awakened root do bud out now.

If, as water stirred more circles be
Produced by one, love such additions take,
Those, like so many spheres, but one heaven make,
For they are all concentric unto thee;
And though each spring do add to love new heat,
As princes do in time of action get
New taxes, and remit them not in peace,
No winter shall abate the spring's increase.

Sonnet 75, From Amoretti
Edmund Spenser

One day I wrote her name upon the strand,
But came the waves and washéd it away:
Agayne I wrote it with a second hand,
But came the tyde, and made my pains his pray.
"Vayne man," sayd she, "that doest in vaine assay,
A mortall thing so to immortalize,
For I my selve shall lyke to to this decay,
And eek my name bee wypéd out lykewize."
"Not so," quod I, "let baser things devize
To dy in dust, but you shall live by fame:
My verse your vertues rare shall eternize,
And in the hevens wryte your glorious name.
Where whenas death shall all the world subdew,
Our love shall live, and later life renew."

Sonnet 68
William Shakespeare

Thus is his cheek the map of days outworn,
When beauty lived and died as flowers do now,
Before these bastard signs of fair were born,
Or durst inhabit on a living brow:
Before the golden tresses of the dead,
The right of sepulchres, were shorn away,

To live a second life on second head,
Ere beauty's dead fleece made another gay:
In him those holy antique hours are seen,
Without all ornament, it self and true,
Making no summer of another's green,
Robbing no old to dress his beauty new,
>   And him as for a map doth Nature store,
>   To show false Art what beauty was of yore.

Sonnet 81

William Shakespeare

Or I shall live your epitaph to make,
Or you survive when I in earth am rotten,
From hence your memory death cannot take,
Although in me each part will be forgotten.
Your name from hence immortal life shall have,
Though I (once gone) to all the world must die,
The earth can yield me but a common grave,
When you entombed in men's eyes shall lie,
Your monument shall be my gentle verse,
Which eyes not yet created shall o'er-read,
And tongues to be, your being shall rehearse,
When all the breathers of this world are dead,
>   You still shall live (such virtue hath my pen)
>   Where breath most breathes, even in the mouths of men.

Sonnet 108

William Shakespeare

What's in the brain that ink may character,
Which hath not figured to thee my true spirit,
What's new to speak, what now to register,
That may express my love, or thy dear merit?
Nothing sweet boy, but yet like prayers divine,
I must each day say o'er the very same,
Counting no old thing old, thou mine, I thine,
Even as when first I hallowed thy fair name.
So that eternal love in love's fresh case,

Weighs not the dust and injury of age,
Nor gives to necessary wrinkles place,
But makes antiquity for aye his page,
Finding the first conceit of love there bred,
Where time and outward form would show it dead.

Sonnet 110

William Shakespeare

Alas 'tis true, I have gone here and there,
And made my self a motley to the view,
Gored mine own thoughts, sold cheap what is most dear,
Made old offences of affections new.
Most true it is, that I have looked on truth
Askance and strangely: but by all above,
These blenches gave my heart another youth,
And worse essays proved thee my best of love.
Now all is done, have what shall have no end,
Mine appetite I never more will grind
On newer proof, to try an older friend,
A god in love, to whom I am confined.
Then give me welcome, next my heaven the best,
Even to thy pure and most most loving breast.

Sonnet 117

William Shakespeare

Accuse me thus, that I have scanted all,
Wherein I should your great deserts repay,
Forgot upon your dearest love to call,
Whereto all bonds do tie me day by day,
That I have frequent been with unknown minds,
And given to time your own dear-purchased right,
That I have hoisted sail to all the winds
Which should transport me farthest from your sight.
Book both my wilfulness and errors down,
And on just proof surmise, accumulate,
Bring me within the level of your frown,
But shoot not at me in your wakened hate:
Since my appeal says I did strive to prove
The constancy and virtue of your love.

SONNET 123

William Shakespeare

No! Time, thou shalt not boast that I do change,
Thy pyramids built up with newer might
To me are nothing novel, nothing strange,
They are but dressings Of a former sight:
Our dates are brief, and therefore we admire,
What thou dost foist upon us that is old,
And rather make them born to our desire,
Than think that we before have heard them told:
Thy registers and thee I both defy,
Not wond'ring at the present, nor the past,
For thy records, and what we see doth lie,
Made more or less by thy continual haste:
    This I do vow and this shall ever be,
    I will be true despite thy scythe and thee.

SONNET 142

William Shakespeare

Love is my sin, and thy dear virtue hate,
Hate of my sin, grounded on sinful loving,
O but with mine, compare thou thine own state,
And thou shalt find it merits not reproving,
Or if it do, not from those lips of thine,
That have profaned their scarlet ornaments,
And sealed false bonds of love as oft as mine,
Robbed others' beds' revenues of their rents.
Be it lawful I love thee as thou lov'st those,
Whom thine eyes woo as mine importune thee,
Root pity in thy heart that when it grows,
Thy pity may deserve to pitied be.
    If thou dost seek to have what thou dost hide,
    By self-example mayst thou be denied.

CHRISTABEL: PART 1

Samuel Taylor Coleridge

'Tis the middle of night by the castle clock,
And the owls have awakened the crowing cock;
Tu—whit! Tu—whoo!
And hark, again! the crowing cock,
How drowsily it crew.
Sir Leoline, the Baron rich,
Hath a toothless mastiff bitch;
From her kennel beneath the rock
She maketh answer to the clock,
Four for the quarters, and twelve for the hour;
Ever and aye, by shine and shower,
Sixteen short howls, not over loud;
Some say, she sees my lady's shroud.

Is the night chilly and dark?
The night is chilly, but not dark.
The thin gray cloud is spread on high,
It covers but not hides the sky.
The moon is behind, and at the full;
And yet she looks both small and dull.
The night is chill, the cloud is gray:
Tis a month before the month of May,
And the Spring comes slowly up this way.

The lovely lady, Christabel,
Whom her father loves so well,
What makes her in the wood so late,
A furlong from the castle gate?
She had dreams all yesternight
Of her own betroth'd knight;
And she in the midnight wood will pray
For the weal of her lover that's far away.

She stole along, she nothing spoke,
The sighs she heaved were soft and low,
And naught was green upon the oak
But moss and rarest misletoe:
She kneels beneath the huge oak tree,
And in silence prayeth she.

The lady sprang up suddenly,
The lovely lady Christabel!
It moaned as near, as near can be,
But what it is she cannot tell.—
On the other side it seems to be,
Of the huge, broad-breasted, old oak tree.

The night is chill; the forest bare;
Is it the wind that moaneth bleak?
There is not wind enough in the air
To move away the ringlet curl
From the lovely lady's cheek—
There is not wind enough to twirl
The one red leaf, the last of its clan,
That dances as often as dance it can,
Hanging so light, and hanging so high,
On the topmost twig that looks up at the sky.

Hush, beating heart of Christabel!
Jesu, Maria, shield her well!
She folded her arms beneath her cloak,
And stole to the other side of the oak.
What sees she there?

There she sees a damsel bright,
Drest in a silken robe of white,
That shadowy in the moonlight shone:
The neck that made that white robe wan,
Her stately neck, and arms were bare;
Her blue-veined feet unsandl'd were,
And wildly glittered here and there
The gems entangled in her hair.
I guess, 'twas frightful there to see
A lady so richly clad as she—
Beautiful exceedingly!

Mary mother, save me now!
(Said Christabel) And who art thou?

The lady strange made answer meet,
And her voice was faint and sweet:—
Have pity on my sore distress,
I scarce can speak for weariness:

Stretch forth thy hand, and have no fear!
Said Christabel, How camest thou here?
And the lady, whose voice was faint and sweet,
Did thus pursue her answer meet:—

My sire is of a noble line,
And my name is Geraldine:
Five warriors seized me yestermorn,
Me, even me, a maid forlorn:
They choked my cries with force and fright,
And tied me on a palfrey white.
The palfrey was as fleet as wind,
And they rode furiously behind.
They spurred amain, their steeds were white:
And once we crossed the shade of night.
As sure as Heaven shall rescue me,
I have no thought what men they be;
Nor do I know how long it is
(For I have lain entranced I wish)
Since one, the tallest of the five,
Took me from the palfrey's back,
A weary woman, scarce alive.
Some muttered words his comrades spoke:
He placed me underneath this oak;
He swore they would return with haste;
Whither they went I cannot tell—
I thought I heard, some minutes past,
Sounds as of a castle bell.
Stretch forth thy hand (thus ended she).
And help a wretched maid to flee.

Then Christabel stretched forth her hand,
And comforted fair Geraldine:
O well, bright dame! may you command
The service of Sir Leoline;
And gladly our stout chivalry
Will he send forth and friends withal
To guide and guard you safe and free
Home to your noble father's hall.

She rose: and forth with steps they passed
That strove to be, and were not, fast.
Her gracious stars the lady blest,
And thus spake on sweet Christabel:
All our household are at rest,
The hall as silent as the cell;
Sir Leoline is weak in health,
And may not well awakened be,
But we will move as if in stealth,
And I beseech your courtesy,
This night, to share your couch with me.

They crossed the moat, and Christabel
Took the key that fitted well;
A little door she opened straight,
All in the middle of the gate;
The gate that was ironed within and without,
Where an army in battle array had marched out.
The lady sank, belike through pain,
And Christabel with might and main
Lifted her up, a weary weight,
Over the threshold of the gate:
Then the lady rose again,
And moved, as she were not in pain.

So free from danger, free from fear,
They crossed the court: right glad they were.
And Christabel devoutly cried
To the lady by her side,
Praise we the Virgin all divine
Who hath rescued thee from thy distress!
Alas, alas! said Geraldine,
I cannot speak for weariness.
So free from danger, free from fear,
They crossed the court: right glad they were.

Outside her kennel, the mastiff old
Lay fast asleep, in moonshine cold.
The mastiff old did not awake,
Yet she an angry moan did make!

And what can ail the mastiff bitch?
Never till now she uttered yell
Beneath the eye of Christabel.
Perhaps it is the owlet's scritch:
For what can ail the mastiff bitch?

They passed the hall, that echoes still,
Pass as lightly as you will!
The brands were flat, the brands were dying,
Amid their own white ashes lying;
But when the lady passed, there came
A tongue of light, a fit of flame;
And Christabel saw the lady's eye,
And nothing else saw she thereby,
Save the boss of the shield of Sir Leoline tall,
Which hung in a murky old niche in the wall.
O softly tread, said Christabel,
My father seldom sleepeth well.

Sweet Christabel her feet doth bare,
And jealous of the listening air
They steal their way from stair to stair,
Now in glimmer, and now in gloom,
And now they pass the Baron's room,
As still as death, with stifled breath!
And now have reached her chamber door;
And now doth Geraldine press down
The rushes of the chamber floor.

The moon shines dim in the open air,
And not a moonbeam enters here.
But they without its light can see
The chamber carved so curiously,
Carved with figures strange and sweet,
All made out of the carver's brain,
For a lady's chamber meet:
The lamp with twofold silver chain
Is fastened to an angel's feet.

The silver lamp burns dead and dim;
But Christabel the lamp will trim.
She trimmed the lamp, and made it bright,

And left it swinging to and fro,
While Geraldine, in wretched plight,
Sank down upon the floor below.

O weary lady, Geraldine,
I pray you, drink this cordial wine!
It is a wine of virtuous powers;
My mother made it of wild flowers.

And will your mother pity me,
Who am a maiden most forlorn?
Christabel answered—Woe is me!
She died the hour that I was born.
I have heard the grey-haired friar tell
How on her death-bed she did say,
That she should hear the castle-bell
Strike twelve upon my wedding-day.
O mother dear! that thou wert here!
I would, said Geraldine, she were!

But soon with altered voice, said she—
"Off, wandering mother! Peak and pine!
I have power to bid thee flee."
Alas! what ails poor Geraldine?
Why stares she with unsettled eye?
Can she the bodiless dead espy?

And why with hollow voice cries she,
"Off, woman, off! this hour is mine—
Though thou her guardian spirit be,
Off, woman, off! 'tis given to me."

Then Christabel knelt by the lady's side,
And raised to heaven her eyes so blue—
Alas! said she, this ghastly ride—
Dear lady! it hath wildered you!
The lady wiped her moist cold brow,
And faintly said, "'tis over now!"

Again the wild-flower wine she drank:
Her fair large eyes 'gan glitter bright,

And from the floor whereon she sank,

The lofty lady stood upright:
She was most beautiful to see,
Like a lady of a far countr'ee.

And thus the lofty lady spake—
All they who live in the upper sky,
Do love you, holy Christabel!
And you love them, and for their sake
And for the good which me befel,
Even I in my degree will try,
Fair maiden, to requite you well.
But now unrobe yourself; for I
Must pray, ere yet in bed I lie.'

Quoth Christabel, So let it be!
And as the lady bade, did she.
Her gentle limbs did she undress,
And lay down in her loveliness.

But through her brain of weal and woe
So many thoughts moved to and fro,
That vain it were her lids to close;
So half-way from the bed she rose,
And on her elbow did recline
To look at the lady Geraldine.

Beneath the lamp the lady bowed,
And slowly rolled her eyes around;
Then drawing in her breath aloud,
Like one that shuddered, she unbound
The cincture from beneath her breast:
Her silken robe, and inner vest,
Dropt to her feet, and full in view,
Behold! her bosom and half her side
A sight to dream of, not to tell!
O shield her! shield sweet Christabel!

Yet Geraldine nor speaks nor stirs;
Ah! what a stricken look was hers!
Deep from within she seems half-way
To lift some weight with sick assáy,

And eyes the maid and seeks delay;
Then suddenly, as one defied,
Collects herself in scorn and pride,
And lay down by the Maiden's side!
And in her arms the maid she took,
Ah wel-a-day!
And with low voice and doleful look
These words did say:
"In the touch of this bosom there worketh a spell,
Which is lord of thy utterance, Christabel!
Thou knowest to-night, and wilt know to-morrow,
This mark of my shame, this seal of my sorrow;
But vainly thou warrest,
For this is alone in
Thy power to declare,
That in the dim forest
Thou heard'st a low moaning,
And found'st a bright lady, surpassingly fair;
And didst bring her home with thee in love and in charity,
To shield her and shelter her from the damp air."

Conclusion To Part I

It was a lovely sight to see
The lady Christabel, when she
Was praying at the old oak tree.
Amid the jagg'ed shadows
Of mossy leafless boughs,
Kneeling in the moonlight,
To make her gentle vows;
Her slender palms together prest,
Heaving sometimes on her breast;
Her face resigned to bliss or bale—
Her face, oh call it fair not pale,
And both blue eyes more bright than clear,
Each about to have a tear.

With open eyes (ah woe is me!)
Asleep, and dreaming fearfully,

Fearfully dreaming, yet, I wis,
Dreaming that alone, which is—
O sorrow and shame! Can this be she,
The lady, who knelt at the old oak tree?
And lo! the worker of these harms,
That holds the maiden in her arms,
Seems to slumber still and mild,
As a mother with her child.

A star hath set, a star hath risen,
O Geraldine! since arms of thine
Have been the lovely lady's prison.
O Geraldine! one hour was thine—
Thou'st had thy will! By tairn and rill,
The night-birds all that hour were still.
But now they are jubilant anew,
From cliffand tower, tu—whoo! tu—whoo!
Tu—whoo! tu—whoo! from wood and fell!

And see! the lady Christabel
Gathers herself from out her trance;
Her limbs relax, her countenance
Grows sad and soft; the smooth thin lids
Close o'er her eyes; and tears she sheds—
Large tears that leave the lashes bright!
And oft the while she seems to smile
As infants at a sudden light!

Yea, she doth smile, and she doth weep,
Like a youthful hermitess,
Beauteous in a wilderness,
Who, praying always, prays in sleep.
And, if she move unquietly,
Perchance, 'tis but the blood so free
Comes back and tingles in her feet.
No doubt, she hath a vision sweet.
What if her guardian spirit 'twere,
What if she knew her mother near?
But this she knows, in joys and woes,
That saints will aid if men will call:
For the blue sky bends over all!

HIGHLAND MARY

Robert Burns

Ye banks, and braes, and streams around
    The castle o' Montgomery,
Green be your woods and fair your flowers,
    Your waters never drumlie!
There simmer first unfauld her robes,
    And there the langest tarry;
For there I took the last fareweel,
O' my sweet Highland Mary.

How sweetly bloom'd the gay green birk,
    How rich the hawthorn's blossom,
As underneath their fragrant shade
    I clasp'd her to my bosom!
The golden hours, on angel wings,
    Flew o'er me and my dearie;
For dear to me as light and life,
    Was my sweet Highland Mary.

Wi' monie a vow and lock'd embrace
    Our parting was fu' tender;
And, pledging aft to meet again,
    We tore oursels asunder;
But O! fell death's untimely frost,
    That nipt my flower sae early!
Now green's the sod, and cauld's the clay,
    That wraps my Highland Mary!

O pale, pale now, those rosy lips,
    I aft hae kiss'd sae fondly!
And closed for aye the sparkling glance,
    That dwelt on me sae kindly!
And mould'ring now in silent dust,
    That heart that lo'ed me dearly!
But still within my bosom's core
    Shall live my Highland Mary.

AND IF AT LAST

Louise Labé

And if at last he drew me to his side
In hot embrace, for whom I waste away;
And if this sick necessity to stay
With him forever so were satisfied;
And if he held me so and sighed, O love,
Let us be true, let such fatality
Join us as neither hurricane nor sea
Nor subtler turbulence shall ever move;
And if a held him bound upon my breast,
Frantic and ardent, as the ivies cling
About the mighty bough; and death should spring
Upon me: I should offer all y breath
Upon his lips at last, and sink to rest,
Knowing in life no lovelier thing than death.

℘ROSPICE

Robert Browning

Fear death?—to feel the fog in my throat,
    The mist in my face,
When the snows begin, and the blasts denote
    I am nearing the place,
The power of the night, the press of the storm,
    The post of the foe;
Where he stands, the Arch Fear in a visible form,
    Yet the strong man must go:
For the journey is done and the summit attained,
    And the barriers fall,
Though a battle's to fight ere the guerdon be gained,
    The reward of it all.
I was ever a fighter, so—one fight more,
    The best and the last!
I would hate that death bandaged my eyes and forbore,
    And bade me creep past.
 No! let me taste the whole of it, fare like my peers

    The heroes of old,
Bear the brunt, in a minute pay glad life's arrears
    Of pain, darkness and cold.
For sudden the worst turns the best to the brave,
    The black minute's at end,
And the elements' rage, the fiend-voices that rave,
    Shall dwindle, shall blend,
Shall change, shall become first a peace out of pain,
    Then a light, then thy breast,
O thou soul of my soul! I shall clasp thee again,
    And with God be the rest!

ᴅELIA: XXXIII

Samuel Daniel

When men shall find thy flower, thy glory, pass,
And thou with careful brow sitting alone
Received hast this message from thy glass,
That tells thee truth and says that all is gone:

Fresh shalt thou see in me the wounds thou madest,
Though spent thy flame, in me the heat remaining;
I that have lov'd thee thus before thou fadest,
My faith shall wax when thou art in thy waning.
The world shall find this miracle in me,
That fire can burn when all the matter's spent;
Then what my faith hath been thyself shall see,
And that thou wast unkind thou mayst repent.
Thou mayst repent that thou hast scorn'd my tears,
When winter snows upon thy golden hairs.

AND THOU ART DEAD, AS YOUNG AND FAIR
Lord Byron (George Gordon)

And thou art dead, as young and fair
As aught of mortal birth;
And form so soft, and charms so rare,
Too soon return'd to Earth!
Though Earth receiv'd them in her bed,
And o'er the spot the crowd may tread
In carelessness or mirth,
There is an eye which could not brook
A moment on that grave to look.

I will not ask where thou liest low,
Nor gaze upon the spot;
There flowers or weeds at will may grow,
So I behold them not:
It is enough for me to prove
That what I lov'd, and long must love,
Like common earth can rot;
To me there needs no stone to tell,
T'is Nothing that I lov'd so well.

Yet did I love thee to the last
As fervently as thou,
Who didst not change through all the past,
And canst not alter now.
The love where Death has set his seal,
Nor age can chill, nor rival steal,
Nor falsehood disavow:

And, what were worse, thou canst not see
Or wrong, or change, or fault in me.

The better days of life were ours;
The worst can be but mine:
The sun that cheers, the storm that lowers,
Shall never more be thine.
The silence of that dreamless sleep
I envy now too much to weep;
Nor need I to repine
That all those charms have pass'd away,
I might have watch'd through long decay.

The flower in ripen'd bloom unmatch'd
Must fall the earliest prey;
Though by no hand untimely snatch'd,
The leaves must drop away:
And yet it were a greater grief
To watch it withering, leaf by leaf,
Than see it pluck'd to-day;
Since earthly eye but ill can bear
To trace the change to foul from fair.

I know not if I could have borne
To see thy beauties fade;
The night that follow'd such a morn
Had worn a deeper shade:
Thy day without a cloud hath pass'd,
And thou wert lovely to the last,
Extinguish'd, not decay'd;
As stars that shoot along the sky
Shine brightest as they fall from high.

As once I wept, if I could weep,
My tears might well be shed,
To think I was not near to keep
One vigil o'er thy bed;
To gaze, how fondly! on thy face,
To fold thee in a faint embrace,
Uphold thy drooping head;
And show that love, however vain,
Nor thou nor I can feel again.

Yet how much less it were to gain,
Though thou hast left me free,
The loveliest things that still remain,
Than thus remember thee!
The all of thine that cannot die
Through dark and dread Eternity
Returns again to me,
And more thy buried love endears
Than aught except its living years.

*A*LBA INNOMINATA

Anonymous

In a garden where the whitethorn spreads her leaves
My lady hath her love lain close beside her,
Till the warder cries the dawn- Ah dawn that grieves!
Ah God! Ah God! That dawn should come so soon!

"Please God that night, dear night, should never cease,
Nor that my love should parted be from me,
nor watch cry 'Dawn' - Ah dawn that slayeth peace!
Ah God! Ah God! That dawn should come so soon!

"Fair friend and sweet, thy lips! Our lips again!
Lo, in the meadow there the birds give song!
Our be the love and Jealousy's the pain!
Ah God! Ah God! That dawn should come so soon!

"Sweet friend and fair take we our joy again
Down in the garden, where the birds are loud,
Till the warder's reed astrain
Cry God! Ah God! That dawn should come so soon!

"Of that sweet wind that comes from Far-Away
Have I drunk deep of my Beloved's breath,
Yea! of my Love's that is so dear and gay,
Ah God! Ah God! That dawn should come so soon!"

Song From Chartivel
Marie de France

Hath any loved you well, down there,
 Summer or winter through?
Down there, have you found any fair
 Laid in the grave with you?
Is death's long kiss a richer kiss
 Than mine was wont to be-
Or have you gone to some far bliss
 And quite forgotten me?

What soft enamoring of sleep
 Hath you in some soft way?
What charmed death holdeth you with deep
 Strange lure by night and day?
A little space below the grass,
 Out of the sun and shade;
But worlds away from me alas,
 Down there where you are laid.

My brightest waved and wasted gold,
 What is it now to thee-
Whether the rose-red life I hold
 Or white death holdeth me?
Down there you love the grave's own green,
 And evermore you rave
Of some sweet seraph you have seen
 Or dreamt of in the grave.

There you shall lie as you have lain,
 Though in the world above,
Another live your life again,
 Loving again your love:
Is it not sweet beneath the palm?
 Is it not warm day rife
With some long mystic golden calm
 Better than love and life?

The broad quaint odorous leaves like hands
 Weaving the fair day through,

While death weaves sleep for you;
And many a strange rich breathing sound
    Ravishes morn and noon:
And in that place you must have found
    Death a delicious swoon-

Hold me no longer for a word
    I used to say or sing:
Ah, long ago you must have heard
    So many a sweeter thing:
For rich earth must have reached your heart
    And turned the faith to flowers;
And warm wind stolen, part by part,
    Your soul through faithless hours.

And many a soft seed must have won
    Soil of some yielding thought,
To bring a bloom up to the sun
    That else had ne'er been brought;
And, doubtless, many a passionate hue
    Hath made that place more fair,
Making some passionate part of you
    Faithless to me down there.

Ulysses And The Siren
Samuel Daniel

SIREN:
Come worthy Greek, Ulysses, come,
Possess these shores with me;
The winds and seas are troublesome,
And here we may be free.
Here may we sit and view their toil
That travail in the deep,
And joy the day in mirth the while,
And spend the night in sleep.

ULYSSES:
Fair nymph, if fame or honour were
To be attain'd with ease,
Then would I come and rest me there,
And leave such toils as these.

But here it dwells, and here must I
With danger seek it forth;
To spend the time luxuriously
Becomes not men of worth.

SIREN:
Ulysses, O be not deceiv'd
With that unreal name;
This honour is a thing conceiv'd
And rests on others' fame.
Begotten only to molest
Our peace, and to beguile
The best thing of our life, our rest,
And give us up to toil.

ULYSSES:
Delicious nymph, suppose there were
Nor honour nor report,
Yet manliness would scorn to wear
The time in idle sport.
For toil doth give a better touch,
To make us feel our joy;
And ease finds tediousness as much
As labour yields annoy..

SIREN:
Then pleasure likewise seems the shore
Whereto tends all your toil,
Which you forego to make it more,
And perish oft the while.
Who may disport them diversely,
Find never tedious day,
And ease may have variety
As well as action may.

ULYSSES:
But natures of the noblest frame
These toils and dangers please,
And they take comfort in the same
As much as you in ease,
And with the thoughts of actions past
Are recreated still;

When pleasure leaves a touch at last
To show that it was ill.

SIREN:

That doth opinion only cause
That's out of custom bred,
Which makes us many other laws
Than ever nature did.
No widows wail for our delights,
Our sports are without blood;
The world we see by warlike wights
Receives more hurt than good.

ULYSSES:

But yet the state of things require
These motions of unrest,
And these great spirits of high desire
Seem born to turn them best,
To purge the mischiefs that increase
And all good order mar;
For oft we see a wicked peace
To be well chang'd for war.

SIREN:

Well, well, Ulysses, then I see
I shall not have thee here,
And therefore I will come to thee
And take my fortunes there.
I must be won that cannot win,
Yet lost were I not won;
For beauty hath created been
T'undo, or be undone.

THE ECSTASY

John Donne

Where, like a pillow on a bed
A pregnant bank swell'd up to rest
The violet's reclining head,
Sat we two, one another's best.
Our hands were firmly cemented

With a fast balm, which thence did spring;
Our eye-beams twisted, and did thread
Our eyes upon one double string;
So t'intergraft our hands, as yet
Was all the means to make us one,
And pictures in our eyes to get
Was all our propagation.
As 'twixt two equal armies fate
Suspends uncertain victory,
Our souls (which to advance their state
Were gone out) hung 'twixt her and me.
And whilst our souls negotiate there,
We like sepulchral statues lay;
All day, the same our postures were,
And we said nothing, all the day.
If any, so by love refin'd
That the soul's language understood,
And by good love were grown all mind,
Within convenient distance stood,
He (though he knew not which soul spake,
Because both meant, both spake the same)
Might thence a new concoction take
And part far purer than he came.
This ecstasy doth unperplex,
We said, and tell us what we love;
We see by this it was not sex,
We see we saw not what did move;
But as all several souls contain
Mixtures of things, they know not what,
Love these mix'd souls doth mix again
And makes both one, each this and that.
A single violet transplant,
The strength, the colour, and the size,
(All which before was poor and scant)
Redoubles still, and multiplies.
When love with one another so
Interinanimates two souls,
That abler soul, which thence doth flow,
Defects of loneliness controls.

We then, who are this new soul, know
Of what we are compos'd and made,
For th' atomies of which we grow
Are souls. whom no change can invade.
But oh alas, so long, so far,
Our bodies why do we forbear?
They are ours, though they are not we; we are
The intelligences, they the spheres.
We owe them thanks, because they thus
Did us, to us, at first convey,
Yielded their senses' force to us,
Nor are dross to us, but allay.
On man heaven's influence works not so,
But that it first imprints the air;
So soul into the soul may flow,
Though it to body first repair.
As our blood labors to beget
Spirits, as like souls as it can,
Because such fingers need to knit
That subtle knot which makes us man,
So must pure lovers' souls descend
T''affections, and to faculties,
Which sense may reach and apprehend,
Else a great prince in prison lies.
To our bodies turn we then, that so
Weak men on love reveal'd may look;
Love's mysteries in souls do grow,
But yet the body is his book.
And if some lover, such as we,
Have heard this dialogue of one,
Let him still mark us, he shall see
Small change, when we're to bodies gone.

$\mathcal{L}$OVE LETTERS

Robert Burns

$\mathscr{D}$ ear Madam,

The passion of love has need to be productive of much delight; as where it takes thorough possession of the man, it almost unfits him for anything else. The lover who is certain of an equal return of affection, is surely the happiest of men; but he who is a prey to the horrors of anxiety and dreaded disappointment, is a being whose situation is by no means enviable. Of this, my present experience gives me much proof. To me, amusement seems impertinent, and business intrusion, while you alone engross every faculty of my mind. My I request you to drop me a line, to inform me when I may wait upon you? For pity's sake, do; and let me have it soon. In the meantime allow me, in all the artless sincerity of truth, to assure you that I truly am,

> my dearest Madam,
>> your ardent lover, and devoted humble servant

Grace Greenwood

$\mathscr{L}$ ove-Letter To A Friend

Dear Anna, hast ne'er heard it told
How florists have the curious power
To graft on some rude garden-plant
A tender and exquisite flower?

Thus are our natures made as one,
In union mystic and divine;
Thus, sweetest rose of womanhood,
Thy life is blooming into mine.

"Forget" thee! Whence the childish fear?
Ah, vain would be such heart-recalling!
Have I not felt thine angel smiles,—
Thy tears upon my bosom falling?

How oft, when, through our lattice stealing,
The moonlight came in quivering gleams,
When thou wert by my side reposing,
Thy spirit busy with its dreams,

—In love that would not let me sleep,
I hung above thy tranquil rest,
Whose soft, low breathings scarcely stirred
The snowy folds upon thy breast,

And watched to see thy starry eyes
Beam from their blue-veined lids' eclipse,
And drank thy very breath, and kissed
The night-dew from thy rose-bud lips!

As one in moon-lit, star-crowned night
Marks not the dark and envious shades
That lurk within the garden-bower,
Or glide along the forest-glades;

Thus heed I not life's shadows dim,
Though gathering fast, around, above,
The blessed while 't is mine to feel
The silvery presence of thy love.

Juliette Drouet

ℒove Letter To Victor Hugo

I need your love as a touchstone of my existence.
It is the sun which breathes life into me.

James Joyce

ℒetter To His Wife

You are my only love. You have me completely in your power. I know and feel that if I am to write anything fine and noble in the future I shall do so only by listening at the doors of your heart. I would like to go through life side by side with you, telling you more and more until we grew to be one being together until the hour should come for us to die.

Ludwig Van Beethoven

𝒯o The "Immortal Beloved"

Good Morning

Though still in bed my thoughts go out to you, my Immortal Beloved, now and then joyfully, then sadly, waiting to learn whether or not fate will hear us. I can live wholly with you or not at all—yes, I am resolved to wander so long away from you until I can fly to your arms and say that I am really at home, send my soul enwrapped in you in the land of spirits.—Yes, unhappily it must be so –you will be the more resolved since you know my fidelity–to you, no one can ever again possess my heart– none–never– Oh, God! why is it necessary to part from one whom one so loves and yet my life in W. (Vienna) is now a wretched life –your love makes me at once the happiest and the unhappiest of men–at my age, I need a steady, quiet life –can that be under our conditions? My angel, I have just been told that the mail coach goes every day–and I must close at once so that you may receive the L. at once. Be calm, only by a calm consideration of our existence can we achieve our purpose to live together— be calm—love me—today –yesterday–what tearful longings for you –you–you––my life—my all—farewell—Oh continue to love me— never misjudge the most faithful heart of your beloved L.

ever thine

ever mine

ever for each other

Nelson

𝒯o Lady Hamilton

"Victory," October 19th, 1805

My dearest beloved Emma, the dear friend of my bosom. The signal has been made that the enemy's combined fleet are coming out of the port. We have very little wind, so that I have no hopes of seeing them before tomorrow. May the God of battles crown my endeavors with success; at all events, I will take care that my name shall ever be most dear to you and Horatio, both of whom I love as much as my own life. And as my last writing, before the battle, will be to you, so I hope, in God, that I shall live to finish my letter after the battle. May heaven bless you, prays your

Nelson

John Keats

𝒦eats To Fanny Brawne

I never knew before, what such love as you have made me feel, was; I did not believe in it; my Fanny was afraid of it, lest it burn me up. But if you will fully love me, though there may be some fire 'twill not be more than we can bear when moistened and bedewed with Pleasures…I love you the more in that I believe you have liked me for my own sake and nothing else. I have met with women whom I really think would like to be married to a Poem and to be given away by a Novel. Ever yours, my love!

I have no limits now to my love. I have been astonished that men could die martyrs of religion. I have shuddered at it. I shudder no more. I could be martyred for religion - love is my religion - I could die for you. My creed is love and you are its only tenet. You have ravished me away by a power I cannot resist...My love is selfish. I cannot breathe without you...Yours for ever.

Henry VIII

𝒯o Anne Boleyn

Mymne awne Sweetheart, this shall be to advetise you of the great ellingness that I find here sonce your departing, for I ensure you, me thinketh the TYme longer since your departing now last than I was wont to do a whole Fortnight; I think your kindness and my Fervence of Love causeth it, for otherwise I wolde not thought it possible, that for so little a while it should have grieved me, but now I am come-ing

toward you, me thinketh my Pains by half released, and also I am right well com-
forted, insomuch that my Book maketh substantially for my Matter, in writing
whereof I have spent above III Hours this Day, which caused me now write the
shorter Letter to you at this TYme, because of some Payne in my Head, wishing my
self (specially an Evening) in my Sweethearts Armes whose pritty Duckys I trust
shortly to kysse. Writne with the Hand of him that was, is, and shall be yours by his
will,

H.R.

Rainer Maria Rilke

ℱROM "LETTERS TO A YOUNG POET"

May 14, 1904, Rome

To love is good, too: love being difficult. For one
human being to love another: that is perhaps the
most difficult of all our tasks, the ultimate, the
last test and proof, the work for which all other
work is but preparation. For this reason young
people, who are beginners in everything, cannot
yet know love: they have to learn it. With their
whole being, with all their forces, gathered close
about their lonely, timid, upward-beating hearts,
they must learn to love. But learning-time is
always a long, secluded time, and so loving, for a
long while ahead and far on into life, is—solitude,
intensified and deepened loneness for him who
loves. Love is at first not anything that means
merging, giving over, and uniting with another
(for what would a union be of something unclarified
and unfinished, still subordinate—?), it is a high
inducement to the individual to ripen, to become
something in himself for another's sake, it is a great
exacting claim upon him, something that chooses
him out and calls him to vast things.

Lord Byron (George Gordon)

𝒯o The Countess Guiccioli

My Dearest Teresa,

I have read this book in your garden;—my love, you were absent, or else I could not have read it. It is a favorite book of yours, and the writer was a friend of mine. You will not understand the English words, and others will not understand them,—which is the reasons I have not scrawled them in Italian. But you will recognize the handwriting of him who passionately loved you, and you will divine that, over a book which was yours, he could only think of love.

In that word, beautiful in all languages, but most so in yours—Amor mio—is comprised my existence here and hereafter. I feel I exist here, and I feel that I shall exist hereafter,—to what purpose you will decide; my destiny rests with you, and you are a woman, eighteen years of age, and two out of a convent, I wish that you had stayed there, with all my heart,—or, at least, that I had never met you in your married state.

But all this is too late. I love you, and you love me,—at least you say so, and act as if you did so, which last is a great consolation in all events. But I more than love you, and cannot cease to love you.

Think of me, sometimes, when the Alps and ocean divide us,—but they never will, unless you wish it.

Robert Browning

𝒯o Elizabeth Barrett, After Their Marriage

You will only expect a few words—what will those be? When the heart is full it may run over, but the real fullness stays within.

You asked me yesterday "if I should repent?" Yes—my own Ba,—I could wish all the past were to do over again, that in it I might somewhat more,—never so little more, conform in the outward homage, to the inward feeling, What I have professed,(for I have performed nothing) seems to fall short of what my first love required even—and when I think of this moment's love…I could repent, as I say.

Words can never tell you, however,—form them, transform them anyway, how perfectly dear you are to me—perfectly dear to my heart and soul.

I look back, and in every one point, every word and gesture, every letter, every silence—you have been entirely perfect to me—I would not change one word, one look.

My hope and aim are to preserve this love, not to fall from it—for which I trust to God who procured it for me, and doubtless can preserve it.

Enough now, my dearest, dearest, own Ba! You have given me the highest, completest proof of love that ever one human being gave another. I am all gratitude—and all pride (under the proper feeling which ascribes pride to the right source) all pride that my life has been so crowned by you.

God bless you prays your very own R.

Mary Tucker

A LOVE-LETTER

You wished for a love-letter, Doctor—but then,
I know you to be most conceited of men;
You'll think I'm in earnest, I vow now I ain't,
For I would not deign to love even a saint.

You must never believe what the fair ladies say:
Take their nay for a yes, and their yes for a nay.
Like doctors, the darlings are very deceiving,
And most that they say is not half worth believing.

But now for my letter. How shall I begin?
If I say, my dear Doctor, that will be a sin!
And a love-letter without dear, darling, or dove,
Would be as insipid as one without love.

Love, glorious love, with its grand mystic art,
Sways each mortal mind, and scathes each human heart;
Without care or regret it inflicts pain or joy,
Tossing high the frail heart that becomes its day's toy.

It drinks up the life-sap, becomes life itself,
Regardless of true love, of beauty or self—
An object most "homely" in love's eye I ween—
Will seem like an angel, as bright as a queen.

It glosses its object, like man's serpent tongue —
Makes even the aged appear as if young;

Waving locks to love's eye, e'en if sprinkled with gray,
Does not lessen, but strengthens its powerful sway.

Love, bright, joyous love, heals each sad, breaking heart,
But breaks it again when it strives to depart:
For the void, when once filled by love, never again
A vision can fill it, save only great pain.

The blessing of blessings, the greatest of woes,
Will leave its bright signet wherever it goes:
Then seek love and find it, whenever you can—
My counsel is needless, for you are a— man.

Now, Doctor, I'm sure that this letter you'll find
Is suited exactly to your turn of mind;
I've sent what I promised—a true loving letter,
—And if it don't suit you, why, just write a better!

Napoleon Bonaparte

Napoleon To Josephine

I don't love you, not at all; on the contrary, I detest you—Tou're a naught, gawky, foollish Cinderella. You never write me; you don't love your husband; you know what pleasures your letters give him, and yet you haven't written him six lines, dashed off so casually!

What do you do all day, Madam? What is the affair so important as to leave you no time to write to your devoted lover? What affection stifles and puts to one side the love, the tender and constant love you promised him? Of what sort can be that marvelous being, that new lover that tyrannizes over your days, and prevents your giving any attention to your husband? Josephine, take care! Some fine night, the doors will be broken open and there I'll be.

Indeed, I am very uneasy, my love, at receiving no news of you; write me quickly four pages, pages full of agreeable things which shall fill my heart with the pleasantest feelings.

I hope before long to crush you in my arms and cover you with a million kisses as though beneath the equator.

Bonaparte

Edgar Allan Poe

𝒱ALENTINE

For her this rhyme is penned, whose luminous eyes,
    Brightly expressive as the twins of Leda,
Shall find her own sweet name, that nestling lies
    Upon the page, enwrapped from every reader.
Search narrowly the lines!-they hold a treasure
    Divine-a talisman-an amulet
That must be worn at heart. Search well the measure-
    The words- the syllables! Do not forget
The trivialest point, or you may lose your labor
    And yet there is in this no Gordian knot
Which one might not undo without a sabre,
    If one could merely comprehend the plot.
Enwritten upon the leaf where now are peering
    Eyes scintillating soul, there lie perdus
Three eloquent words oft uttered in the hearing
    Of poets, by poets- as the name is a poet's, too,
Its letters, although naturally lying
    Like the knight Pinto-Mendez Ferdinando-
Still form a synonym for Truth—Cease trying!
    You will not read the riddle, though you do the best you can do.

Percy Bysshe Shelley

𝒯O JANE

The keen stars were twinkling, And the fair moon was rising among them,
Dear Jane.
The guitar was tinkling,
But the notes were not sweet till you sung them
Again.
As the moon's soft splendour
O'er the faint cold starlight of Heaven
Is thrown,
So your voice most tender
To the strings without soul had then given
Its own.

The stars will awaken,
Though the moon sleep a full hour laterTo-night;
No leaf will be shaken
Whilst the dews of your melody scatter Delight.
Though the sound overpowers,
Sing again, with your dear voice revealing
A tone
Of some world far from ours,
Where music and moonlight and feeling
Are one.

*L*OVE AND LOSS

Broken Hearted I Wandered

Anonymous

1.

Broken hearted I wandered,
For the loss of my true lover,
He's a jolly, jolly horseman,
In the battle he was slain.

He had but one sixpence,
And he broke it in two,
And he gave to me the half o't
Before he went away.

He wrote me a letter
In the month of November,
And he told me not to worry
As he was coming home.

2.

Broken-hearted we parted
At the loss of my beloved
He was a jolly sailor
And in battle he was killed.

He had a silver sixpence
And he broke it in two
And he gave me the one half
Before he went away.

He wrote me a letter
And sealed it with his hands
And he told me not to worry
For he was coming home.

Oh were I an angel
And had I wings that I might fly
I'd go to yonder valley
Where my beloved lies.

3.

Broken-hearted I wander,
At the loss of my brother;
He's a jolly, jolly fellow,
At the battle he was slain;

He had a silver sixpence,
And he broke it in twae,
And he gave me the half o't
Before he went away.

If I were an angel
I would fly to the skies,
And far beyond the mountains
Where my dear brother lies.

Moonlit Night

Tu Fu

Tonight at Fu-chou, this moon she watches
Alone in our room. And my little, far-off
Children, too young to understand what keeps me
Away, or even remember Chang'an. By now,
Her hair will be mist-scented, her jade-white
Arms chilled in its clear light. When
Will it find us together again, drapes drawn
Open, light traced where it dries our tears?

A Lost Dream

Paul Laurence Dunbar

Ah, I have changed, I do not know
Why lonely hours affect me so.

In days of yore, this were not wont,
No loneliness my soul could daunt.

For me too serious for my age,
The weighty tome of hoary sage,

Until with puzzled heart astir,
One God-giv'n night, I dreamed of her.

I loved no woman, hardly knew,
More of the sex that strong men woo,

Than cloistered monk within his cell;
But now the dream is lost, and Hell

Holds me her captive tight and fast
Who prays and struggles for the past.

No living maid has charmed my eyes,
But now, my soul is wonder-wise.

For I have dreamed of her and seen
Her red-brown tresses, ruddy sheen,

Have known her sweetness, lip to lip,
The joy of her companionship.

When days were bleak and winds were rude,
She shared my smiling solitude,

And all the bare hills walked with me
To hearken winter's melody.

And when the spring came o'er the land
We fared together hand in hand

Beneath the linden's leafy screen
That waved above us faintly green.

In summer, by the river-side,
Our souls were kindred with the tide

That floated onward to the sea
As we swept toward Eternity.

The bird's call and the water's drone
Were all for us and us alone.

The water-fall that sang all night
Was her companion, my delight,

And e'en the squirrel, as he sped
Along the branches overhead,

Half kindly and half envious,
Would chatter at the joy of us.

'Twas but a dream, her face, her hair,
The spring-time sweet, the winter bare,

The summer when the woods we ranged,
—'Twas but a dream, but all is changed.

Yes, all is changed and all has fled,
The dream is broken, shattered, dead.

And yet, sometimes, I pray to know
How just a dream could hold me so.

Angelina Baker

Traditional Folk Song

Angelina Baker, Angelina Baker
Angelina Baker lives on the village green
The way the I love her beats all to be seen
Angelina Baker her age is 43
I gave her candy by the peck, but she won't marry me
She wont do the bakin', because she is too stout
She makes cookies by the peck and throws the coffee out
The last time I saw her, it was at the county fair
Her daddy chased me halfway home and told me to stay there
Angelina taught me to weep, and she taught me to moan
Angelina taught me to weep and play on the old jawbone.

Barbara Allen

Anonymous, Traditional English

In Scarlet Town where I was born,
There was a fair maid dwellin'
Made every youth cry Well-a-day,
Her name was Barb'ra Allen.
All in the merry month of May,
When green buds they were swellin'
Young Willie Grove on his death-bed lay,
For love of Barb'ra Allen.

He sent his man unto her then
To the town where he was dwellin'
You must come to my master, dear,
If your name be Barb'ra Allen.
So slowly, slowly she came up,
And slowly she came nigh him,
And all she said when there she came:
"Young man, I think you're dying!"

He turned his face unto the wall
And death was drawing nigh him.
Adieu, adieu, my dear friends all,
And be kind to Bar'bra Allen
As she was walking o'er the fields,
She heard the death bell knellin',
And ev'ry stroke did seem to say,
Unworthy Barb'ra Allen.

When he was dead and laid in grave,
Her heart was struck with sorrow.
"Oh mother, mother, make my bed
For I shall die tomorrow."
And on her deathbed she lay,
She begged to be buried by him,
And sore repented of the day
That she did e'er deny him.
"Farewell," she said, "ye virgins all,
And shun the fault I fell in,
Henceforth take warning by the fall
Of cruel Barb'ra Allen."

$\mathcal{I}$ Made A Big Mistake

Anonynmous, Traditional American

On the day I left my home
Said, Goodbye, sweetheart, I'm goin'
I'll come back to you when I get my big break
It wasn't long 'til my heart yearned
Couldn't wait 'til I returned
Looked around and found I made a big mistake
And then I saw you passing by
With your new love by your side
And I felt my heart cry out and start to break
You looked so happy now, it's true
My heart cried, I still love you
Oh, I can't explain; I made a big mistake
But give me one star's candle-light
For the moon is dark tonight
And I'm lost, but I can't lose this empty ache
Your new love lies where I once lay
My heart still cries; I long to stay
I regret too late, I made a big mistake.

$\mathcal{G}$rown And Flown

Christina Rossetti

I loved my love from green of Spring
Until sere Autumn's fall;
But now that leaves are withering
How should one love at all?
One heart's too small
For hunger, cold, love, everything.
I loved my love on sunny days
Until late Summer's wane;
But now that frost begins to glaze
How should one love again ?
Nay, love and pain
Walk wide apart in diverse ways.
I loved my love——alas to see
That this should be, alas!
I thought that this could scarcely be,
Yet has it come to pass:
Sweet sweet love was,
Now bitter bitter grown to me.

Her Bright Smile Haunts Me Still

Traditional, American

It's been a year since last we met
We may never meet again
I have struggled to forget,
But the struggle was in vain.
For her voice lives in the breeze,
Her spirit comes at will.
In the midnight on the seas
Her bright smile haunts me still.

   In the midnight on the seas
   Her bright smile haunts me still.

I have sailed a falling sky
And I've charted hazard's paths
I have seen the storm arise
Like a giant in his wrath.
Every danger I have known
That a reckless life can fill,
Though her presence is now flown
Her bright smile haunts me still.

   Though her presence is now flown
   Her bright smile haunts me still.

At the first sweet dawn of light
When I gaze upon the deep,
Her form still greets my sight
While the stars their vigil keep.
When I close my aching eyes
Sweet dreams my memory fill.
And from sleep when I arise
Her bright smile haunts me still.

   And from sleep when I arise
   Her bright smile haunts me still.

The Irish Girl

Anonymous, American

I stepped out one morning
Down by the riverside;
I cast my eyes all around me,
That blue-eyed girl I spied.
So red and rosy were her cheeks,
And yellow was her hair,
How costly was the jewelry
That blue-eyed girl did wear.
Tears came rolling down her cheeks,
How mournful she did cry:
"My love has gone and left me,
And surely I will die."
Love, it is a killing thing
Did you ever feel the pang?
How hard it is to be in love

And can't be loved again.
I wish I were in New Orleans,
A-sitting in my chair,
A glass of brandy in my hand,
My arms around my dear.
I'd wish for whiskey, Roman wine,
I'd drink before I'd go;
I'd sail through the deepest ocean,
Let the wind blow high or low.

Let the winds blow high or low, me boys
Let the seas be mountain high.
It is the seaman's duty
The helm to stand by.

Sonnet II

Edna St. Vncent Millay

Time does not bring relief; you all have lied
Who told me time would ease me of my pain!
I miss him in the weeping of the rain;
I want him at the shrinking of the tide;
The old snows melt from every mountain-side,
And last year's leaves are smoke in every lane;
But last year's bitter loving must remain
Heaped on my heart, and my old thoughts abide!
There are a hundred places where I fear
To go,—so with his memory they brim!
And entering with relief some quiet place
Where never fell his foot or shone his faceI say,
"There is no memory of him here!"
And so stand stricken, so remembering him!

Absence

Charlotte Mew

Sometimes I know the way
You walk, up over the bay;
It is a wind from that far sea
That blows the fragrance of your hair to me.
Or in this garden when the breeze
Touches my trees
To stir their dreaming shadows on the grass
I see you pass.
In sheltered beds, the heart of every rose
Serenely sleeps to-night. As shut as those
Your guarded heart; as safe as they form the beat, beat
Of hooves that tread dropped roses in the street.
Turn never again
On these eyes blind with a wild rain
Your eyes; they were stars to me.—
There are things stars may not see.
But call, call, and though Christ stands
Still with scarred hands
Over my mouth, I must answer. So
I will come—He shall let me go!

Drifting Duckweed

Ts'ao Chih

Drifting duckweed floats on the clear water
Blown by the wind east and west.
Hair done up, I bade farewell to my parents,
To come to be my lord's mate.
Respectful and careful morning and night,
Without cause I got your accusations and blame.
In the past I was favoured with love and kindness,
In harmony and joy like harp and lute.
Why do you now reject me,
And separate us like east-star and west-star?
Dogwood itself has fragrance,
But not like the cassia and orchid;

Though you can love a new woman
It will be nothing like your old happiness.
Passing clouds return in time;
Shall, by chance, your love return?
Unsatisfied, unsatisfied, I look to the sky and sigh;
To what shall my anxious heart appeal?
The sun and moon stay not always in the same place;
Man's life is as insignificant as an overnight stay.
A sad wind comes and enters my breast;
Tears drop like falling dew.
I'll open this box and make some clothes,
Cut and sew the glossy silk and plain silk.

The Day Is Gone, And All Its Sweets Are Gone!
John Keats

The day is gone, and all its sweets are gone!
   Sweet voice, sweet lips, soft hand, and softer breast,
Warm breath, light whisper, tender semi-tone,
   Bright eyes, accomplish'd shape, and lang'rous waist!
Faded the flower and all its budded charms,
   Faded the sight of beauty from my eyes,
Faded the shape of beauty from my arms,
   Faded the voice, warmth, whiteness, paradise-
Vanish'd unseasonably at shut of eve,
   When the dusk holiday or holinight
Of fragrant-curtain'd love begins to weave
   The woof of darkness thick, for hid delight;
But, as I've read love's missal through to-day,
   He'll let me sleep, seeing I fast and pray.

Lost Joy
Emily Dickinson

I had a daily bliss
I half indifferent viewed,
Till sudden I perceived it stir,—
It grew as I pursued,

Till when, around a crag,
It wasted from my sight,
Enlarged beyond my utmost scope,
I learned its sweetness right

La Belle Dame Sans Merci

John Keats

O what can ail thee, knight-at-arms,
Alone and palely loitering?
The sedge has wither'd from the Lake,
And no birds sing!

O what can ail thee, Knight-at-arms,
So haggard and so woe-begone?
The squirrel's granary is full,
And the harvest's done.

I see a lily on thy brow
With anguish moist and fever dew,
And on thy cheeks a fading rose
Fast withereth too.

"I met a Lady in the Meads,
Full beautiful—a faery's child,
Her hair was long, her foot was light,
And her eyes were wild.

"I made a Garland for her head,
And bracelets too, and fragrant Zone;
She look'd at me as she did love,
And made sweet moan.

"I set her on my pacing steed,
And nothing else saw all day long,
For sidelong would she bend, and sing
A faery's song.

She found me roots of relish sweet,
And honey wild, and manna dew,
And sure in language strange she said—
'I love thee true.'

"She took me to her elfin grot
And there she wept and sigh'd full sore,
And there I shut her wild wild eyes
With kisses four.

"And there she lulled me asleep,
And there I dream'd—Ah! Woe betide!
The latest dream I ever dream'd
On the cold hill's side.

"I saw pale Kings and Princes too,
Pale warriors, death-pale were they all;
They cried—'la belle dame sans merci
Hath thee in thrall!'

"I saw their starved lips in the gloam
With horrid warning gaped wide,
And I awoke and found me here
On the cold hill's side.

"And this is why I sojourn here,
Alone and palely loitering;
Though the sedge is wither'd from the Lake,
And no birds sing.

The Widower

John Brainard

O doth it walk—that spirit bright and pure,
And may it disembodied, ever come
Back to this earth? I do not, dare not hope,
A reappearance of that kindest eye,
Or of that smoothest cheek or sweetest voice,

—But can she see my tears, when I, alone,
Weep by her grave? and may she leave the throng
Where angels minister and saints adore,
To visit this sad earth! When, as the nights
Of fireside winter gather chilly round,
I kiss our little child, and lay me down
Upon a widowed pillow, doth she leave
Those glorious, holy, heavenly essences,
Those sacred perfumes round the throne on high,
To keep a watch on me? and upon ours?
—Her I did love, and I was loved again, —
And had it been my mortal lot, instead,
I would, were I accepted, ask my God,
For one more look upon my wife and child.

I Saw My Lady

Anonnymous

I saw my Lady weep,
And Sorrow proud to be advanced so
In those fair eyes, where all perfections keep;
 Her face was full of woe,
But such a woe (believe me) as wins more hearts
Than mirth can do, with her enticing parts.
Sorrow was there made fair,
And Passion, wise; Tears, a delightful thing;
Silence, beyond all speech, a wisdom rare;
 She made her sighs to sing,
And all things with so sweet a sadness move;
As made my heart both grieve and love.
O Fairer than aught else
The world can shew, leave off, in time, to grieve,
Enough, enough! Your joyful look excels;
 Tears kill the heart, believe,
O strive not to be excellent in woe,
Which only breeds your beauty's overthrow.

WAKE

Tess Gallagher

Three nights you lay in our house.
Three nights in the chill of the body.
Did I want to prove how surely
I'd been left behind? In the room's great dark
I climbed up beside you onto our high bed, bed
We'd loved in and slept in, married
and unmarried.

There was a halo of cold around you
as if the bosy's messages carry farther
in death, my own warmth taking on the silver-white
of a voice sent unbroken across snow just to hear
itself in its clarity of calling. We were dead
a little while together then,
serene and afloat on the strange broad canopy
of the abandoned world.

SONNET V

Edna St. Vincent Millay

If I should learn, in some quite casual way,
That you were gone, not to return again—
Read from the back-page of a paper, say,
Held by a neighbor in a subway train,
How at the corner of this avenue
And such a street (so are the papers filled)
A hurrying man—who happened to be you—
At noon to-day had happened to be killed,
I should not cry aloud—I could not cry
Aloud, or wring my hands in such a place—
I should but watch the station lights rush by
With a more careful interest on my face,
Or raise my eyes and read with greater care
Where to store furs and how to treat the hair.

REMEMBER
Christina Rossetti

Remember me when I am gone away,
    Gone far away into the silent land;
    When you can no more hold me by the hand,
Nor I half turn to go, yet turning stay.
Remember me when no more day by day
    You tell me of our future that you planned:
    Only remember me; you understand
It will be late to counsel then or pray.
Yet if you should forget me for a while
    And afterwards remember, do not grieve:
    For if the darkness and corruption leave
    A vestige of the thoughts that once I had,
Better by far you should forget and smile
    Than that you should remember and be sad.

SWEET-BRIAR IN ROSE
Michael Field

So sweet, all sweet — the body as the shyer
Sweet senses, and the Spirit sweet as those:
For me the fragrance of a whole sweet-briar
Beside the rose!
"Lo, my loved is dying "
Lo, my loved is dying, and the call
Is come that I must die,
All the leaves are dying, all
Dying, drifting by.
Every leaf is lonely in its fall,
Every flower has its speck and stain;
The birds from hedge and tree
Lisp mournfully,
And the great reconciliation of this pain
Lies in the full soft rain.

Three Songs of Shattering

Edna St. Vincent Millay

I

The first rose on my rose-tree
   Budded, bloomed, and shattered,
During sad days when to me
   Nothing mattered.

Grief of grief has drained me clean;
   Still it seems a pity
No one saw,—it must have been
   Very pretty.

II

Let the little birds sing;
   Let the little lambs play;
Spring is here; and so 'tis spring; —
   But not in the old way!

I recall a place
   Where a plum-tree grew;
There you lifted up your face,
   And blossoms covered you.

If the little birds sing,
   And the little lambs play,
Spring is here; and so 'tis spring—
   not in the old way!

III

All the dog-wood blossoms are underneath the tree!
   Ere spring was going—ah, spring is gone!
And there comes no summer to the like of you and me,—
   Blossom time is early, but no fruit sets on.

All the dog-wood blossoms are underneath the tree,
   Browned at the edges, turned in a day;
And I would with all my heart they trimmed a mound for me,
   And weeds were tall on all the paths that led that way!

In The Willow Shade

Christina Rossetti

I sat beneath a willow tree,
Where water falls and calls;
While fancies upon fancies solaced me,
Some true, and some were false.
Who set their heart upon a hope
That never comes to pass,
Droop in the end like fading heliotrope
The sun's wan looking-glass.
Who set their will upon a whim
Clung to through good and ill,
Are wrecked alike whether they sink or swim,
Or hit or miss their will.
All things are vain that wax and wane,
For which we waste our breath;
Love only doth not wane and is not vain,
Love only outlives death.
A singing lark rose toward the sky,
Circling he sang amain;
He sang, a speck scarce visible sky-high,
And then he sank again.
A second like a sunlit spark
Flashed singing up his track;
But never overtook that foremost lark,
And songless fluttered back.
A hovering melody of birds
Haunted the air above;
They clearly sang contentment without words,
And youth and joy and love.
O silvery weeping willow tree
With all leaves shivering,
Have you no purpose but to shadow me
Beside this rippled spring?
On this first fleeting day of Spring,
For Winter is gone by,
And every bird on every quivering wing
Floats in a sunny sky;

On this first Summer-like soft day,
While sunshine steeps the air,
And every cloud has got itself away,
And birds sing everywhere.
Have you no purpose in the world
But thus to shadow me
With all your tender drooping twigs unfurled,
O weeping willow tree?
With all your tremulous leaves outspread
Betwixt me and the sun,
While here I loiter on a mossy bed
With half my work undone;
My work undone, that should be done
At once with all my might;
For after the long day and lingering sun
Comes the unworking night.
This day is lapsing on its way,
Is lapsing out of sight;
And after all the chances of the day
Comes the resourceless night.
The weeping willow shook its head
And stretched its shadow long;
The west grew crimson, the sun smoldered red,
The birds forbore a song.
Slow wind sighed through the willow leaves,
The ripple made a moan,
The world drooped murmuring like a thing that grieves;
And then I felt alone.
I rose to go, and felt the chill,
And shivered as I went;
Yet shivering wondered, and I wonder still,
What more that willow meant;
That silvery weeping willow tree
With all leaves shivering,
Which spent one long day overshadowing me
Beside a spring in Spring.

The Valentine
Lizette Woodward Reese

Against this thorny Present shows
Your memory like the dew;
Each maid a wrinkled Beauty goes,
When I do think of you.
Folded away in the deep grass,
What is it can befall?
Nor Clouds that fade, nor Gusts that pass,
Nor any Grief at all.
Now lovers write their verses brave;
Now buds start on the tree;
But Love went with you to the grave,
The sere leaf bides with me.
I have not any word save this;
My tears are all my store;
The fairer that the weather is
I miss you but the more.

Interim
Edna St. Vincent Millay

The room is full of you! — As I came in
And closed the door behind me, all at once
A something in the air, intangible,
Yet stiff with meaning, struck my senses sick!—
Sharp, unfamiliar odors have destroyed
Each other room's dear personality.
The heavy scent of damp, funereal flowers,—
The very essence, hush-distilled, of Death —
Has strangled that habitual breath of home
Whose expiration leaves all houses dead;
And wheresoe'er I look is hideous change.
Save here. Here 'twas as if a weed-choked gate
Had opened at my touch, and I had stepped
Into some long-forgot, enchanted, strange,
Sweet garden of a thousand years ago
And suddenly thought, "I have been here before!"

You are not here. I know that you are gone,
And will not ever enter here again.
And yet it seems to me, if I should speak,
Your silent step must wake across the hall;
If I should turn my head, that your sweet eyes
Would kiss me from the door.—So short a time
To teach my life its transposition to
This difficult and unaccustomed key!—
The room is as you left it; your last touch —
A thoughtless pressure, knowing not itself
As saintly—hallows now each simple thing;
Hallows and glorifies, and glows between
The dust's grey fingers like a shielded light.

There is your book, just as you laid it down,
Face to the table,—I cannot believe
That you are gone!—Just then it seemed to me
You must be here. I almost laughed to think
How like reality the dream had been;
Yet knew before I laughed, and so was still.
That book, outspread, just as you laid it down!
Perhaps you thought, "I wonder what comes next,
And whether this or this will be the end";
So rose, and left it, thinking to return.

Perhaps that chair, when you arose and passed
Out of the room, rocked silently a while
Ere it again was still. When you were gone
Forever from the room, perhaps that chair,
Stirred by your movement, rocked a little while,
Silently, to and fro…

And here are the last words your fingers wrote,
Scrawled in broad characters across a page
In this brown book I gave you. Here your hand,
Guiding your rapid pen, moved up and down.
Here with a looping knot you crossed a "t",
And here another like it, just beyond
These two eccentric "e's". You were so small,
And wrote so brave a hand!

How strange it seems
That of all words these are the words you chose!
And yet a simple choice; you did not know
You would not write again. If you had known —
But then, it does not matter,—and indeed
If you had known there was so little time
You would have dropped your pen and come to me
And this page would be empty, and some phrase
Other than this would hold my wonder now.
Yet, since you could not know, and it befell
That these are the last words your fingers wrote,
There is a dignity some might not see
In this, "I picked the first sweet-pea to-day."
To-day! Was there an opening bud beside it
You left until to-morrow?—O my love,
The things that withered,—and you came not back!
That day you filled this circle of my arms
That now is empty. (O my empty life!)
That day—that day you picked the first sweet-pea,—
And brought it in to show me! I recall
With terrible distinctness how the smell
Of your cool gardens drifted in with you.
I know, you held it up for me to see
And flushed because I looked not at the flower,
But at your face; and when behind my look
You saw such unmistakable intent
You laughed and brushed your flower against my lips.
(You were the fairest thing God ever made,
I think.) And then your hands above my heart
Drew down its stem into a fastening,
And while your head was bent I kissed your hair.
I wonder if you knew. (Beloved hands!
Somehow I cannot seem to see them still.
Somehow I cannot seem to see the dust
In your bright hair.) What is the need of Heaven
When earth can be so sweet?—If only God
Had let us love,—and show the world the way!
Strange cancellings must ink th' eternal books

When love-crossed-out will bring the answer right!
That first sweet-pea! I wonder where it is.
It seems to me I laid it down somewhere,
And yet,—I am not sure. I am not sure,
Even, if it was white or pink; for then
'Twas much like any other flower to me,
Save that it was the first. I did not know,
Then, that it was the last. If I had known—
But then, it does not matter. Strange how few,
After all's said and done, the things that are
Of moment.
             Few indeed!
     When I can make
Of ten small words a rope to hang the world!
"I had you and I have you now no more."
There, there it dangles,—where's the little truth
That can for long keep footing under that
When its slack syllables tighten to a thought?
Here, let me write it down! I wish to see
Just how a thing like that will look on paper!
"I had you and I have you now no more."

*M*EMORIES

Fenton Johnson

When at evening in the vale I walk,
Wrapt in memories of dear Lucille;
When among the violets I lie,
All my hours of love before me steal.

Earth and heaven was this maid to me,
And her voice the song of lark and wren;
Now that she hath left my heart I know
Through the love of women God makes men.

If in distant countries I should dwell
With a people strange and proudly cold,
I would always see my long lost love
In the heart of dying marigold.

AFTER

Lizette Woodward Reese

Oh, the littles that remain!
Scent of mint out in the lane;
Flare of window; sound of bees;
—These, but these.

Three times sitting down to bread;
One time climbing up to bed;
Table-setting o'er and o'er;
Drying herbs for winter's store;

This thing; that thing;
—nothing more.
But just now out in the lane,
Oh, the scent of mint was plain!

TEARS, IDLE TEARS

Lord Alfred Tennyson

Tears, idle tears, I know not what they mean,
Tears from the depth of some divine despair
Rise in the heart, and gather to the eyes,
In looking on the happy Autumn-fields,
And thinking of the days that are no more.
Fresh as the first beam glittering on a sail,
That brings our friends up from the underworld,
Sad as the last which reddens over one
That sinks with all we love below the verge;
So sad, so fresh, the days that are no more.
Ah, sad and strange as in dark summer dawns
The earliest pipe of half-awaken'd birds
To dying ears, when unto dying eyes
The casement slowly grows a summering square;
So sad, so strange, the days that are no more.
Dear as remember'd kisses after death,
And sweet as those by hopeless fancy feign'd
On lips that are for others; deep as love,
Deep as first love, and wild with all regret;
O Death in Life, the days that are no more!

Once More Into My Arid Days
Edna St. Vincent Millay

Once more into my arid days like dew,
Like wind from an oasis, or the sound
Of cold sweet water bubbling underground,
A treacherous messenger—the thought of you
Comes to destroy me; once more I renew
Firm faith in your abundance, whom I found
Long since to be but just one other mound
Of sand, whereon no green thing ever grew.
And once again, and wiser is no wise,
I chase your colored phantom on the air,
And sob and curse and fall and weep and rise
And stumble pitifully on to where,
Miserable and lost, with stinging eyes,
Once more I clasp—and there is nothing there.

The Visit
Ralph Waldo Emerson

Askest "How long thou shall stay?"
Devastator of the day!
Know, each substance and relation
Thorough nature's operation,
Hath its unit, bound, and metre,
And every new compound
Is some product and repeater,
Product of the early found.
But the unit of the visit,
The encounter of the wise,
Say what other metre is it
Than the meeting of the eyes?
Nature poureth into nature
Through the channels of that feature.
Riding on the ray of Sight,
More fleet than waves or whirlwinds go,
Or for service or delight,
Hearts to hearts their meaning show,
Sum their long experience,
And import intelligence.
Single look has drained the breast,
Single moment years confessed.
The duration of a glance
Is the term of convenance,
And, though thy rede be church or state,
Frugal multiples of that.
Speeding Saturn cannot halt;
Linger,—thou shall rue the fault,
If Love his moment overstay,
Hatred's swift repulsions play.

Sorrowful Dreams
Edna St. Vincent Millay

Sorrowful dreams remembered after waking
Shadow with dolour all the candid day;
Even as I read, the silly tears out-breaking
Splash on my hands and shut the page away.
Grief at the root, a dark and secret dolour,
Harder to bear than wind-and-weather grief,
Clutching the rose, draining its cheek of colour,
Drying the bud, curling the opened leaf.
Deep is the pond—although its edge be shallow,
Frank in the sun, revealing fish and stone,
Climbing ashore to turtle-head and mallow;
Black at the centre beats a heart unknown.
Desolate dreams pursue me out of sleep;
Weeping I wake; waking, I weep, I weep.

David's Lament For Jonathan
Peter Abelard

Low in they grave with thee,
Happy to lie,
Since there's no greater thing left Love to do;
And to live after thee
Is but to die,
For with but half a soul what can Life do?

So share thy victory,
Or else thy grave,
Either to rescue thee, or with thee lie:
Ending that life for thee,
That thou didst save,
So Death that sundereth might bring more nigh.

Peace, O my stricken lute!
Thy strings are sleeping.
Would that my heart could still
Its bitter weeping!

Sonnet 73

William Shakespeare

That time of year thou mayst in me behold
When yellow leaves, or none, or few, do hang
Upon those boughs which shake against the cold,
Bare ruined choirs, where late the sweet birds sang.
In me thou seest the twilight of such day
As after sunset fadeth in the west,
Which by and by black night doth take away,
Death's second self that seals up all in rest.
In me thou seest the glowing of such fire
That on the ashes of his youth doth lie,
As the death-bed whereon it must expire,
Consumed with that which it was nourished by.
    This thou perceiv'st, which makes thy love more strong,
    To love that well which thou must leave ere long.

Annabel Lee

Edgar Allan Poe

It was many and many a year ago,
    In a kingdom by the sea,
That a maiden there lived whom you may know
    By the name of ANNABEL LEE;
And this maiden she lived with no other thought
    Than to love and be loved by me.

I was a child and she was a child,
    In this kingdom by the sea;
But we loved with a love that was more than love-
    I and my Annabel Lee;
With a love that the winged seraphs of heaven
    Coveted her and me.

And this was the reason that, long ago,
    In this kingdom by the sea,
A wind blew out of a cloud, chilling
    My beautiful Annabel Lee;
So that her highborn kinsman came

And bore her away from me,
To shut her up in a sepulchre
   In this kingdom by the sea.

The angels, not half so happy in heaven,
   Went envying her and me-
Yes!- that was the reason (as all men know,
   In this kingdom by the sea)
That the wind came out of the cloud by night,
   Chilling and killing my Annabel Lee.
But our love it was stronger by far than the love
   Of those who were older than we-
   Of many far wiser than we-
And neither the angels in heaven above,
   Nor the demons down under the sea,
Can ever dissever my soul from the soul
   Of the beautiful Annabel Lee.

For the moon never beams without bringing me dreams
   Of the beautiful Annabel Lee;
And the stars never rise but I feel the bright eyes
   Of the beautiful Annabel Lee;
And so, all the night-tide, I lie down by the side
Of my darling- my darling- my life and my bride,
   In the sepulchre there by the sea,
   In her tomb by the sounding sea.

III

Emily Dickinson

To lose thee, sweeter than to gain
   All other hearts I knew.
'T is true the drought is destitute,
   But then I had the dew!
The Caspian has its realms of sand,
   Its other realm of sea;
Without the sterile perquisite
   No Caspian could be

Three Poems

Kakinomoto no Asomi Hitomaro

Your hair has turned white
While your heart stayed
Knotted against me.
I shall never
Loosen it now.

May those who are born after me
Never dream of such ways of love.

The plovers cry
Over the evening waves
On Lake Omi.
In my withering heart
I remember the past.

Recollections Of Love

Samuel Taylor Coleridge

I.
How warm this woodland wild Recess !
Love surely hath been breathing here ;
And this sweet bed of heath, my dear !
Swells up, then sinks with faint caress,
As if to have you yet more near.

II.
Eight springs have flown, since last I lay
On sea-ward Quantock's heathy hills,
Where quiet sounds from hidden rills
Float hear and there, like things astray,
And high o'er head the sky-lark shrills.

III.
No voice as yet had made the air
Be music with your name; yet why
That asking look ? that yearning sigh?
That sense of promise every where?
Beloved ! flew your spirit by?

IV.
As when a mother doth explore
The rose-mark on her long-lost child,
I met, I loved you, maiden mild!
As whom I long had loved before—
So deeply had I been beguiled.

V.
You stood before me like a thought,
A dream remembered in a dream.
But when those meek eyes first did seem
To tell me, Love within you wrought—
O Greta, dear domestic stream !

VI.
Has not, since then, Love's prompture deep,
Has not Love's whisper evermore
Been ceaseless, as thy gentle roar?
Sole voice, when other voices sleep,
Dear under-song in clamor's hour.

What My Lips Have Kissed, and Where, and Why
Edna St. Vincent Millay

What my lips have kissed, and where, and why,
I have forgotten, and what arms have lain
Under my head till morning; but the rain
Is full of ghosts tonight, that tap and sigh
Upon the glass and listen for reply,
And in my heart there stirs a quiet pain
For unremembered lads that not again
Will turn to me at midnight with a cry.
Thus in winter stands the lonely tree,
Nor knows what birds have vanished one by one,
Yet knows its boughs more silent than before:
I cannot say what loves have come and gone,I
 only know that summer sang in me
A little while, that in me sings no more.

A Valediction: Forbidding Mourning
John Donne

As virtuous men passe mildly away,
And whisper to their soules, to goe,
Whilst some of their sad friends do say,
The breath goes now, and some say, no;

So let us melt, and make no noise,
No teare-floods, nor sigh-tempests move,
T'were prophanation of our joyes
To tell the layetie our love.

Moving of th' earth brings harmes and feares,
Men reckon what it did and meant,
But trepidation of the speares,
Though greater farre, is innocent.

Dull sublunary lovers love
(Whose soule is sense) cannot admit
Absence, because it doth remove
Those things which elemented it.

But we by a love, so much refin'd,
That our selves know not what it is,
Inter-assured of the mind,
Care lesse, eyes, lips, and hands to misse.

Our two soules therefore, which are one,
Though I must goe, endure not yet
A breach, but an expansion,
Like gold to ayery thinnesse beate.

If they be two, they are two so
As stiffe twin compasses are two,
Thy soule the fixt foot, makes no show
To move, but doth, if th' other doe.

And though it in the center sit,
Yet when the other far doth rome,
It leanes, and hearkens after it,
And growes erect, as that comes home.

Such wilt thou be to mee, who must
Like th' other foot, obliquely runne;
Thy firmnes drawes my circle just,
And makes me end, where I begunne

Sonnet 30
William Shakespeare

When to the sessions of sweet silent thought,
I summon up remembrance of things past,
I sigh the lack of many a thing I sought,
And with old woes new wail my dear time's waste:
Then can I drown an eye (unused to flow)
For precious friends hid in death's dateless night,
And weep afresh love's long since cancelled woe,
And moan th' expense of many a vanished sight.
Then can I grieve at grievances foregone,
And heavily from woe to woe tell o'er
The sad account of fore-bemoaned moan,
Which I new pay as if not paid before.
But if the while I think on thee (dear friend)
All losses are restored, and sorrows end.

Sonnet XXIX

Edna St. Vincent Millay

Pity me not because the light of day
At close of day no longer walks the sky;
Pity me not for beauties passed away
From field and thicket as the year goes by;
Pity me not the waning of the moon,
Nor that the ebbing tide goes out to sea,
Nor that a man's desire is hushed so soon,
And you no longer look with love on me.
This have I known always: Love is no more
Than the wide blossom that the wind assails,
Than the great tide that treads the shifting shore,
Strewing fresh wreckage gathered inthe gales:
Pity me that the heart is slow to learn
What the swift mind beholds at every turn.

Sonnet XVII

Petrarch

A rain of bitter tears falls from my face
And a tormenting wind blows with my sighs
Whenever toward you I turn my eyes,
Whose absence cuts me from the human race.
It is true that the mild and gentle smiles
Do soothe the ardour of my strong desire
And rescue me from my martyrdom's fire
While I intently look upon your guiles;
But my spirits become suddenly cold
When I see, leaving, the acts I behold
Stolen from me by my stars' fateful ray;
Loosened at last by the amorous keys,
The soul deserts the heart to seek your breeze,
And in deep thought it tears itself away.

XIII

Emily Dickinson

Heart, we will forget him!
You and I, to-night!
You may forget the warmth he gave,
I will forget the light.
When you have done, pray tell me,
That I my thoughts may dim;
Haste! lest while you're lagging,
I may remember him!

To One In Paradise

Edgar Allan Poe

Thou wast all that to me, love,
　For which my soul did pine-
A green isle in the sea, love,
　A fountain and a shrine,
All wreathed with fairy fruits and flowers,
　And all the flowers were mine.
Ah, dream too bright to last!

　Ah, starry Hope! that didst arise
But to be overcast!
　A voice from out the Future cries,
"On! on!"—but o'er the Past
　(Dim gulf!) my spirit hovering lies
Mute, motionless, aghast!

For, alas! alas! me
　The light of Life is o'er!
"No more- no more- no more-"
　(Such language holds the solemn sea
To the sands upon the shore)
　Shall bloom the thunder-blasted tree
Or the stricken eagle soar!

And all my days are trances,
　And all my nightly dreams
Are where thy grey eye glances,
　And where thy footstep gleams-
In what ethereal dances,
　By what eternal streams.

XV

Emily Dickinson

We outgrow love, like other things
And put it in the drawer,
Till it an antique fashion shows
Like costumes grandsires wore.

Pilgrim's Peak

H. Amanda Schueler

I came up to this high peak today
and saw Wind pull Cloud's shadow
over dozing Meadow,
heard Breeze hushing
Birds' staccato calls into
trilling lullaby,
smelled warm Pine
coaxing deeper, slower breaths
as I lay cradled in the moment -
the perfect moment of
perfect memory.

This is a place for lovers.
I saw them today.
Life throbs here like the heartbeat
in a lover's breast.

I come here to remember.

You led me here long ago,
lay me on the sloped ground
sending heat radiating
through me from inside out,
like Sun shining through
Leaves above my head,
revealing hard veins
accellerating blood and sap
to Heart's core.

Memory encases love's thrill
like a bug stuck in resin.
But Bug is not the same
as when he burrowed into wood.
This peak is not the same
as when we embraced here long ago.
I am not the same.
You are not the same.
Memory cannot stop life's pulse.

I am awakened by the
rush of gas to piston engine -
lovers' careening back to the valley
below.
Trailing behind mixed with exhaust -
my moment.

I turn to leave
but in the rearview mirror
my eye catches a fleeting once.

When I return this peak will not be the same.
I will not be the same.

The Night Has A Thousand Eyes

Frances William Bourdillon

The night has a thousand eyes,
And the day but one;
Yet the light of a bright world dies
When day is done.

The mind has a thousand eyes,
And the heart but one;
Yet the light of a whole life dies
When love is done.

Poem To Lou

Guillaume Apollinaire

If I should die out there on the battle-front,
You'd weep, O Lou my darling, a single day,
And then my memory would die away
As a shell dies bursting over the battle-front,
A beautiful shell like a flowered mimosa spray.

And then this memory exploded in space
Would flood the whole wide world beneath my blood:
The mountains, valleys, seas and the stars that race,
The wondrous suns that ripen far in space,
As golden fruit round General Baratier would.

Forgotten memory, living in all things,
I'd redden the nipples of your sweet pink breasts,
I'd blush your mouth, your hair's now blood-like rings.
You wouldn't grow old at all; these lovely things
Would ever make you young for their brave behests.

The fatal spurting of my blood on the world
Would give more lively brightness to the sun,
More color to flowers, to waves more speedy run.
A marvelous love would descend upon the world,
Would be, in your lonely flesh, more strongly grown.

If I die there, memory you'll forget—
Sometimes remember, Lou, the moments of madness
Of youth and love and passion's dazzling fret-
My blood will be the burning fountain of gladness!
And be the happiest being the prettiest yet,

O my only love and my great madness!

L ong night is fallin;
On us foreboding
Ushers a long, long fate of blood.

Ashes Of Life
Edna St. Vincent Millay

Love has gone and left me and the days are all alike;
Eat I must, and sleep I will,—and would that night were here!
But ah!—to lie awake and hear the slow hours strike!
Would that it were day again!—with twilight near!

Love has gone and left me and I don't know what to do;
This or that or what you will is all the same to me;
But all the things that I begin I leave before I'm through,—
There's little use in anything as far as I can see.

Love has gone and left me,—and the neighbors knock and borrow,
And life goes on forever like the gnawing of a mouse,—
And to-morrow and to-morrow and to-morrow and to-morrow
There's this little street and this little house.

Bridal Ballad
Edgar Allan Poe

The ring is on my hand,
    And the wreath is on my brow;
Satin and jewels grand
    Are all at my command,
And I am happy now.

And my lord he loves me well;
    But, when first he breathed his vow,
I felt my bosom swell-
For the words rang as a knell,
And the voice seemed his who fell
In the battle down the dell,
    And who is happy now.

But he spoke to re-assure me,
    And he kissed my pallid brow,
While a reverie came o'er me,
    And to the church-yard bore me,
    And I sighed to him before me,
    Thinking him dead D'Elormie,
    "Oh, I am happy now!"

And thus the words were spoken,
And this the plighted vow,
And, though my faith be broken,
And, though my heart be broken,
Here is a ring, as token
That I am happy now!

Would God I could awaken!
For I dream I know not how!
And my soul is sorely shaken
Lest an evil step be taken,-
Lest the dead who is forsaken
May not be happy now.

Her Immortality

Thomas Hardy

Upon a noon I pilgrimed through
    A pasture, mile by mile,
Unto the place where I last saw
    My dead Love's living smile.
And sorrowing I lay me down
    Upon the heated sod:
It seemed as if my body pressed
    The very ground she trod.

I lay, and thought; and in a trance
    She came and stood me by—
The same, even to the marvellous ray
    That used to light her eye.
"You draw me, and I come to you,
    My faithful one," she said,
In voice that had the moving tone
    It bore in maidenhead.

She said: "'Tis seven years since I died:
    Few now remember me;
My husband clasps another bride;
    My children mothers she.
My brethren, sisters, and my friends
    Care not to meet my sprite:
Who prized me most I did not know
    Till I passed down from sight."

I said: "My days are lonely here;
    I need thy smile alway:
I'll use this night my ball or blade,
    And join thee ere the day."

A tremor stirred her tender lips,
    Which parted to dissuade:
"That cannot be, O friend," she cried;
    "Think, I am but a Shade!
"A Shade but in its mindful ones
    Has immortality;
By living, me you keep alive,
    By dying you slay me.

"In you resides my single power
    Of sweet continuance here;
On your fidelity I count
    Through many a coming year."
—I started through me at her plight,
    So suddenly confessed:
Dismissing late distaste for life,
    I craved its bleak unrest.

"I will not die, my One of all!—
    To lengthen out thy days
I'll guard me from minutest harms
    That may invest my ways!"
She smiled and went. Since then she comes
    when her birth-moon climbs,
Or at the seasons' ingresses
    Or anniversary times;

But grows my grief. When I surcease,
    Through whom alone lives she,
Ceases my Love, her words, her ways,
    Never again to be!

Quote

Unknown

Marriage is a permanent contract based upon temporary feelings,
Casual sex is a temporary contract based upon permanent feelings.

ℒYRICS OF LOVE, LYRIC THREE
Fenton Johnson

Sweet pigeon carrier upon my roof,
Oh, tell me, tell me how my lover fares!
Last night to war he marched, his breast aglow,
Within his heart his troubled country's cares.

"O lovely maiden, many tears shall fall
Ere to thy bosom shall thy lover fly;
Beneath the Belgian moon, in bloody death,
With thousands does your ardent lover lie."

Oh, woe is me! The moon and stars have died,
No more for me the dance on village green;
My couch is spread upon the meadowland,
Six feet of darkness 'neath the churchyard green.

XVI
Emily Dickinson

Not with a club the heart is broken
Nor with a stone;
A whip so small you could not see it
I 've known
To lash the magic creature
Till it fell,
Yet that whip's name
Too noble then to tell.
Magnanimous as bird
By boy descried,
Singing unto the stone
Of which it died;
Shame need not crouch
In such an earth as ours—
Stand—stand erect;
The universe is yours.

THE HILL WIFE

Robert Frost

LONELINESS
(Her Word)
One ought not to have to care
So much as you and I
Care when the birds come round the house
To seem to say good-bye;
Or care so much when they come back
With whatever it is they sing;
The truth being we are as much
Too glad for the one thing
As we are too sad for the other here—
With birds that fill their breasts
But with each other and themselves
And their built or driven nests.

HOUSE FEAR
Always—I tell you this they learned—
Always at night when they returned
To the lonely house from far away
To lamps unlighted and fire gone gray,
They learned to rattle the lock and key
To give whatever might chance to be
Warning and time to be off in flight:
And preferring the out- to the in-door night,
They learned to leave the house-door wide
Until they had lit the lamp inside.

THE SMILE
(Her Word)
I didn't like the way he went away.
That smile! It never came of being gay.
Still he smiled—did you see him?—I was sure!
Perhaps because we gave him only bread
And the wretch knew from that that we were poor.
Perhaps because he let us give instead
Of seizing from us as he might have seized.

Perhaps he mocked at us for being wed,
Or being very young (and he was pleased
To have a vision of us old and dead).
I wonder how far down the road he's got.
He's watching from the woods as like as not.

THE OFT-REPEATED DREAM

She had no saying dark enough
For the dark pine that kept
Forever trying the window-latch
Of the room where they slept.

The tireless but ineffectual hands
That with every futile pass
Made the great tree seem as a little bird
Before the mystery of glass!

It never had been inside the room,
And only one of the two
Was afraid in an oft-repeated dream
Of what the tree might do.

THE IMPULSE

It was too lonely for her there,
And too wild,
And since there were but two of them,
And no child,

And work was little in the house,
She was free,
And followed where he furrowed field,
Or felled tree.

She rested on a log and tossed
The fresh chips,
With a song only to herself
On her lips.

And once she went to break a bough
Of black alder.
She strayed so far she scarcely heard
When he called her—

And didn't answer—didn't speak—
Or return.

She stood, and then she ran and hid
In the fern.
He never found her, though he looked
Everywhere,
And he asked at her mother's house
Was she there.
Sudden and swift and light as that
The ties gave,
And he learned of finalities
Besides the grave.

Not Dead

Robert Grave

Walking through trees to cool my heat and pain,
I know that David's with me here again.
All that is simple, happy, strong, he is.
Caressingly I stroke
Rough bark of the friendly oak.
A brook goes bubbling by: the voice is his.
Turf burns with pleasant smoke;
I laugh at chaffinch and at primroses.
All that is simple, happy, strong, he is.
Over the whole wood in a little while
Breaks his slow smile.

My Friend, The Things That Do Attain

Henry Howard, Earl of Surrey

My friend, the things that do attain
The happy life be these,
I find:The riches left, not got with pain;
The fruitful ground; the quiet mind;
The equal friend; no grudge; no strife;
No charge of rule, nor governance;
Without disease, the healthy life;
The household of continuance;

The mean diet, no dainty fare;
Wisdom joined with simpleness;
The night discharged of all care,
Where wine the wit may not opress:
The faithful wife, without debate;
Such sleeps as may beguile the night;
Content thyself with thine estate,
Neither wish death, nor fear his might.

Superficial Voltage
for Arnie
Sharon Mesmer

You are sick of this museum.
Tired of the restless lap at last.

You are finally quiet,
finally the child that your parents desired for thirty years,
finally blossoming at the bar mitzvah that is neverending
until Cleveland,
or in the last turning off of that bare bulb behind your father's old
clothing store.

You are elemental now,
definitive and invisible as algebra,
gone back to sand and air and aqua.
Your life is worthless now,
nothing more than the low blue flame that prevents
a primitive death.

Your bent back (embarassing, for a young man)
was a mismatched barrel of bones,
staggered as the skyline,
your black hair a dusty, blunt-cut pyramid.
Your smell was leather in a small foreign car,
soft dirty beds, and shirts draped from drawers like spanish moss.
And after you left, your smell hung in your ransacked
record store for days,
as if you could still be alive in the backroom,
a patron saint of hunchbacks,
sending out Life through a great black transmitter.
You were a cheap nautical shirt,
the carpet of pornography,
the mother with the restraining order,
a lying palmist in a shopping mall.
You were the rickety kitchen, blue tv Sunday nights,
a winter pregnancy under the Magikist sign,
and a tragic orange in Washington Square.

You were the big box that arrived every birthday.
Your death was a kiss stolen in a sportscar.

Your Strange Hair

Rene Vivien

Your strange hair, cold light,
Has pale glows and blond dullness;
Your gaze has the blue of ether and waves;
Your gown has the chill of the breeze and the woods.
I burn the whiteness of your fingers with kisses.
The night air spreads the dust from many worlds.
Still I don't know anymore, in the heart of those deep nights,
How to see you with the passion of yesterday.
The moon grazed you with a slanted glow…
It was terrible, like prophetic lightning
Revealing the hideous below your beauty.
I saw—as one sees a flower fade—
On your mouth, like summer auroras,
The withered smile of an old whore.

Bricklayer Love

Carl Sandburg

I thought of killing myself because I am only a bricklayer
and you a woman who loves the man who runs a drug store.
I don't care like I used to;
I lay bricks straighter than I used to
and I sing slower handling the trowel afternoons.
When the sun is in my eyes and the ladders are shaky
and the mortar boards go wrong, I think of you.

Sonnet 9

William Shakespeare

Is it for fear to wet a widow's eye,
That thou consum'st thy self in single life?
Ah, if thou issueless shalt hap to die,
The world will wail thee like a makeless wife,
The world will be thy widow and still weep,
That thou no form of thee hast left behind,
When every private widow well may keep,

By children's eyes, her husband's shape in mind:
Look what an unthrift in the world doth spend
Shifts but his place, for still the world enjoys it;
But beauty's waste hath in the world an end,
And kept unused the user so destroys it:
  No love toward others in that bosom sits
  That on himself such murd'rous shame commits.

Sonnet 34

William Shakespeare

Why didst thou promise such a beauteous day,
And make me travel forth without my cloak,
To let base clouds o'ertake me in my way,
Hiding thy brav'ry in their rotten smoke?
'Tis not enough that through the cloud thou break,
To dry the rain on my storm-beaten face,
For no man well of such a salve can speak,
That heals the wound, and cures not the disgrace:
Nor can thy shame give physic to my grief,
Though thou repent, yet I have still the loss,
Th' offender's sorrow lends but weak relief
To him that bears the strong offence's cross.
  Ah but those tears are pearl which thy love sheds,
  And they are rich, and ransom all ill deeds.

Sonnet 42

William Shakespeare

That thou hast her it is not all my grief,
And yet it may be said I loved her dearly,
That she hath thee is of my wailing chief,
A loss in love that touches me more nearly.
Loving offenders thus I will excuse ye,
Thou dost love her, because thou know'st I love her,
And for my sake even so doth she abuse me,
Suff'ring my friend for my sake to approve her.
If I lose thee, my loss is my love's gain,
And losing her, my friend hath found that loss,
Both find each other, and I lose both twain,

And both for my sake lay on me this cross,
But here's the joy, my friend and I are one,
Sweet flattery, then she loves but me alone.

Sonnet 50

William Shakespeare

How heavy do I journey on the way,
When what I seek (my weary travel's end)
Doth teach that case and that repose to say
'Thus far the miles are measured from thy friend.'
The beast that bears me, tired with my woe,
Plods dully on, to bear that weight in me,
As if by some instinct the wretch did know
His rider loved not speed being made from thee:
The bloody spur cannot provoke him on,
That sometimes anger thrusts into his hide,
Which heavily he answers with a groan,
More sharp to me than spurring to his side,
For that same groan doth put this in my mind,
My grief lies onward and my joy behind.

Sonnet 88

William Shakespeare

When thou shalt be disposed to set me light,
And place my merit in the eye of scorn,
Upon thy side, against my self I'll fight,
And prove thee virtuous, though thou art forsworn:
With mine own weakness being best acquainted,
Upon thy part I can set down a story
Of faults concealed, wherein I am attainted:
That thou in losing me, shalt win much glory:
And I by this will be a gainer too,
For bending all my loving thoughts on thee,
The injuries that to my self I do,
Doing thee vantage, double-vantage me.
Such is my love, to thee I so belong,
That for thy right, my self will bear all wrong.

Sonnet 146

William Shakespeare

Poor soul the centre of my sinful earth,
My sinful earth these rebel powers array,
Why dost thou pine within and suffer dearth
Painting thy outward walls so costly gay?
Why so large cost having so short a lease,
Dost thou upon thy fading mansion spend?
Shall worms inheritors of this excess
Eat up thy charge? is this thy body's end?
Then soul live thou upon thy servant's loss,
And let that pine to aggravate thy store;
Buy terms divine in selling hours of dross;
Within be fed, without be rich no more,
> So shall thou feed on death, that feeds on men,
> And death once dead, there's no more dying then.

Song: My Silks And Fine Array

William Blake

My silks and fine array,
> My smiles and languish'd air,
By love are driv'n away;
> And mournful lean Despair
Brings me yew to deck my grave:
> Such end true lovers have.
His face is fair as heav'n,
> When springing buds unfold;
O why to him was't giv'n,
> Whose heart is wintry cold?
His breast is love's all worship'd tomb,
> Where all love's pilgrims come.
Bring me an axe and spade,
> Bring me a winding sheet;
When I my grave have made,
> Let winds and tempests beat:
Then down I'll lie, as cold as clay,
> True love doth pass away!

Mad Song
William Blake

The wild winds weep
And the night is a-cold;
Come hither, Sleep,
And my griefs infold:
But lo! the morning peeps
Over the eastern steeps,
And the rustling birds of dawn
The earth do scorn.

Lo! to the vault
Of paved heaven,
With sorrow fraught
My notes are driven:
They strike the ear of night,
Make weep the eyes of day;
They make mad the roaring winds,
And with tempests play.

Like a fiend in a cloud,
With howling woe,
After night I do crowd,
And with night will go;
I turn my back to the east,
From whence comforts have increas'd;
For light doth seize my brain
With frantic pain.

Song: When June Is Past, The Fading Rose
Thomas Carew

Ask me no more where Jove bestows,
When June is past, the fading rose;
For in your beauty's orient deep
These flowers as in their causes, sleep.

Ask me no more whither doth stray
The golden atoms of the day;

For in pure love heaven did prepare
Those powders to enrich your hair.

Ask me no more whither doth haste
The nightingale when May is past;
For in your sweet dividing throat
She winters and keeps warm her note.

Ask me no more where those stars light
That downwards fall in dead of night;
For in your eyes they sit, and there,
Fixed become as in their sphere.

Ask me no more if east or west
The phoenix builds her spicy nest;
For unto you at last she flies,
And in your fragrant bosom dies.

The Forsaken Merman
Matthew Arnold

Come, dear children, let us away;
Down and away below!
Now my brothers call from the bay,
Now the great winds shoreward blow,
Now the salt tides seaward flow;
Now the wild white horses play,
Champ and chafe and toss in the spray.
Children dear, let us away!
This way, this way!

Call her once before you go—
Call once yet!
In a voice that she will know:
"Margaret! Margaret!"
Children's voices should be dear
(Call once more) to a mother's ear;
Children's voices, wild with pain—
Surely she will come again!
Call her once and come away;

This way, this way!
"Mother dear, we cannot stay!
The wild white horses foam and fret."
Margaret! Margaret!

Come, dear children, come away down;
Call no more!
One last look at the white-wall'd town
And the little grey church on the windy shore,
Then come down!
She will not come though you call all day;
Come away, come away!

Children dear, was it yesterday
We heard the sweet bells over the bay?
In the caverns where we lay,
Through the surf and through the swell,
The far-off sound of a silver bell?
Sand-strewn caverns, cool and deep,
Where the winds are all asleep;
Where the spent lights quiver and gleam,
Where the salt weed sways in the stream,
Where the sea-beasts, ranged all round,
Feed in the ooze of their pasture-ground;
Where the sea-snakes coil and twine,
Dry their mail and bask in the brine;
Where great whales come sailing by,
Sail and sail, with unshut eye,
Round the world for ever and aye?
When did music come this way?
Children dear, was it yesterday?

Children dear, was it yesterday
(Call yet once) that she went away?
Once she sate with you and me,
On a red gold throne in the heart of the sea,
And the youngest sate on her knee.
She comb'd its bright hair, and she tended it well,
When down swung the sound of a far-off bell.
She sigh'd, she look'd up through the clear green sea;

She said: "I must go, to my kinsfolk pray
In the little grey church on the shore to-day.
'Twill be Easter-time in the world—ah me!
And I lose my poor soul, Merman! here with thee."
I said: "Go up, dear heart, through the waves;
Say thy prayer, and come back to the kind sea-caves!"
She smiled, she went up through the surf in the bay.
Children dear, was it yesterday?

Children dear, were we long alone?
"The sea grows stormy, the little ones moan;
Long prayers," I said, "in the world they say;
"Come!" I said; and we rose through the surf in the bay.
We went up the beach, by the sandy down
Where the sea-stocks bloom, to the white-wall'd town;
Through the narrow paved streets, where all was still,
To the little grey church on the windy hill.
From the church came a murmur of folk at their prayers,
But we stood without in the cold blowing airs.
We climb'd on the graves, on the stones worn with rains,
And we gazed up the aisle through the small leaded panes.
She sate by the pillar; we saw her clear:
"Margaret, hist! come quick, we are here!
Dear heart," I said, "we are long alone;
The sea grows stormy, the little ones moan."
But, ah, she gave me never a look,
For her eyes were seal'd to the holy book!
Loud prays the priest; shut stands the door.
Come away, children, call no more!
Come away, come down, call no more!

Down, down, down!
Down to the depths of the sea!
She sits at her wheel in the humming town,
Singing most joyfully.
Hark what she sings: "O joy, O joy,
For the humming street, and the child with its toy!
For the priest, and the bell, and the holy well;
For the wheel where I spun,

And the blessed light of the sun!"
And so she sings her fill,
Singing most joyfully,
Till the spindle drops from her hand,
And the whizzing wheel stands still.
She steals to the window, and looks at the sand,
And over the sand at the sea;
And her eyes are set in a stare;
And anon there breaks a sigh,
And anon there drops a tear,
From a sorrow-clouded eye,
And a heart sorrow-laden,
A long, long sigh;
For the cold strange eyes of a little Mermaiden
And the gleam of her golden hair.

Come away, away children
Come children, come down!
The hoarse wind blows coldly;
Lights shine in the town.
She will start from her slumber
When gusts shake the door;
She will hear the winds howling,
Will hear the waves roar.
We shall see, while above us
The waves roar and whirl,
A ceiling of amber,
A pavement of pearl.
Singing: "Here came a mortal,
But faithless was she!
And alone dwell for ever
The kings of the sea."

But, children, at midnight,
When soft the winds blow,
When clear falls the moonlight,
When spring-tides are low;
When sweet airs come seaward
From heaths starr'd with broom,

And high rocks throw mildly
On the blanch'd sands a gloom;
Up the still, glistening beaches,
Up the creeks we will hie,
Over banks of bright seaweed
The ebb-tide leaves dry.
We will gaze, from the sand-hills,
At the white, sleeping town;
At the church on the hill-side—
And then come back down.
Singing: "There dwells a loved one,
But cruel is she!
She left lonely for ever
The kings of the sea."

Requiescat

Matthew Arnold

Strew on her roses, roses,
And never a spray of yew!
In quiet she reposes;
Ah, would that I did too!

Her mirth the world required;
She bathed it in smiles of glee.
But her heart was tired, tired,
And now they let her be.

Her life was turning, turning,
In mazes of heat and sound.
But for peace her soul was yearning,
And now peace laps her round.

Her cabin'd, ample spirit,
It flutter'd and fail'd for breath.
To-night it doth inherit
The vasty hall of death.

New Love

Brown Penny

W. B. Yeats

I whispered, 'I am too young,'
And then, 'I am old enough';
Wherefore I threw a penny
To find out if I might love.
'Go and love, go and love, young man,
If the lady be young and fair.'
Ah, penny, brown penny, brown penny,
I am looped in the loops of her hair.

And the penny sang up in my face,
'There is nobody wise enough
To find out all that is in it,
For he would be thinking of love
That is looped in the loops of her hair,
Till the loops of time had run.'
Ah, penny, brown penny, brown penny,
One cannot begin it too soon.

Planning The Perfect Evening

Rita Dove

I keep him waiting, tuck in the curtains,
buff my nails (such small pink eggshells).
As if for the last time, I descend the stair.

He stands there penguin-stiff in a room
that's so quiet we forget it is there
Now nothing, not even breath can come

between us, not even the aroma of punch
and sneakers as we dance the length
of the gymnasium and crepe paper streams

down like cartoon lightning. Ah,
Augustus, where did you learn to samba?
And what is that lump below your cummerbund?

Stardust. The band fold up
resolutely, with plum-dark faces.
The night still chirps. Sixteen cars

caravan to Georgia for a terrace,
beer and tacos, Even this far south
a thin blue ice shackles the moon,

and I'm happy my glass sizzles with stars.
How far away the world! And how hulking
you are, my dear, my sweet black bear!

First Love

John Clare

I ne'er was struck before that hour
   With love so sudden and so sweet,
Her face it bloomed like a sweet flower
   And stole my heart away complete.

My face turned pale as deadly pale,
   My legs refused to walk away,
And when she looked, what could I ail?
   My life and all seemed turned to clay.

And then my blood rushed to my face
   And took my eyesight quite away,
The trees and bushes round the place
   Seemed midnight at noonday.

I could not see a single thing,
   Words from my eyes did start -
They spoke as chords do from the string,
   And blood burnt round my heart.

Are flowers the winter's choice?
   Is love's bed always snow?
She seemed to hear my silent voice,
I never saw so sweet a face
   As that I stood before.
My heart has left its dwelling-place
   And can return no more.

The First Day

Christina Rossetti

I wish I could remember the first day,
First hour, first moment of your meeting me;
If bright or dim the season, it might be
Summer or winter for aught I can say.
So unrecorded did it slip away,
So blind was I to see and to foresee,
So dull to mark the budding of my tree
That would not blossom yet for many a May.
If only I could recollect it? Such
A day of days! I let it come and go

As traceless as a thaw of bygone snow.
It seemed to mean so little, meant so much!
If only now I could recall that touch,
First touch of hand in hand! Did one but know!

ℐ Found You Standing There
Catie Farrell

I wasn't looking
I didn't prepare
To feel your touch
And find you standing there

My mind is still reeling from the wonder
Of it all
I need to take a breath
Before the walls
About me
Fall

My life was flowing nicely
I wasn't seeking love
Then suddenly
From nowhere, like a gift from
Up above

Your being appeared before me your soul
Entwined with mine. Now
I am thirsty for your sweet
And sparkling wine.

Sonnet 49
William Shakespeare

Against that time (if ever that time come)
When I shall see thee frown on my defects,
When as thy love hath cast his utmost sum,
Called to that audit by advised respects,
Against that time when thou shalt strangely pass,
And scarcely greet me with that sun thine eye,
When love converted from the thing it was
Shall reasons find of settled gravity;
Against that time do I ensconce me here
Within the knowledge of mine own desert,
And this my hand, against my self uprear,
To guard the lawful reasons on thy part,
    To leave poor me, thou hast the strength of laws,
    Since why to love, I can allege no cause.

When I Think

Elizabeth Barrett Browning

Beloved, my Beloved, when I think
That thou wast in the world a year ago,
What time I sat alone here in the snow
And saw no footprint, heard the silence sink
No moment at thy voice,...but, link by link,
When counting all my chains, as if that so
They never could fall off at any blow
Struck by thy possible hand...why, thus I drink
Of life's great cup of wonder!
Wonderful
Never to feel the thrill the day or night
With personal act or speech—nor ever cull
Some prescience of thee with the blossoms white
Thou sawest growing! Atheists are as dull
Who cannot guess God's presence out of sight.

To

Sidney Lanier

The Day was dying; his breath
Wavered away in a hectic gleam;
And I said, if Life's a dream, and Death
And Love and all are dreams—I'll dream.

A mist came over the bay
Like as a dream would over an eye.
The mist was white and the dream was grey
And both contained a human cry,

The burden whereof was "Love,"
And it filled both mist and dream with pain,
And the hills below and the skies above
Were touched and uttered it back again.

The mist broke: down the rift
A kind ray shot from a holy star.
Then my dream did waver and break and lift—
Through it, O Love, shone thy face, afar.

So Boyhood sets: comes Youth,
A painful night of mists and dreams;
That broods till Love's exquisite truth,
The star of a morn-clear manhood, beams.

*I*N SPITE OF MY EFFORTS
Taira no Kanemori

In spite of my efforts
        to hide my love,
    it shows in my face
    and makes people ask,
"Is something bothering you?"

*S*ONNET LXI
Petrarch

Blessed may be the day, the month, the year,
And the season, the time, the hour, the point,
And the country, the place where I was joined
By two fair eyes that now have tied me here.
And blessed be the first sweet agony
That I felt in becoming bound to Love,
And the bow and the arrows piercing me,
And the wounds that go down so deep to move
Blessed the many voices that I raised,
Calling my lady, to scatter her name,
And blessed be my tears, my sighs, my heart;
Blessed may be the paper where more fame
I earn for her, my thought by which she is praised,
Only her own: no one else has a part.

A LECTURE UPON THE SHADOW
John Donne

Stand still, and I will read to thee
A lecture, love, in love's philosophy.
    These three hours that we have spent,
    Walking here, two shadows went

Along with us, which we ourselves produc'd.
But, now the sun is just above our head,
We do those shadows tread,
And to brave clearness all things are reduc'd.
So whilst our infant loves did grow,
Disguises did, and shadows, flow
From us, and our cares; but now 'tis not so.
That love has not attain'd the high'st degree,
Which is still diligent lest others see.
Except our loves at this noon stay,
We shall new shadows make the other way.
As the first were made to blind
Others, these which come behind
Will work upon ourselves, and blind our eyes.
If our loves faint, and westwardly decline,
To me thou, falsely, thine,
And I to thee mine actions shall disguise.
The morning shadows wear away,
But these grow longer all the day;
But oh, love's day is short, if love decay.
Love is a growing, or full constant light,
And his first minute, after noon, is night.

Meeting And Passing

Robert Frost

As I went down the hill along the wall
There was a gate I had leaned at for the view
And had just turned from when I first saw you
As you came up the hill. We met. But all
We did that day was mingle great and small
Footprints in summer dust as if we drew
The figure of our being less than two
But more than one as yet. Your parasol
Pointed the decimal off with one deep thrust.
And all the time we talked you seemed to see
Something down there to smile at in the dust.
(Oh, it was without prejudice to me!)
Afterward I went past what you had passed
Before we met and you what I had passed.

Love's Delay

Elia W. Peattie

Nay, do not haste your coming, love.
Wait for a little while. And why?
I would postpone the sweets of your first kiss,
And let you, too, feed on expectancy.
You write you love me.

Ay, and I love you!
I love you with a love as delicate
As moon-gold on a tropic sea, or
Webs of gossamer in the morning sun, or
Gleam of dew on early flowers,
Or bloom that makes the moth's regalia.

I put you in my most enchanting dreams
When night is here, and in the day
Frame thoughts of you in music.

Ah, dear heart, I pray that you and nature are in league.
If heaven drops rain, I say, "My love is sad."
If birds sing in the morn, I kiss my hand
Westward toward you and cry,
"Here's hail unto my own, who suns himself
In my bright love, and sends this dawn
To tell me so!"
And every day I cull my thoughts to send the fairest ones
To you.

Ah, be content a little while,
Nor know my baser moods, my selfishness!
Keep all your thoughts of me as they are now,
So fine, and high, and chaste!
Haste not, Dear love, your coming.

Wait awhile! I dream,
In solitary twilight hours, how sweet,
How tender-sweet and pure your kiss will be,—
Your first kiss, love!
Delay—lest it be past!

Last Love

Fyodor Tyutchev

Love at the closing of our days
is apprehensive and very tender.
Glow brighter, brighter farewell rays
of one last love in its evening splendor.

Blue shade takes half the world away;
through western clouds alone some light is slanted.
O tarry. O tarry, declining day,
enchantment, let me stay enchanted.

The blood runs thinner, yet the heart
remains as ever deep and tender.
O last belated love, thou art
a blend of joy and of hopeless surrender.

Sonnet 2

William Shakespeare

When forty winters shall besiege thy brow,
And dig deep trenches in thy beauty's field,
Thy youth's proud livery so gazed on now,
Will be a tattered weed of small worth held:
Then being asked, where all thy beauty lies,
Where all the treasure of thy lusty days;
To say within thine own deep sunken eyes,
Were an all-eating shame, and thriftless praise.
How much more praise deserved thy beauty's use,
If thou couldst answer 'This fair child of mine
Shall sum my count, and make my old excuse'
Proving his beauty by succession thine.
    This were to be new made when thou art old,
    And see thy blood warm when thou feel'st it cold.

With Rue My Heart Is Laden

A.E. Houseman

With rue my heart is laden
  For golden friends I had,
For many a rose-lipt maiden
  And many a lightfoot lad.
By brooks too broad for leaping
  The lightfoot boys are laid;
The rose-lipt girls are sleeping
  In fields where roses fade.

Sonnet 22

William Shakespeare

My glass shall not persuade me I am old,
So long as youth and thou are of one date,
But when in thee time's furrows I behold,
Then look I death my days should expiate.
For all that beauty that doth cover thee,
Is but the seemly raiment of my heart,
Which in thy breast doth live, as thine in me,
How can I then be elder than thou art?
O therefore love be of thyself so wary,
As I not for my self, but for thee will,
Bearing thy heart which I will keep so chary
As tender nurse her babe from faring ill.
    Presume not on thy heart when mine is slain,
    Thou gav'st me thine not to give back again.

Untitled

Bertrand Russell

I did not know I loved you until I heard myself telling so, for one instance
I thought, "Good God, what have I said?" and then I knew it was true.

Healing
Abraham Reisen

Kiss away my gray hair, oh, my love,
You may yet
Kiss away the gray, and bring
Back the jet.

Kiss away the anguish from my eye,
And the doubt;
I may yet turn good again,
And devout.

Kiss the venom, oh, my love,
From my tongue,
And perhaps I'll be a fool
Again, and young.

Sonnet 104
William Shakespeare

To me, fair friend, you never can be old,
For as you were when first your eye I eyed,
Such seems your beauty still. Three winters cold
Have from the forests shook three summers' pride,
Three beauteous springs to yellow autumn turned
In process of the seasons have I seen,
Three April perfumes in three hot Junes burned,
Since first I saw you fresh, which yet are green.
Ah yet doth beauty, like a dial hand,
Steal from his figure, and no pace perceived;
So your sweet hue, which methinks still doth stand,
Hath motion, and mine eye may be deceived.
    For fear of which, hear this thou age unbred.
    Ere you were born was beauty's summer dead.

To Love
Albert Camus

To love a person means to agree to grow old with him.

Two Songs

Abraham Reisen

1

The sweetest melody
Your heart can sing,
Keep for your autumn hour,
Not for the spring.

Glad is the blossom time
With its own tune and chime;
Ah, but the sunset day —
Sing it away.

2

On with another new love,
Burning and bright and keen,
Yet terribly dear in the distance
Shines the love that has been.

On with another new love,
Kisses and hands that meet —
Yet, oh to be close to the old love
And beg for content at her feet!

A Quoi Bon Dire

Charlotte Mew

Seventeen years ago you said
Something that sounded like Good-bye;
And everybody thinks that you are dead,
But I.
So I, as I grow stiff and cold
To this and that say Good-bye too;
And everybody sees that I am old
But you.
And one fine morning in a sunny lane
Some boy and girl will meet and kiss and swear
That nobody can love their way again
While over there
You will have smiled, I shall have tossed your hair.

A Song Of A Young Lady To Her Ancient Lover

John Wilmot, Second Earl of Rochester

Ancient person, for whom I
All the flittering youth defy
Long be it ere thou grow old,
Aching, shaking, crazy, cold;
But still continue as thou art,
Ancient person of my heart

On thy withered lips and dry,
Which like barren furrow, lie,
Brooding kisses I will pour
Shall thy youthful heat restore
Shall thy youthful heat restore
Such kind showers in autumn fall,
And a second spring recall);
   Nor from thee will ever part,
   Ancient person of my heart.

The nobler part, which but to name
In our sex would be counted shame,
By age's frozen grasp possessed,
From his ice shall be released,
And soothed by my reviving hand,
In former warmth and vigour stand.
All a lover's wish can reach
For thy joy my love shall teach,
And for thy pleasure shall improve
All that art can add to love.
   Yet still I love thee without art,
   Ancient person of my heart.

ℱORTY IS SPORTY

Anonymous, American

If forty is sporty
Then fifty is nifty
And I am delighted
I'm middle aged too.
I've got the generic —
The standard climacteric—
But I've still got the hots over you.
I love you
I want you to know
"I want you."
I love you to say.
I've reached middle age
And I'm out of the Cage

So mama, come on and let us play!
Though the autumn wind sighs through the trees
And the snow clouds hunker on the hills
And the swimmin' hole threatens to freeze
I lust for you— and I always will.
If forty is sporty
Then fifty is nifty
And I am delighted
I'm middle-aged too.
It's clearly generic —
The plain old climacteric —
And yet I've got the hots over you.

Silver Threads Among The Gold

Eben E. Rexford and Hart Pease Danks

Darling, I am growing old,
Silver threads among the gold
Shine upon my brow today,
Life is fading fast away.
> But, my darling, you will be,
> Always young and fair to me,
> Yes, my darling, you will be,
> Always young and fair to me.

Darling, I am growing old,
Silver threads among the gold,
Shine upon my brow today,
Life is fading fast away.
> When your hair is silver white,
> And your cheeks no longer bright,
> With the roses of the May,
> I will kiss your lips and say:

Oh! my darling, mine alone, alone,
You have never older grown,

Yes, my darling, mine alone,
You have never older grown.
Love can never more grow old.
Locks may lose their brown and gold,
Cheeks may fade and hollow grow,
But the hearts that love will know
> Never, never, winter's frost and chill,
> Summer warmth is in them still;
> Never winter's frost and chill,
> Summer warmth is in them still.

Love is always young and fair.
What to us is silver hair,
Faded cheeks or steps grown slow,
To the heart that beats below?
> Since I kissed you, mine alone, alone,
> You have never older grown;
> Since I kissed you, mine alone,
> You have never older grown.

Sonnet 19

William Shakespeare

Devouring Time, blunt thou the lion's paws,
And make the earth devour her own sweet brood;
Pluck the keen teeth from the fierce tiger's jaws,
And burn the long-lived phoenix, in her blood;
Make glad and sorry seasons as thou fleets,
And do whate'er thou wilt, swift-footed Time,
To the wide world and all her fading sweets;
But I forbid thee one most heinous crime,
O, carve not with thy hours my love's fair brow,
Nor draw no lines there with thine antique pen.
Him in thy course untainted do allow,
For beauty's pattern to succeeding men
> Yet do thy worst, old Time; despite thy wrong,
> My love shall in my verse ever live young.

GRIEVE NOT, LADIES

Anna Hempstead Branch

Oh, grieve not, ladies, if at night
Ye wake to feel your beauty going.
It was a web
Of frail delight
Inconstant as an April snowing.

In other eyes, in other lands,
In deep fair pools, new beauty lingers,
But like spent water in your hands
It runs from your reluctant fingers,

Ye shall not keep the singing lark
That owes to earlier skies its duty.
Weep not to hear along the dark
The sound of your departing beauty.

The fine and anguished car of night is
tuned to bear the smallest sorrow.
Oh, wait until the morning light!
It may not seem so gone to-morrow!
But honey-pale and rosy-red!

Brief lights that made a little shining!
Beautiful looks about us shed
They leave us to the old repining.
Think not the watchful dim despair

Has come to you the first, sweet-hearted!
For oh, the gold in Helen's hair!
And how she cried when that departed!
Perhaps that one that took the most,

The swiftest borrower, wildest spender,
May count, as we would not, the cost—
And grow more true to us and tender.
Happy are we if in his eyes
We see no shadow of forgetting.
Nay— if our star sinks in those skies
We shall not wholly see its setting.

Then let us laugh as do the brooks
That such immortal youth is ours,
If memory keeps for them our looks
As fresh as are the spring-time flowers.

Oh, grieve not, Ladies, if at night
Ye wake, to feel the cold December!
Rather recall the early light
And in your loved one's arms, remember.

*M*EMORIES

Catie Farrell

Hands
Reaching out
Finding
Once again

The memory
Lingers still
Reunited
With a friend

Remember once
When skin was soft
I do

*R*ECUERDO

Edna St. Vincent Millay

We were very tired, we were very merry—
We had gone back and forth all night on the ferry.
It was bare and bright, and smelled like a stable—
But we looked into a fire, we leaned across a table,
We lay on a hilltop underneath the moon;
And the whistles kept blowing, and the dawn came soon.

We were very tired, we were very merry—
We had gone back and forth all night on the ferry,
And you ate an apple, and I ate a pear,

From a dozen of each we had bought somewhere;
And the sky went wan, and the wind came cold,
And the sun rose dripping, a bucketful of gold.

We were very tired, we were very merry—
We had gone back and forth all night on the ferry,
We hailed "Good morrow, mother!" to a shawl-covered head,
And bought a morning paper, which neither of us read;
And she wept, "God bless you!" for the apples and pears,
And we gave her all our money but our subway fares.

Heart Of My Heart
Madison Cawein

Here where the season turns the land to gold,
Among the fields our feet have known of old,
When we were children who would laugh and run,
Glad little playmates of the wind and sun,
Before came toil and care and years went ill,
And one forgot and one remembered still;
Heart of my heart, among the old fields here,
Give me your hands and let me draw you near,

Heart of my heart.
Stars are not truer than your soul is true
What need I more of heaven then than you?
Flowers are not sweeter than your face is sweet
What need I more to make my world complete?

O woman nature, love that still endures,
What strength has ours that is not born of yours?
Heart of my heart, to you, whatever come,
To you the lead, whose love hath led me home.
Heart of my heart.

Observation
Benjamin Disraeli

I have lived long enough to know that the evening glow of love has
its own riches and splendor.

$\mathcal{Y}$EARS

Alicia Ostriker

for J.P.O.

I have wished you dead and myself dead.
How could it be otherwise.
I have broken into you like a burglar.
And you've set your dogs on me.
You have been a hurricane to me.
And a pile of broken sticks.
A child could kick.
I have climbed you like a monument, gasoing,
For the exercise and the view,
And leaned over the railng at the top——
Strong and warm, the summer wind.

$\mathcal{W}$HEN THE LAMP IS SHATTER'D

Percy Bysshe Shelley

When the lamp is shatter'd,
The light in the dust lies dead.
When the cloud is scatter'd,
The rainbow's glory is shed.
When the lute is broken,
Sweet tones are remember'd not;
When the lips have spoken,
Loved accents are soon forgot.
As music and splendour
Survive not the lamp and the lute,
The heart's echoes render
No song when the spirit is mute.
No song but sad dirges
Like the wind through a ruin'd cell,
Or the mournful surges
That ring the dead seaman's knell.

When hearts have once mingled
Love first leaves the well-built nest;
The weak one is singled
To endure what it once possess'd.
O Love! who bewailest
The frailty of all things here,
Why choose you the frailest
For your cradle, your home, and your bier?
Its passions will rock thee
As the storms rock the ravens on high.
Bright Reason will mock thee
Like the sun from a wintry sky.
From thy nest every rafter
Will rot, and thine eagle home
Leave thee naked to laughter
When leaves fall and cold winds come.

SONNET 32

William Shakespeare

If thou survive my well-contented day,
When that churl death my bones with dust shall cover
And shalt by fortune once more re-survey
These poor rude lines of thy deceased lover:
Compare them with the bett'ring of the time,
And though they be outstripped by every pen,
Reserve them for my love, not for their rhyme,
Exceeded by the height of happier men.
O then vouchsafe me but this loving thought,
'Had my friend's Muse grown with this growing age,
A dearer birth than this his love had brought
To march in ranks of better equipage:
    But since he died and poets better prove,
    Theirs for their style I'll read, his for his love'.

SONNET 67

William Shakespeare

Ah wherefore with infection should he live,
And with his presence grace impiety,
That sin by him advantage should achieve,
And lace it self with his society?
Why should false painting imitate his cheek,
And steal dead seeming of his living hue?
Why should poor beauty indirectly seek,
Roses of shadow, since his rose is true?
Why should he live, now nature bankrupt is,
Beggared of blood to blush through lively veins,
For she hath no exchequer now but his,
And proud of many, lives upon his gains?
    O him she stores, to show what wealth she had,
    In days long since, before these last so bad.

Sonnet 76

William Shakespeare

Why is my verse so barren of new pride?
So far from variation or quick change?
Why with the time do I not glance aside
To new-found methods, and to compounds strange?
Why write I still all one, ever the same,
And keep invention in a noted weed,
That every word doth almost tell my name,
Showing their birth, and where they did proceed?
O know sweet love I always write of you,
And you and love are still my argument:
So all my best is dressing old words new,
Spending again what is already spent:
    For as the sun is daily new and old,
    So is my love still telling what is told.

Sonnet 89

William Shakespeare

Say that thou didst forsake me for some fault,
And I will comment upon that offence,
Speak of my lameness, and I straight will halt:
Against thy reasons making no defence.
Thou canst not (love) disgrace me half so ill,
To set a form upon desired change,
As I'll my self disgrace, knowing thy will,
I will acquaintance strangle and look strange:
Be absent from thy walks and in my tongue,
Thy sweet beloved name no more shall dwell,
Lest I (too much profane) should do it wronk:
And haply of our old acquaintance tell.
    For thee, against my self I'll vow debate,
    For I must ne'er love him whom thou dost hate.

Sonnet 106

William Shakespeare

When in the chronicle of wasted time,
I see descriptions of the fairest wights,
And beauty making beautiful old rhyme,
In praise of ladies dead, and lovely knights,
Then in the blazon of sweet beauty's best,
Of hand, of foot, of lip, of eye, of brow,
I see their antique pen would have expressed,
Even such a beauty as you master now.
So all their praises are but prophecies
Of this our time, all you prefiguring,
And for they looked but with divining eyes,
They had not skill enough your worth to sing:
    For we which now behold these present days,
    Have eyes to wonder, but lack tongues to praise.

Sonnet 122

William Shakespeare

Thy gift, thy tables, are within my brain
Full charactered with lasting memory,
Which shall above that idle rank remain
Beyond all date even to eternity.
Or at the least, so long as brain and heart
Have faculty by nature to subsist,
Till each to razed oblivion yield his part
Of thee, thy record never can be missed:
That poor retention could not so much hold,
Nor need I tallies thy dear love to score,
Therefore to give them from me was I bold,
To trust those tables that receive thee more:
    To keep an adjunct to remember thee
    Were to import forgetfulness in me.

Sonnet 152

William Shakespeare

In loving thee thou know'st I am forsworn,
But thou art twice forsworn to me love swearing,
In act thy bed-vow broke and new faith torn,
In vowing new hate after new love bearing:
But why of two oaths' breach do I accuse thee,
When I break twenty? I am perjured most,
For all my vows are oaths but to misuse thee:
And all my honest faith in thee is lost.
For I have sworn deep oaths of thy deep kindness:
Oaths of thy love, thy truth, thy constancy,
And to enlighten thee gave eyes to blindness,
Or made them swear against the thing they see.
    For I have sworn thee fair: more perjured I,
    To swear against the truth so foul a be.

Rabbi Ben Ezra

Robert Browning

Grow old along with me!
   The best is yet to be,
   The last of life, for which the first was made:
   Our times are in His hand
   Who saith "A whole I planned,
Youth shows but half; trust God: see all, nor be afraid!"

Not that, amassing flowers,
   Youth sighed "Which rose make ours,
Which lily leave and then as best recall?"
   Not that, admiring stars,
   It yearned "Nor Jove, nor Mars;
Mine be some figured flame which blends, transcends them all!"

Not for such hopes and fears
   Annulling youth's brief years,
Do I remonstrate: folly wide the mark!
   Rather I prize the doubt

Low kinds exist without,
Finished and finite clods, untroubled by a spark.

Poor vaunt of life indeed,
Were man but formed to feed
On joy, to solely seek and find and feast:
Such feasting ended, then
As sure an end to men;
Irks care the crop-full bird? Frets doubt the maw-crammed beast?

Rejoice we are allied
To that which doth provide
And not partake, effect and not receive!
A spark disturbs our clod;
Nearer we hold of God
Who gives, than of His tribes that take, I must believe.

Then, welcome each rebuff
That turns earth's smoothness rough,
Each sting that bids nor sit nor stand but go!
Be our joys three-parts pain!
Strive, and hold cheap the strain;
Learn, nor account the pang; dare, never grudge the throe!

For thence,—a paradox
Which comforts while it mocks,—
Shall life succeed in that it seems to fail:
What I aspired to be,
And was not, comforts me:
A brute I might have been, but would not sink i' the scale.

What is he but a brute
Whose flesh has soul to suit,
Whose spirit works lest arms and legs want play?
To man, propose this test—
Thy body at its best,
How far can that project thy soul on its lone way?

Yet gifts should prove their use:
I own the Past profuse
Of power each side, perfection every turn:

Eyes, ears took in their dole,
Brain treasured up the whole;
Should not the heart beat once "How good to live and learn?"

Not once beat "Praise be Thine!
I see the whole design,
I, who saw power, see now love perfect too:
Perfect I call Thy plan:
Thanks that I was a man!
Maker, remake, complete,—I trust what Thou shalt do!"

For pleasant is this flesh;
Our soul, in its rose-mesh
Pulled ever to the earth, still yearns for rest;
Would we some prize might hold
To match those manifold
Possessions of the brute,—gain most, as we did best!

Let us not always say,
"Spite of this flesh to-day
I strove, made head, gained ground upon the whole!"
As the bird wings and sings,
Let us cry "All good things
Are ours, nor soul helps flesh more, now, than flesh helps soul!"

Therefore I summon age
To grant youth's heritage,
Life's struggle having so far reached its term:
Thence shall I pass, approved
A man, for aye removed
From the developed brute; a god though in the germ.

And I shall thereupon
Take rest, ere I be gone
Once more on my adventure brave and new:
Fearless and unperplexed,
When I wage battle next,
What weapons to select, what armour to indue.

Youth ended, I shall try
My gain or loss thereby;

Leave the fire ashes, what survives is gold:
And I shall weigh the same,
Give life its praise or blame:
Young, all lay in dispute; I shall know, being old.

For note, when evening shuts,
A certain moment cuts
The deed off, calls the glory from the grey:
A whisper from the west
Shoots—"Add this to the rest,
Take it and try its worth: here dies another day."

So, still within this life,
Though lifted o'er its strife,
Let me discern, compare, pronounce at last,
This rage was right i' the main,
That acquiescence vain:
The Future I may face now I have proved the Past."

For more is not reserved
To man, with soul just nerved
To act to-morrow what he learns to-day:
Here, work enough to watch
The Master work, and catch
Hints of the proper craft, tricks of the tool's true play.

As it was better, youth
Should strive, through acts uncouth,
Toward making, than repose on aught found made:
So, better, age, exempt
From strife, should know, than tempt
Further. Thou waitedst age: wait death nor be afraid!

Enough now, if the Right
And Good and Infinite
Be named here, as thou callest thy hand thine own
With knowledge absolute,
Subject to no dispute
From fools that crowded youth, nor let thee feel alone.

Be there, for once and all,
Severed great minds from small,
Announced to each his station in the Past!
Was I, the world arraigned,
Were they, my soul disdained,
Right? Let age speak the truth and give us peace at last!

Now, who shall arbitrate?
Ten men love what I hate,
Shun what I follow, slight what I receive;
Ten, who in ears and eyes
Match me: we all surmise,
They this thing, and I that: whom shall my soul believe?

Not on the vulgar mass
Called "work," must sentence pass,
Things done, that took the eye and had the price;
O'er which, from level stand,
The low world laid its hand,
Found straightway to its mind, could value in a trice:

But all, the world's coarse thumb
And finger failed to plumb,
So passed in making up the main account;
All instincts immature,
All purposes unsure,
That weighed not as his work, yet swelled the man's amount:

Thoughts hardly to be packed
Into a narrow act,
Fancies that broke through language and escaped;
All I could never be,
All, men ignored in me,
This, I was worth to God, whose wheel the pitcher shaped.

Ay, note that Potter's wheel,
That metaphor! and feel
Why time spins fast, why passive lies our clay,—
Thou, to whom fools propound,
When the wine makes its round,
"Since life fleets, all is change; the Past gone, seize to-day!"

Fool! All that is, at all,
Lasts ever, past recall;
Earth changes, but thy soul and God stand sure:
What entered into thee,
That was, is, and shall be:
Time's wheel runs back or stops: Potter and clay endure.

He fixed thee mid this dance
Of plastic circumstance,
This Present, thou, forsooth, wouldst fain arrest:
Machinery just meant
To give thy soul its bent,
Try thee and turn thee forth, sufficiently impressed.

What though the earlier grooves,
Which ran the laughing loves
Around thy base, no longer pause and press?
What though, about thy rim,
Skull-things in order grim
Grow out, in graver mood, obey the sterner stress?

Look not thou down but up!
To uses of a cup,
The festal board, lamp's flash and trumpet's peal,
The new wine's foaming flow,
The Master's lips a-glow!
Thou, heaven's consummate cup, what need'st thou with earth's wheel?

But I need, now as then,
Thee, God, who mouldest men;
And since, not even while the whirl was worst,
Did I,—to the wheel of life
With shapes and colours rife,
Bound dizzily,—mistake my end, to slake Thy thirst:

So, take and use Thy work:
Amend what flaws may lurk,
What strain o' the stuff, what warpings past the aim!
My times be in Thy hand!
Perfect the cup as planned!
Let age approve of youth, and death complete the same!

Air And Angels

John Donne

Twice or thrice had I lov'd thee,
Before I knew thy face or name;
So in a voice, so in a shapeless flame
Angels affect us oft, and worshipp'd be;
Still when, to where thou wert, I came,
Some lovely glorious nothing I did see.
But since my soul, whose child love is,
Takes limbs of flesh, and else could nothing do,
More subtle than the parent is
Love must not be, but take a body too;
And therefore what thou wert, and who,
I bid Love ask, and now
That it assume thy body, I allow,
And fix itself in thy lip, eye, and brow.

Whilst thus to ballast love I thought,
And so more steadily to have gone,
With wares which would sink admiration,
I saw I had love's pinnace overfraught;
Ev'ry thy hair for love to work upon
Is much too much, some fitter must be sought;
For, nor in nothing, nor in things
Extreme, and scatt'ring bright, can love inhere;
Then, as an angel, face, and wings
Of air, not pure as it, yet pure, doth wear,
So thy love may be my love's sphere;
Just such disparity
As is 'twixt air and angels' purity,
Twixt women's love, and men's, will ever be.

$\mathcal{A}$CKNOWLEDGMENTS

"Lust, Love and Loss, Part 3: Appomattox", from *Greed* by Ai. Copyright © 1993 by Ai. Reprinted by permissoin of W. W. Norton & Company, Inc.

"Why Can't I Leave You" from *Cruelty* by Ai. Copyright © 1970 by Ai. Used by permission of the author.

"You Don't Know Me" by Eddy Arnold and Cindy Walker ©1955 (Renewed) Unichappell Music Inc. (BMI). All rights reserved. Used by permission of WARNER BROS. PUBLICATIONS U.S. INC., Miami, FL 33014.

"To Praise" by Ellen Bass, reprinted by permission of the publisher from *Florilezia,* Ed. by Debbie Berrow, et. al. (Calyx Books, 1987).

"In Celebration" from *I'm Not Your Laughing Daughter* by Ellen Bass. Copyright © 1973 by Ellen Bass. Used by permission of the author.

"Two Sleepy People" written by Hoagy Carmichael *(music)* and Frank Loesser *(lyrics)* © 1938 (renewed 1965) Famous Music Corporation. Reprinted by Permission. All rights reserved.

"The Nearness of You" written by Hoagy Carmichael *(music)* and Ned Washington *(lyrics)* © 1937, 1940 (renewed 1964, 1967) Famous Music Corporation. Reprinted by Permission. All rights reserved.

"Marriage" from *Fires* by Raymond Carver reprinted with permission of Capra Press. Copyright © 1983 by Raymond Carver.

"Poem in Praise of My Husband (Taos)" Copyright © 1976 by Diane di Prima. All rights reserved.

"Planning the Perfect Evening" from Rita Dove, *The Yellow House on the Corner,* © 1980 by Rita Dove. Reprinted by permission of the author.

"The Kiss" reprinted with the permission of Simon & Schuster from *Mirror of the Heart: Poems of Sara Teasdale,* edited by William Drake (New York: Macmillan Publishing Company © 1984).

"At Midsummer", from *Selected and New Poems* by Norman Dubie. Copyright © 1983 by Norman Dubie. Reprinted by permission of W. W. Norton & Company, Inc.

"The Orchard" by Gretel Ehrlich. Used by permission of A. Thomas Trusky, Ashata Press.

"Where You Go When She Sleeps" reprinted by permission of Louisiana State University Press from *The Angelic Orders:* Poems by T. R. Hummer. Copyright © 1982 by T. R. Hummer.

"Getting Out" by Cleopatra Mathis reprinted by permission of the author.